NOMADS, TRIBES, AND THE STATE IN THE ANCIENT NEAR EAST

NOMADS, TRIBES, AND THE STATE IN THE ANCIENT NEAR EAST
CROSS-DISCIPLINARY PERSPECTIVES

edited by

JEFFREY SZUCHMAN

with contributions by

Jeffrey Szuchman, Hans Barnard, Robert Ritner, Steven A. Rosen, Benjamin A. Saidel, Eveline van der Steen, Anatoly M. Khazanov, Abbas Alizadeh, Thomas E. Levy, Bertille Lyonnet, Anne Porter, Daniel E. Fleming, Donald Whitcomb, *and* Frank Hole

THE ORIENTAL INSTITUTE OF THE UNIVERSITY OF CHICAGO
ORIENTAL INSTITUTE SEMINARS • NUMBER 5
CHICAGO • ILLINOIS

Library of Congress Control Number: 2008943404
ISBN-13: 978-1-885923-61-5
ISBN-10: 1-885923-61-9
ISSN: 1559-2944

The Oriental Institute, Chicago

THE UNIVERSITY OF CHICAGO

ORIENTAL INSTITUTE SEMINARS • NUMBER 5

Series Editors

Leslie Schramer

and

Thomas G. Urban

with the assistance of

Katie L. Johnson

Cover Illustrations

Front: Semitic tribe in traditional costume and Egyptians. Egyptian painting. 19th century B.C.E.
Mural from the tomb of Beni-Hassan. Photo credit: Erich Lessing / Art Resource, NY.
Kunsthistorisches Museum, Vienna, Austria

Back: Figure (on right) with open cloak. Rock art from the site of Uan Amil, Libya.
Figure 3.5 in this volume. Photo by Robert Ritner

Publication of this volume was made possible through generous funding
from the Arthur and Lee Herbst Research and Education Fund

Printed by Edwards Brothers, Ann Arbor, Michigan

TABLE OF CONTENTS

SECTION THREE: RESPONSE

LIST OF ABBREVIATIONS

ca.	circa
cf.	*confer*, compare
cm	centimeter(s)
col(s).	column(s)
diss.	dissertation
e.g.	*exempli gratia*, for example
esp.	especially
et al.	*et alii*, and others
etc.	*et cetera,* and so forth
fig(s).	figure(s)
ha	hectare(s)
ibid.	*ibidem*, in the same place
i.e.	*id est*, that is
km	kilometer(s)
lit.	literally
m	meter(s)
mm	millimeter(s)
n(n).	note(s)
n.d.	no date
no(s).	number(s)
obv.	obverse
p(p).	page(s)
pers. comm.	personal communication
pl(s).	plate(s)
rev.	reverse
sq.	square
vs.	versus

LIST OF FIGURES

LIST OF TABLES

PREFACE

This volume is the result of a two-day seminar held at the Oriental Institute at the University of Chicago on March 7–8, 2008. It was an honor and a pleasure to organize the seminar as a postdoctoral fellow at the Oriental Institute, which has been associated with decades of groundbreaking research on Near Eastern tribes and nomads. One might draw a direct line from the Braidwood's work on pastoral and agricultural communities along the "hilly flanks" of the Fertile Crescent, to Michael Rowton's famous papers on enclosed nomadism and dimorphic chiefdoms, to Robert McC. Adams' work on the Mesopotamian frontier, to that of six of the contributors to this volume who hold Ph.D.s from the University of Chicago. All that work played a part in revolutionizing the way we understand the role of nomads and tribe-state interaction in Near Eastern history. I hope that this volume marks a further step forward along a research path that the Oriental Institute has been instrumental in paving.

I am grateful for the enthusiasm and dedication with which all of the participants approached the conference and am thankful for the help of Steve Camp, Chris Woods, Seth Richardson, McGuire Gibson, Adam T. Smith, David Schloen, and the entire faculty and staff of the Oriental Institute, who were more than welcoming, and graciously offered practical and intellectual support that contributed to shaping this volume. Mariana Perlinac and Kaye Oberhausen provided vital help organizing the seminar and keeping me sane throughout. Thomas Urban, Leslie Schramer, and Katie L. Johnson guided me through the publication process with patience and humor. I am especially grateful to Gil Stein, whose interest, encouragement, and input have been enormously constructive.

Finally, Sonya Edelman has been more supportive, helpful, patient, and inspiring than she knows.

Seminar Participants, from left to right. Front row: Jeffrey Szuchman, Bertille Lyonnet, Daniel Fleming, Anne Porter, Anatoly Khazanov, Robert Ritner, Thomas Barfield.
Back row: Frank Hole, Steven Rosen, Eveline van der Steen, Hans Barnard, Benjamin Saidel, Thomas Levy, David Schloen.

1

INTEGRATING APPROACHES TO NOMADS, TRIBES, AND THE STATE IN THE ANCIENT NEAR EAST

JEFFREY SZUCHMAN, UNIVERSITY OF CHICAGO

The chapters in this volume represent the contributions of a group of archaeologists, anthropologists, and historians who, in March 2008, gathered at a seminar at the Oriental Institute of the University of Chicago. Our aim was to present and discuss ways to integrate approaches to and ideas about the roles of pastoral nomads and tribe-state interactions in the ancient Near East. These concerns are by no means new; they have been of interest to researchers for decades, and recent work continues to be shaped by the classic theories of Ibn Khaldun, Kupper (1957), and Rowton (e.g., 1973; 1974; 1976), along with accounts and ethnographies of Near Eastern nomads in the nineteenth and twentieth centuries too numerous to list. However, despite calls for the integration of archaeology, anthropology, and history in the study of ancient pastoral nomadism in the Near East (LaBianca and Witzel 2007: 63), each discipline has been addressing these issues in relative isolation. Although great strides have recently been made,[1] a pressing need remains for cross-disciplinary dialog to establish a common framework for the study of pastoral nomadism and tribe-state interactions specific to the ancient Near East.

It was this overriding concern that lay behind the Oriental Institute seminar and the contributions in this book. The goal of the seminar was to find commonalities among the work of those studying nomadic and tribal groups throughout the greater Near East, from Iran to Egypt, and from prehistory to the early Islamic period. Where approaches and theories differed, we aimed to evaluate those differences in order to learn new ways to think and talk about nomads and tribes in our own research. This book thus represents an attempt to bring disparate scholars together to push forward a new agenda for studying pastoral nomads, tribes, and the state in the ancient Near East.

One particularly thorny problem associated with organizing a small seminar on such a large topic presented itself from the outset: how to convey the themes of the seminar without falling into the semantic trap of establishing social categories that may not represent reality. For example, the term "tribe," itself, and many of the attributes associated with it, such as segmentary lineages and egalitarianism, notions that have troubled anthropologists for some time, seem even more fluid and amorphous according to recent literature. In recent years, scholars of both texts and archaeology have acknowledged a degree of integration between urban and pastoral sectors, and between tribes and states that Rowton's standard dimorphic model did not anticipate (Fleming 2004; McClellan 2004; Porter 2002, 2004). Although this approach appears to capture more accurately the complexity of ancient tribe-state interactions,

---

[1] Notably those stemming from the research program "Difference and Integration" at the Universities of Halle-Wittenberg and Leipzig (Mitteilungen des SFB "Differenz und Integration"), and the recent University of California, Los Angeles, conference on the achaeology of mobility (Barnard and Wendrich 2008).

it also introduces questions about the very categories we use to describe pastoral nomadic tribes. Did such bounded categories really exist in antiquity, or are they fabrications or ideal-izations created by modern ethnographers (Abu-Lughod 1989; Marx 1992; Salzman 1999)? If so, should they be applied to mobile and sedentary communities in the past? Does it even make sense to discuss tribe and state as separate social, political, or economic sectors? As the division between tribe and state in antiquity continues to blur, we may seem hyperaware of the inadequacy of those terms that make up the title of this book: "nomad," "tribe," and "state." One is often compelled to define or defend their use at the outset of a publication (Abdi 2003: 398; Bar-Yosef and Khazanov 1992: 2; Leder 2004; Saidel and van der Steen 2007: 2). As a way to frame the issues with which the following chapters grapple, this introduction avoids offering specific definitions of the terms, but focuses on an examination of why these terms are so contentious.

NOMADS

The term nomad, or more precisely pastoral, or sheep- and goat-herding nomad, is itself a complex concept, and scholars have long struggled to identify and overcome the multiple biases that affect interpretations of Near Eastern nomadism. Although the word "nomad" no longer conjures up the image of mythic and inscrutable creatures, fiercely independent and existing outside the purview of the civilized world, this romantic notion was not easily van-quished, and one can trace a long tradition of Western travelers and scholars who perpetuated the myth of the stateless nomad, along with a false binary state-nomad opposition. A second myth that has been put to rest is that of the barbaric nomad, sweeping in from the desert to occasionally overwhelm bucolic villages and their defenseless inhabitants.

In place of the mythical noble nomad and the barbaric nomad, scholars have focused not on the nomad per se, but on the nature of pastoral nomadism as an economic adaptation. This focus on pastoral economies has brought to light the fact that there are indeed many different types of pastoral nomadism in the Near East, depending in part on the natural environment. As Alizadeh (this volume) shows, the variety of pastoral economies has diverse ramifications, so that one pastoral nomadic community is not always comparable to another. For the most part, however, whether they deal with nomads in the highlands of southwest Iran, the Syrian steppe, or the Negev Desert, the chapters in this book are primarily concerned with multi-resource pastoral nomadism, an economic adaptation that depends upon a variety of resources that are acquired from a variety of economic pursuits in addition to pastoralism: small-scale cultivation, trade, crafts, raiding, smuggling, or other activities. That is, as Salzman (1971: 190) puts it, "to say 'pastoral' does not necessarily entail 'nomadic,' and to say 'nomadic,' does not necessarily entail 'pastoral.'"

The economic aspect of pastoral nomadism has occupied anthropological research for some time. Khazanov (1994; this volume), for example, has long held that pastoral nomad-ism is fundamentally an economic adaptation that entails mobility only as a by-product of a specialized pastoral economy. The work of Khazanov and others has also shown that economic necessity requires that nomadic communities are closely intertwined with village and city life. Emanuel Marx, for example, sees the integration of pastoral nomads with sedentary popula-tions as so complete that he questions the relevance of the concept at all. He has asked in a 1992 article, "Are There Pastoral Nomads in the Middle East?"; in 1996, "Are there Pastoral Nomads in the Arab Middle East?"; and, as recently as 2006 (p. 93), "is the concept 'pastoral nomads' still useful"? What Marx is wrestling with is not only the utility of the term "pastoral nomad" itself, but with the very category of a distinct pastoral nomadic economy, which according to him is merely "an attenuated version of the city's complex economic specialization and differentiation" (Marx 2007: 77).[2]

Marx's question is perhaps a natural response to the ever-increasing evidence that the distinction between nomadic and sedentary communities is not always clear. It is now commonplace to assert that pastoral nomads operate along a continuum of economic and social activities, at times pursuing pastoral activities to a greater extent than other forms of subsistence, and at other times engaging in agriculture more than in pastoral production. The emphasis on either economic pursuit can often correlate with an individual's or group's level of mobility. Since the 1970s, when Rowton (1973: 201) showed that ancient steppe and mountain nomads often comprised polities that represented "a curious blend of city-state, tribe, and nomadism," a number of whose members were becoming sedentary and nomadic in varying proportions and at varying times, archaeologists have stressed even greater levels of integration between nomadic and sedentary populations. Thus, nomads may become sedentary without severing ties to their nomadic kin or even their nomadic identity. Furthermore, behind Porter's (2004) notion of the "urban nomad" lies the suggestion that nomads can form, sustain, and dwell within urban locales. Does this mean that sedentary nomads and mobile nomads are both equally nomadic? At what point, if ever, then, does a sedentarized nomad cease to be a nomad (Whitcomb, this volume)? And, if identifying nomadic remains presents special challenges to archaeologists because of the nature of their mobile lifestyle (Barnard, this volume), what other challenges face archaeologists who seek evidence of ancient nomadism in urban contexts, perhaps in response to the economic and social demands of a nomadic livelihood (Lyonnet, Porter, this volume)?

These questions seem to revolve around two competing theories about the implications of the intimate integration of nomads into village, town, and city life. On the one hand, this integration means that, as an economic specialization, pastoral nomadism is so intertwined with the other sectors of a regional economy, that nomadic groups themselves are nearly indistinguishable from other elements of society. On the other hand, the integration of nomad and sedentary means that even sedentary nomads are still nomadic, in that they are culturally distinct from other members of a sedentary community. The conflict here is thus between understanding pastoral nomadism as either an economic or a cultural phenomenon. Yet neither of these factors alone is enough to explain the contrasts between nomadic and sedentary populations. Often, a nomadic community's self-identity goes well beyond its economic base. A sedentarized nomad remains intimately bound to tribe and tribal kin who remain mobile. Tents commonly erected alongside a mudbrick house (Beck 2003: 293; Mortensen 1993: 118, fig. 6.54), or the re-creation of temporary tent plans in more permanent mudbrick structures (Beck 1991: 336–40; Katakura 1977: 74–76; Layne 1987), are visual expressions of a persistent nomadic identity even in the context of residential stability. Mobility, then, in addition to a pastoral economy, is indeed an essential component of pastoral nomadism, one which must have an effect on the social structures that develop within a mobile community (Porter, this volume).

---

[2] For Marx, these concerns remain constant, though he appears to answer the questions differently on different occasions: "It is no longer useful to describe a particular population as pastoral nomads" (Marx 1992: 259); "The answer [to the question 'are there pastoral nomads in the Middle East?'] is emphatically yes, provided a new emphasis is given to the political-economic environment, and to the constantly changing conditions, in which pastoral nomads operate" (Marx 1996: 112; cf. Marx 2006: 93).

TRIBES

The pastoral economy/nomadic culture conundrum may be related to the fact that settled nomads identify not only as nomadic but also as members of their tribe, the second contentious word in the title of this volume. The notion of the tribe has a long history of use and abuse in the social sciences. In its early incarnation, according to the scheme most closely associated with Sahlins (1961; 1968) and Service (1971), the tribe was a stage of cultural evolution characterized by a group of cohesive but separate segments of society, integrated through mechanisms of lineage and other forms of organizational solidarity. While the social evolutionary framework of Sahlins and Service has been the target of a number of critiques, the segmented quality of tribal organization continues to be a useful classificatory feature of the tribe (Baştuğ 1998; Ritner 2007), despite criticisms leveled against the notion of tribe itself and false assumptions associated with tribal social organization (see Parkinson 2002 for an overview).

Some scholars have pointed out that one problem with the term "tribe" is that it is commonly described in opposition to the state. Tapper (1997: 6–9), for example, notes that "'Tribe' as an analytical concept ... is best viewed as — and best matches indigenous concepts for — a state of mind, a construction of reality, a model for action, a mode of social organization *essentially opposed to that of the centralized state*" (emphasis added). This conception of the tribe, rooted in a definition that describes what a tribe is *not*, rather than what it is, is one that is often applied, whether consciously or not (Fowles 2002: 18). Cribb (1991: 54–55), for example, who understands the tribe as a more concrete mechanism by which territory is allocated, suggests that "'tribe' simply refers to a territorial system in which control is not vested in the state apparatus, or at least where certain areas of control are relinquished to local interests and collectives." But Tapper and Cribb represent only two of the multiple approaches that describe tribes in ways that can best be characterized as flexible, adaptive, and highly variable. Tribes have been understood as cultural systems, political systems, and economic systems. They have been described in so many shapes and sizes that many anthropologists have advocated abandoning the term "tribe" altogether.

Some archaeologists have also avoided the term "tribal" in favor of more descriptive designations like "heterachical" (Ehrenreich, Crumley, and Levy 1995), "communal," or "corporate" social systems (Blanton et al. 1996; Porter 2002), terms that evoke the nature of tribes as communities in which power is shared across the group, rather than vested in an individual or small group of people. Corporate structures of authority involve communal decision making and relatively unrestricted access to the instruments of power, in contrast to hierarchical forms of authority and exclusive access to power. Moreover, several forms of political authority could occur within the same community (Fleming, this volume), and apparent co-occurrence of these features reflected in the archaeological record have been interpreted as the material correlate of a tribally organized society (Cooper 2006a; 2006b).

Tribalism has also been recently understood not as a static social form, but as a dynamic process that undergoes and generates a range of social transformations over varying time scales (Fowles 2002; Parkinson, ed. 2002; Parkinson and Galaty 2007). Thus, as Fowles (2002: 18) notes, "With respect to the problem of tribal society, we therefore stand to profit from an analytic framework that ... concerns itself less with characterizing the political, ideological, or economic qualities of a society — in other words, with what a tribe is — and more with what happens over time in tribal contexts." In other words, "'Tribal' is as 'tribal' does"

(Fowles 2002: 18). In the chapters that follow, changes in tribal structure are examined over differing time scales, some relatively short, others spanning thousands of years.

Finally, just as there seems to be a "culture of nomadism" that values mobility as an ideology and generates unique modes of habitation and even literary expression (e.g., Bailey 2002), tribalism too has an ideological and cultural element that, in modern contexts at least, values characteristics like honor, piety, hospitality, courage, and restraint (Caton 1990: 25–35; van der Steen, this volume; cf. Dresch 1989: 250). This feature of tribes has also played a role in their development over time and the way they interact with state authorities.

TRIBES AND THE STATE

Although we should avoid defining the tribe solely in contrast to the state, the two entities do come into contact, and their interactions are mediated in a variety of ways. The obstacles to understanding the general nature of tribe-state interactions are clearly apparent in the context of modern geopolitics, which offers a more immediate sense of the unease and ambiguity that results when these three independent concepts — nomads, tribes, and the state — are integrated. In places like Kenya and Iraq, the tensions at play between tribal and state allegiances are perhaps most visible (Salzman 2008). For example, Fox (2007) recently addressed this very tension by explaining that in Iraq, "the family, clan, tribe and sect command major allegiance, and the idea of the individual autonomous voter, if necessary and commonplace in our own systems, is totally foreign." Although Fox addresses tribes and the modern democratic nation-state, issues that are not germane to the ancient world, his statement is nonetheless telling because it speaks to the enduring myth of the tribe-state dichotomy — to the idea that tribal structures cannot coexist with state structures. On the contrary, several chapters in this book show that not only can tribes and states coexist and even share social elements, but that we must begin to question the very idea that tribes and states are categorically *not the same thing*. What Fox's statement shows, concerning modern Iraq as much as anywhere else, is just how tangled the integration of tribe and state can be.[3] Each individual element can be called upon to either increase solidarity among disparate groups, or emphasize distinctions between groups (Dresch and Haykel 1995). Thus, just as nomads can become sedentary without giving up their nomadic identity, tribes may not only become states, but they can also become state-like, exhibiting urban features and political hierarchies, while still remaining in some sense, fundamentally tribal.

INTEGRATING APPROACHES TO NOMADS, TRIBES, AND THE STATE IN THE ANCIENT NEAR EAST

What all this means is that none of these concepts — nomad, tribe, and state — can be divorced from the other. Any study of sociopolitical change or interaction in the ancient Near East will have to take each element into account to build a comprehensive picture. We need to understand how each element interacts with, affects, and changes the other in ways that feed back, and either alter or reinforce existing patterns of economic, social, and political behavior.

---

[3] In the case of modern Iraq, religious affiliation also plays a fundamental role in shaping identity, a role that was also likely to have been important for ancient Near Eastern tribes (e.g., Hole, this volume; Porter 2002, this volume; Rosen et al. 2007).

This book raises several questions that address how that goal might be accomplished. Does it make sense to talk about nomads, tribes, and states as separate, if none can really be understood without the others? How should we integrate them? What evidence should we draw upon? How can we even understand one another if we are using a vocabulary that is often so imprecise? At a basic level, these are the same questions scholars have been asking for a long time, though never before has a group of scholars come together to address specific issues of integrating these approaches in the ancient Near East. Some recent conferences have helped move the general debate along in various ways, but while some have been more expansive in scope (Leder and Streck 2005), others have been narrower in either geographic (Saidel and van der Steen 2007) or methodological (Barnard and Wendrich 2008) focus. The chapters in this volume describe a variety of types of nomadism and tribal organization in different regions of the Near East (Syria, Jordan, Egypt, Israel, Iran), and different time periods (from prehistory to the early Islamic period), and draw on archaeological, textual, ethnographic, ethnoarchaeological, and ethnohistoric data.

Within this diversity, however, the contributors share a concern with both the methods by which nomads and tribes can be accessed in the archaeological and historical record, and with how mobile populations and tribal groups actually behaved — how they organized their economies, how they structured their society and interactions with other societies, where they lived, etc. That these concerns were predominant became especially clear during discussions over the course of the seminar that touched on the role of ethnographic analogy, the categories of data that may indicate the presence of pastoral nomads at a site, the extent of participation of nomads in craft activities, or even whether tribal kingdoms were ever capable of being sustained. The organization of the book follows those organically generated themes that guided and derived from discussions during the conference and reflect the most pressing issues, according to the participants, in the study of pastoral nomads and tribe-state interaction in the ancient Near East.

INTEGRATING METHODS AND DATA: ARCHAEOLOGY, ETHNOARCHAEOLOGY, AND TEXTS

The first part of the book focuses on the first step in solving some of these problems: how to identify ancient pastoral nomads and tribes. These papers all deal with collecting and interpreting problematic or scarce data: How do we interpret the past when texts confront archaeology? How do we interpret archaeological data in the absence of texts? How do our own assumptions about modern nomads affect the way we analyze ancient remains? The first two chapters (Barnard, Ritner) offer contrasting approaches for studying nomadic populations in the deserts of Egypt. Both of these papers, and many others that follow, deal with the intersection of texts and archaeology. For example, Barnard assails the tendency of researchers to assume that a certain complex of material remains must equate with a named nomadic population simply because that name appears in texts. Those texts, however, were often composed by people who in fact knew very little about the populations to which they refer. Ritner highlights this very incongruity as evidence for the nature of the relationship between the Egyptian state and Libyan nomads.

The reliability of archaeological and ethnographic data was a subject of some debate during the seminar. For example, although several participants agreed that Lyonnet's suggestion that *Kranzhügel* sites may have been the locus of seasonal communal activity among pastoralists made intuitive sense, some participants also stressed the need for more conclusive quantitative data to support or disprove the hypothesis. These data can come from faunal remains that may point to seasonality or patterns of sheep/goat exploitation, presence of wool production tools or agricultural implements, or chemical residue analysis that might point to cultural or economic links between pastoral and non-pastoral populations. Rosen's paper makes a clear case that when several categories of archaeological data exist, they can be combined to analyze long-term trends in nomadic and sedentary interactions.

During the seminar, discussion also centered on the appropriateness of ethnographic analogy for understanding ancient nomadism. The archetypal black tent, upon which many ethnoarchaeological studies of camp layout, domestic space, and personal effects have been based (Cribb 1991; Hole 1979), is probably not an appropriate analog for ancient nomadic environments or behavior (Barnard, Rosen, this volume; Saidel 2008). Furthermore, the behavior of modern pastoral groups in one region may be very different from that of pastoralists in another region, either as a result of geographic, political, social, or a host of other contingent factors (Alizadeh). Porter makes a strong case that archaeologists have long operated according to a misguided model, derived from modern ethnography, of ancient nomads as "essentially alien to urban and agricultural society in the Near East of the third and second millennia BC."

Despite the critique of ethnographic analogy that is woven into several of the chapters in this volume, other chapters suggest that new technologies (Saidel) and a nuanced ethnohistorical approach (van der Steen) can indeed offer new ways of understanding changes in social, economic, or domestic behavior in the past. Hole also reminds us that there is much to be gained from a careful analysis of the behavior of modern pastoral nomadic groups in the Middle East, especially when those behaviors are a response, in part, to geography and climate, features that have changed very little since antiquity (see also Alizadeh, this volume), or indeed to mobility itself, which Porter sees as the fundamental feature of pastoral nomadism that shapes social structure. Hole's response serves to caution us that although new approaches to ancient pastoral nomadism are both necessary and often fruitful, we must be careful not to stray too far from understanding nomadism as much more than an adaptive response to generally stable environmental factors.

INTEGRATING PARADIGMS OF TRIBE-STATE INTERACTION

The chapters in the book's second section focus on a second recurring topic of discussion during the seminar — what exactly Near Eastern tribes and nomads were capable of accomplishing. This includes not only the potential for nomads to undertake large construction projects (Lyonnet) or craft activities on an industrial scale (Levy), but also how the social structures of mobile tribes enable particular patterns of political or social interactions with non-tribal actors (Alizadeh, Fleming, Khazanov, Porter), or how mobile tribes transition to states (Whitcomb). These topics naturally generated a great deal of debate. For example, Alizadeh disagreed with Khazanov about the extent of the military capabilities of nomads prior to the domestication of the horse and camel. Levy's proposal that the copper production that took place at Khirbet en-Nahas was carried out by the same nomadic pastoralists who utilized a nearby cemetery and who may have been the Shasu of Egyptian texts was also the subject of some debate. Whereas some participants wondered how, or indeed if, the site might look different if copper production was controlled by a state (i.e., Egypt) rather than by nomads, others agreed that the tenth century was a period in which no centralized state in the region had the means to control such an operation. Here, the debate seemed as much about the archaeological data supporting tribal organization of copper production as it was about whether a tribe of pastoral nomads was capable of organizing and practicing metallurgy on an industrial scale.

There was also discussion of what constituted a "tribal state," and whether such a thing could have existed at all. Barfield suggested that what some referred to as a tribal state was more likely a situation in which a tribal leader, by means of military advantage and charisma, became the leader of a state, but did not maintain tribal traditions or organizational structures. Whitcomb suggested that Mu'awiya was indeed the ruler of a tribal state, but that this was short-lived, having devolved as a result of political factionalization. Although we came to no consensus, this was, as one participant pointed out, perhaps partly the result of the differing definitions of tribal states, one of the very problems that the seminar intended to address. The fact that this issue surfaced near the end of the second day of the seminar should serve to remind us that semantic disagreements may underlie similar debates. If we are to continue to make progress in understanding the ways tribes and states interacted in the ancient Near East, we must strive to be unambiguous in our terminology and specific in our analysis.

The final section of the book contains a response by Hole to the preceding chapters. His response is informed by personal experience and therefore offers a case study in the integration of methodological and conceptual approaches to Near Eastern nomadism and tribe-state interactions.

Although this book is organized according to the thematic links that I found most salient, another editor may have made different choices. The fact is that several conceptual threads weave all the chapters together in different ways.[4] For example, several contributors take an approach to particular regions or communities to assess long-term changes in the nature of pastoral nomadism or tribe-state interactions. The time scales vary — Rosen looks at thousands of years of nomad-sedentary interaction, whereas Levy looks at sociopolitical changes among nomads in Jordan over the course of the Iron Age. What is significant, however, is that pastoral nomadic tribes do change. The way they develop and interact with their neighbors at a given moment, whether those are states or other tribes, is as much the result of the contingent historical, economic, or social circumstances both within and external to the tribe that have led up to that moment, as it is the result of more predictable, immediate factors like ecology, for example. The dynamic nature of pastoral nomadism, tribal structures, and tribe-state interactions is a key element of these papers, which seem to build upon recent approaches that view tribalism as a process, rather than as a static category (Fowles 2002).

FUTURE RESEARCH

In many ways, these papers turn the notion of tribe-state interdependency on its head and demonstrate that in some cases not only can tribes act entirely independently, but states can sometimes be dependent on tribes. At other times, many of the features of nomadic tribes begin to look very state-like, which suggests that we will need to continue to wrestle with our definitions of tribe and state. It is likely that the line between tribes and states will continue to blur, as several of these chapters argue that nomadic tribes can take a rather sophisticated role in regional interactions, industrial and administrative organization, the development of

---

[4] In this respect, it is worth noting that the seminar papers were originally presented in three thematic sessions that were organized along different lines from the presentation of chapters in this book

urban centers, and state formation. Many of these papers stretch previous ideas concerning what tribes can do. Construction of urban sites, monumental architecture, and the formation of powerful kingdoms turn out to be well within the realm of tribal accomplishments. Each of the contributors to this book raises vital questions that future research will need to address. One of the more exciting questions these papers raise is whether, if we are only just beginning to identify nomadic tribes as the agents of significant social change in the ancient Near East — changes we had previously thought were instigated by states or even empires — in how many other cases have we overlooked the autonomous role of nomads or tribes in regional developments?

BIBLIOGRAPHY

Abdi, Kamyar
    2003   "The Early Development of Pastoralism in the Central Zagros Mountains." *Journal of World Prehistory* 17: 395–448.

Abu-Lughod, Lila
    1989   "Zones of Theory in the Anthropology of the Arab World." *Annual Review of Anthropology* 18: 267–306.

Bailey, Clinton
    2002   *Bedouin Poetry from Sinai and the Negev*. London: Saqi Books.

Bar-Yosef, Ofer, and Anatoly M. Khazanov
    1992   "Introduction." In *Pastoralism in the Levant: Archaeological Materials and Anthropological Perspectives*, edited by Ofer Bar-Yosef and Anatoly M. Khazanov, pp. 1–9. Madison: Prehistory Press.

Barnard, Hans, and Willeke Wendrich, editors
    2008   *The Archaeology of Mobility. Nomads in the Old and in the New World*. Cotsen Advanced Seminars. Los Angeles: Cotsen Institute of Archaeology.

Baştuğ, Sharon
    1998   "The Segmentary Lineage System: A Reappraisal." In *Changing Nomads in a Changing World*, edited by Joseph Ginat and Anatoly M. Khazanov, pp. 94–123. Brighton and Portland: Sussex Academic Press.

Beck, Lois
    1991   *Nomad: A Year in the Life of a Qasha'i Tribesman in Iran*. Berkeley: University of California.
    2003   "Qashqa'i Nomadic Pastoralists and Their Use of Land." In *Yeki Bud, Yeki Nabud: Essays on the Archaeology of Iran in Honor of William M. Sumner*, edited by Naomi F. Miller and Kaymar Abdi, pp. 289–304. Los Angeles: The Cotsen Institute of Archaeology; The American Institute of Iranian Studies; The University of Pennsylvania Museum of Archaeology and Anthropology.

Blanton, Richard E.; Gary M. Feinman; Stephen A. Kowalewski; and Peter N. Peregrine
    1996   "A Dual-Processual Theory for the Evolution of Mesoamerican Civilization." *Current Anthropology* 37: 1–14.

Caton, Steven
    1990   "Anthropological Theories of Tribe and State Formation in the Middle East: Ideology and Semiotics of Power." In *Tribes and State Formation in the Middle East*, edited by Philip Khoury and Joseph Kostiner, pp. 74–108. Berkeley: University of California Press.

Cooper, Lisa
    2006a   "The Demise and Regeneration of Bronze Age Urban Centers in the Euphrates Valley of Syria." In *After Collapse: The Regeneration of Complex Societies*, edited by Glenn M. Schwartz and John J. Nichols, pp. 18–37. Tucson: University of Arizona Press.
    2006b   *Early Urbanism on the Syrian Euphrates*. New York: Routledge.

Cribb, Roger
    1991   *Nomads in Archaeology*. Cambridge: Cambridge University Press.

Dresch, Paul
    1989   *Tribes, Government, and History in Yemen*. Oxford: Oxford University Press.

Dresch, Paul, and Bernard Haykel
    1995   "Stereotypes and Political Styles: Islamists and Tribesfolk in Yemen." *International Journal of Middle East Studies* 27 (4 November): 405–31.

Ehrenreich, Robert M.; Carole L. Crumley; and Janet E. Levy, eds.
  1995   *Heterarchy and the Analysis of Complex Societies.* Arlington: American
              Anthropological Association.

Fleming, Daniel
  2004   *Democracy's Ancient Ancestors: Mari and Early Collective Governance.* Cambridge:
              Cambridge University Press.

Fowles, Severin M.
  2002   "From Social Type to Social Process: Placing 'Tribe' in a Historical Framework."
              In *The Archaeology of Tribal Societies*, edited by William A. Parkinson, pp. 13–33.
              Ann Arbor: International Monographs in Prehistory.

Fox, Robin
  2007   "The Kindness of Strangers." *Society* 44(6): 164–70.

Hole, Frank
  1979   "Rediscovering the Past in the Present: Ethnoarchaeology in Luristan, Iran." In
              Ethnoarchaeology: Implications of Ethnography for Archaeology, edited by Carol
              Kramer, pp. 192–218. New York: Columbia University.

Ibn Khaldun
  1967   *The Muqaddimah.* Edited by N. J. Dawood. Translated by Franz Rosenthal. London:
              Routledge and Kegan Paul.

Katakura, Motoko
  1977   *Bedouin Village: A Study of a Saudi Arabian People in Transition.* Tokyo: University
              of Tokyo.

Khazanov, Anatoly M.
  1994   *Nomads and the Outside World.* Translated by Julia Crookenden. 2nd edition.
              Madison: University of Wisconsin Press.

Kupper, Jean-Robert
  1957   *Les nomades en Mésopotamie au temps des rois de Mari.* Paris: Bibliothèque de la
              Faculté de Philosophie et Lettres de l'Université de Liège.

LaBianca, Øystein, and Kristen Witzel
  2007   "Nomads, Empires and Civilizations: Great and Little Traditions and the Historical
              Landscape of the Southern Levant." In *On the Fringe of Society: Archaeological and
              Ethnoarchaeological Perspectives on Pastoral and Agricultural Societies*, edited by
              Benjamin A. Saidel and Eveline J. van der Steen, pp. 63–74. British Archaeological
              Reports, International Series 1657. Oxford: Archaeopress.

Layne, Linda
  1987   "Village-Bedouin: Patterns of Change from Mobility to Sedentism in Jordan." In
              Method and Theory for Activity Area Research, edited by Susan Kent, pp. 345–73.
              New York: Columbia University.

Leder, Stefan
  2004   "Nomadische Lebensformen und ihre Wahrnehmung im Spiegel der arabischen
              Terminologie." *Die Welt des Orients* 34: 72–104.

Leder, Stefan, and Bernhard Streck, eds.
  2005   *Shifts and Drifts in Nomad-Sedentary Relations.* Nomaden und Sesshaften 2.
              Wiesbaden: Reichert.

Marx, Emanuel
  1992   "Are There Pastoral Nomads in the Middle East?" In *Pastoralism in the Levant:
              Archaeological Material in Anthropological Perspectives*, edited by Ofer Bar-Yosef
              and Anatoly Khazanov, pp. 255–60. Monographs in World Archaeology 10. Madison:
              Prehistory Press.

1996   "Are There Pastoral Nomads in the Arab Middle East?" In *The Anthropology of Tribal and Peasant Pastoral Societies: The Dialectics of Social Cohesion and Fragmentation = Antropologia delle Società Pastorali Tribali e Contadine: La Dialettica della Coesione e della Frammentazione Sociale*, edited by Ugo Fabietti and Philip Carl Salzman, pp. 101–15. Pavia: Collegio Ghislieri; Como: Ibis.

2006   "The Political Economy of Middle Eastern and North African Pastoral Nomads." In *Nomadic Societies in the Middle East and North Africa: Entering the 21st Century*, edited by Dawn Chatty, pp. 78–97. Leiden: Brill.

2007   "Nomads and Cities: Changing Conceptions." In *On the Fringe of Society: Archaeological and Ethnoarchaeological Perspectives on Pastoral and Agricultural Societies*, edited by Benjamin A. Saidel and Eveline J. van der Steen, pp. 75–78. British Archaeological Reports, International Series 1657. Oxford: Archaeopress.

McClellan, Thomas C.

1992   "The 12th Century BC in Syria: Comments on H. Sader's Paper." In *The Crisis Years: The 12th Century BC, from Beyond the Danube to the Tigris*, edited by William A. Ward and Martha Sharp Joukowsky, pp. 164–73. Dubuque: Kendall/Hunt.

Mortensen, Inge Deman

1993   *Nomads of Luristan: History, Material Culture, and Pastoralism in Western Iran*. London and New York: Thames & Hudson; Copenhagen: Rhodos International Science and Art Publishers.

Parkinson, William A., ed.

2002   *The Archaeology of Tribal Societies*. Ann Arbor: International Monographs in Prehistory.

Parkinson, William A.

2002   "Introduction: Archaeology and Tribal Societies." In *The Archaeology of Tribal Societies*, edited by William A. Parkinson, pp. 1–12. Ann Arbor: International Monographs in Prehistory.

Parkinson, William A., and Michael L. Galaty

2007   "Secondary States in Perspective: An Integrated Approach to State Formation in the Prehistoric Aegean." *American Anthropologist* 109: 113–29.

Porter, Anne

2002   "The Dynamics of Death: Ancestors, Pastoralism, and the Origins of a Third-Millennium City in Syria." *Bulletin of the American Schools of Oriental Research* 325: 1–36.

2004   "The Urban Nomad: Countering the Old Clichés." In *Nomades et Sédentaires dans le Proche-Orient Ancien* (Rencontre Assyriologique Internationale 46, Paris), edited by Christophe Nicolle, pp. 69–74. Amurru 3. Paris: Éditions Recherche sur les Civilisations.

Ritner, Robert

2007   "Fragmentation and Re-integration in the Third Intermediate Period." Paper presented at the conference "The Libyan Period in Egypt," Leiden.

Rosen, Steven A.; Fanny Bocquentin; Yoav Avni; and Naomi Porat

2007   "Investigations at Ramat Saharonim: A Desert Neolithic Sacred Precinct in the Central Negev." *Bulletin of the American Schools of Oriental Research* 346: 1–27.

Rowton, Michael B.

1973   "Urban Autonomy in a Nomadic Environment." *Journal of Near Eastern Studies* 32: 201–15.

1974   "Enclosed Nomadism." *Journal of the Economic and Social History of the Orient* 17: 1–30.

1976   "Dimorphic Structure and Topology." *Oriens Antiquus* 15: 17–31.

Sahlins, Marshall D.

1961 "The Segmentary Lineage: An Organization of Predatory Expansion." *American Anthropologist* 63: 322–45.

1968 *Tribesmen*. Englewood Cliffs: Prentice-Hall.

Saidel, Benjamin A.

2008 "The Bedouin Tent: An Ethno-Archaeological Portal to Antiquity or a Modern Construct?" In *The Archaeology of Mobility: Old World and New World Nomadism*, edited Hans Barnard and Willeke Z. Wendrich, pp. 465–86. Los Angeles: Cotsen Institute of Archaeology.

Saidel, Benjamin A., and Eveline J. van der Steen, eds.

2007 *On the Fringe of Society: Archaeological and Ethnoarchaeological Perspectives on Pastoral and Agricultural Societies*. British Archaeological Reports, International Series 1657. Oxford: Archaeopress.

Salzman, Philip C.

1971 "Movement and Resource Extraction among Pastoral Nomads: The Case of the Shah Nawazi Baluch." *Anthropological Quarterly* 44 (3, Comparative Studies of Nomadism and Pastoralism): 185–97.

1999 "Is Inequality Universal?" *Current Anthropology* 40: 31–61.

2008 *Culture and Conflict in the Middle East*. Amherst: Humanity Books.

Service, Elman R.

1971 *Primitive Social Organization: An Evolutionary Perspective*. New York: Random House.

Tapper, Richard

1997 *Frontier Nomads of Iran: A Political and Social History of the Shahsevan*. Cambridge: Cambridge University.

2

THE ARCHAEOLOGY OF THE PASTORAL NOMADS BETWEEN THE NILE AND THE RED SEA

HANS BARNARD, UNIVERSITY OF CALIFORNIA, LOS ANGELES

The archaeology of Egypt has long been overshadowed by the wealth of textual sources, from monumental to informal, further augmented by the relatively early translation of hieroglyphic Egyptian and the initial emphasis on finds of museum quality. Initially, Egyptian archaeology was perceived as a technique to find more texts and objects, while archaeological observations were readily explained from the textual data. Only recently has the archaeology of Egypt become a specialism in its own right, generating its own specific data, although often still haunted by legacies of the past. The latter also concerns the study of the pastoral nomads that regularly occur in the Egyptian textual records, most famously the *Medjay* during the Middle Kingdom (1975–1640 B.C.) and the *Blemmyes* in Greco-Roman and Byzantine times (332 B.C.–A.D. 641). These groups are often associated with specific archaeological phenomena; the Medjay with the pan-graves, so called because they are shaped like a frying pan; the Blemmyes with Eastern Desert Ware, well-burnished hand-made cups and bowls with incised decorations.

A recent study of Eastern Desert Ware, which included chemical analysis of the ceramic matrix and the organic residues in the vessels, as well as ethnography and experimental archaeology, indicated that it was probably made and used by a group of pastoral nomads, but did not provide any evidence toward their identification nor an association with any specific group mentioned in the textual sources. Such is further hampered by the scholarly interest in the remains left in the Eastern Desert by outsiders, miners, traders and quarry-men, while little research has been done on the pastoral nomads living in the area. The archaeological study of the latter requires a specialized approach, combining the study of ephemeral campsites and low-density surface scatters with data on the environment, the available resources, and the routes of the nomads. This methodology will be very similar for the study of pastoral nomads, mobile groups of hunter-gatherers, or sections of a settled population that have temporarily been displaced. Specialists in these fields should work together to come to an archaeology of mobility to increase our understanding of people on the move.

HISTORICAL BACKGROUND

Egypt is not just a gift of the Nile, as famously stated by Herodotus, but also of the deserts surrounding it (Friedman 2002). At the end of the Holocene pluvial period (or Holocene "wet phase," 8500–5300 B.C.) the desiccation of North Africa drove most of the mobile herder-hunter-gatherers inhabiting the area into the Nile Valley, where they settled and gave rise to the Pharaonic civilization (Kuper 2006; Kuper and Kröpelin 2006). The desert west of the Nile, the Libyan or Western Desert, became all but uninhabitable save for a few oases (such as Fayum, Siwa, Bahariya, Farafra, Dakhla, Kharga, Kufra, and Salima). In contrast, the desert between the Nile and the Red Sea, the Nubian or Eastern Desert, has no oases but can support a small number of inhabitants due to shallow aquifers that are replenished by occasional rainfall in the Red Sea Hills (Kaper 1998; Krzywinski and Pierce 2001). As Pharaonic Egypt developed, any communal memory of the past quickly disappeared and was replaced with respectful apprehension for the vast arid areas referred to as "dšr.t" (*desheret* = red land) and a deep affection for "km.t" (*kemet* = black land), the fertile Nile Valley that was previously mostly avoided because of its marshes and dangerous wildlife (Butzer 1997; Kuper and Kröpelin 2006). As a consequence, the inhabitants of the desert were usually mistrusted. The fear for the desert and the marginalization of its inhabitants carried on into modern times, in Egypt and beyond. On the other hand, there were frequent contacts between the population of the Nile Valley and the desert dwellers, at times hostile but more often friendly (Adams 1984; Barnard 2005; Cappers 2006; Christides 1980; Dafaᶜalla 1987; Dahl and Hjort-af-Ornas 2006; Dijkstra 2008; Eide et al. 1998; Giuliani 1998; Hafsaas 2006; Kaper 1998; Krzywinski and Pierce 2001; Lassányi 2005; Sadr 1987, 1990; Sidebotham, Barnard, and Pyke 2002; Updegraff 1988; Zibelius-Chen 2007). Cooperation included the employment of the desert dwellers as mercenaries, guards, or guides and their aid with the harvest, in exchange for part of the yield and the right to have their flocks graze on the stubbles afterward, leaving their droppings as fertilizer for the next crop. The desert dwellers are also known to have brought medicinal herbs, charcoal of acacia trees, and of course their animals to markets in the Nile Valley, as they still do today (Cappers 2006; Dahl and Hjort-af-Ornas 2006; Kaper 1998; Krzywinski and Pierce 2001; Sidebotham, Barnard, and Pyke 2002).

In Egypt, the enormous wealth of Pharaonic monuments and the early translation of Egyptian hieroglyphs (in 1822–1824 by Jean-François Champollion, partly based on the work of Thomas Young, Johan David Åkerblad, and the baron Silvestre de Sacy) have long overshadowed the archaeology of settlements and daily life. Historical and archaeological research each produces data sets that can be analogous, complementary, or contradictory (Bietak 1979; Rosen 2006; Wendrich et al. 2006). These different sources of information should be pursued more or less independently, although their confrontation can serve as an additional heuristic tool, and one cannot replace the other, or be considered superior. The dearth of archaeological data is all the more significant in areas not comprehensively covered by the texts, such as pastoral nomads or the Eastern Desert. Here we are confronted with extremely limited information, written by outsiders and strongly biased toward a settled life in the Nile Valley, which nevertheless dominates the interpretation of the relevant archaeological finds (table 2.1). At the very beginning of his monumental work on the Middle Nile region, Adams writes that "Egypt at the lower end of the Nile has the longest recorded history in the world. Inner Africa, at the headwaters of the same river has almost the shortest. Nubia, the land between, alternates for 5,000 years between history and dark ages" (Adams 1984: 1). During that time, Nubia was often perceived as a potential threat to the ancient Egyptian universe and often amalgamated with the Eastern Desert, not only by ancient authors but subsequently also in the minds of modern scholars. The authority of the written sources is thus responsible for the ongoing ambiguous association of people, archaeological objects, and even places both with Nubia and with the Eastern Desert (Barnard 2005; Burstein 2008). The fact that much of our current knowledge is based on research done within the framework of the UNESCO International Campaign to Save the Monuments of Nubia, working in Lower Nubia before it was lost under the water of Lake Nasser in the 1960s (Bietak 1966; Ricke 1967; Strouhal 1984; Williams 1983), only adds to this confusion.

MEDJAY AND PAN-GRAVES

Three groups are usually associated with the Eastern Desert: the Medjay (in Pharaonic times), the Blemmyes (in Greco-Roman times), and the Beja (in modern times). The Medjay (*mḏʒj.w*, fig. 2.1; Faulkner 1962; Gardiner 1947) are mentioned in a number of Egyptian sources, mostly dated to the Middle Kingdom and the Second Intermediate (Hyksos) Period (table 2.1), but they also feature in earlier and later texts (Bietak 1966; Giuliani 1998; Hafsaas 2006; Sadr 1990; Zibelius-Chen 2007). From these, they appear to be part of a southern Nilotic, "Nubian," and dark-skinned conglomerate (Gardiner 1947; Giuliani 1998; Hafsaas 2006; Posener 1958), or to live as pastoral nomads in the Eastern Desert (Bietak 1966; Hafsaas 2006; Sadr 1990; Smither 1945). Elsewhere, especially in later texts, "mḏʒ.w" seems to refer to mercenaries (bowmen) or guards, often without obvious ethnic connotation (Bietak 1966; Gardiner 1947; Zibelius-Chen 2007). Such different modern interpretations of one ancient Egyptian term could indicate changes over time (Bietak 1966; Hafsaas 2006; Sadr 1990), or the simultaneous existence of different sections of the same ethnic group (Sadr 1987, 1988, 1990). More likely, however, it results from the ancient classification system, in which ethnic terms were differently defined and less static than expected from a modern point of view (Barnard 2007; Burstein 2008; Dolukhanov 1994; Hutchinson and Smith 1996; Jones 1997; Mayerson 1993; Ratcliffe 1994; Rosen 2006; Sadr 1990; Yinger 1994). Instead of referring to an entity resembling a nation-state, "mḏʒj.w" was probably used in a way closer to modern and equally problematic terms like "Gypsy" or "Jew" (Barnard 2005; Kershaw 1998: 563–72).

Other ancient Egyptian names of nomadic groups include "Aamu" (now usually placed in the Sinai and said to have survived by cattle raiding; Weinstein 1975), "jwntj.w" (Cairn-people, although descriptive is believed to refer to a specific ethnic group, like the Medjay said to be bowmen from the Eastern Desert; Behrens 1982; Lansing 1947; Meredith 1957), and "Tjehenu" or "Tjemehu" (now usually identified as Libyans, but said to be at war with Nubian peoples; Breasted 1962; Murray 1965). More general terms for (pastoral) nomads include "ḥrjw.šˁ" (sand-people), "nmjw.šˁ" (sand-walkers) and "ẖtjw.tʒ" (vagabonds); these could possibly have been used for representatives of more than one of the peoples mentioned above. The existence of such descriptive terms suggests that the other terms, with no obvious meaning in ancient Egyptian, are based on a foreign language. These terms could indeed have referred specifically to a certain people, like modern "Beja" (Barnard 2007; Dahl and Hjort-af-Ornas 2006). They could also have been related to the lifestyle of segments of the group, such as "Bedouin" (Cole 2003), or have a more complicated etymology like "barbarian" (βάρβαρος), originally an ancient Greek derogatory onomatopoeia with no previous meaning in any language; or "Eskimo" (Algonquian for "eaters of raw meat" or Montagnais for "speakers of a different language," Mailhot 1978), a pejorative taken from the language of a third people.

Two often cited ancient texts that mention the Medjay are the *Biography of Weni* (*Uni*) and the *Semna Dispatches*, dated circa 2250 B.C. and circa 1800 B.C. respectively. The *Biography of Weni* was carved into a slab of limestone that was part of the tomb or cenotaph in Abydos for the high government official Weni, who served under Pharaohs Teti, Pepi I, and Merenre (Sixth Dynasty). Near the beginning of the text, Medjay are listed among the people recruited for the army of Pepi I, as part of a larger group, the *Nḥsyw*, which is alternatively interpreted as "southerners," "Nubians," or "colored people." Near the end of the text, the rulers of the Medjay are said to have provided some of the wood for the seven boats that Pharaoh Merenre requested of Weni (Giuliani 1998; Lichtheim 1975). The Semna dispatches are a collection of official missives from occupied Nubia, written during the reign of Pharaoh Amenemhet III (Seventh Dynasty) and shortly afterwards copied onto a length of papyrus that was found in a Middle Kingdom tomb on the grounds of the Ramesseum (near Luxor) in 1896. Medjay occur in several of the dispatches, when they arrive from the desert or are encountered on its edge (Sadr 1990; Smither 1945). The latter source may indeed refer to (pastoral) nomads, but seems hardly consistent with the former, while neither provides a basis for the proposed link between the Medjay and the pan-graves.

Pan-graves were first described at Hu (ancient Seshesh, the capital of the seventh *nome* of Upper Egypt, between modern Denderah and Abydos) and later found in relative abundance in Lower Nubia, the Nile Valley between the First and Second Cataracts (fig. 2.2; Bietak 1966; Hafsaas 2006; Sadr 1987, 1990). Originally they were interpreted as atypical manifestations of the C-Group (table 2.1), later they were recognized to represent a contemporaneous but distinctly different group: the Pan-Grave Culture (Bietak 1966; Säve-Söderbergh 1941). Pan-graves are round to oval pits in which the body of the deceased is buried, in a crouched position, on its right side with the head either to the north or to the west (fig. 2.3; Bietak 1966; Friedman 2001, 2004; Hafsaas 2006; Sadr 1987, 1990; Säve-Söderbergh 1941). Some graves are lined or covered with stones or have a simple superstructure, others preserve evidence that the burial was preceded by the application of resins or ashes to the floor of the grave (Friedman 2001, 2004; Hafsaas 2006). Grave goods usually include pan-grave pottery (fig. 2.3), mostly hand-made bowls characterized by thin walls, thick rims, and cross-hatched incisions (Bietak 1966; Kemp 1977; Williams 1983). Other gifts include weapons, bracelets and necklaces of seashell beads, sometimes with characteristic "spacers" (Bietak 1966: pls. 32, 36; Hafsaas 2006: pl. 7), and, often in a secondary pit, one or more painted skulls of goats, gazelles, or cattle (fig. 2.4; Friedman 2001, 2004; Hafsaas 2006). Pan-grave cemeteries are usually small, although cemeteries with more than 100 pan-graves have been described at Dibeira and Ashkeit, near the Second Cataract, and at Mostagedda (north of Abydos). Most are some distance from the Nile, others are located on the fringes of cemeteries of the C-Group (Bietak 1966; Hafsaas 2006; Sadr 1987, 1990).

Scholars often connect the pan-graves with the Medjay (Adams 1984; Bietak 1966, 1979; Friedman 2001; Hafsaas 2006; Sadr 1987; Säve-Söderbergh 1941, but see Friedman 2004; Sadr 1990), an association that is reflected in more popular literature (Berg and Berg 1998). This conclusion was originally based on the abundance of weapons in the pan-graves near the Egyptian forts in Lower Nubia and the robust appearance of the bones, which led to the inference that these must be the graves of Medjay mercenaries known from the historical sources (Bietak 1966, 1979; Sadr 1987; Säve-Söderbergh 1941). The fact that these Medjay were considered to be directly related to the pastoral nomads of the Eastern Desert was seen reflected in the shell beads, mostly of Red Sea *Nerita* and *Conus* sp., and the interment of animal crania (Bietak 1966; Friedman 2001, 2004; Hafsaas 2006; Posener 1958; Sadr 1987, 1990).

There are obviously several problems with this interpretation (Bietak 1966; Sadr 1990). First is that the Medjay feature in the ancient sources from the Old to the New Kingdom, while most pan-graves were relatively securely dated, by associated finds, to the Second Intermediate Period (table 2.1). This could be explained by assuming that pan-graves and the associated material culture went in and out of fashion among the Medjay. Funerary practices, however, are usually an essential part of the cultural heritage or ethnic identity of a people and tend to be preserved throughout their history. Second is the distribution of the graves (fig. 2.3), which were mostly found in or very near the Nile Valley, on both the east and the west bank, and not in the Eastern Desert proper. Intensive archaeological surveys in the Kassala area of eastern Sudan (fig. 2.3) have revealed many potsherds with great similarity to those of the Pan-Grave Culture (Sadr 1987, 1988, 1990). These were dated to around 1500–1000 B.C., just after pan-graves and Medjay disappear from the Egyptian archaeological and historical records. The producers and users of these vessels were identified as the Mokram Group, after Mount Mokram near Kassala. This shows that archaeological research of the pastoral nomads in this area, although at times logistically and politically vexing, is technically eminently possible (Bar-Yosef and Khazanov 1992; Chang and Koster 1994; Cribb 1991; Sadr 1988; Veth, Smith, and Hiscock 2005; Wendrich and Barnard 2008). The relationship between the Mokram Group and the Pan-Grave Culture of the archaeological record, or the Medjay of the historical sources, however, remains unclear (Sadr 1988, 1990). Third, as discussed above, "mḏ₃j.w" may not have referred to a political, ethnic, or cultural entity that can be connected one-to-one with a corpus of archaeological finds. Finally, there is no evident reason to connect the archaeological finds with the Medjay, rather than with the Aamu, "jwntj.w" or the Tjehenu (Tjemehu), or even the "ḥrjw.š⸢," the "nmjw.š⸢," or the "ḥtjw.t₃." There may have been a group of people in ancient Egypt that was specifically identified, or identified themselves, as "mḏ₃j.w" and it is possible that the pan-graves were indeed constructed by groups of pastoral nomads, but their equation can only be assumed and is, so far, quite tentative.

BLEMMYES AND EASTERN DESERT WARE

An argument remarkably similar to that on Medjay and pan-graves above can be made concerning the proposed connection between the Blemmyes (Βλέμμυες or Βλέμυες) of the Greco-Roman sources on Egypt and its hinterland, dating from 332 B.C. to A.D. 641 (table 2.1), and Eastern Desert Ware (fig. 2.5; Bietak 2006; Rose 1995; Sidebotham and Wendrich 1996, 2001). The Blemmyes appear in the historical record between 620–600 B.C., on the enthronement stele of King Anlamani, and A.D. 500–600, in the so-called "Blemmyan documents" (Barnard 2005, 2007; Burstein 2008; Christides 1980; Dafaʿalla 1987; Eide et al. 1996, 1998, 2000; Krall 1900; Lassányi 2005; Updegraff 1988; Vycichl 1958; Zaborski 1989). They are depicted as "nomads and neither many nor warlike" (Strabo 17.1.53–54) and are "reported to have no heads, their mouths and eyes attached to their chests" (Pliny the Elder, *Natural History* 5.46). More comprehensive sources, such as Procopius' *De Bellis*, Priscus (fragment 21), and Olympiodorus (quoted in Photius, *Bibliotheca* 80, 62a9–26), describe the Blemmyes as living in a kingdom (or chiefdom) in Lower Nubia (Dijkstra 2008; Updegraff 1988), but somehow controlling the *Mons Smaragdus* region in the Eastern Desert (fig. 2.6), or as brigands raiding Egypt and Lower Nubia (presumably from the surrounding desert). This again illustrates both the confusion between Nubia and the Eastern Desert and the problems with understanding ancient ethnographies from a modern perspective (Barnard 2005, 2007; Burstein 2008; Dolukhanov 1994; Hutchinson and Smith 1996; Jones 1997; Mayerson 1993; Ratcliffe 1994; Rosen 2006; Sadr 1990; Yinger 1994). Many more names of people that appear to live a nomadic life in the Eastern Desert are mentioned in the written sources, including Adulites, *Akridophagoi* (Locust-eaters), Annoubades, Balahau, Bougaites, Catadupians, *Elephantophagoi* (Elephant-eaters), *Ichthyophagoi* (Fish-eaters), *Kreophagoi* (Meat-eaters), *Kynamolgoi* (Dog-milkers), Nobatai, Noubades, Noubai, *Rhizophagoi* (Root-eaters), *Spermaphagoi* (Seed-eaters), *Strouthophagoi* (Ostrich-eaters), *Troglodytes* (Cave-dwellers), and Trogodytes (Barnard 2005, 2007; see also Murray and Warmington 1967).

Only few contemporary texts have been preserved that may contain reliable information on the Blemmyes (Barnard 2005, 2007; Eide et al. 1998, 2000). Two often cited are the *Inscription of Silko* and the *Letter of Phonen*, dated to around A.D. 450. The inscription of Silko is incised in the west wall of the forecourt of the temple of Mandulis at Kalabsha (ancient Talmis near Aswan). It celebrates the victories of Silko, "Little King (βασιλίσκος) of all Aithiopians," over the Blemmyes and the Noubades, allowing him to occupy their cities (Eide et al. 1998). The letter of Phonen, found in 1976 in Qasr Ibrim (in Lower Nubia), is written on papyrus in poor Greek which makes it rather difficult to interpret (Eide et al. 1998). It was written by Phonen, who identifies himself as King (βασιλεύς) of the Blemmyes, and is addressed to Abourni, King of the Noubades, and his sons. Phonen acknowledges the conquering of Talmis (Kalabsha) by Silko and Abourni respectively and claims this city back, together with its temple and surrounding lands, in exchange for a ransom of silver, sheep, and camels (part of which has apparently already been paid). This letter is a rare instance of self-definition as Blemmyes, probably because Phonen, writing in a language that was obviously not his own, chose this convenient term to classify himself, much like a Chief of the Navajo may identify himself as Indian, Native American, Navajo, or as an inhabitant of *Diné* (the Navajo Nation), Arizona or the United States of America, all depending on the context. It is more remarkable that Phonen claims to be king, with all the implications associated with such a title, and demands his belongings back, notably a city in the Nile Valley. All this seems hardly concurrent with the notion of the Blemmyes as pastoral nomads and marauders roaming the Eastern Desert and it certainly provides no basis for the proposed link between the Blemmyes and Eastern Desert Ware (EDW).

Eastern Desert Ware vessels are hand-made cups and bowls that are usually smoothed or burnished and frequently decorated with impressed or incised decorations (fig. 2.5). Their remains have been found in fourth to sixth-century A.D. contexts in the Nile Valley between the First and the Fifth Cataract, as well as in the Eastern Desert between there and the Red Sea coast (fig. 2.6). Eastern Desert Ware invariably forms only a small percentage of the ceramic finds, the majority being the remains of Cream Ware and Red Ware associated with the Late Meroitic Nubia (table 2.1; Barnard 2007; Strouhal 1984), or with Egyptian Red Slip A and B associated with Late Roman Egypt (table 2.1; Barnard 2007; Tomber 1998, 1999). Eastern Desert Ware has now been studied in some detail (Barnard 2006; Barnard and Rose 2007), including chemical analysis of the ceramic matrix and the organic residues in the vessels (Barnard, Dooley, and Faull 2006; Barnard and Magid 2006; Barnard and Strouhal 2004), as well as ethnographic and experimental archaeology (Barnard 2008). It was concluded that Eastern Desert Ware was probably made and used by one of the indigenous groups in the area at the time, which is concurrent with earlier assumptions based on more cursory studies of the material (Luft et al. 2002; Ricke 1967; Rose 1995; Sidebotham and Wendrich 1996, 2001). The identification of this group with the Blemmyes, however, remains problematic for the same reasons that the pan-graves cannot readily be associated with the Medjay.

Like the Medjay, the Blemmyes feature in the historical sources well before and after Eastern Desert Ware appears in the archaeological record (Barnard 2005, 2007). Furthermore, Eastern Desert Ware is found far outside the area in which the written sources seem to place the Blemmyes, near or in the Nile Valley between the First and Second Cataracts (fig. 2.6; Barnard and Rose 2007; Burstein 2008; Dijkstra 2008; Updegraff 1988). Obviously, pottery can be traded over long distances (Tomber 1998, 1999), either for its contents or its intrinsic value; and production methods, shapes, and styles can change rapidly without an evident relation to historical events (Adams et al. 1979). On the other hand, the highly recognizable appearance of Eastern Desert Ware, which comprised mostly serving vessels, would have set its users apart and it may well have functioned as a cultural or ethnic marker (Barnard 2007;

Barnard and Rose 2007; Smith 2008). Like "mdȝj.w," Βλέμμυες did probably not refer to a political, ethnic, or cultural entity, but was more likely used as a convenient term to talk about outsiders (Barnard 2005), or to outsiders if the need for that occurred (as, for instance, in the case of Phonen). And again, there is no apparent reason to connect the archaeological finds, including the tumulus graves (sometimes referred to as *ekratels*) in the desert (Krzywinski and Pierce 2001; Sadr et al. 1994; Strouhal 1984) in which Eastern Desert Ware has been found and several enigmatic petroglyphs in the Eastern Desert (Barnard 2007; Huyge 1998; Winkler 1938), with the Blemmyes rather than with any of the many other groups mentioned in the ancient sources.

MEDJAY = BLEMMYES = BEJA?

Although the Eastern Desert continues to desiccate and human activity has caused considerable ecological degradation during the last century (Colston 1879; Floyer 1893; Krzywinski and Pierce 2001; Vermeeren 1999, 2000), the region can still support a number of nomadic and semi-nomadic inhabitants (Cappers 2006; Dahl and Hjort-af-Ornas 2006; Hobbs 1990; Keimer 1951, 1952a–b, 1953a–b, 1954a–b; Krzywinski and Pierce 2001; Magid 2008; Murray 1935; Paul 1954; Wendrich 2008). Many of them are considered, and also consider themselves, part of the Beja confederacy; others are Maʿaza or Rashaida Bedouin, who came from the Arabian Peninsula during the eighteenth and nineteenth century A.D. respectively (Hobbs 1990; Paul 1954). The Beja conglomerate is an amalgam of clans and tribes, including the Ababda, Amarar, Arteiga, Ashraf, Beni Amer, Bishareen, Fellata Melle, Hadendowa, Halenga, Hamran, Hassanab, Kammalab, Kimmeilab, Melhitkinab, Morghumab, Shaiab, and the Sigolab (fig. 2.6, table 2.2). Many speak Arabic as a first or a second language, others the Cushitic (Afro-Asiatic) *Beja* language (*To-Badawi*) or the Semitic *Tigre* (*Xasa*). Some are pastoral nomads, herding sheep, goats, and camels; many others are semi-nomadic cattle herders, settled agriculturalists, or day-laborers. It is often stated that the Beja are the direct descendents of the Blemmyes and the Medjay and have lived in the Eastern Desert since time immemorial (Dahl and Hjort-af-Ornas 2006; Zibelius-Chen 2007). This seems to be supported by elements of their material culture (fig. 2.7), but in fact replaces the "tyranny of texts" (Rosen 2006), discussed above, with a "tyranny of ethnography" (Wobst 1978), as this point of view is based on the misapprehension that the mobile groups in the past were identical or very similar to the pastoral nomads in the desert today (Bernbeck 2008; Burstein 2008; Khazanov 1984; Saidel 2008; Wobst 1978). Our annotations and connotations with words like "nomad," "Bedouin," "tribe," and "clan" may be too much influenced by modern biases (Abu-Lughod 1989; Bar-Yosef and Khazanov 1992; Barnard and Wendrich 2008; Cole 2003; Porter 2002; Ratnagar 2003; Salzman et al. 1999; Veth, Smith, and Hiscock 2005), effectively denying the modern pastoral nomads at least 4,500 years of ethnic, cultural, and historical development, while at the same time freezing the people of the past in both space and time.

The iconic Bedouin "black tent" (بيت الشعر, *bayt al-sha ʿar*), although not often seen in the Eastern Desert, may be a relatively recent phenomenon (Saidel 2008), whereas the Medjay did not raise camels, the Blemmyes did not drink coffee, and neither adhered to the Muslim faith. There has been a constant influx of people into the area (Christides 1980; Dafaʿalla 1987; Dahl and Hjort-af-Ornas 2006), Maʿaza Bedouin and Banu Kanz from the north (the Arabian Peninsula and Mesopotamia; Adams 1984; Hobbs 1990), Rashaida Bedouin from the east (the Arabian Peninsula; Paul 1954), *Tigre* speakers and Funj from the south (Erithrea and the Sudd; Adams 1984), and possibly also groups from the Nile Valley, such as the Medjay

(Sadr 1987, 1990). Others seem to have left for the Nile Valley, as reflected in the historical sources, and presumably also elsewhere. Cultural developments include the constant adjustments of the inhabitants of the Eastern Desert to the changing climate and ecology of the region, their conversion to Christianity and later Islam, and the introduction of camels, coffee, the Arabic language, and, more recently, plastic containers, cars, and cellular telephones into the area (Krzywinski and Pierce 2001; Wendrich 2008). Contacts with the successive kingdoms, empires, and governments must have also left their traces on the desert communities (table 2.1; Adams 1984; Barnard 2007). Even if the modern dwellers of the Eastern Desert have preserved remnants of the past (fig. 2.7; Cappers 2006), these are appreciated very differently now than they were during a previous era, like our Christmas trees and Easter eggs. The difficulties with the interpretation of the data have led some to denounce the use of ethnoarchaeological research and parallels in the study of ancient mobile people (Bernbeck 2008; Wobst 1978), whereas others urge to do so only with great caution (Bar-Yosef and Khazanov 1992; Cribb 1991; Saidel 2001; Wendrich 2008). One thing that may be inferred from comparing the present and the past is that the ethnic and cultural landscape of the Eastern Desert was always a patchwork of interlinking groups and that the history of the region is far more complex than that of the three static groups now usually associated with the area (tables 2.1–2).

It is also often maintained that the current (nineteenth–twentieth century A.D.) Beja culture is disappearing because of the increasing influence of the outside world (Cappers 2006; Dahl and Hjort-af-Ornas 2006; Krzywinski and Pierce 2001). Such remarks echo the notion of the "noble savage" and implicitly deny the Beja access to their cars and telephones, but also modern education and health care (Barnard 2007; Wendrich 2008). The fact that the culture of the Beja can "disappear" or, in more positive terms, adapt and develop, illustrates how similar changes happened in the past and will continue to happen in the future. The society of the dwellers of the Eastern Desert was never frozen in time or more rigid than that of the inhabitants of the Nile Valley (table 2.1). Like the Medjay and the Blemmyes and all other groups mentioned above, the Beja deserve the recording and study of their culture and history, but they also deserve to be the principal agents of their own destiny.

TOWARD AN ARCHAEOLOGY OF MOBILITY

Further research on the available archaeological material and data is unlikely to produce significant new insights into the history of the Eastern Desert and, unless substantial new textual sources are discovered, the historical research on the region seems exhausted. Archaeological research in Lower Nubia, between the First and Second Cataracts, is no longer possible and the same is true for the area between the Fourth and Fifth Cataracts after the Merowe High Dam near Hamdab will be closed in 2008. The data collected during the rescue excavations in this area, similar to the UNESCO International Campaign to Save the Monuments of Nubia, will be published in the near future and shed more light on life in the Eastern Desert in ancient times (Welsby and Anderson 2004). Much more can be expected, however, from additional archaeological and ethnographic work in the Eastern Desert itself as the archaeological research in this area has so far mostly concentrated on the quarries, mines, settlements, roads, and petroglyphs left by outsiders, while much of the ethnographical research has looked for the simplistic parallels discussed above.

During the past decades the anthropological theory on the relationship between the settled majority and the mobile minority in the Near East has developed from the permanent conflict reflected by the historical sources to the more symbiotic relationship that can be deduced from archaeological and ethnoarchaeological data. Our current terminology, with fixed categories for mobile and sedentary groups, is no more applicable to the ancient situation, in which these groups were even more intertwined, than to the present situation. Much like the ancient ethnic names, such as Medjay and Blemmyes, do not correspond with our modern use of similar terms, so may our understanding of words like "clan," "tribe," "Bedouin," or "nomad" not correspond to reality (Abu-Lughod 1989; Bar-Yosef and Khazanov 1992; Barnard and Wendrich 2008; Cole 2003; Porter 2002; Ratnagar 2003; Salzman et al. 1999; Veth, Smith, and Hiscock 2005). It has recently been appreciated that nomadic people are not archaeologically invisible (Childe 1951; Finkelstein 1992, but see Rosen 1992), but leave traces that are discernible and often specific for a nomadic way of life (Bar-Yosef and Khazanov 1992; Barnard and Wendrich 2008; Chang and Koster 1994; Cribb 1991; Haiman 1995; Rosen and Avni 1993; Veth, Smith, and Hiscock 2005). New archaeological tools and techniques (such as Google Earth, geographic information systems, chemical fingerprinting and residue analysis, etc.), and techniques adapted from other scientific disciplines (such as geology, paleontology, climatology, statistics, etc.) will dramatically increase the amount of sites and artifacts, as well as the information gleaned from them (Barnard, Dooley, and Faull 2006; Barnard and Strouhal 2004; Sadr 1987, 1988, 1990; Sadr et al. 1994; Wendrich and Barnard 2008). Only after such an archaeology of mobility has been developed, applied to the Eastern Desert as well as to selections of finds from that region, and confronted with the historical sources in a heuristic rather than a bellicose fashion (Bietak 1979; Rosen 2006; Wendrich et al. 2006), can the above issues be comprehensively addressed and more convincing associations be made between the Medjay, the Blemmyes, and the archaeological record of the Eastern Desert. Until then, the inadequate links between material culture and historical terminology must be severed to allow each discipline to freely expand and interpret its own specific data set. We must keep in mind that archaeology, ethnography, and history are independent disciplines that will produce different narratives. Inferring links between those is often too simplistic to be heuristic and we must be prepared to find that it may prove impossible to pinpoint the material culture of all the groups mentioned in the historical sources, or to connect all archaeological finds to a specific name from those sources.

ACKNOWLEDGMENTS

Sincere thanks are due to Jitka Barochová, Manfred Bietak, Roswitha Egner, Sharon Herbert, Knut Krzywinski, Anwar Abdel-Magid, Richard Pierce, Elfriede Reiser-Haslauer, Pamela Rose, Valery and John Seeger, Steve Sidebotham, Jana Součková, Eugen Strouhal, Roberta Tomber, Isabella and Derek Welsby, and Henry Wright, for making the necessary material available; to Ram Alkali, Alek Dooley, Kym Faull, Hector Neff, and Dave Verity, for their help with the analysis of Eastern Desert Ware; to Anna Barnard-van der Nat, Kym Faull, Hector Neff, and Chip Stanish, for their logistical and financial support; to Jacco Dieleman, Jitse Dijkstra, and Claudia Näser, for their comments; and to Willeke Wendrich, for her unending encouragement and love.

Southeast Egypt		Northeast Sudan		Eastern Desert
Lower Paleolithic 500,000–100,000 B.C.				

Lower Paleolithic 500,000–100,000 B.C.

Middle Paleolithic 100,000–35,000 B.C.

Upper Paleolithic 35,000–20,000 B.C.

Late Paleolithic 20,000–8,000 B.C.

Epipaleolitic (Mesolithic) 8000–6000 B.C.

Early Neolithic 6000–5000 B.C.

	Fayum–Badarian 5000–4200 B.C.	Khartoum Neolithic 5000–3000 B.C.		
Prehistoric Egypt	Merimde–Naqada 4200–3100 B.C.	A-Group 3800–3000 B.C.	Khartoum Neolithic	
	Predynastic Egypt 3100–2575 B.C.	Lower Nubia Depopulated?	Pre-Kerma Culture 3000–2500 B.C.	
	Old Kingdom 2725–2125 B.C.			Medjay
	First Intermediate Period 2125–1975 B.C.	C-Group 2300–1520 B.C.	Kingdom of Kerma 2500–1520 B.C.	
	Middle Kingdom 1975–1640 B.C.			
Pharaonic Egypt	Second Intermediate Period (Hyksos) 1630–1520 B.C.			
	Pan-Graves			
	New Kingdom 1540–1075 B.C.			
	Third Intermediate Period 1075–715 B.C.	Kingdom of Napata (Kushite Kingdom) 1075–300 B.C.		
	25th Dynasty 770–657 B.C.			
	Late Period (Persian Invasions) 664–332 B.C.			
Greco-Roman Egypt	Ptolemaic Empire 332 B.C.–A.D. 30	Kingdom of Meroe (Kushite Kingdom) 300 B.C.–A.D. 350		
	Roman Empire A.D. 30–330			
	Eastern Desert Ware			
Byzantine Egypt	Byzantine Empire A.D. 330–616	Kingdom of Nobatia (Ballana Culture) A.D. 300–700	Kingdom of Makuria (protected by the *baqt*) A.D. 500–1323	Blemmyes
	Persian Invasion A.D. 616–628			
	Byzantine Empire A.D. 629–641			
Islamic Egypt	Rashidun Caliphs A.D. 641–658			
	Umayyad Caliphate A.D. 658–750			
	Abbasid Caliphate A.D. 750–969			
	Fatimid Caliphs A.D. 969–1171			
	Ayyubid Sultanate A.D. 1171–1250			
	Mamluk Sultans A.D. 1250–1517	Banu Kanz (Awlad Kenz) A.D. 1323–1517		
Ottoman Egypt	Ottoman Empire A.D. 1517–1798	Sultanate of Sinnar (Funj) A.D. 1504–1821		
	Invasion of Napoleon A.D. 1798–1801			
Modern Egypt	Khedives and Kings of the Dynasty of Mohamed Ali Mohamed Ali (1805–1848)–Fu'ad II (1952–1953)			
	Increasingly Controlled by the British Empire	Mahdi Revolt A.D. 1883–1898		Beja
	Unilateral Independence 22 February 1922	Anglo-Egyptian Sudan A.D. 1899–1956		
	Republic of Egypt 18 June 1953			
	Full Independence 18 June 1956	Republic of Sudan 1 January 1956		

Table 2.1. General chronology of the Lower and Middle Nile region from 500,000 B.C. to A.D. 1956, also indicating the three groups generally believed to have inhabited the desert between the Nile Valley and the Red Sea (after Adams 1984; Baines and Malek 2000; Barnard 2007) as well as the finds usually associated with them. Note the extremely limited differentiation in the history of the Eastern Desert (on the far right)

Beja Clans and Tribes (after Murray 1935: 423; Paul 1954: 137–39; Wendrich 2008: 513–15)				Ancient Desert Dwellers (after Eide et al. 1996, 1998)
CLAN (*aila, wasm*)		TRIBE (*qabila, bayt*)		
ABABDA(?)	Bilalab	ʿAmirab		Aamu
		Batranab		Adulites
		Firhanab		*Akridophagoi* (Locust-eaters)
		Jahadab		Annoubades
		Jidalab		Balahau
		Kiriab		Blemmyes
		Rajabab		Bougaites
		Saadallab		Catadupians
		Selimab		*Elephantophagoi* (Elephant-eaters)
		Tamanab		*ḥrjw.šʿ* (Sand-people)
		Zeidab		*ḫtjw.tȝ* (Vagabonds)
	Haranaab			*Ichthyophagoi* (Fish-eaters)
	Hareinab	Hareinab		*jwntj.w* (Cain-people)
		Nafaiab		*Kreophagoi* (Meat-eaters)
	ʿIbudiyeen			*Kynamolgoi* (Dog-milkers)
	Jileiliyeen			Medjay
	Meleikab	Meleikab		*nmjw.šʿ* (Sand-walkers)
		Fuqara		Nobatai
	Muhammedab	ʿAbdeinab		Noubades
		ʿAmranab		Noubai
		ʿAtiyaiab		*Rhizophagoi* (Root-eaters)
		ʿAdwallaiab		*Spermaphagoi* (Seed-eaters)
		Edidanab		*Strouthophagoi* (Ostrich-eaters)
		Faraiab		Tjehenu
		Fishaiab		Tjemehu
		Hameidab		*Troglodytes* (Cave-dwellers)
		Jaralab		Trogodyte

Table 2.2. Selection of known ethnic names associated with the dwellers of the desert between the Nile Valley and the Red Sea coast at present (on left) and in the past (on far right). The social organization in ancient times may prove dif₅cult to reconstruct from the historical and archaeological records

Beja Clans and Tribes (after Murray 1935: 423; Paul 1954: 137–39; Wendrich 2008: 513–15)				Ancient Desert Dwellers (after Eide et al. 1996, 1998)
CLAN (*aila, wasm*)		TRIBE (*qabila, bayt*)		
		Jubranab		*jwntj.w* (Cain-people)
		Malakab		
		Rahalab		
		Siedanab		
		Shafab		
		Sheinab		
		Shuweimab		
	Shanatir			
	"Broken Tribes"	Anqaraiab		
		Hamei		
		Heteimiyah		
		Hukm		
		Kimeilab		
		Qireiab		
AMARAR	Amarar	Esheibab		
		Fadlab		
	Otman	Ailaib	Arfoiab	
			Keilab	
			Manfolab	
			Minniab	
		Gwilai	Abdel Rahimab	
			Abdel Rahmanab	
			Musiab	
			Omar Hassanaiab	
			Sindereit	
		Kurbab		
		Nurab		
ARTEIGA				
ASHRAF				
BENI AMER	Egeilab			
	Hadareb	Ad al Khasa		
		Ad Kokoi		
		Beit Awat		
		Beit Goreish		

Beja Clans and Tribes (after Murray 1935: 423; Paul 1954: 137–39; Wendrich 2008: 513–15)				Ancient Desert Dwellers (after Eide et al. 1996, 1998)
CLAN (*aila, wasm*)		TRIBE (*qabila, bayt*)		
		Beit Musa		
		Hadoigoboiab		
		Labat		
		Libis		
		Sinkatkinab		
		Sogaiet		
	Nabtab			
	Tigré	Abhasheila		
		Ad Fadil		
		Aflanda		
		Almada		
		Asfada		
		Hamasein		
		Meikal		
		Rigbat		
		Targeila		
		Wilinnoho		
BISHAREEN	Umm Ali	Alaib		
		Amrab		
		Hamadorab		
		Shinterab		
	Umm Nagi	Adloiab		
		Batran		
		Eiraiab		
		Garab		
		Hammadab		
		Madakir		
		Mansurab		
		Mashbolab		
		Nafi'ab		
		Wailaliab		
FELLATA MELLE(?)				
HADENDOWA	Beiranab			
	Buglinai			
	Bushariab			
	Emirab			
	Gemilab			

Beja Clans and Tribes (after Murray 1935: 423; Paul 1954: 137–39; Wendrich 2008: 513–15)			Ancient Desert Dwellers (after Eide et al. 1996, 1998)
CLAN (*aila, wasm*)	TRIBE (*qabila, bayt*)		
	Ger'ib		
	Gurhabab		
	Hakolab		
	Hamdab		
	Kalolai		
	Meishab		
	Rabamak		
	Samarandowab		
	Samarar		
	Shaboidinab		
	Shara'ab		
	Tirik		
	Wailaliab		
HALENGA			
HAMRAN			
HASSANAB			
KAMMALAB			
KIMMEILAB			
MELHITKINAB			
MORGHUMAB			
SHAIAB			
SIGOLAB			

Figure 2.1. *Mḏ3j.w* (Medjay; Faulkner 1962; Gardiner 1947) is written with the bound prisoner or the throw stick and seated man determinatives (*top*), in this context signifying enemies of Egypt (Redford 1963), or with the foreign land determinative (*bottom*), indicating a geographical area outside the Egyptian heartland (the Nile Valley north of Aswan)

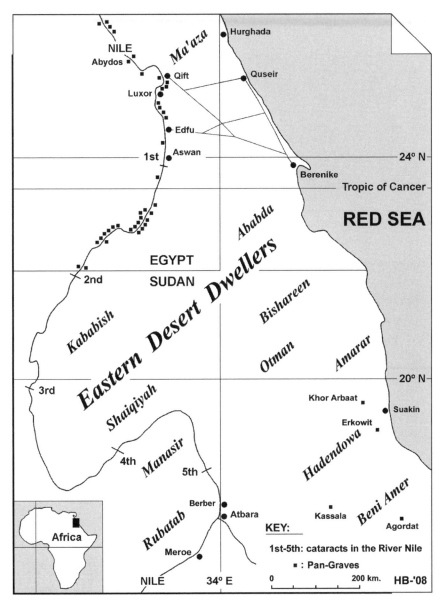

Figure 2.2. Map of southern Egypt and northern Sudan, showing the distribution of pan-graves (after Bietak 1966: 66; Sadr 1987: 266), as well as the approximate territories of the modern Bedouin tribes in the area (after Hobbs 1990; Magid 2008: 442; Paul 1954; Sadr 1988: 386)

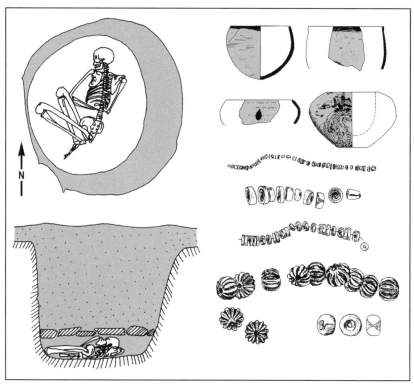

Figure 2.3. Layout of a typical pan-grave (B/8 in Sayala, Lower Nubia, now lost
under Lake Nasser) with associated finds (after Bietak 1966: pls. 21, 29)

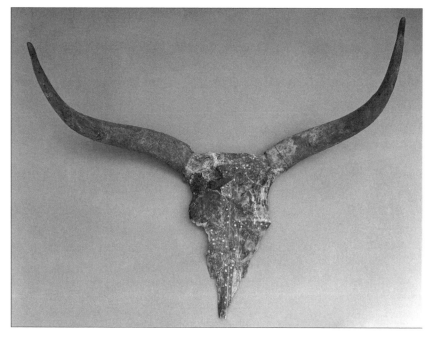

Figure 2.4. Bucranium (41.5 × 75.0 cm) decorated with blocks and bands of red and black paint;
white dots have been applied to the red areas. Found in a pan-grave at Abydos in a context dating
to the Second Intermediate Period (1630–1520 B.C.), now in the Metropolitan Museum of Art,
Roger Fund 1916 (16.2.23). Image courtesy of the Metropolitan Museum of Art, New York

Figure 2.5. Examples of Eastern Desert Ware (EDW), KHM 76918 is from Sayala (courtesy of the Kunsthistorisches Museum, Vienna), EDW 17 is from Berenike, P 840 is from Wadi Qitna (courtesy of the Náprstek Museum, Prague), and EDW 234 is from Wadi Sikait in the Mons Smaragdus region (after Barnard 2008: fig. 19.1)

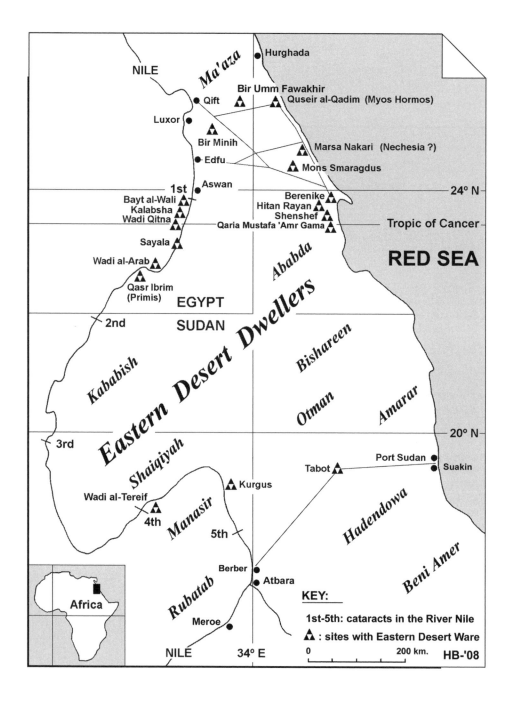

Figure 2.6. Map of southern Egypt and northern Sudan, showing the distribution of Eastern Desert Ware (after Barnard 2006; Barnard, Dooley, and Faull 2006; Barnard and Magid 2006; Barnard and Rose 2007; Barnard and Strouhal 2004), as well as the approximate territories of some of the modern Bedouin tribes in the area (after Hobbs 1990; Magid 2008: 442; Paul 1954; Sadr 1988: 386)

Figure 2.7. The headrests used by the Beja show great similarity with those found in ancient Egyptian tombs and have been interpreted as evidence for cultural continuity (Cappers 2006; Dahl and Hjort-af-Ornas 2006; Hafsaas 2006; Keimer 1951, 1952a–b, 1953a–b, 1954a–b; Krzywinski and Pierce 2001; Zibelius-Chen 2007), despite evidence to the contrary (Barnard 2005, 2007; Burstein 2008; Christides 1980; Cole 2003; Dafaʿalla 1987; Wendrich 2008). Photograph courtesy of the EDAPP/Bayt al-Ababda Museum (after Wendrich 2008: fig. 23.7)

BIBLIOGRAPHY

Abu-Lughod, Lila

    1989   "Zones of Theory in the Anthropology of the Arab World." *Annual Review of Anthropology* 18: 267–306.

Adams, William Y.

    1984   *Nubia: Corridor to Africa.* 2nd edition. London: Allen Lane; Princeton: Princeton University Press.

Adams, William Y.; Leland J. Abel; Dean E. Arnold; Neville Chittick; Whitney M. Davis; Pierre de Maret; Rodolfo Fattovich; H. J. Franken; Charles C. Kolb; Thomas P. Myers; Michael P. Simmons; and E. Leigh Syms

    1979   "On the Argument from Ceramics to History: A Challenge Based on Evidence from Medieval Nubia." *Current Anthropology* 20: 727–44.

Baines, John, and Jaromír Málek

    2000   *Cultural Atlas of Ancient Egypt.* Revised edition. New York: Facts on File.

Bar-Yosef, Ofer, and Anatoly M. Khazanov, editors

    1992   *Pastoralism in the Levant: Archaeological Materials in Anthropological Perspectives.* Monographs in World Archaeology 10. Madison: Prehistory Press.

Barnard, Hans

    2005   "Sire, il n'y a pas de Blemmyes: A Re-evaluation of Historical and Archaeological Data." In *People of the Red Sea* (Proceedings of the Red Sea Project 2, at the British Museum, October 2004), edited by Janet C. M. Starkey, pp. 23–40. Society for Arabian Studies Monographs 3; British Archaeological Reports, International Series 1395. Oxford: Archaeopress.

    2006   "The Macroscopic Description of Eastern Desert Ware (1935–2002)." In *Acta Nubica* (Proceedings of the Tenth International Conference on Nubian Studies, in Rome, 9–14 September 2002), edited by Isabella Caneva and Alessandro Roccati, pp. 51–62. Rome: Libreria dello Stato.

    2007   "Additional Remarks on Blemmyes, Beja and Eastern Desert Ware." *Ägypten und Levante* 17: 23–31.

    2008   "Suggestion for a Chaîne Opératoire of Nomadic Pottery Sherds." In *The Archaeology of Mobility: Old World and New World Nomadism*, edited by Hans Barnard and Willeke Z. Wendrich, pp. 413–39. Cotsen Advanced Seminars 4. Los Angeles: Cotsen Institute of Archaeology, University of California.

Barnard, Hans; Alek N. Dooley; and Kym F. Faull

    2006   "New Data on the Eastern Desert Ware from Sayala (Lower Nubia) in the Kunsthistorisches Museum, Vienna." *Ägypten und Levante* 15: 49–64.

Barnard, Hans, and Anwar A. Magid

    2006   "Eastern Desert Ware from Tabot (Sudan): More Links to the North." *Archéologie du Nil Moyen* 10: 15–34.

Barnard, Hans, and Pamela J. Rose

    2007   "Eastern Desert Ware from Berenike and Kab Marfu'a." In *Berenike 1999/2000: Report on the Excavations At Berenike, Including Excavations in Wadi Kalalat and Siket, and the Survey of the Mons Smaragdus Region*, edited by Steven E. Sidebotham and Willeke Z. Wendrich, pp. 183–99. Berenike Report 6. Los Angeles: Cotsen Institute of Archaeology, University of California.

Barnard, Hans, and Eugen Strouhal

    2004   "Wadi Qitna Revisited." *Annals of the Náprstek Museum* (Prague) 25: 29–55.

Barnard, Hans, and Willeke Z. Wendrich, editors
    2008   *The Archaeology of Mobility: Old World and New World Nomadism.* Cotsen
                Advanced Seminars 4. Los Angeles: Cotsen Institute of Archaeology, University of
                California.

Behrens, Peter
    1982   "Nomaden (und Bauern)." In *Lexikon der Ägyptologie,* Volume 4: *Megiddo–
                Pyramiden,* edited by Wolfgang Helck and Eberhard Otto, pp. 522–23. Wiesbaden:
                Otto Harrassowitz.

Berg, Robert, and Lorraine Berg
    1998   "Nomads and Pharaohs." *Saudi Aramco World* 49.3 (May/June): 26–35.

Bernbeck, Reinhard
    2008   "An Archaeology of Multisited Communities." In *The Archaeology of Mobility:
                Old World and New World Nomadism,* edited by Hans Barnard and Willeke Z.
                Wendrich, pp. 43–77. Cotsen Advanced Seminars 4. Los Angeles: Cotsen Institute
                of Archaeology, University of California.

Bietak, Manfred
    1966   *Ausgrabungen in Sayala-Nubien 1961–1965: Denkmäler der C-Gruppe und der
                Pan-Graäber-Kultur.* Österreichische Akademie der Wissenschaften, Philosophisch-
                Historische Klasse Denkschriften 92; Berichte des Österreischen Nationalkomitees
                der UNESCO-Aktion für die Rettung der Nubischen Altertümer 3. Vienna: H. Böhlaus
                Nachf.
    1979   "Review Article: 'The Present State of Egyptian Archaeology.'" *Journal of Egyptian
                Archaeology* 65: 156–60.
    2006   "Introduction." *Ägypten und Levante* 15: 11–13.

Breasted, James Henry
    1962   *Ancient Records of Egypt: Historical Documents from the Earliest Times to the
                Persian Conquest; Collected, Edited, and Translated with Commentary,* Part 1.
                Reprint of 1906 original. New York: Russell & Russell.

Burstein, Stanley M.
    2008   "Trogodytes = Blemmyes = Beja? The Misuse of Ancient Ethnography." In *The
                Archaeology of Mobility: Old World and New World Nomadism,* edited by Hans
                Barnard and Willeke Z. Wendrich, pp. 250–63. Cotsen Advanced Seminars 4. Los
                Angeles: Cotsen Institute of Archaeology, University of California.

Butzer, Karl W.
    1997   "Late Quaternary Problems of the Egyptian Nile: Stratigraphy, Environments,
                Prehistory." *Paléorient* 23: 151–73.

Cappers, René T. J.
    2006   *Roman Foodprints at Berenike: Archaeobotanical Evidence of Subsistence and Trade
                in the Eastern Desert of Egypt.* Cotsen Institute of Archaeology Monograph 55. Los
                Angeles: Cotsen Institute of Archaeology, University of California.

Chang, Claudia, and Harold A. Koster, editors
    1994   *Pastoralists at the Periphery: Herders in a Capitalist World.* Tucson: University of
                Arizona Press.

Childe, V. Gordon
    1951   *Man Makes Himself.* A Mentor Book 64. New York: New American Library.

Christides, Vassilios
    1980   "Ethnic Movements in Southern Egypt and Northern Sudan: Blemmyes-Beja in Late
                Antiquity and Early Arab Egypt until 707 A.D." *Listy Filologické* 103: 129–43.

Cole, Donald P.
2003   "Where Have the Bedouin Gone?" *Anthropological Quarterly* 76: 235–67.

Colston, R. E.
1879   "Life in the Egyptian Deserts." *Journal of the American Geographical Society* 11: 301–33.

Cribb, Roger
1991   *Nomads in Archaeology*. New Studies in Archaeology. Cambridge: Cambridge University Press.

Dafaʿalla, Samia B.
1987   "The Historical Role of the Blemmyes in Late Meroitic and Early X-Group Periods." *Beiträge zur Sudanforschung* 2: 34–40.

Dahl, Gudrun, and Anders Hjort-af-Ornas
2006   "Precolonial Beja: A Periphery at the Crossroads." *Nordic Journal of African Studies* 15: 473–98.

Dijkstra, Jitse H. F.
2008   *Philae and the End of Ancient Egyptian Religion: A Regional Study of Religious Transformation*. Orientalia Lovaniensia Analecta 173. Leuven: Uitgeverij Peeters.

Dolukhanov, Pavel M.
1994   *Environment and Ethnicity in the Ancient Middle East*. World Archaeology Series 7. Aldershot: Avebury.

Eide, Tormod; Tomas Hägg; Richard Holton Pierce; and László Török
1996   *Fontes Historiae Nubiorum*, Volume 2: *From the Mid-Fifth Century BC to the First Century AD*. Bergen: University of Bergen.

1998   *Fontes Historiae Nubiorum*, Volume 3: *From the First to the Sixth Century AD*. Bergen: University of Bergen.

2000   *Fontes Historiae Nubiorum*, Volume 4: *Corrigenda and Indices*. Bergen: University of Bergen.

Faulkner, Raymond O.
1962   *A Concise Dictionary of Middle Egyptian*. Oxford: The Griffith Institute at the University Press.

Finkelstein, Israel
1992   "Invisible Nomads: A Rejoinder." *Bulletin of the American Schools of Oriental Research* 287: 87–88.

Floyer, Ernest Ayscoghe
1893   *Étude sur le Nord-Etbai entre le Nil et la Mer Rouge*. Cairo: Imprimerie National.

Friedman, Renée F.
2001   "Nubians at Hierakonpolis." *Sudan and Nubia* 5: 29–45.

2002   *Egypt and Nubia: Gifts of the Desert*. London: British Museum Press.

2004   "The Nubian Cemetery at Hierakonpolis, Egypt: Results of the 2003 Season." *Sudan and Nubia* 8: 47–59.

Gardiner, Alan H.
1947   *Ancient Egyptian Onomastica*. 3 volumes. Oxford: Oxford University Press.

Giuliani, Serena
1998   "Medja Sources in the Old Kingdom." *Discussions in Egyptology* 42: 41–54.

Hafsaas, Henriette
2006   *Cattle Pastoralists in a Multicultural Setting: The C-Group People in Lower Nubia 2500–1500 BCE*. The Lower Jordan River Basin Programme Publications 10. Bergen: University of Bergen; Ramallah: Birzeit University.

Haiman, Mordechai
    1995   "Agriculture and Nomad-State Relations in the Negev Desert in the Byzantine and Early Islamic Periods." *Bulletin of the American Schools of Oriental Research* 297: 29–53.

Hobbs, Joseph John
    1990   *Bedouin Life in the Egyptian Wilderness*. Cairo: American University in Cairo Press.

Hutchinson, John, and Anthony D. Smith, editors
    1996   *Ethnicity*. Oxford Readers. Oxford: Oxford University Press.

Huyge, Dirk
    1998   "Art on the Decline? Egyptian Rock Art Drawings from Late and Graeco-Roman Periods." In *Egyptian Religion: The Last Thousand Years; Studies Dedicated to the Memory of Jan Quaegebeur*, Part 2, edited by Willy Clarysse, Antoine Schoors, and Harco Willems, pp. 1377–92. Orientalia Lovaniensia Analecta 84. Leuven: Uitgeverij Peeters.

Jones, Sian
    1997   *The Archaeology of Ethnicity: Constructing Identities in the Past and Present*. London: Routledge.

Kaper, Olaf E., editor
    1998   *Life on the Fringe: Living in the Southern Egyptian Deserts during Roman and Early-Byzantine Periods*. Research School of Asian, African, and Amerindian Studies (CNWS) Publications 71; Contributions by the Netherlands-Flemish Institute in Cairo 2. Leiden: Research School of Asian, African, and Amerindian Studies (CNWS).

Keimer, Louis
    1951   "Notes prises chez les Bišarîn et les Nubiens d'Assouan: Première partie." *Bulletin de l'Institut d'Égypte* 32, Session 1949–1950: 49–101.
    1952a   "Notes prises chez les Bišarîn et les Nubiens d'Assouan: Deuxième partie." *Bulletin de l'Institut d'Égypte* 33, Session 1950–1951: 42–84.
    1952b   "Notes prises chez les Bišarîn et les Nubiens d'Assouan: Troisième partie." *Bulletin de l'Institut d'Égypte* 33, Session 1950–1951: 85–135.
    1953a   "Notes prises chez les Bišarîn et les Nubiens d'Assouan: Quatrième partie." *Bulletin de l'Institut d'Égypte* 34, Session 1951–1952: 329–400.
    1953b   "Notes prises chez les Bišarîn et les Nubiens d'Assouan: Cinquième partie (1)." *Bulletin de l'Institut d'Égypte* 34, Session 1951–1952: 401–49.
    1954a   "Notes prises chez les Bišarîn et les Nubiens d'Assouan: Cinquième partie (2)." *Bulletin de l'Institut d'Égypte* 35, Session 1953–1954: 447–70.
    1954b   "Notes prises chez les Bišarîn et les Nubiens d'Assouan: Sixième partie." *Bulletin de l'Institut d'Égypte* 35, Session 1953–1954: 471–533.

Kemp, Barry J.
    1977   "An Incised Sherd from Kahun." *Egypt, Journal of Near Eastern Studies* 36: 289–92.

Kershaw, Ian
    1998   *Hitler: 1889–1936; Hubris*. London: Allen Lane.

Khazanov, Anatoly M.
    1984   *Nomads and the Outside World*. Cambridge Studies in Social Anthropology 44. Cambridge: Cambridge University Press.

Krall, Jakob
    1900   *Beiträge zur Geschichte der Blemyer und Nubier*. Denkschriften der Kaiserlichen Akademie der Wissenschaften, Philosophisch-Historische Klasse 46. Vienna: Kaiserliche Akademie der Wissenschaften.

Krzywinski, Knut, and Richard Holton Pierce, editors
2001   *Deserting the Desert: A Threatened Cultural Landscape between the Nile and the Sea.* Bergen: University of Bergen.

Kuper, Rudolph
2006   "After 5000 BC: The Libyan Desert in Transition." *Comptes Rendus Palevol* 5: 409–19.

Kuper, Rudolph, and Stefan Kröpelin
2006   "Climate-Controlled Holocene Occupation in the Sahara: Motor of Africa's Evolution." *Science* 313: 803–07.

Lansing, Ambrose
1947   "An Old Kingdom Captive." *The Metropolitan Museum of Art Bulletin, New Series* 5: 149–52.

Lassányi, Gábor
2005   "The Blemmyes and the Frontier Defence in Egypt in Late Antiquity: Some Archaeological Notes." In *Limes* 19: *Proceedings of the Nineteenth International Congress of Roman Frontier Studies held in Pécs, Hungary* (September 2003), edited by Zsolt Visy, pp. 783–90. Pécs: University of Pécs.

Lichtheim, Miriam
1975   *Ancient Egyptian Literature: A Book of Readings,* Volume 1: *The Old and Middle Kingdoms.* Berkeley: University of California Press.

Luft, Ulrich; Adrienn Almásy; Marton Attila Farkas; Ildiko Furka; Zoltan Horváth; and Gabor Lassányi
2002   "Preliminary Report on the Fieldwork at Bir Minih, Arabian Desert." *Mitteilungen des Deutschen Archäologischen Instituts, Abteilung Kairo* 58: 373–90.

Magid, Anwar A.
2008   "History of the Nomadic Architecture of the Hadendowa in Northeast Sudan." In *The Archaeology of Mobility: Old World and New World Nomadism*, edited by Hans Barnard and Willeke Z. Wendrich, pp. 441–64. Cotsen Advanced Seminars 4. Los Angeles: Cotsen Institute of Archaeology, University of California.

Mailhot, Jose
1978   "L'étymologie de 'Esquimau': Revue et corrigée." *Etudes/Inuit/Studies* 2: 59–69.

Mayerson, Philip
1993   "A Confusion of Indias: Asian India and African India in the Byzantine Sources." *Journal of the American Oriental Society* 113: 169–74.

Meredith, David
1957   "Berenice Trogloditica." *Journal of Egyptian Archaeology* 43: 56–70.

Murray, George W.
1935   *Sons of Ishmael: A Study of the Egyptian Bedouin.* London: George Routledge.
1965   "Harkhuf's Third Journey." *The Geographical Journal* 131: 72–75.

Murray, George W., and Eric H. Warmington
1967   "Trogodytica: The Red Sea Littoral in Ptolemaic Times." *The Geographical Journal* 133: 24–33.

Paul, Andrew
1954   *A History of the Beja Tribes of the Sudan.* Cambridge: Cambridge University Press.

Porter, Anne
2002   "The Dynamics of Death: Ancestors, Pastoralism, and the Origins of a Third-Millennium City in Syria." *Bulletin of the American Schools of Oriental Research* 325: 1–36.

Posener, Georges
1958   "Nhsj.w et Md3j.w." *Zeitschrift für Ägyptische Sprache und Altertumskunde* 83: 38–43.

Ratcliffe, Peter, editor
1994   *"Race," Ethnicity and Nation: International Perspectives on Social Conflict.* London: University College London Press.

Ratnagar, Shereen
2003   "Our Tribal Past." *Social Scientist* 31: 17–36.

Redford, Donald B.
1963   "Exodus I 11." *Vetus Testamentum* 13: 401–18.

Ricke, Herbert
1967   *Ausgrabungen von Khor-Dehmit bis Bet el-Wali.* University of Chicago Oriental Institute Nubian Expedition Publications 2. Chicago: University of Chicago.

Rose, Pamela J.
1995   "Report on the Handmade Sherds." In *Berenike 1994: Preliminary Report of the 1994 Excavations at Berenike (Egyptian Red Sea Coast) and the Survey of the Eastern Desert,* edited by Steven E. Sidebotham and Willeke Z. Wendrich, pp. 41–43. Research School of Asian, African, and Amerindian Studies (CNWS) Publications, Special Series 1. Leiden: Research School of Asian, African, and Amerindian Studies (CNWS).

Rosen, Steven A.
1992   "Nomads in Archaeology: A Response to Finkelstein and Perevolotsky." *Bulletin of the American Schools of Oriental Research* 287: 75–85.

2006   "The Tyranny of Texts: A Rebellion against the Primacy of Written Documents in Defining Archaeological Agendas." In *"I Will Speak the Riddles of Ancient Times": Archaeological and Historical Studies in Honor of Amihai Mazar on the Occasion of His Sixtieth Birthday,* Volume 2, edited by Aren M. Maeir and Pierre de Miroschedji, pp. 879–93. Winona Lake: Eisenbrauns.

Rosen, Steven A., and Gideon Avni
1993   "The Edge of the Empire: The Archaeology of Pastoral Nomads in the Southern Negev Highlands in Late Antiquity." *Biblical Archaeologist* 56: 189–99.

Sadr, Karim
1987   "The Territorial Expanse of the Pan-Grave Culture." *Archéologie du Nil Moyen* 2: 265–93.

1988   "Settlement Patterns and Land Use in the Late Prehistoric Southern Atbai, East Central Sudan." *Journal of Field Archaeology* 15: 381–401.

1990   "The Medjay in Southern Atbai." *Archéologie du Nil Moyen* 4: 63–86.

Sadr, Karim; Alfredo Castiglioni; Angelo Castiglioni; and Giancarlo Negro
1994   "Archaeology in the Nubian Desert." *Sahara* 6: 69–75.

Saidel, Benjamin A.
2001   "Ethnoarchaeological Investigations of Abandoned Tent Camps in Southern Jordan." *Near Eastern Archaeology* 64: 150–57.

2008   "The Bedouin Tent: An Ethno-Archaeological Portal to Antiquity or a Modern Construct?" In *The Archaeology of Mobility: Old World and New World Nomadism,* edited Hans Barnard and Willeke Z. Wendrich, pp. 465–86. Cotsen Advanced Seminars 4. Los Angeles: Cotsen Institute of Archaeology, University of California.

Salzman, Philip Carl; Michael Bollig; Pierre Bonte; Michael J. Casimir; Elliot M. Fratkin; John G. Galaty; William Irons; Robert L. Kelly; Fidelity Lancaster; William Lancaster; Peter D. Little; Emanuel Marx; Terrence McCabe; François Pouillon; Lin Poyer; Aparna Rao; Bahram Tavakolian; and William C. Young
1999   "Is Inequality Universal?" *Current Anthropology* 40: 31–61.

Säve-Söderbergh, Torgny

1941   *Ägypten und Nubien: Ein Beitrag zur Geschichte altägyptischer Aussenpolitik.* Lund: Håkan Ohlssons Boktryckeri.

Sidebotham, Steven E.; Hans Barnard; and Gillian Pyke

2002   "Five Enigmatic Late Roman Settlements in the Eastern Desert." *Journal of Egyptian Archaeology* 88: 187–225.

Sidebotham, Steven E., and Willeke Z. Wendrich

1996   "Berenike: Roman Egypt's Maritime Gateway to Arabia and India." *Egyptian Archaeology* 8: 15–18.

2001   "Berenike, Roms Tor am Roten Meer nach Arabien und Indien." *Antike Welt* 32: 251–63.

Smith, Stuart T.

2008   "Crossing Boundaries: Nomadic Groups and Ethnic Identities." In *The Archaeology of Mobility: Old World and New World Nomadism*, edited by Hans Barnard and Willeke Z. Wendrich, pp. 343–65. Cotsen Advanced Seminars 4. Los Angeles: Cotsen Institute of Archaeology, University of California.

Smither, Paul C.

1945   "The Semnah Despatches." *Journal of Egyptian Archaeology* 31: 3–10.

Strouhal, Eugen

1984   *Wadi Qitna and Kalabsha-South: Late Roman–Early Byzantine Tumuli Cemeteries in Egyptian Nubia,* Volume 1: *Archaeology.* Czechoslovak Institute of Egyptology, Charles University Publications. Prague: Charles University.

Tomber, Roberta S.

1998   "The Pottery." In *Berenike 1996: Report of the 1996 Excavations at Berenike (Egyptian Red Sea Coast) and the Survey of the Eastern Desert,* edited by Steven E. Sidebotham and Willeke Z. Wendrich, pp. 163–80. Research School of Asian, African, and Amerindian Studies (CNWS) Publications, Special Series 3. Leiden: Research School of Asian, African, and Amerindian Studies (CNWS).

1999   "The Pottery." In *Berenike 1997: Report of the 1996 Excavations at Berenike and the Survey of the Egyptian Eastern Desert, Including Excavations at Shenshef,* edited by Steven E. Sidebotham and Willeke Z. Wendrich, pp. 123–59. Research School of Asian, African, and Amerindian Studies (CNWS) Publications, Special Series 4. Leiden: Research School of Asian, African, and Amerindian Studies (CNWS).

Updegraff, Robert T.

1988   "The Blemmyes I: The Rise of the Blemmyes and the Roman Withdrawal from Nubia under Diocletian." In *Aufstieg und Niedergang der römische Welt,* Volume 2, edited by Wolfgang Haase and Hildegard Temporini, pp. 44–97. Berlin, New York: Walter de Gruyter.

Vermeeren, Caroline E.

1999   "Wood and Charcoal." In *Berenike 1997: Report of the 1996 Excavations at Berenike and the Survey of the Egyptian Eastern Desert, Including Excavations at Shenshef,* edited by Steven E. Sidebotham and Willeke Z. Wendrich, pp. 307–24. Research School of Asian, African, and Amerindian Studies (CNWS) Publications, Special Series 4. Leiden: Research School of Asian, African, and Amerindian Studies (CNWS).

2000   "Wood and Charcoal." In *Berenike 1998: Report of the 1997 Excavations at Berenike and the Survey of the Egyptian Eastern Desert, Including Excavations at Wadi Kalalat,* edited by Steven E. Sidebotham and Willeke Z. Wendrich, pp. 311–42. Research School of Asian, African, and Amerindian Studies (CNWS) Publications, Special Series 4. Leiden: Research School of Asian, African, and Amerindian Studies (CNWS).

Veth, Peter M.; Mike A. Smith; and Peter Hiscock, editors
2005   *Desert Peoples: Archaeological Perspectives*. Malden: Blackwell.

Vycichl, Werner
1958   "The Name of the Blemmyes." *Kush* 6: 179.

Weinstein, James M.
1975   "Egyptian Relations with Palestine in the Middle Kingdom." *Bulletin of the American Schools of Oriental Research* 217: 1–16.

Welsby, Derek A., and Julie R. Anderson, editors
2004   *Sudan Ancient Treasures: An Exhibition of Recent Discoveries from the Sudan National Museum*. London: British Museum Press.

Wendrich, Willeke Z.
2008   "From Objects to Agents: The Ababda Nomads and the Interpretation of the Past." In *The Archaeology of Mobility: Old World and New World Nomadism*, edited by Hans Barnard and Willeke Z. Wendrich, pp. 509–42. Cotsen Advanced Seminars 4. Los Angeles: Cotsen Institute of Archaeology, University of California.

Wendrich, Willeke Z.; Roger S. Bagnall; Rene T. J. Cappers; James A. Harrell; Steven E. Sidebotham; and Roberta S. Tomberw
2006   "Berenike Crossroads: The Integration of Information." In *Excavating Asian History: Interdisciplinary Studies in Archaeology and History*, edited by Norman Yoffee and Bradley L. Crowell, pp. 15–66. Tucson: University of Arizona Press.

Wendrich, Willeke Z., and Hans Barnard
2008   "The Archaeology of Mobility: Definitions and Research Approaches." In *The Archaeology of Mobility: Old World and New World Nomadism*, edited by Hans Barnard and Willeke Z. Wendrich, pp. 1–21. Cotsen Advanced Seminars 4. Los Angeles: Cotsen Institute of Archaeology, University of California.

Williams, Bruce B.
1983   *C-Group, Pan Grave, and Kerma Remains at Adindan Cemeteries T, K, U, and J*. The University of Chicago Oriental Institute Nubian Expedition 5; Excavations between Abu Simbel and the Sudan Frontier 5. Chicago: The Oriental Institute.

Winkler, Hans A.
1938   *Rock-Drawings of Southern Egypt*, Volume 1: *Sir Robert Mond Desert Expedition: Season 1936–1937; Preliminary Report*. Archaeological Survey of Egypt. London: The Egypt Exploration Fund.

Wobst, Martin
1978   "The Archaeo-Ethnology of Hunter-Gatherers, or the Tyranny of the Ethnographic Record in Archaeology." *American Antiquity* 43: 303–09.

Yinger, John M.
1994   *Ethnicity: Source of Strength? Source of Conflict?* State University of New York Series in Ethnicity and Race in American Life. Albany: State University of New York Press.

Zaborski, Andrzej
1989   "The Problem of Blemmyes-Beja: An Etymology." *Beiträge zur Sudanforschung* 4: 169–77.

Zibelius-Chen, Karola
2007   "Die Medja in altägyptischen Quellen." *Studien zur Altägyptischen Kultur* 36: 391–405.

3

EGYPT AND THE VANISHING LIBYAN: INSTITUTIONAL RESPONSES TO A NOMADIC PEOPLE

ROBERT RITNER, UNIVERSITY OF CHICAGO

General studies of the ancient Near East invariably extend no farther west than Egypt, with perhaps a few references to its Saharan oases. In sharp contrast to numerous colloquia held over the years on Egypt and its eastern or southern neighbors, only one scholarly conference has ever been devoted to the broad interactions between Egypt and Libya (in 1990; Leahy 1990), with a second, in 2007, concerned exclusively with the period of domination by intrusive families of Libyan descent during Egypt's Third Intermediate Period (ca. 1100 to 650 B.C.).[1] Despite extensive, if fragmentary, evidence of ancient Libyan cultural groups, broad attempts to provide a synthetic treatment of ancient Libya include only the 1914 volume *The Eastern Libyans,* by Oric Bates, and the 1936 dissertation by Wilhelm Hölscher, *Libyer und Ägypter* (Hölscher 1955).[2] So poorly known is Libya among Egyptologists that it even merited a brief article in the University College London Egyptological volume *Mysterious Lands*, whose tone is set by the introduction: "Mapping the Unknown in Ancient Egypt" (O'Connor and Quirke 2003: 5; Snape 2003).

A primary reason for this "mysterious" status, as the editors recognize (O'Connor and Quirke 2003: 3–5), is the lack of indigenous Libyan written records for these ancient periods. The same situation, however, is equally applicable to early Nubia, which has not suffered the same scholarly neglect. The more significant factor in our ignorance of ancient Libya lies in the nature of Libyan societies themselves: constantly moving tribes of pastoral nomads who have left little archaeological evidence of their presence or passage.[3] The general assumption that the Libyan homeland was confined to the Cyrenaica and the western (modern Egyptian) oases is unsubstantiated by archaeology.[4] What is known has been gleaned almost exclusively from (often unsympathetic) Egyptian texts and representations. Although it has been asserted that pastoral nomadism in Libya cannot be recognized before the "beginning of the first millennium B.C." (Khazanov 1984: 107–08), Egyptian records of all eras provide uniform, and conclusive, evidence of the pastoral nature of Libyan groups. Libyan "cattle culture" is evident from the Predynastic "Libya Palette" with its emphasis on the region's files of cattle and flocks (Ridley 1974: 43–46), to the Old Kingdom Annals of Senefru with its accession year capture of 13,100 Libyan animals (Sethe 1933: 237, line 13), to the yet more numerous captured Libyan cattle noted in victory texts of Sahure, Niuserre, Pepy I and II of the Old Kingdom, Merneptah and Ramesses III of the New Kingdom, and Taharqa of the

---

[1] "The Libyan Period in Egypt, Leiden University," 25–27 October 2007.

[2] Osing 1980.

[3] Archaeological deficiency is discussed in detail in both Snape 2003 and Hope 2007. See further White 1994.

[4] "This 'cultural horizon' ... is present over an area which exists far to the west of the zone of Libyan occupation noted above," (Snape 2003: 96 see also pp. 95, 98). For general assumptions, see Mattingly 2003: 344; Spalinger 1979.

Third Intermediate Period. Beyond such official records, the Middle Kingdom literary tale of Sinuhe notes the seizure of Libyan "cattle of all kinds beyond number" (Simpson 2003: 54), while in the New Kingdom, the first evidence of a new Libyan tribe, the Meshwesh, is tied to economic dockets of their primary trade good: bull fat (Hayes 1951: figs. 2 and 10, no. 130). Geographical limitations for sedentary cattle breeding, parallels with classical-era nomads, the general lack of identified settlements, and the Egyptian evidence of infrequent contact all strongly support the nomadic nature of Libyan societies, as was recognized initially by Bates (1914: 14, 31, 92), and most recently, by David O'Connor and Steven Snape (O'Connor 1990; cf. Snape 2003: 94, 98).

O'Connor in particular has surveyed the compelling evidence for Libyan pastoral nomadism as part of his broader, and less compelling, thesis suggesting a Libyan "nomadic state" during the New Kingdom (O'Connor 1990: 95–98). As I have already responded to this central thesis for the 2007 conference on the Third Intermediate Period, and the present participants received pre-publication copies of that article (Ritner in press), I shall devote the core of this chapter to a further issue raised by O'Connor, who insists that the Egyptians "were well informed about conditions and events within the lands of Libu and Meshwesh" (O'Connor 1990: 66). On the contrary, as I shall show, the Egyptian state was far more often at a loss to comprehend, or even to maintain contact with, any of the Libyan peoples to their west.

At the pyramid complex of the Fifth Dynasty King Sahure at Abusir, near modern Cairo, is the earliest evidence for a series of documents that well illustrate this point.[5] In multiple reliefs, King Sahure's victory over the Libyans is celebrated, with the king as a sphinx trampling the fallen Libyan ruler. Throughout the scenes, Libyans display one of the two basic representational styles for these western peoples, with (for both adult sexes) phallus sheaths below the waist and long, pendant necklaces below crossed bandoliers on the chest.[6] Tufts of hair at the brow approximate the uraeus serpent worn on the brow of Egyptian kings, and — again recalling royal Egyptian iconography — males wear bull tails suspended from the back of their belts.[7] To the right of the primary scene, Libyan notables implore peace, captured herds and flocks are numbered in the hundreds of thousands, and at the bottom, the remainder of the Libyan "royal family" observes their defeat, followed by the deities of the West and Libya (Borchardt 1913: 10–23, pls. 1–8, especially no. 1). Names accompany the family, labeling the queen as Khuites and her two sons as Wesa and Weni. This "royal family" scene (ca. 2506–2492 B.C.),[8] reappears with only minor variation in the later pyramid complex of King Niuserre of the Fifth Dynasty (ca. 2474–2444 B.C.),[9] the pyramid temples of Pepi I (ca. 2354–2310 B.C.)[10] and Pepi II (ca. 2300–2206 B.C.)[11] of the Sixth Dynasty, and yet again, some 1,600 years after their first attestation, in the Kawa temple built by the Twenty-fifth Dynasty Nubian Pharaoh Taharqa (690–664 B.C.). Additional examples were

---

[5] For the series, see Stockfisch 1996.

[6] Bates (1914: 132, n. 1) estimated that these bands were attested on about 70 percent of the Libyans represented on Egyptian monuments.

[7] For these parallels to Egyptian iconography, see Müller 1910: 61–62, 135; Martin 1986: columns 864–65. Note also the similar use of feathers in the earliest periods, discussed in Wilkinson 2003: 83–85. In Egypt, this usage continued in the hieroglyph for "soldier" 𓀀 . Such parallels suggest a once closer

relation between these North African peoples that weakened as "Egyptians" settled in the Nile Valley while "Libyans" continued a hunting and pastoral lifestyle in the Sahara.

[8] For simplicity, all dates given are those of Redford 2001: back endsheets.

[9] Borchardt 1907: 46–49, pls. 8–11.

[10] Leclant 1980: 49–54, pl. 2.

[11] Jéquier 1938: 13–14, pls. 8–9, 11.

probably created for King Unas at the end of the Fifth Dynasty and for King Montuhotep I of the Eleventh Dynasty.[12] Where names are preserved, they are invariably the familiar Khuites, Wesa, and Weni.

In 1,600 years, Libyans certainly had other names than these three (two of which, Khuites and Weni, are Egyptian), and it is obvious that the scene was continually repeated from a standard pattern book. For some Egyptologists, notably Sir Alan Gardiner, this scene was evidence of the inherent unreliability of Egyptian historical reliefs,[13] but what has often been overlooked is the unique character of this repetition. There are no parallels in Egyptian historical reliefs. The issue is not really the historicity of Egyptian records, but the theo-political need for a detailed scene of absent Libyan enemies. As the king was theologically master of the four directions, his funerary memorials necessarily required depictions of his victories in each area. For Asia and Nubia, this was not a problem, but the peripatetic Libyans were less easy to confront, and a standard substitution became obligatory. Given the nature of the problem, it cannot be taken as certain that the Sahure exemplar was in fact the original combat. It may also be a copy of a lost, earlier version.

Intermittent contact with Libyans in the Old Kingdom is certain, as detailed not just in formal royal accounts, but in the personal expedition records of Weni (reign of Pepi I) and Harkhuf (reign of Merenre; Simpson 2003: 404 [Weni], 409–10 [Harkhuf]), as well as Sixth Dynasty finds from Abu Ballas (ca. 200 km southwest of the Dakhla Oasis) that include Egyptian pottery and graffiti of cattle and Libyans hunting.[14] These encounters, however, were not military conquests. The situation changes briefly at the end of the First Intermediate Period. Military scenes for Montuhotep I at Gebelein provide a clear exception for this Eleventh Dynasty Theban ruler (2061–2011 B.C.), and it is significant that the scenes have no boilerplate "Libyan family" and include a distinct name for the defeated Libyan chieftain (von Bissing 1914: no. 33A). The scenes also add a critical feature of all later Libyan depictions: a feather signifying rank or tribal affiliation. The king's title (Netjeryhedjet) indicates an event in the second phase of his career, prior to his year 39.[15] However, once the king had secured rule over the entire country and constructed his royal mortuary complex (under new titles) at Deir el-Bahari, the decorative scheme was again influenced by traditional northern patterns, as surviving fragments of the standard Libyan scene indicate.[16] The style of the reliefs shows a clear reversion to Memphite models.[17]

---

[12] For the Taharqa examples, see Macadam 1955: 61, 63–65, pls. 9, 48–49; and Ritner 2008. For the Unas examples, see Labrousse, Lauer, and Leclant 1977: 89–92, pl. 32 (documents 39–41). For the Montuhotep example, to be published by Ritner, see Ritner 2008: 305, n. 4, and below.

[13] Gardiner (1961: 57): "they did not hesitate to ascribe to themselves deeds of heroism or piety in reality borrowed from others. The funerary temple of King Sahure' of Dyn. V depicts a group of Libyan chieftains brought in as prisoners and specifies the number of cattle taken as booty; the identical scene is found depicted in the pyramid temple of Piopi II of Dyn. VI, where the Libyan princes bear precisely the same names; so too, for a third time in a far distant Nubian temple under the Ethiopian king Taharka (c. 690 B.C.)."

[14] See Kuper 2002: 9–10, pls. 18–20. A comparable Libyan hunter (with distinguishing feather in his hair) is depicted on a bowl from Qubbet el-Hawa at Aswan, a frequent point of departure for Egyptian desert expeditions (such as that of Harkhuf).

[15] See the overview of the king's career in Werner 2001.

[16] See Naville, Hall, and Ayrton 1907: 41 (H. R. Hall: "possibly a Libyan"); and Naville and Hall 1913: 23 (unrecognized by Naville, but cf. n. 2 by H. R. Hall: "certainly Libyans") and pl. 13/2–3. Surely associated with these fragments is the text of OIM 8856, to be published by R. K. Ritner. The king was formerly designated as Montuhotep II.

[17] For the reign's deliberate return to Memphite relief typology, see Robins 1997: 90–96.

The following Middle Kingdom presents a comparable picture of infrequent contact. In the Twelfth Dynasty tomb of Khnumhotep I at Beni Hasan, dated to the reign of Amenemhat I (1991–1962 B.C.), an Egyptian superintendent is shown escorting a small group of traveling Libyans, with males, females, children, and herds (Newberry 1893: 85, pls. 45 and 47 [tomb 14]). The males display the second traditional dress for Libyans, with both hair feathers and long cloaks. Such depictions with long, and usually open, cloaks are found as early as the Predynastic period, and they continue throughout the New Kingdom in combination or alternation with figures showing the phallus sheath.[18] The Beni Hasan Libyan males do not display the most distinctive Libyan characteristic, the sidelock, otherwise associated with Libyans at all periods.[19] If this scene shows a brief local contact, and the literary text of Sinuhe describes a victorious campaign of Amenemhat I against the Libyans (Simpson 2003: 54), a more valuable index of Middle Kingdom knowledge of Libya is provided by contemporary magical cursing rites, known as the "execration texts."[20]

Inscribed on red pots or bound prisoner figures later ritually damaged, standardized texts provide lists of individually named enemy regions and rulers, as well as hostile Egyptians and general evil forces. The names in these lists were updated to reflect foreign regnal changes and new Egyptian opponents and were products of the royal chancellery. The sections on Asia, Nubia, and Egypt are highly detailed, but the contrast with Libya is striking. Thus for Nubia, one version of the section begins:

> The ruler of Kush, Auau, born of [...], and all the stricken ones who are with him.
> The ruler of Saï, Seteqtenkekh, and all the stricken ones who are with him.
> The ruler of Webasepet, Bakuayt, called Tchay, born of Ihaas, born to Wenkat, and all the stricken ones who are with him.
>
> The ruler of Webasepet, Iauny, born of Gemhu[(?)...], born to Ti[...], and all the stricken ones who are with him (Ritner 1997: 50–51).

The Asian section is similarly specific:

> The ruler of Iy-anq, Erum, and all the stricken ones who are with him.
> The ruler of Iy-anq, Abi-yamimu, and all the stricken ones who are with him.
> The ruler of Iy-anq, Akirum, and all the stricken ones who are with him.
> The ruler of Shutu, Ayyabum, and all the stricken ones who are with him (Ritner 1997: 51–52).

The specifically Libyan section, in its entirety, is as follows:

> The chiefs in Libya, all Libyans and their rulers" (Ritner 1997: 52).

---

[18] Compare the depiction of Libyans among the "four races of mankind" in the tomb of King Seti I (KV 17) showing cloaks, sidelocks, feathers, and phallus sheaths (Hornung 1990: 147, fig. 105), and the contemporary scenes of the king's Libyan campaign recorded at Karnak, with feathers, sidelocks, and phallus sheaths but no cloaks (Epigraphic Survey 1986: 87–101, pls. 27–32). Both types are again shown in the Libyan battle reliefs of Ramsses III at Medinet Habu. The stereotyped nature of these representations undercuts the skeptical assessment regarding Libyan robes in Hope 2007: 410, n. 1. The link between the "Battlefield Palette" Libyan and later examples is based as much upon the sidelock as the cloak. Hope's further criticisms of Nibbi are valid.

[19] See Smith 1967; Arkell 1963; and Bates 1914: 134–37. For the sidelock in the Niuserre "Libyan scene," see Bates 1914: 134; Borchardt 1907: 48, fig. 31.

[20] For an overview of the rite, including texts and procedures, see Ritner 1993: 136–90.

All sections end with the formulaic coda:

> Their strong men, their messengers, their confederates, their allies, who will rebel, who will plot, who will fight, who will say that they will fight, who will say that they will rebel, in this entire land.

Ironically, for the Libyan section the coda is longer than the text it concludes.

Devoid of multiple personal, regional, settlement, or even tribal names, the Libyan section is the shortest of the entire series, and — like the boilerplate victory scenes — is included simply to ensure geographic completeness. In its unique terseness, it is eloquent testimony to the Egyptian court's ignorance of Libyan social components, territories, or rulers. If the Libyan razzia mentioned in Sinuhe did occur, it had notably little effect on Egyptian chancellery records.

The abstentee Libyan posed a different problem for the court of Queen Hatshepsut (1502–1482 B.C.) during Egypt's New Kingdom. Celebration of a great procession of the goddess Hathor required the presence of a troupe of Libyan dancers with clappers. As depicted on a side wall in the queen's Hathor shrine at Deir el-Bahari, the "Libyans" are quite unusual (Naville 1901: pl. 90). Although the scene is designated in the accompanying text as "Dance of the Libyans" and the performers do have a number of feathers in their hair, they wear modified Egyptian kilts in addition to cloaks and (in one case) a phallus sheath or tail. Most strikingly, their hair is indistinguishable from that of other Egyptians in the procession and is simply an Egyptian hairstyle into which feathers have been inserted as decoration. As already recognized by Hölscher in 1936 (Hölscher 1955: 30–31), these "Libyans" are really costumed Egyptians performing as "mummers" for the celebration. The unavailability of genuine Libyans probably necessitated the substitution.

As climatological changes and population movements of the Sea Peoples forced Libyans into closer contact with the Nile in the later New Kingdom, new cultural confrontations and misunderstandings would arise. Thus, according to inscriptions at Karnak, the year five campaign of Merneptah (1233 B.C.) against the Libyans was begun when a coalition of tribes under the Libu reached the western border of the Nile,[21] bringing not just warriors, but wives, children, and herds,[22] so that the Delta "was abandoned as pasture land for the cattle" belonging to the enemies.[23] The Egyptian texts make reference to past, repeated penetrations of the western border up to the great river, probably describing a changing Libyan pastoral cycle,[24] and they give indications of a general famine. Thus the Libyans are said to be "fighting in order to fill their bellies daily. They have come to the land of Egypt just to seek the necessities of their mouths."[25] In the same context, Merneptah mentions a grain shipment to sustain the land of the Hittites.[26] Following the Egyptian victory, the Athribis stela records that Libyan camps were abandoned, their plants gone, and their wells lacking through acts of the king, since the sun god "Pre himself had cursed their people since they had transgressed" Egyptian territory.[27] One is left to wonder whether these statements describe real punitive acts by

---

[21] Kitchen 1982: 3, line 6, and p. 4, lines 3–4 (Karnak Inscription lines 7 and 15).

[22] Kitchen 1982: 4, lines 2–3, p. 8, line 5, and p. 9, line 2 (Karnak Inscription lines 14, 50, 57).

[23] Kitchen 1982: 3, line 7 (Karnak Inscription line 8).

[24] Kitchen 1982: 4, lines 9–10 (Karnak Inscription line 19).

[25] Kitchen 1982: 4, lines 14–15 (Karnak Inscription line 22).

[26] Kitchen 1982: 5, line 3 [Karnak Inscription line 24).

[27] Kitchen 1982: 20, lines 8–9, and p. 21, line 1 (Kom el-Ahmar/Athribis stela lines 7–10).

Egyptians in the Libyan heartlands or are simply a theological explanation of the famine that drove the Libyans to the Egyptian frontier. The true nature of this Libyan "invasion" is clear from the conclusion of Merneptah's triumphal hymn: Egypt attained peace with no herdsmen crossing at will, no frightening foreign speech requesting assistance, and no stolen cattle or crops (Wente 2003: 360; Kitchen 1982: 18, lines 9–15).

Similar pressures probably underlay the next great Libyan invasion in year 5 of Ramesses III (1194 B.C.). Egypt is again said to have been continually exposed to marauding by Libyan tribesmen,[28] but now Ramesses III attempted a clever diplomatic solution, by causing a Libyan delegation to request that he appoint a supreme chief to act as their ruler and Egypt's puppet: "His Majesty brought a little one from the land of the Tjemhu, a child supported by his strong arms, appointed for them to be a chief to regulate their land. It had not been heard of before, since Egyptian kings had come into existence."[29] The situation is paralleled by other settled societies' attempts to designate a single tribal ruler for negotiations. In the words of Marshall Sahlins, this inclination to "find a chief" is "a need so compelling that nomad chiefs may have to be invented if they do not already exist" (Sahlins 1968: 38). Like many such colonial efforts, the Egyptian attempt to impose a single ruler over the tribal groups proved a failure. War resulted, and the Libyans were defeated and settled by tribe in reservations, from which they would rise in rank as mercenaries and ultimately as kings in Egypt's Third Intermediate Period. Their tribal structure, effectively preserved in their isolated camps, would have profound impact on the Egyptian society of that period, which I have discussed elsewhere (Ritner in press).

If Libyans were so infrequently encountered in the periods prior to the New Kingdom, some explanation can be found in the extreme distances they traveled in their pastoral cycles. Evidence for this travel comes not from Egypt, but — at last — from sources provided by the Libyans themselves. Generally unknown to Egyptology, these Libyan records consist of painted or carved rock art in the far southwestern corner of the Libyan province of Fezzan, among the cliffs of the Tadrart Acacus adjacent to modern Algeria.[30] Attempts to date the rock art on the basis of style and surface weathering are necessarily speculative,[31] but the images are striking confirmation of the depictions of Libyans in Egyptian records. Scenes of cattle dominate the rock art (see figs. 3.1–2).[32] Standing near captured cattle, figures with throwsticks (the basic component of the earliest Egyptian name for Libya, Tchehenu) and the prominent frontal hairlock or "uraeus" are shown in the supposedly early "round-head" style at Grotto Wadi Kessan (Mori 1965: 162, fig. 64). One man probably wears a feather in his hair (cf. fig. 3.3). In the ensuing "older pastoralist style," men display hairlocks and throwsticks at Teshuniat (Mori 1965: 174, fig. 83), while a scene of the dressing of these locks is found at Uan Amil (see fig. 3.4; Mori 1965: 177, fig. 86). Hunters with tails clearly appended to their

[28] Epigraphic Survey 1930: pl. 27, lines 20–22 = Edgerton and Wilson 1936: 23 = Kitchen 1983: 22, lines 4–6.

[29] Epigraphic Survey 1930: pl. 27, lines 26–31 = Edgerton and Wilson 1936: 24–26 = Kitchen 1983: 22, lines 12–23, 4.

[30] For a general discussion, see the brief overview in Ayoub 1968: 32–40. Specific images and commentary are found in Mori 1965. For maps of the relevant

area of the rock art, see Mori 1965: 17–18. I have lectured publicly on this art since 1988, and now a brief reference to the parallels appears in Manassa 2003: 89, n. 77.

[31] Such attempts are found in Mori 1965; Barich 1989; Jelinek 1989; Gattinara 1998: 122–54; and Mattingly 2003: 279–326.

[32] Mori 1965: 162, 173, 175–76, 181, 184, 186–91, 194–95, 200, 202, 204–07.

waists are shown at Hararig.[33] Even the Libyan bandolier appears on a carved female figure at Ti-n-lalan (Mori 1965: 88, figs. 38–39 and 89, fig. 42).

With distinctive weapon, hairstyle, feather, bull's tail, and bandolier all attested, it is little surprising that even the alternate representation with open cloak is well represented in the "older pastoralist style" at Uan Amil, in the succeeding "new pastoralist style" at Ti-n-lalan and In Eidi, and in the later "horse style" at Teshuinat and Uan Muhaggig (see fig. 3.5).[34] At Ti-n-lalan and Uan Muhaggig, individuals also sport horizontally placed feathers, later an indication of the Meshwesh tribe. In contrast, at In Eidi, open cloaks are worn with vertical feathers, later an indication of the Libu tribe. A painted male figure in the "new pastoralist style" at Uadi Kessi includes not only the frontal hairlock, but the distinctive sidelock and body tattoos expected from Egyptian reliefs (Mori 1965: 191, fig. 108). Although it is only the latest "horse" or "horse-and-chariot" style that rock art specialists have readily linked to Egyptian types,[35] it should be clear that all these phases are relevant to the Egyptian representations, and the retention of certain critical features across stylistic periods is of note. At intervals, Libyans with these features appeared on the Egyptian borders and then vanished into the Sahara well beyond the reach of the Egyptian state.[36] The remarkable extent of the travels of some Libyan groups as far as the Tadrart Acacus readily explains their "mysterious" status to the Egyptians, who often failed not only to understand them but even to see them.

---

[33] Mori 1965: 173, fig. 81. Tails are also shown at Tassili; see the central figure in Gattinara 1998: 84.

[34] See Mori 1965: 179, fig. 89, and 180, fig. 91 (Uan Amil); 200, figs. 122, 201, fig. 123 (Ti-n-lalan); 196, fig. 115 (In Eidi); 206, fig. 130 (Teshuinat); and 207, fig. 133 (Uan Muhaggig).

[35] Links to contemporary Egypt are noted in Mori 1965: 206 ("scene di tipo egizio" for the "horse style") and in Barich 1989: 504–05, for the same period called "Horse-and-Chariot" men. The chariots are also considered evidence of Nilotic contact in Mattingly 2003: 345. Earlier contacts have been suggested occasionally. Frobenius in 1937 had linked ("roundhead style") ithyphallic figures to the Egyptian god Bes; see Mori 1965: 68–69. See also Gattinara (1998: 115–17) on Anubis and Libyan "Jackal-man" images. Mattingly 2003: 343–44, based on Bates, notes the general similarity of plumes, hairstyles, penis sheaves, and tattoos but offers no specific citations of relevant Libyan rock art.

[36] In his discussion of these seminar papers, Frank Hole has rightly raised the issues of the sustainability of Saharan cattle cultures and their routes of mobility. These matters have been discussed by scholars previously, but they deserve a synopsis here. The possibility of mobile cattle herds west of the Nile Valley is certain, not only from the explicit Egyptian records of Libyan movements surveyed in this paper, but from evidence of wild cattle herds in the western desert during the Egyptian New Kingdom. In year 2 of Amenhotep III, a sighting of 170 wild bulls on the desert near the Wadi Natrun prompted a royal hunting party whose success was commemorated on a series of official scarabs; see Ritner 1986 and Blankenberg-van Delden 1969: 13–14, 17, 57–61, 189, pl. 10. The desert route taken by these wild cattle is unknown, but they may have followed oasis tracks from the Mediterranean coast, as suggested by Hole for the Libyans themselves. Likely Libyan pastoral zones are discussed by Bates 1914: 30–35, and by O'Conner 1990: 33–38 (who locates the Tjemhu, Libu, and Meshwesh tribes in the Cyrenaica, while noting that similar conditions for cattle culture extend along the coast as far west as Tripolitania) and pp. 89–98. For established tracks leading south and east along the Libyan coast, see Bates 1914: 5–17. Common routes from the coast via small oases toward the areas of Libyan rock art are discussed in ibid., pp. 14–15. Possible (multiple) Libyan invasion routes (with cattle and goats) in the time of Merneptah are surveyed in Manassa 2003: 94–100. The diversity of Libyan tribal units and occupation zones, as well as the extent and harshness of known oasis routes undoubtedly influenced the intermittent visibility of Libyan groups in Egypt. Limited mobility of herd animals is necessarily an additional factor. Libyan herders with sheep may be limited to the coast and major oasis routes. In contrast, sheep are absent from herds depicted in the Tadrart Acacus.

Figure 3.1. Scene of cattle (Uan Amil; this and all photos taken by the author, 2006)

Figure 3.2. Rare depiction of a goat (Tadrart Acacus)

Figure 3.3. Figure with hair feather and throwstick (Tadrart Acacus)

Figure 3.4. Scene of dressing frontal hair lock (Uan Amil)

Figure 3.5. Figure (on right) with open cloak (Uan Amil)

BIBLIOGRAPHY

Arkell, A. J.
1963   "Was King Scorpion Menes?" *Antiquity* 37: 31–35.

Ayoub, M. S.
1968   *Fezzan: A Short History*. Libya: Kingdom of Libya, Ministry of Tourism and
            Antiquities.

Barich, Barbara E.
1989   "Uan Muhuggiag Rock Shelter (Tadrart Acacus) and the Late Prehistory of the
            Libyan Sahara." In *Late Prehistory of the Nile Basin and the Sahara*, edited by Lech
            Krzyzaniak and Michael Kobusiewicz, pp. 499–505. Studies in African Archaeology
            2. Poznan: Poznan Archaeological Museum.

Bates, Oric
1914   *The Eastern Libyans: An Essay*. London: Macmillan. Reprinted London: F. Cass,
            1970.

Blankenberg-van Delden, C.
1969   *The Large Commemorative Scarabs of Amenhotep III*. Documenta et monumenta
            Orientis antiqui 15. Leiden: E. J. Brill.

Borchardt, Ludwig
1907   *Das Grabdenkmal des Königs Ne-User-Re ʿ*. Ausgrabungen der Deutschen Orient-
            Gesellschaft in Abusir 1902–1904; Wissenschaftliche Veröffentlichung der Deutschen
            Orient-Gesellschaft 7. Leipzig: J. C. Hinrichs.
1913   *Das Grabdenkmal des Königs Sʾaʒḥu-Re ʿ*, Volume 2: *Die Wandbilder*. Ausgrabungen
            der Deutschen Orient-Gesellschaft 1902–1908; Wissenschaftliche Veröffentlichung
            der Deutschen Orient-Gesellschaft 26/2. Leipzig: J. C. Hinrichs.

Edgerton, William F., and John A. Wilson
1936   *Historical Records of Ramses III: The Texts in Medinet Habu, Translated with
            Explanatory Notes*. 2 volumes. Studies in Ancient Oriental Civilization 12. Chicago:
            The University of Chicago Press.

The Epigraphic Survey
1930   *Medinet Habu, Volume 1: Earlier Historical Records of Ramses III*. Oriental Institute
            Publications 8. Chicago: The University of Chicago Press.
1986   *The Battle Reliefs of King Sety I*. Oriental Institute Publications 107; Reliefs and
            Inscriptions at Karnak 4. Chicago: The Oriental Institute.

Gardiner, Alan H.
1961   *Egypt of the Pharaohs: An Introduction*. Oxford: Clarendon Press.

Gattinara, Giulia Castelli
1998   *Libia: Arte rupestre del Sahara*. Florence: Polaris.

Hayes, William C.
1951   "Inscriptions from the Palace of Amenhotep III." *Journal of Near Eastern Studies*
            10: 35–56.

Hölscher, Wilhelm
1955   *Libyer und Ägypter: Beiträge zur Ethnologie und Geschichte libyscher Völkerschaften
            nach den altägyptischen Quellen*. Ägyptologische Forschungen 4. Glückstadt: J. J.
            Augustin. Unaltered reprint of Munich dissertation, 1936.

Hope, Colin A.
2007   "Egypt and 'Libya' to the End of the Old Kingdom: A View from the Dakhleh Oasis."
            In *The Archaeology and Art of Ancient Egypt: Essays in Honor of David B. O'Connor*

edited by Zahi A. Hawass and Janet E. Richards, pp. 399–415. Annales du service des antiquités de l'Égypte 36. Cairo: Conseil Suprême des Antiquités de l'Égypte.

Hornung, Eriks
1990   *The Valley of the Kings: Horizon of Eternity*. New York: Timken.

Jelinek, Jan
1989   "Saharan Neolithic Rock Art." In *Late Prehistory of the Nile Basin and the Sahara*, edited by Lech Krzyzaniak and Michael Kobusiewicz, pp. 513–30. Studies in African Archaeology 2. Poznan: Poznan Archaeological Museum.

Jéquier, Gustave
1938   *Le monuments funéraires de Pepi II,* Volume 2: *Le temple*. Fouilles à Saqqarah. Cairo: Imprimerie de l'Institut français d'archéologie orientale.

Khazanov, Anatoly M.
1984   *Nomads and the Outside World*. Cambridge Studies in Social Anthropology 44. Cambridge: Cambridge University Press.

Kitchen, Kenneth A.
1982   *Ramesside Inscriptions: Historical and Biographical*, Volume 4. Oxford: B. H. Blackwell.
1983   *Ramesside Inscriptions: Historical and Biographical*, Volume 5. Oxford: B. H. Blackwell.

Kuper, Rudolph
2002   "Routes and Roots in Egypt's Western Desert: The Early Holocene Resettlement of the Eastern Sahara." In *Egypt and Nubia: Gifts of the Nile*, edited by Renée F. Friedman, pp. 1–12. London: British Museum Press.

Labrousse, A.; Jean-Philippe Lauer; and Jean Leclant
1977   *Le temple haut du complexe funéraire du roi Ounas*. Bibliothèque d'étude 73; Mission archéologique de Saqqarah 2; Publications de l'Institut français d'archéologie orientale du Caire. Cairo: Institut français d'archéologie orientale du Caire.

Leahy, Anthony, editor
1990   *Libya and Egypt, c 1300–750 BC*. London: Centre of Near and Middle Eastern Studies and the Society for Libyan Studies, School of Oriental and African Studies.

Leclant, Jean
1980   "La 'Famille Libyenne' au temple haut de Pépi Ier." In *Livre de Centenaire (1880–1980)*, edited by Jean Vercoutter, pp. 49–54. Mémoires publiés par les membres de l'Institut français d'archéologie orientale du Caire 104. Cairo: Institut français d'archéologique orientale du Caire.

Macadam, M. F. Laming
1955   *The Temples of Kawa,* Volume 2: *History and Archaeology of the Site*. Oxford Excavations in Nubia. London: The Griffith Institute.

Manassa, Colleen
2003   *The Great Karnak Inscription of Merneptah: Grand Strategy in the 13th Century B.C.* Yale Egyptological Studies 5. New Haven: Yale Egyptological Seminar.

Martin, Karl
1986   "Uräus." In *Lexikon der Ägyptologie*, Volume 6: *Stele–Zypresse*, edited by Wolfgang Helck and Eberhard Otto, columns 864–68. Wiesbaden: Otto Harrassowitz.

Mattingly, David J., editor
2003   *The Archaeology of Fazzān,* Volume 1: *Synthesis*. London: Society for Libyan Studies.

Mori, Fabrizio
    1965   *Tadrart Acacus: Arte rupestre e culture del Sahara preistorico.* Turin: Giulio Einaudi.

Müller, Wilhelm Max
    1910   *Egyptological Researches,* Volume 2: *Results of a Journey in 1906.* Washington, D.C.: Carnegie Institution of Washington.

Naville, Edouard
    1901   *The Temple of Deir el-Bahari,* Part 4. Excavation Memoir 19. London: Egypt Exploration Fund.

Naville, Edouard; H. R. Hall; and E. R. Ayrton
    1907   *The XIth Dynasty Temple of Deir el-Bahari,* Part 1. Egypt Exploration Fund Memoir 28. London: Egypt Exploration Fund.

Naville, Edouard, and H. R. Hall
    1913   *The XIth Dynasty Temple of Deir el-Bahari,* Part 3. Egypt Exploration Fund Memoir 32. London: Egypt Exploration Fund.

Newberry, Percy E.
    1893   *Beni Hasan,* Part 1. Archaeological Survey of Egypt 1. London: Egypt Exploration Fund.

O'Connor, David
    1990   "The Nature of Tjemhu (Libyan) Society in the Later New Kingdom." In *Libya and Egypt: c 1300–750 BC,* edited by Anthony Leahy, pp. 29–113. London: Centre of Near and Middle Eastern Studies and Society for Libyan Studies, School of Oriental and African Studies.

O'Connor, David B., and Stephen Quirke, editors
    2003   *Mysterious Lands.* Encounters with Ancient Egypt. London: University College of London.

Osing, J.
    1980   "Libyen, Libyer." In *Lexikon der Ägyptologie,* Volume 3: *Horhekenu–Megeb,* edited by Wolfgang Helck and Eberhard Otto, columns 1015–33. Wiesbaden: Otto Harrassowitz.

Redford, Donald B., editor
    2001   *The Oxford Encyclopedia of Ancient Egypt.* 3 volumes. Oxford: Oxford University Press.

Ridley, Ronald T.
    1973   *The Unification of Egypt.* Deception Bay: Shield Press.

Ritner, Robert K.
    1986   "The Site of the Wild Bull-hunt of Amenophis III." *Journal of Egyptian Archaeology* 72: 193–94.
    1993   *The Mechanics of Ancient Egyptian Magical Practice.* Studies in Ancient Oriental Civilization 54. Chicago: The Oriental Institute.
    1997   "Execration Texts." In *The Context of Scripture,* Volume 1: *Canonical Compositions from the Biblical World,* edited by William W. Hallo and K. Lawson Younger, pp. 50–52. Leiden: E. J. Brill.
    2008   "Libyan vs. Nubian as the Ideal Egyptian." In *Egypt and Beyond: Studies Presented to Leonard H. Lesko upon His Retirement from Brown University, June 2005,* edited by Stephen Thompson, pp. 305–14. Providence: Brown University.
    In press   "Fragmentation and Re-integration in the Third Intermediate Period." In *Proceedings of the Conference "The Libyan Period in Egypt."* Leiden.

Robins, Gay
  1997   *The Art of Ancient Egypt.* Cambridge: Harvard University Press.

Sahlins, Marshall D.
  1968   *Tribesmen.* Foundations of Modern Anthropology Series. Englewood Cliffs: Prentice-Hall.

Sethe, Kurt
  1933   *Urkunden des Alten Reiche*s. 2nd edition. Urkunden des ägyptischen Altertums 1. Leipzig: J. C. Hinrichs.

Simpson, William K., editor
  2003   *The Literature of Ancient Egypt: An Anthology of Stories, Instructions, Stelae, Autobiographies, and Poetry.* 3rd edition. New Haven: Yale University Press.

Smith, W. S.
  1967   "Two Archaic Egyptian Sculptures." *Bulletin: Museum of Fine Arts, Boston* 65(340): 70–84.

Snape, Steven
  2003   "The Emergence of Libya on the Horizon of Egypt." In *Mysterious Lands,* edited by David O'Connor and Stephen Quirke, pp. 93–106. Encounters with Ancient Egypt. London: University College of London.

Spalinger, Anthony J.
  1979   "Some Notes on the Libyans of the Old Kingdom and Later Historical Reflexes." *Society for the Study of Egyptian Antiquities Journal* 9/3: 125–60.

Stockfisch, Dagmar
  1996   "Bemerkungen zur sog. 'libyschen Familie.'" In *Wege Öffnen: Festschrift für Rolf Gundlach zum 65. Geburtstag,* edited by Mechthild Schade-Busch, pp. 315–25. Ägypten und Altes Testament 35. Wiesbaden: Otto Harrassowitz.

Wente, Edward F., translator
  2003   "The Israel Stela." In *The Literature of Ancient Egypt: An Anthology of Stories, Instructions, Stelae, Autobiographies, and Poetry,* Third edition, edited by William K. Simpson, pp. 356–60. New Haven: Yale University Press.

Werner, Edward K.
  2001   "Montuhotep I, Nebhepetre." In *The Oxford Encyclopedia of Ancient Egypt*, Volume 2, edited by Donald Redford, pp. 436–38. Oxford: Oxford University Press.

White, Donald
  1994   "Before the Greeks Came: A Survey of the Current Archaeological Evidence for the Pre-Greek Libyans." *Libyan Studies* 25: 31–44.

Wilkinson, Toby A. H.
  2003   *Genesis of the Pharaohs: Dramatic New Discoveries Rewrite the Origins of Ancient Egypt.* London: Thames & Hudson.

von Bissing, Friedrich W.
  1914   *Denkmäler ägyptischer Skulptur.* Munich: F. Bruckmann.

4

HISTORY DOES NOT REPEAT ITSELF: CYCLICITY AND PARTICULARISM IN NOMAD-SEDENTARY RELATIONS IN THE NEGEV IN THE LONG TERM

STEVEN A. ROSEN, BEN-GURION UNIVERSITY

INTRODUCTION

The study of nomads from pre-ethnographic times is difficult. Traditionally seen through a lens of contemporary texts usually reflecting some degree of animosity, and always reflecting a naïve depiction of the "other," scholars attempting to explore the nature of nomadic pastoralism in ancient times have faced both a scarcity of sources and basic limitations within those sources. Even when we temper the biases and lacunae in these sources using modern historical and anthropological critique, we are left with tremendous gaps in our direct basic knowledge of ancient pastoral societies.

While not a panacea to these problems of sources, archaeology provides an old-new avenue for exploring ancient pastoral nomadism. Even given the obvious limitations of the archaeological record (preservation, precision in dating, telescoping of events, selective coverage, etc.), the mere fact that we can and do find ancient nomadic camps, often in large numbers, allows us to "do archaeology" on them, generating not only new data sets offering insights to various traditional historical questions, but also, as a matter of course, generating new questions.

In particular, beyond the enriched data set that archaeology can bring to the study of ancient nomadism, the archaeological record studied as an integrated sequence provides a deeper time perspective on the development of the phenomenon. It contrasts with the textual record in two ways. First, the earliest periods in the development of specialized pastoralism, the Neolithic and Chalcolithic, are beyond the chronological range of writing — archaeology is the only means for examining the rise of the phenomenon. Second, even within the span of time for which texts have documented pastoral societies, for obvious reasons, the earlier the period, the fewer the historical texts. Although the archaeological record of pastoral sites in the settled zone has suffered significantly from the destruction wrought by development, beginning in ancient times (and including the practice of agriculture), and in such cases the archaeological record is patchy at best, the record in the desert is relatively even. We can trace the archaeology of desert pastoralism back to its origins and the different periods are roughly comparable in terms of the representativeness of the record. This facilitates comparison between periods and cultures, providing the means for a *longue durée* approach to the analysis.

Focusing on the Negev as a case study, shifting patterns of relations between nomadic and sedentary groups can be traced over the long term, beginning with the origins of the phenomenon in the Late Neolithic and extending forward through classical and indeed recent times. These are reflected in fluctuating demographic patterns, changes in desert subsistence systems, changing patterns of trade relations, shifting settlement systems (including movement of the border between desert and sown), and evolving material culture systems. Archaeologically I suggest that the long span in the Negev may be divided into four basic complexes, the earliest Timnian complex, the early historical complex (second millennium and early first millennium B.C.), the Classical complex (beginning with the Nabateans and extending through the Early Islamic period), and the recent Bedouin. Each complex shows a specific package of social, economic, technological, and ecological adaptations.

THE NEGEV AS A CASE STUDY: SETTLEMENT PATTERNS

Archaeological investigations in the Negev highlands in the early 1980s, initiated as a large salvage project before the redeployment of the Israeli army out of the Sinai Peninsula, resulted in the systematic documentation of thousands of previously unknown sites spanning the entire breadth of the archaeological record (fig. 4.1). Numerous excavations were also conducted. The surveys were published (and are still being published) in a series of standardized monographs each covering 100 sq. km (for the central Negev, see Avni 1991; Baumgarten 2004; Cohen 1981, 1985; Haiman 1986, 1991, 1993, 1999; Lender 1990; Rosen 1994; and in ecological and cultural contrast, for the northern Negev, see Beit-Arieh 2003a; Gazit 1996; Govrin 1991). Excavations were published in various forums and formats. Other research conducted in adjacent areas like the southern Negev (e.g., Avner 1990, 1998; Rothenberg 1972c), Sinai (e.g., Amiran, Beit-Arieh, and Glass 1973; Bar-Yosef 1984; Beit-Arieh 2003b; Dahari 2000; Rothenberg 1972a–b), and southern Jordan (Henry 1992, 1995) complements the picture from the central Negev and indeed is often the key to understanding the phenomena reflected in the record of the central Negev.

Beyond the specifics of the different periods, several general features of this record are integral to the themes of this paper. The surveys in the central Negev present a consistent picture of major demographic peaks and declines (Rosen 1987b) and seem to contrast with more stable sequences in the southern Negev (e.g., Avner 1998; Avner, Carmi, and Segal 1994). The northern Negev shows periods of rise and decline, but these are not necessarily coincident with those of the central Negev and seem to reflect different social and historical trends or events. To a major extent, these demographic fluctuations seem to reflect shifts in the edge of systematic agricultural settlement, coincident in some cases with shifting pastoral territories. Figure 4.2 summarizes roughly the north–south shifts of the agricultural settlement over time, as reflected in the presence of evidence for agriculture and associated sites during a particular time period on a latitudinal scale. The types of evidence vary with different periods, as agricultural practices change. For the earlier periods (Bronze Age and earlier), the presence of high proportions of flint sickle blades in a lithic assemblage is a good proxy for the intensity of agricultural practices (Rosen 1997: 58), and the clear contrasts between desert and Mediterranean zone lithic assemblages in the proportions of sickles must surely be a reflection of intensity of practice.[1] For later periods, the presence of agricultural terracing, direct evidence for run-off irrigation systems, is a clear reflection of systematic farming. Although

---

[1] Although ethnographically some modern Bedouin groups reap by hand, without the use of sickles of any kind, given the presence of flint sickles in the Mediterranean zone, and their presence in agricultural enclaves in the desert, corresponding to microenvironments appropriate for agriculture, and given the environmental limitations of the desert for agriculture, relative proportions of sickles indeed seem to reflect intensity of practice.

the dating of these terrace systems has been the subject of some debate (e.g., Haiman 1990, 1995a), and certainly they have been reused by recent Bedouin, the presence of homesteads in association with the dam systems is a strong indicator of agricultural settlement. In classical and recent times, texts and ethnography also inform on agricultural practices (e.g., Bailey 1980; Bruins 1986; Evenari, Shanan, and Tadmor 1982; Kraemer 1958; Marx 1967; Mayerson 1960). Figure 4.2 provides a simplified north–south perspective on agricultural penetration; the real distribution of agricultural[2] practices obviously does not follow east–west latitudinal lines, but rather the natural geography, and enclaves of farming may exist in otherwise non-agricultural regions. The true pattern is less even and perhaps even somewhat patchy. Figure 4.3 presents maps suggesting the edge of agricultural practices in two different periods, the Byzantine period and the Early Bronze Age II, and figure 4.4 presents an impressionistic perspective on the actual edges of systematic agricultural exploitation in different periods, with an emphasis on "impressionistic." Thus, figure 4.2 is intended to summarize the fluctuations and should be taken as an indicator of depth of penetration rather than a detailed geographic statement. As an aside, it is quite important to note that these shifts in the agricultural zone do not correspond in any one-to-one sense with climatic fluctuations in some absolute sense of the word. It is clear that the Early Bronze Age (and for that matter, the Chalcolithic period) were times of considerably greater rainfall than the Byzantine period (e.g., A. Rosen 2007: 150–71 and references; also Bar-Matthews, Ayalon, and Kaufman 1998), yet with considerably less agricultural penetration into the desert.

Complementing this picture of agricultural expansion and contraction, we can also construct similar schematics of fluctuating pastoral occupation in the central Negev. However, in contrast to agricultural settlements, defining pastoral presence requires some discussion, both in terms of what exactly we mean by presence in referring to mobile peoples, and what types of evidence can be used to infer that presence.

For the purposes of this analysis, defining pastoral presence perhaps is more easily accomplished by stating what it is not: it is not the presence of a shepherd opportunistically grazing in an area, nor is it the occasional (non-cyclical) penetration of a group into or through a region. Furthermore, it is clear that desert pastoralists commonly penetrate the agricultural zone, either in the course of seasonal migration or during seasonal dispersal. Thus by pastoral presence I intend the presence of primary residential camps in what Binford (1980) has termed a system of residential mobility. Although Binford was referring to hunting-gathering groups and contrasted residential mobility (the movement of the entire residential social unit) with logistical mobility (movement of individuals or subgroups to and from base camps to secondary resource exploitation sites), the key here is the distinction between residential camps and other sites. Thus, pastoral presence is the common use of a territory by families and clans as expressed in the presence of residential base camps. I refer to this kind of presence from here on as pastoral tribal presence, to distinguish it from sedentary occupations and from opportunistic exploitation. In the classical era, there is clear overlap between the agricultural and pastoral zones (Avni 1996; Haiman 1995a; Rosen 1987a; Rosen and Avni 1993), but the primary pastoral tribal presence, in this case in the sense of the largest aggregate encampments, is in the areas south of the Ramon Crater.

---

[2] I refer here to cereal agriculture and horticulture, and distinguish between plant agriculture and pastoralism, often also considered a form of agriculture.

Furthermore, it should be noted in particular that the recent discovery of rock shelters with dung layers attributable to periods for which there are no campsites in the region (Rosen et al. 2005) does not constitute tribal presence, but obviously reflects the use of the central Negev for seasonal grazing. The near total absence of material culture in these rock shelters is typical for such types of exploitation since the range of activities is severely limited.

The second issue is that of archaeological visibility. The central Negev is rich in archaeological sites not associated with agricultural systems, interpreted universally as the remains of residential camps reflecting pastoral systems (e.g., Cohen 1999; Cohen and Dever 1978, 1979, 1980; Haiman 1995a–b; Rosen 1987a; Rosen and Avni 1997).[3] On the other hand, debate has arisen around those periods for which there is little evidence of residential camps of any kind, pastoral or sedentary, for example, in the second millennium B.C. In particular, Finkelstein (1995; Finkelstein and Perevoletsky 1990) has argued that these periods (in the Negev) represent times of increased mobility, with correspondingly less hard archaeological evidence. It is beyond the scope of this paper to deal in depth with this issue (see Rosen 1992), but the arguments for archaeological invisibility are flawed for the earlier periods (at least as late as the end of the third millennium B.C.), when lithic industries which leave large quantities of waste provide a clear marker for occupation sites (in much the same way as for the Paleolithic), and for later periods, when ceramics are common. Furthermore, given the likelihood that tents are a later phenomenon among nomadic groups (Rosen and Saidel in press), architectural remains should also provide markers. Finally, it is also worth noting that tents too leave their archaeological signature (for ethnoarchaeological examples, see Avni 1992; Banning and Kohler-Rollefson 1986, 1992; Eldar, Nir, and Nahlieli 1992; Saidel 2001; Simms 1988; and for archaeological examples, see Banning 1986; Rosen 1993; Rosen and Avni 1997: 19, 44, 54–55, 59).

Given these provisos, figure 4.5 summarizes the north–south extent of pastoral tribal presence in the Negev in different periods. As with the schematic of agricultural penetration (fig. 4.2), the long-term record shows shifting territories, with some periods showing penetration fairly far north, and others a contraction into the southern Negev and Sinai. Significantly, while there appears to be partial correlation between the agricultural and pastoral systems, such that during some periods the two systems seem geographically linked with their borders more or less coinciding and even overlapping, there are other long periods when there appears to be significant distance between the two systems, in essence leaving a blank space in the middle, in the heartland of the central Negev. These blank periods coincide, of course, with those periods of demographic decline mentioned earlier. In particular, this phenomenon can be noted during the second millennium B.C. and during the Middle Ages, in the first half of the second millennium A.D. For comparative purposes, figure 4.3, showing the settlement systems of the Early Bronze Age (ca. 3000 B.C.) (ignoring for the moment the Early Bronze Age IV, at the end of the third millennium B.C.) and the classical era can be compared to figures 4.6 and 4.7, presenting impressionistic maps of the tribal pastoral system/agricultural systems of the Middle Ages and of the Middle Bronze Age, circa 1800 B.C.

The spatial and chronological variability reflected in these figures has its source in social dynamics, and I would suggest especially in the nature of relations between the sedentary societies of the Mediterranean (and steppe) zone, and the nomadic societies of the desert.

---

[3] There has been some debate as to whether some of these sites are best associated with pastoral systems or with penetrations from the northern zone (e.g., the Early Bronze sites of south Sinai [Beit-Arieh 1986]), but everyone agrees that other sites are indeed associated with local pastoral cultures.

Periods of proximity between the systems reflect close relations and indeed, some degree of economic and perhaps cultural integration. Periods of spatial separation reflect different levels of integration, indeed different kinds of relations, at least in the regions surveyed. These spatial patterns and fluctuations combine well with analyses of material culture and texts, suggesting that the long span of pastoral adaptations, from origins to modern times in the Negev, may be divided into four general complexes. Explanation of the patterns of contraction and expansion requires explication of each individual complex in its historical and cultural context.

THE TIMNIAN COMPLEX

The Timnian complex (Eddy and Wendorf 1998; Henry 1992, 1995: 353–74; Kozloff 1972/73, 1981; Rothenberg and Glass 1992; also see Ronen 1970 for lithic descriptions without direct attribution; Rosen in press for recent update; and Zarins 1990, 1992 for counterpart in Arabia), the earliest pastoral complex in the desert, developed in the sixth millennium B.C. as herding replaced hunting, and as social and cultural institutions evolved concomitant to this new subsistence base. In particular the following features are characteristic of the complex, and contrast with the preceding Early Neolithic (Pre-Pottery Neolithic B) cultures: (1) Enclosure and attached-room architecture (contrasting with the clustered rooms of the Early Neolithic); (2) Increasing site sizes such that the larger sites consist of aggregates of several enclosures and attached rooms; (3) The prevalence of desert kites (gazelle hunting drive traps); (4) The presence of desert shrines with cosmological symbolism, sometimes achieving megalithic proportions; (5) The presence of constructed burial fields (tumuli, nawamis) often in association with the shrines; and (6) A material culture assemblage dominated by the chipped stone industry, including small and transverse stone arrowheads, microlithic drills, tabular scrapers, ad hoc blade tools, and a wide range of ad hoc flake tools. Beads made of seashells and other materials are also common. Ceramics appear late in the sequence and are dominated by globular hole-mouth cooking pots.

In general, the package seems to reflect the evolution of a tribal society, contrasting with earlier smaller-scale social formulations. Thus, desert kites reflect cooperative hunting, probably requiring a larger community than earlier hunting strategies, as well as investment in hunting furniture on a scale not seen previously.[4] The shrines, especially in their megalithic aspect (Rosen et al. 2007) indicate labor organization of a degree previously not seen in the desert. The presence of burial structures organized in extensive fields and standing upright and visible from some distance most likely reflects a higher order of territoriality, probably a response to the needs of herding. Indeed, the presence of large shrines (with cosmological alignments) and large tombs strongly suggests a social organization capable of drafting labor for construction and the development of an ideological system for legitimizing these new power relations. Geographic variability in site size and material culture suggests seasonal aggregation and dispersion (e.g., Haiman 1992; Kozloff 1981; also see Henry 1992 for an example from Jordan).

---

[4] There is still some debate on the date of the earliest desert kites. Although Betts and Russell (2000) have suggested a Pre-Pottery Neolithic B date for a kite on the basis of stratigraphic association with Pre-Pottery Neolithic B structures, Meshel (1980) prefers a Pottery Neolithic/Chalcolithic date (= Timnian) and A. Goren (cited in Rosen 1997: 39) claims to have recovered transverse arrowheads, an attribute of the Timnian, in his excavation of one kite.

The Timnian as an archaeological complex spans more than three millennia, from circa 5500 B.C. to circa 2000 B.C. It can be divided into four phases (Early, Middle, Late, and Terminal) distinguishable on the basis of material culture variability, especially arrowhead typology in the early stages and ceramics in the latter. Other chronological markers include tabular scrapers and associated attributes, other lithic types, burial styles, the introduction of metallurgy, and the introduction of ceramics, and for the later stages, ceramic variability.

For the purposes of this paper, the important issues are the changes in external relations between Timnian pastoral groups and the sedentary farming societies of the Mediterranean zone. The increasing ties between the two culture regions can be traced from relative autonomy in the Early Phase of the Timnian sequence to increasing ties (based especially on metallurgy) in the Middle Phase, and on to intensive ties leading to economic asymmetries in the Late and Terminal Phases. Specifically, the Early Phase shows only minor connections between the desert and the Mediterranean zone, reflected primarily in shell bead exchange (Bar-Yosef Mayer 1997) and perhaps the diffusion of arrowhead paradigms (the direction of which is not always clear) (e.g., Gopher 1989, 1994). Economically, Timnian groups in this period are basically autonomous. In the Middle Phase copper moved regularly, if not in truly large quantities, from Feinan, and perhaps Timna, into the Beersheva Basin. Two points are crucial for understanding why the Timnian should still be seen as a relatively autonomous economy in this period. First, with the exception of the copper, objects originating in the desert are very rare in sites in the agricultural Chalcolithic Beersheva-Ghassul culture of the northern Negev. Second, in parallel, there is virtually no movement of goods south, and material culture in the desert is virtually all local in origin. Essentially, the Early and Middle Phases of the Timnian reflect a subsistence pastoral economy, one which I have referred to elsewhere as herding-gathering (Rosen 2002).

In distinct contrast, by the Late Timnian (Early Bronze Age II in northern terms), both the diversity and the quantity of goods moving between north and south increased dramatically. Thus, the material culture assemblage from Arad, the Early Bronze Age desert gateway town in the northern Negev, includes the following desert derived goods: copper, milling stones, shell beads, other beads, tabular scrapers, and pottery. Pottery and milling stones are a new addition to the exchange system, and all other goods significantly increased quantitatively. Good evidence for production for export of milling stones and beads at the level of the cottage industry has been documented in the central Negev (Abadi and Rosen 2008; Rosen 2003). Trade in copper is also evident (for central Negev, Segal and Rosen 2005; for other regions, e.g., Beit-Arieh 1974; Rothenberg 1972c; Rothenberg and Glass 1992). Import of ceramics into the desert has also been demonstrated, and the presence of trade stations in south Sinai is well established (Amiran, Beit-Arieh, and Glass 1973; Beit-Arieh 2003b; Porat 1989). This change in the basic tenor of relations is also reflected in a major increase in the number of sites in this period (fig. 4.8). The combination of increasing intensity of exchange, increase in number of desert sites (undoubtedly reflecting a demographic expansion), and the apparent collapse of this trade system with the abandonment of Arad suggests that relations by the Late Timnian can be characterized as economically asymmetric, such that herding-gathering was no longer a viable subsistence system and trade had now become crucial to the desert polities. This economic asymmetry is one of the defining features of recent pastoral nomadic systems (Khazanov 1984). When the trade system collapsed, the large population was no longer viable and the system was abandoned.

The desert Early Bronze Age IV (= Intermediate Bronze Age = Middle Bronze Age I) sites, dated to the late third millennium B.C., have been attributed to the Terminal Timnian on the basis of ceramic and lithic technological continuities with the preceding phase (e.g., Rosen et al. 2006; Vardi 2005). Notably, the Early Bronze Age IV corresponds to the pan-Near Eastern collapse of urban society, but reflects a settlement peak in the arid region.

Despite these material culture continuities, the central Negev shows a culture stratigraphic break between the phases, associated with the Early Bronze Age III and the abandonment of Arad.[5] Both the settlement patterns and basic domestic architecture in the Terminal Timnian differ from the preceding Late Timnian and some of the sites achieve sizes not previously seen in the region (e.g., Ein Ziq has some 200 domestic structures) (see especially Cohen 1999: 83–298 for summary). It is beyond the scope of this paper to review these materials in detail, but site distributions (Cohen 1992, 1999: 267–82; Haiman 1996), ceramic petrography (Goren 1996), and the presence of copper ingots originating in Feinan (with a possibility of origin at Timna) at several sites (Segal and Roman 1999) suggest close connections with areas east of the Rift Valley. That is, the Early Bronze Age IV "recolonization" may derive from Jordan, and continuities with the Timnian are through the east. The point to be stressed here is that despite the size of the sites there is no evidence for significant agriculture, nor would the desert environment of the period have permitted it. Instead, this pastoral society seems to have had its raison d'etre in the desert in the exchange systems with the north and perhaps with Egypt (e.g., Yekutieli 1998), with a primary focus on copper.

THE EARLY HISTORICAL COMPLEX

By the beginning of the second millennium B.C., Terminal Timnian/Early Bronze Age IV sites in the Negev were abandoned and the central Negev remained devoid of pastoral tribal presence (or agricultural presence for that matter) until the beginning of the first millennium B.C., this in spite of Middle and Late Bronze Age sites in the southern Negev, southern Jordan, and Sinai (e.g., Avner, Carmi, and Segal 1994; Pratico 1985; Rothenberg 1972a–b). Unfortunately, these have been too little investigated, and their nature has not been adequately explicated. Coinciding with the contraction of the desert pastoral expanse, the agricultural regime also retreated to areas north of the Beersheva Basin, this retreat accompanied by reurbanization after the third-millennium collapse. Exceptions in the Beersheva Basin at fortified sites such as Masos and Malhata seem to reflect military rather than settlement expansion (Beit-Arieh 2003b: 11*).

Thus archaeological evidence in the Negev is limited, but the geographical contraction on both sides of the central Negev indicates a fundamental change in pastoral-agricultural relations. I suggest, as a hypothesis to be explored and not as a proven fact, that this period in the southern Levant sees the rise of enclosed nomadism, the pastoral adaptation described by Rowton (e.g., 1974, 1977), wherein tribal groups lived in the interstices between the urban sites, with seasonal migrations beyond the settled zone. Rowton's analyses were based primarily on the Mari archives with their large number of references to nomads (e.g., Kupper 1957; Luke 1965; Matthews 1978) and reflect the spatial expanses of the Syrian steppe. As such his portrayal is probably not a perfect fit for the Levant given its complex mosaic of human and

---

[5] This issue of abandonment and collapse is complex. The pan-Near Eastern urban collapse at the end of the third millennium B.C. follows the heavily urban Early Bronze Age III, a period which in the Negev is already a period of abandonment. The actual period of collapse, the Early Bronze Age IV, in the southern Levant, a period with no cities, corresponds to significant pastoral tribal presence in the central Negev (although a scarcity of sites in the northern Negev).

physical geography (e.g., Marfoe 1979), but still describes a system with a far higher level of integration between the pastoralists and the state (with all its accoutrements, including agriculture) than we have seen in earlier periods in the Negev.

The evidence for enclosed nomadism in the southern Levant is textual. References to groups such as the Apiru (e.g., Na'aman 1986; Rowton 1977), serving primarily as a social or class designation, and the Shasu, either a class designation or an ethnic attribution (e.g., Dever 1997), suggest extra-urban tribal levels of organization (Redford 1992: 269–73). The Shasu are even referred to as tent-dwellers (Redford 1992: 278). Both groups are found within or in proximity to the settled zone. To judge from such texts as the Amarna letters (e.g., Aharoni 1967: 163–64), these tribal groups comprised a significant force to be reckoned with in terms of the internal political balance of the settled zone. Levy and Holl (2002) have recently gone so far as to suggest that such groups were the primary populations of Feinan during the Iron Age, perhaps in fact controlling the copper sources, and at least providing the manpower for their exploitation (also see Levy, this volume). Integration with the settled zone is total in this period and can be compared to the various Mari tribal groups where recent claims have even suggested that some of the Mari kings were tribal in origin (Fleming, this volume). This is a fundamentally different system from the preceding period, as Rowton (1974) himself was aware in his distinction between enclosed and external nomadism.

There are two methodological difficulties with the claim that enclosed nomadism begins in the second millennium B.C. The first is the problem of tracing these groups archaeologically, and the second is the question of whether enclosed nomadism existed earlier.

The absence of archaeology for these groups is difficult. The traditional explanation is one of archaeological visibility, that tents and other light structures of organic materials would not be likely to leave an archaeological signature, or that such a signature might be obscured by vegetation, alluviation, or other processes of destruction or burial. On the other hand, in the desert, sites with stone foundations from the Timnian have been found easily and tent remains have been found dating to classical times (and of course, later). Although one might argue that tents do not leave recoverable archaeological remains in the settled zone, tents in fact seem to be a late phenomenon, used for habitation structures among desert nomads only after the domestication of the camel (Rosen and Saidel in press). Taking a cue from Mari, the enclosed nomads of the second millennium B.C. probably lived in villages, with subgroups engaged in pastoral transhumance. Thus, they may indeed be present in the archaeological record, but as villagers and not as putative tent nomads.

With respect to the existence of enclosed nomadism in the third millennium B.C. (thus earlier than the proposed beginning of the phenomenon in the second millennium B.C.), the difficulty lies in the asymmetry of the evidence. The historical record from the third millennium B.C. is not comparable to that of the second so that it is conceivable that enclosed nomadism is, in fact, an earlier phenomenon which simply does not appear in the scant written records of the period. On the other hand, if we assume that the nomads of the desert and those of the Mediterranean zone were culturally affiliated, then in the settled zone in the third millennium B.C. there are no known sites similar architecturally or in terms of material culture to those of the desert Timnian. In somewhat more detail, the round habitation structures of the Terminal Timnian (Early Bronze IV) are absent from the settled zone, despite the presence of village sites of smaller dimensions than the Terminal Timnian sites of the Negev. Furthermore, the material culture of these regions contrasts, both in the difference in ceramic family groups between north and south (e.g., Amiran 1969; Dever 1973) and in lithic typology and function

(Rosen 1997: 103–11; Rosen et al. 2006; Vardi 2005). A similar argument can be made for earlier periods, based on differences in the configuration of ceramic and lithic assemblages.

The question remains open, but the idea of second- and early first-millennium B.C. enclosed nomadism in Palestine has been used in explanations of the origins of the Israelites (e.g., Finkelstein 1988), the nomads in effect sedentarizing into a new ethnos, the Israelites (also Faust 2006). In this context, the concept may also help explain the nature of the Negev Iron Age, a period with small hill forts enmeshed in what can perhaps be described as a rural steppe. If a Mediterranean zone state expanded into the desert in the eleventh–tenth centuries B.C.,[6] then this expansion may well have incorporated an extra-urban agro-pastoral component, perhaps a co-option of tribal groups. Such a scenario, of pastoral territories enclosed within the settled zone, would also explain the fact that, unlike the preceding Timnian and succeeding Classical complex, there was no separate pastoral tribal presence beyond the zone settled in the Negev during the Iron Age.

The collapse of the Iron Age polities in the central Negev is inferred from the abandonment of the region from the eleventh/tenth century B.C. until the Persian period (cf. Cohen 1980). Unlike the Timnian contraction, apparently to the south, the Iron Age populations most likely moved back to the north. The re-emergence of a pastoral system in the central Negev occurs only with the penetration of Nabatean pastoralists, several centuries after the establishment of the spice trade system.

THE CLASSICAL COMPLEX

The pastoral nomadic complement to the settled system in the Negev, on the edge of the Roman empire and its successors has been described in a number of studies (e.g., Avni 1996; Haiman 1995a; S. Rosen 1987a, 2007; Rosen and Avni 1993; and for a text historical perspective, see especially Mayerson 1994). These studies have tended to focus on the reconstruction of the pastoral system and on the role that nomads may have played in specific historical events or trends. Thus Nahlieli (2007) has recently summarized the views concerning the end of Byzantine urban system, suggesting that, contra Haiman (1995a) and Avni (1996), nomads played little role in the establishment of the Umayad rural agricultural system which succeeded the Byzantine towns. Similarly, in Jordan, research and debate have focused on the nature of the relations between the pastoralists and the empire and a dichotomy between symbiosis and hostility (Banning 1986; Parker 1986, 1987).

In view of the longer-term perspective taken here, the first issue is to establish the existence of a Classical complex for the nomads of the Negev. Beginning in the first centuries A.D./B.C. a new kind of site appears in the central Negev consisting of single lines or rows of individual round or semi-circular structures aligned along the lower terraces of wadis (fig. 4.9). Sometimes these structures are surface sites, probably reflecting tent construction, and sometimes they are pit structures with stone lining, cut 30–40 cm into the surface. These may have had organic superstructures, as in earlier periods, or perhaps were tented. Certainly by this period the camel has been well integrated into desert society and tents would have posed no logistic problem. Some sites have both types of structure. Site organization and

---

[6] Given the disputes on the chronology of the Iron Age IIa, chronological attribution of settlement horizon in the central Negev awaits re-evaluation.

micro-location (on the lower terraces as opposed to the interfluves typical of the Timnian) contrast with earlier periods. The general settlement pattern also contrasts with earlier periods with the aggregate camps of the Classical complex located in the southern Negev highlands, south of the Ramon Crater and south of the general distribution of run-off agricultural systems.[7] Notably, the distribution of the smaller pastoral sites, consisting of single or only a few round structures, overlaps with the distribution of agricultural sites, perhaps reflecting seasonal dispersion into the sedentary zone. Geographically the zones abut one another and show high densities of sites.

Material culture is that of the surrounding states. In the early stages of the Classical complex, ceramics are typical Nabatean and Roman wares, while in later stages they are Byzantine[8] and Early Islamic, clearly imported from production centers associated with the sedentary urban and village systems. Low proportions of handmade pots have been found in some Early Islamic sites (Rosen and Avni 1997: 62–80) and were probably produced in the desert. Other components of the preserved material culture, including rotary milling stones, metal objects, and coins, were all imported into the pastoral system.

As indicated above, this general system appears in the late Nabatean period, and, significantly, there is no evidence for it in the preceding Hellenistic period. It continues through eighth century A.D., showing continuity in architectural type, site organization, and settlement pattern, as well as in general material culture throughout this long period. The system ceases sometime in the eighth or ninth century A.D., followed by a period of little pastoral tribal presence in the central Negev until the infiltration of the modern Bedouin tribes in the eighteenth century A.D. (e.g., Bailey 1980; also see Israel 2007 for the chronology of Gaza Ware, the primary material culture marker for modern Bedouin groups).

Our ability to precisely date shifting patterns of settlement is limited by the coarseness of the archaeological chronology as based on ceramics collected in surveys, especially the ceramics collected from pastoral sites with limited typological repertoires. Nevertheless, three general periods can be distinguished, the Nabatean and Early Roman (ca. A.D. 1–300), the Byzantine (ca. A.D. 300–640), and the Early Islamic (ca. A.D. 640–800), even though the analyses can only be considered preliminary.

The Nabatean sedentary system in this period is difficult to characterize since the larger sites often lie beneath the massive later Byzantine towns. Village and hamlet sites have been documented, along with small-scale watch towers. A Roman military camp is present at Avdat. The towns were incipient in this phase. The pastoral settlement system is geographically more weighted toward the Spice Route and the sedentary sites especially around Avdat than in later periods (Rosen 2007). The largest pastoral sites also seem somewhat smaller than in later periods, reflecting perhaps somewhat less of a tendency to large tribal aggregation, or alternatively, perhaps somewhat greater mobility. Based on the general impression, sites are somewhat less "dug in" in this period. It is important to note that, although sites such as Avdat show Hellenistic presence (beginning in the late fourth century B.C.) (Negev 1986), the

---

[7] In the highlands southwest of the Ramon Crater there is overlap between the agricultural sites and the pastoral encampments. Rosen and Avni (Rosen and Avni 1993; Avni 1996) have suggested that this reflects the practice of agriculture by pastoralists.

[8] The term "Byzantine" in south Levantine archaeology refers to the fourth through early seventh centuries, the period when Christianity dominated the region. It is parallel to Late Roman in Egyptian and European terminologies, but notably ends with the Islamic conquests and does not overlap with the medieval Byzantine period in European terms.

earliest evidence for pastoral tribal presence is several centuries later, dating to the expansion of Nabatean sedentary presence both at Avdat and in its hinterland. That is, the pastoral system post-dates the early caravan trade and was established only with the larger-scale sedentary settlement in the area. Of course, this has its implications for understanding the nature of relations, and suggests a form of dependence relationship from the outset, immediately evident on at least one more level in the import of Nabatean ceramics into the pastoral system, in fact the only ceramics found in these sites. It also renders the issue of the ethnic identity of the pastoralists moot since we have no material culture made by them that might be used for establishing ethnicity.

It is difficult to trace the actual transition to the succeeding Byzantine phase, but comparison of the site distributions (fig. 4.10; Rosen 1987a) shows two changes: (1) The agricultural regime has shifted south and become denser; and (2) The pastoral sites have shifted south and west, and there are more of them. Like the preceding Nabatean phase, there is considerable overlap between the distributions of different kinds of sites, but the basic contrasts are clear. The northern cliff of the Ramon Crater marks the distinction between agricultural and purely pastoral territories. Notably, this also marks a significant geographic transition, from steppe to desert, abrupt here because of the cliff of the Ramon Crater. Regardless, the coincidence of physical and cultural geography strengthens the interpretations. These shifts reflect the changed nature of the Byzantine presence in the central Negev, now an urban system with a village farming hinterland, serving as the frontier zone of the empire (Mayerson 1990). As with the Nabatean period, virtually all ceramics are imported into the pastoral system in this period. Historical texts (e.g., Kraemer 1958; also Mayerson 1980) provide important information on relations in this period. The desert nomads sold camels to the towns, they acted as guides for pilgrimages to Santa Katerina, they utilized the urban markets, and at least one massacre of desert monks has been recorded. On the other hand, they also are described as living miserable lives. Significantly, the presence of numerous isolated farmhouses in the village hinterland of the towns, in close proximity to the exclusively pastoral zone, suggests that relations were not generally hostile. In contrast to the American Wild West (cf. Mayerson 1990), the settled-nomad system in the Negev was maintained for some 800 years; stability seems to have been a primary attribute of the relations.

The Early Islamic period is more difficult to trace in terms of survey since ceramic distinctions are difficult due to typological and technological continuities. On the other hand, excavations of both hamlets (e.g., Haiman 1990, 1995b; Nevo 1985, 1991) and pastoral camps (Avni 1996; Rosen and Avni 1993, 1997) provide primary data for reconstructing basic relations between the sedentary system and the nomadic.

The historical contexts are important to consider here. In terms of the sedentary sites, although not totally abandoned, the urban sites of the Byzantine period were in significant decline by the Early Islamic period, a decline which probably began in the sixth century B.C. On the other hand, a village florescence seems to have filled the demographic void created by the urban decline (Nahlieli 2007). There is no evidence for a violent Islamic conquest or even disruption in the Negev.

In contrast to the urban decline, the desert pastoral system seems to flourish. Thus, this period appears to have the largest pastoral sites of the Classical complex. The excavated 'Oded sites (Rosen and Avni 1997) are large encampments south of the Ramon Crater, each with more than a dozen round pit habitation structures and a mosque, with no evidence for agriculture in the region. Avni (1996) has documented even larger sites of similar architecture and material culture in the Har Saggi area, although some of these are associated with terraced fields. The material culture from these sites provides crucial data for understanding relations between the settled region somewhat farther north and the pastoral groups. More than 90 percent of the pottery is imported from the sedentary zone and is typical ware of the Late Byzantine/Early Islamic period. Milling stones, also imported, also indicate grain processing, despite the distance from agricultural fields, suggesting either import of grain or perhaps opportunistic agricultural practices in other seasons. A coin minted in Tiberias (Amitai-Preiss 1997) indicates trade and integration with other areas of the Caliphate. A fragment of an *Aspartia* shell indicates linkages with the Nile Valley, and a fish spine indicates the transport of fish at least 100 km from the nearest body of water (the Mediterranean), and perhaps from as far as the Nile (Horwitz, Tchernov, and Mineis 1997). Thus, the evidence reflects increased ties with the village (and relict urban) system in the rest of the Negev, concomitant with relative economic improvement and perhaps some sedentarization.

Reviewing the Classical complex as a whole, several features are to be emphasized. Over the course of some 800 years, despite political fluctuations, the general system of pastoral-sedentary relations maintains itself, with aggregate pastoral sites in the desert (Saharo-Arabian vegetation) zone, south of the agricultural regions, more or less coincident with the steppe (Irano-Turanian) zone. The desert towns and villages seem to have provided the sedentary infrastructure for the existence of the pastoral system. Comparing this general system to that of the preceding phase, the absence of enclosed nomadism in the Mediterranean zone is notable. Between the strong centralized state of the Classical era, the high urban population, and the density of agricultural exploitation, there seems to have been little room for pastoral nomadic presence, even at the level of enclosed nomadism, in the core areas of the Levant, at least not in the sense comparable to that of the second millennium B.C.

THE RECENT BEDOUIN

Following the abandonment of the Early Islamic village system in the central Negev in the ninth century A.D., the pastoral tribal presence also ceases and is not renewed until the eighteenth century A.D. with the infiltration of the modern tribes into the region (Bailey 1980). It is beyond the scope of this paper to review in depth the nature of recent Bedouin history and society, but a few observations are pertinent.

The modern adaptation differs from the preceding Classical complex in significant particulars. The round structures, whether tented or covered with organic superstructures, are totally absent from recent Bedouin encampments, replaced by the black tent. This is not an insignificant difference given that the specific organization of space in the black tent reflects basic social structures within recent Bedouin society, and which therefore must contrast markedly with the earlier periods (e.g., Saidel 2008).

The contraction of the agricultural zone following the collapse of the terrace farming systems associated (in their last stages) with the Early Islamic period was accompanied in the early stages of the Middle Ages by a similar contraction in the pastoral sphere, leaving the central Negev in a "vacuum" similar in character to that of the second millennium B.C. Recolonization by the modern tribes seems to have accompanied the strengthening of the Ottoman state in Palestine. We may speculate that the Middle Ages was a time of enclosed nomadism. Interestingly, during the late Ottoman period, when state control in Palestine was weak, there is considerable penetration of Bedouin tribes into the settled region, primarily from the east (e.g., Cohen 1973; Hütteroth 1975; Hütteroth and Abdulfattah 1977; Sharon 1975; Zeevi 1996). Beyond facile analogy, van der Steen (1995, 2006) makes explicit comparisons between the tribal structures and relations of recent Bedouin in the Jordan Valley and pastoral groups in the late second millennium B.C., implicitly supporting the notion of enclosed or geographically integrated nomadism.

FINAL NOTES

The modern Israeli Negev is a product of twentieth-century politics. As a unit, it never existed in the past (for discussions, see Bienkowski 2006; also Rosen 1991). For a truer understanding of the historical processes behind the phenomena outlined here, in a sense sampled by the Negev materials, southern Jordan, northern Arabia, and Sinai must be incorporated into the story. Indeed, given the origins of the modern Bedouin tribes of the Negev, in Jordan and Arabia, and some of their migrations into Egypt, a larger perspective is clearly necessary. Unfortunately, we do not yet have an archaeology of nomadic groups from those regions. Nevertheless, the patterns outlined here for the Negev, both geographical and chronological, are strong enough to indicate that there are important long-term historical trends and processes reflected here and that we should find corresponding, if not identical, phenomena in adjacent areas.

The shape of the settlement contractions and expansions, both with respect to the nomads as well as the farmers, seems to be a function of the geography of the region (see Johnson 1969 for the effects of geography on shorter-term patterns), with a rather broad steppe zone between the desert and the Mediterranean zone (see also Lewis 1987 for the similar contractions and expansions in Syria in more recent times). The fact of these changing configurations in relations seems to reflect fundamental changes in the nature of the nomadic systems, such that we can apparently divide the sequence into large-scale complexes.

On the other hand, lest we lapse into some crude geographical determinism, it is also clear that the adaptations themselves change significantly, even when the settlement configurations seem to be roughly similar. Both technological changes and social changes, internal and external, are cumulative. It is well beyond the scope of this paper to try to delineate these changes. Technologically, obvious additions to nomadic society are the introduction of the camel, and the various accoutrements necessary to fully exploit it (e.g., Bulliet 1990): the tent, the gun, ceramics, water cisterns, etc. Socially and culturally, demographic growth, the rise of markets and trade systems, the evolution of tribal organization, the expansion of empires, and the rise of trans-tribal ideologies such as Islam, all had major and unique effects on desert societies. The superposition of these complex cumulative changes onto a fixed geography is a classic Braudelian case study. It makes for rich and fascinating history.

ACKNOWLEDGMENTS

I am grateful to Jeff Szuchman for inviting me to the seminar at the Oriental Institute for which this paper was prepared. Patrice Kaminsky, of Ben-Gurion University, helped me considerably with the maps. Gunnar Lehmann, also of Ben-Gurion University, was especially helpful in his comments on the early historic periods reviewed in this paper. Oded Tammuz helped me with some of the historic references. Ben Saidel added important comments to the draft.

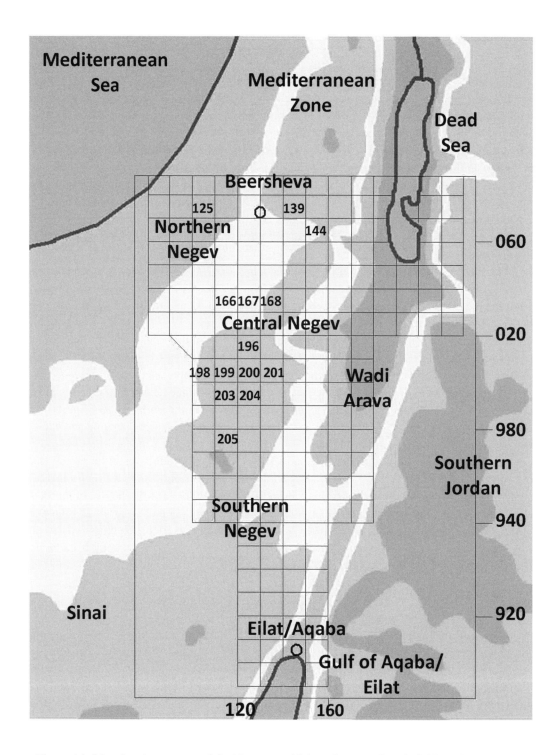

Figure 4.1. Map showing surveys of the Negev on which analyses are based. Grid numbers are local Israel grid, according to which the surveys were organized

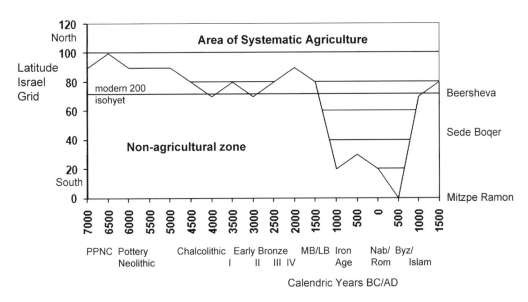

Figure 4.2. Schematic of the fluctuating boundary of systematic agricultural practice in the Negev

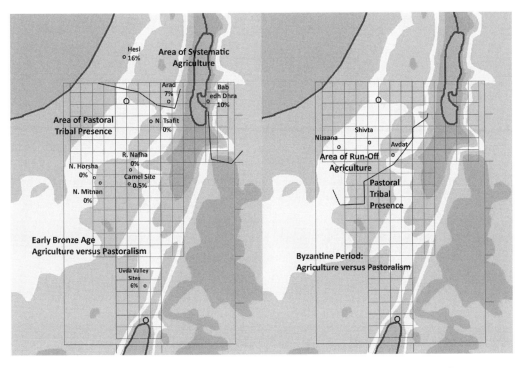

Figure 4.3. Distribution of Early Bronze Age and Byzantine agriculture in the Negev. Percentage figures are proportions of sickle segments in lithic assemblages. Byzantine agricultural zone is defined by reference to terrace systems in wadis

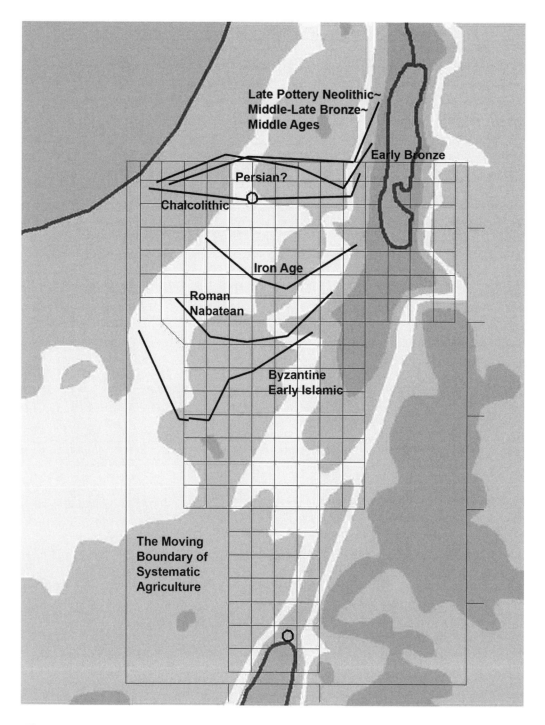

Figure 4.4. Estimated extent of systematic agricultural exploitation in different periods in the Negev. Note that the Persian period is more or less coincident with the Middle and Late Bronze Ages, and the Middle Ages

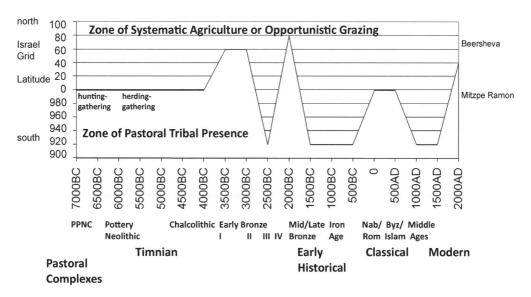

Figure 4.5. Schematic of the fluctuating boundaries of pastoral tribal presence in the Negev

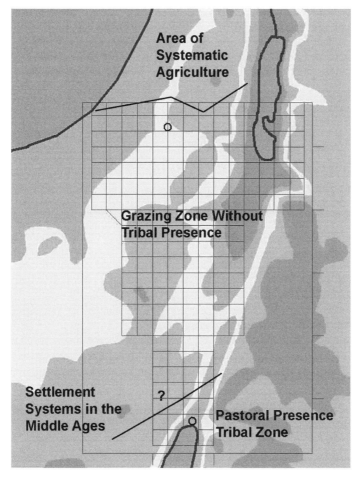

Figure 4.6. Distribution of the tribal pastoral and agricultural systems of the Middle Ages

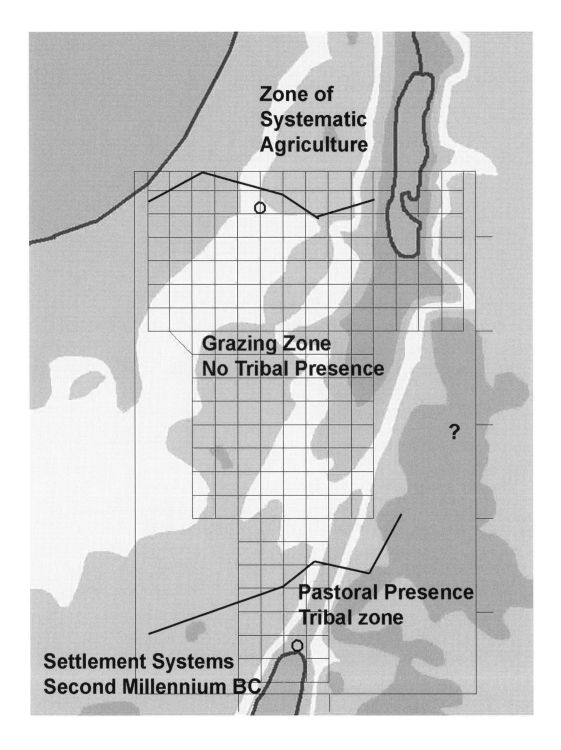

Figure 4.7. Distribution of the tribal pastoral and agricultural systems of the
Middle Bronze Age, circa 1800 B.C.

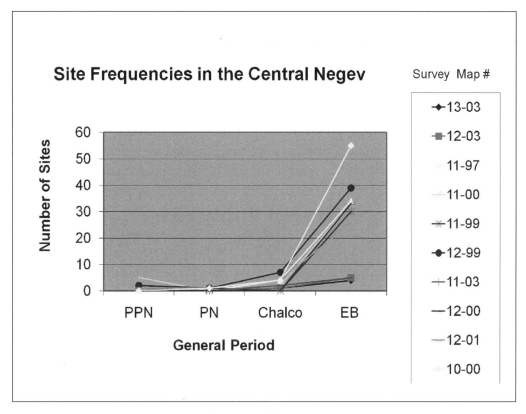

Figure 4.8. Increase in number of desert sites in the third millennium B.C.

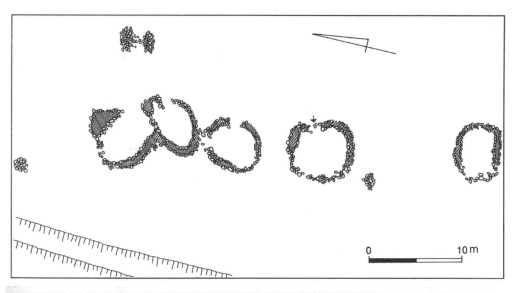

Figure 4.9. Classical Complex architecture. Site 204-93 (Rosen 1994). Note that number in
photograph is a field designation

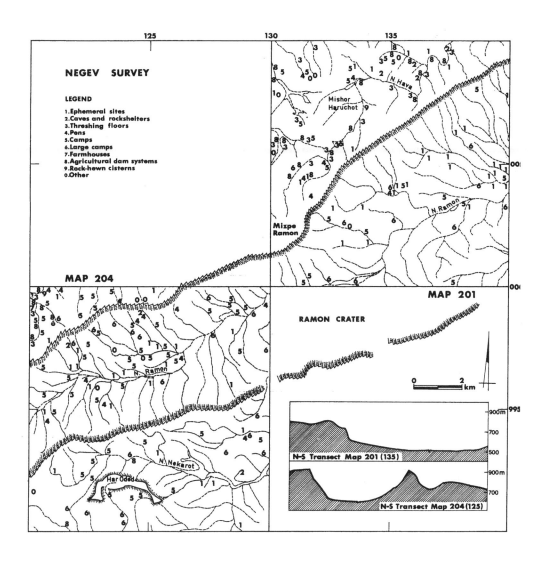

Figure 4.10. Distribution of Byzantine/Early Islamic pastoral encampments versus agriculture sites in and around the Ramon Crater (Rosen 1987a). Reproduced from *The Journal of Field Archaeology* with the permission of the Trustees of Boston University. All rights reserved

BIBLIOGRAPHY

Abadi, Yael, and Steven A. Rosen
  2008   "A Chip Off the Old Millstone: Grinding Stone Production and Distribution in the
             Early Bronze Age of the Negev." In *New Approaches to Old Stones: Recent Studies of
             Ground Stone Artifacts,* edited by Yorke M. Rowan and Jenni R. Ebeling, pp. 99–115.
             Approaches to Anthropological Archaeology. London: Equinox.

Aharoni, Yohanan
  1967   *The Land of the Bible: A Historical Geography.* Philadelphia: Westminster.

Amiran, Ruth
  1969   *Ancient Pottery of the Holy Land: From Its Beginnings in the Neolithic Period to the
             End of the Iron Age.* Jerusalem: Massada.

Amiran, Ruth; Itzhak Beit-Arieh; and Jonathan Glass
  1973   "The Interrelationship between Arad and Sites in the Southern Sinai in the Early
             Bronze II." *Israel Exploration Journal* 23: 33–38.

Amitai-Preiss, Nitzan
  1997   "Appendix Four: A Bronze Coin from the Ummayid Period." In *The 'Oded Sites:
             Investigations of Two Early Islamic Pastoral Camps South of the Ramon Crater,*
             by Steven A. Rosen and Gideon Avni, pp. 128–29. Beer-Sheva 11; Studies by the
             Department of Bible and Ancient Near East. Beersheva: Ben-Gurion University.

Avner, Uzi
  1990   "Ancient Agricultural Settlement and Religion in the Uvda Valley in Southern Israel."
             Biblical Archaeologist 53: 125–41.
  1998   "Settlement, Agriculture, and Paleoclimate in 'Uvda Valley, Southern Negev Desert,
             6th–3rd Millennia BC." In *Water, Environment and Society in Times of Climatic
             Change* (Contributions from an International Workshop within the framework of
             International Hydrological Program [IHP] UNESCO, at Ben-Gurion University,
             Sede Boker, Israel, 7–12 July 1996), edited by Arieh Issar and Neville Brown, pp.
             147–202. Water and Science Technology Library 31. Dordrecht: Kluwer.

Avner, Uzi; Israel Carmi; and Dror Segal
  1994   "Neolithic to Bronze Age Settlement of the Negev and Sinai in Light of Radiocarbon
             Dating: A View from the Southern Negev." In *Late Quaternary Chronology and
             Paleoclimates of the Eastern Mediterranean,* edited by Ofer Bar-Yosef and Renee S.
             Kra, pp. 26–300. Tucson: Radiocarbon.

Avni, Gideon
  1991   *Archaeological Survey of Israel: Map of Har Saggi Northeast (225).* Jerusalem: Israel
             Antiquities Authority.
  1992   "Survey of Deserted Bedouin Campsites in the Negev Highlands and Its Implications
             for Archaeological Research." In *Pastoralism in the Levant: Archaeological Materials
             in Anthropological Perspectives,* edited by Ofer Bar-Yosef and Anatoly M. Khazanov,
             pp. 241–54. Monographs in World Archaeology 10. Madison: Prehistory Press.
  1996   *Nomads, Farmers, and Town-Dwellers: Pastoralist-Sedentist Interaction in the Negev
             Highlands, Sixth–Eighth Centuries C.E.* Supplement to the Archaeological Survey of
             Israel. Jerusalem: Israel Antiquities Authority.

Bailey, Clinton
  1980   "The Negev in the 19th Century: Reconstructing History from Bedouin Oral
             Traditions." *Asian and African Studies* 14: 35–80.

Banning, E. B.
  1986   "Peasants, Pastoralists, and *Pax Romana*: Mutualism in the Southern Highlands of
             Jordan." *Bulletin of the American Schools of Oriental Research* 261: 25–50.

Banning, E. B., and Ilse Kohler-Rollefson
  1986   "Ethnoarchaeological Survey in the Beda Region, Southern Jordan." *Zeitschrift des Deutschen Palästina-Vereins* 102: 152–70.

  1992   "Ethnographic Lessons for the Pastoral Past: Camp Locations and Material Remains Near Beidha, Southern Jordan." In *Pastoralism in the Levant: Archaeological Materials in Anthropological Perspectives*, edited by Ofer Bar-Yosef and Anatoly M. Khazanov, pp. 181–204. Monographs in World Archaeology 10. Madison: Prehistory Press.

Bar-Matthews, Miryam; Avner Ayalon; and Aaron Kaufman
  1998   "Middle to Late Holocene (6,500 Yr. Period) Paleoclimate in the Eastern Mediterranean Region from Stable Isotopic Composition of Speleothems from Soreq Cave, Israel." In *Water, Environment and Society in Times of Climatic Change* (Contributions from an International Workshop within the framework of International Hydrological Program [IHP] UNESCO, at Ben-Gurion University, Sede Boker, Israel, 7–12 July 1996), edited by Arieh Issar and Neville Brown, pp. 203–14. Water and Science Technology Library 31. Dordrecht: Kluwer.

Bar-Yosef, Ofer
  1984   "Seasonality Among Neolithic Hunter-Gatherers in Southern Sinai." In *Animals and Archaeology* 3: *Early Herders and Their Flocks*, edited by Juliette Clutton-Brock and Caroline Grigson, pp. 145–60. British Archaeological Reports, International Series 202. Oxford: British Archaeological Reports.

Bar-Yosef Mayer, Daniella
  1997   "Neolithic Shell Production in Southern Sinai." *Journal of Archaeological Science* 24: 97–111.

Baumgarten, Yakov
  2004   *Archaeological Survey of Israel: Map of Shivta (166)*. Jerusalem: Israel Antiquities Authority.

Beit-Arieh, Itzhak
  1974   "An Early Bronze Age II Site at Nabi Salah in Southern Sinai." *Tel Aviv* 1: 144–56.
  1986   "Two Cultures in South Sinai in the Third Millennium B.C." *Bulletin of the American Schools of Oriental Research* 263: 27–54.

  2003a   *Archaeological Survey of Israel: Map of Tel Malhata (144)*. Jerusalem: Israel Antiquities Authority.

  2003b   *Archaeology of Sinai: The Ophir Expedition*. Monograph Series 21. Tel Aviv: Emery and Claire Yass Publications in Archaeology.

Betts, Alison V. G., and Kenneth W. Russell
  2000   "Prehistoric and Historic Pastoral Strategies in the Syrian Steppe." In *The Transformation of Nomadic Society in the Arab East*, edited by Martha Mundy and Basim Musallam, pp. 24–32. Cambridge: Cambridge University.

Bienkowski, Piotr
  2006   "The Wadi Arabah: Meanings in a Contested Landscape." In *Crossing the Rift: Resources, Routes, Settlement Patterns, and Interaction in the Wadi Arabah*, edited by Piotr Bienkowski and Katharina Galor, pp. 7–28. Levant Supplementary Series 3. Oxford: Oxbow Books.

Binford, Louis R.
  1980   "Willow Smoke and Dogs' Tails: Hunter-Gatherer Settlement Systems and Archaeological Site Formation." *American Antiquity* 45: 4–20.

Bruins, Hendrick J.
  1986   *Desert Environment and Agriculture in the Central Negev and Kadesh-Barnea during Historical Times*. Nijkirk: Midbar Foundation.

Bulliet, Richard W.
    1990   *The Camel and the Wheel.* New York: Columbia University.

Cohen, Amnon
    1973   *Palestine in the 18th Century: Patterns of Government and Administration.* Uriel
                    Heyd Memorial Series. Jerusalem: Magnes Press.

Cohen, Rudolf
    1980   "The Iron Age Fortresses in the Central Negev." *Bulletin of the American Schools of
                    Oriental Research* 236: 61–79.

    1981   *Archaeological Survey of Israel: Map of Sede Boqer-East (168) 13-03.* Jerusalem:
                    Archaeological Survey of Israel.

    1985   *Archaeological Survey of Israel: Map of Sede Boqer-West (167) 12-03.* Jerusalem:
                    Archaeological Survey of Israel.

    1999   *Ancient Settlement in the Negev Highlands.* Israel Antiquities Reports 6. Jerusalem:
                    Israel Antiquities Reports.

    1992   "Nomadic or Semi-Nomadic Middle Bronze Age I Settlements in the Central
                    Negev." In *Pastoralism in the Levant: Archaeological Materials in Anthropological
                    Perspectives*, edited by Ofer Bar-Yosef and Anatoly M. Khazanov, pp. 105–31.
                    Monographs in World Archaeology 10. Madison: Prehistory Press.

Cohen, Rudolf, and William G. Dever
    1978   "Preliminary Report of the Pilot Season of the 'Central Negev Highlands Project.'"
                    Bulletin of the American Schools of Oriental Research 232: 29–45.

    1979   Preliminary Report of the Second Season of the 'Central Negev Highlands Project.'"
                    Bulletin of the American Schools of Oriental Research 236: 41–60.

    1981   "Preliminary Report of the Third and Final Season of the 'Central Negev Highlands
                    Project.'" *Bulletin of the American Schools of Oriental Research* 243: 57–77.

Dahari, Uzi
    2000   *Monastic Settlements in South Sinai in the Byzantine Period: The Archaeological
                    Remains.* Israel Antiquities Reports 9. Jerusalem: Israel Antiquities Authority.

Dever, William G.
    1973   "The EBIV/MBI Horizon in Transjordan and Southern Palestine." *Bulletin of the
                    American Schools of Oriental Research* 210: 37–63.

    1997   "Archaeology and the Emergence of Early Israel." In *Archaeology and Biblical
                    Interpretation*, edited by John R. Bartlett, pp. 20–50. London: Routledge.

Eddy, Frank W., and Fred Wendorf
    1998   "Prehistoric Pastoral Nomads in the Sinai." *Sahara* 10: 7–20.

Eldar, Iris; Yaacov Nir; and Dov Nahlieli
    1992   "The Bedouin and Their Campsites in the Dimona Region of the Negev: Comparative
                    Models for the Study of Ancient Desert Settlements." In *Pastoralism in the Levant:
                    Archaeological Materials in Anthropological Perspectives*, edited by Ofer Bar-
                    Yosef and Anatoly M. Khazanov, pp. 205–19. Monographs in World Archaeology
                    10. Madison: Prehistory Press.

Evenari, Michael; Leslie Shanan; and Naftali Tadmor
    1982   *The Negev: The Challenge of a Desert.* Cambridge: Harvard University Press.

Faust, Avraham
    2006   *Israel's Ethnogenesis: Settlement, Interaction, Expansion and Resistance.* Approaches
                    to Anthropological Archaeology. London: Equinox.

Finkelstein, Israel
    1984   "The Iron Age 'Fortresses' of the Negev Highlands: Sedentarization of the Nomads."
                    Tel Aviv 11: 189–209.

1988   *The Archaeology of Israelite Settlement.* Jerusalem: Israel Exploration Society.

1992   "Pastoralism in the Highlands of Canaan in the Third and Second Millennia B.C.E." In *Pastoralism in the Levant: Archaeological Materials in Anthropological Perspectives*, edited by Ofer Bar-Yosef and Anatoly M. Khazanov, pp. 133–42. Monographs in World Archaeology 10. Madison: Prehistory Press.

1995   *Living on the Fringe: The Archaeology and History of the Negev, Sinai, and Neighbouring Regions in the Bronze and Iron Ages.* Monographs in Mediterranean Archaeology 6. Sheffield: Sheffield Academic Press.

Finkelstein, Israel, and Avi Perevoletsky

1990   "Processes of Sedentarization and Nomadization in the History of the Negev and Sinai." *Bulletin of the American Schools of Oriental Research* 279: 67–88.

Gazit, Dan

1996   *Archaeological Survey of Israel: Map of Urim (125).* Archaeological Survey of Israel. Jerusalem: Israel Antiquities Authority.

Gopher, Avi

1989   "Diffusion Process in the Pre-Pottery Neolithic Levant: The Case of the Helwan Point. In *People and Culture in Change: Proceedings of the Second Symposium on Upper Palaeolithic, Mesolithic, and Neolithic Populations of Europe and the Mediterranean Basin*, edited by Israel Hershkovitz, pp. 91–105. British Archaeological Reports, International Series 508. Oxford: British Archaeological Reports.

1994   *Arrowheads of the Neolithic Levant: A Seriation Analysis.* American Schools of Oriental Research, Dissertation Series 10. Winona Lake: Eisenbrauns.

Goren, Yuval

1996   "The Southern Levant in the Early Bronze Age IV: The Petrographic Perspective." *Bulletin of the American Schools of Oriental Research* 303: 33–72.

Govrin, Yehuda

1991   *Archaeological Survey of Israel: Map of Nahal Yattir (139).* Archaeological Survey of Israel. Jerusalem: Israel Antiquities Authority.

Haiman, Mordecai

1986   *Archaeological Survey of Israel: Map of Har Hamran Southwest (198).* Archaeological Survey of Israel. Jerusalem: Israel Antiquities Authority.

1990   "Agricultural Settlement in the Ramat Barnea Area in the 7th and 8th Centuries A.D." *Atiqot* 10: 111–24. [in Hebrew]

1991   *Archaeological Survey of Israel: Map of Mizpe Ramon Southwest (200).* Jerusalem: Israel Antiquities Authority.

1992   "Sedentism and Pastoralism in the Negev Highlands in the Early Bronze Age: Results of the Western Negev Highlands Emergency Survey." In *Pastoralism in the Levant: Archaeological Materials in Anthropological Perspective,* edited by Ofer Bar-Yosef and Anatoly M. Khazanov, pp. 93–105. Monographs in World Archaeology 10. Madison: Prehistory Press.

1993   *Archaeological Survey of Israel: Map of Har Hamran Southeast (199).* Archaeological Survey of Israel. Jerusalem: Israel Antiquities Authority.

1995a   "Agriculture and Nomad-State Relations in the Negev Desert in the Byzantine and Early Islamic Periods." *Bulletin of the American Schools of Oriental Research* 297: 29–54.

1995b   "An Early Islamic Period Farm at Nahal Mitnan." *Atiqot* 26: 1–13.

1996   "Early Bronze Age IV Settlement Pattern of the Negev and Sinai Seserts: View from Small Marginal Temporary Sites." *Bulletin of the American Schools of Oriental Research* 303: 1–32.

1999   *Archaeological Survey of Israel: Map of Har Ramon (203).* Archaeological Survey of Israel. Jerusalem: Israel Antiquities Authority.

Henry, Donald O.

1992   "Seasonal Movements of Fourth Millennium Pastoral Nomads in Wadi Hisma."
               Studies in the History and Archaeology of Jordan 4: 137–41.

1995   *Prehistoric Cultural Ecology and Evolution: Insights from Southern Jordan.*
               Interdisciplinary Contributions to Archaeology; The Language of Science. New York:
               Plenum.

Horwitz, Liora Kolska; Eitan Tchernov; and Henk Mineis

1997   "Faunal Remains from Nahal 'Oded." In *The 'Oded Sites: Investigations of Two Early
               Islamic Pastoral Camps South of the Ramon Crater*, by Steven A. Rosen and Gideon
               Avni, pp. 107–08. Beer-Sheva 11; Studies by the Department of Bible and Ancient
               Near East. Beersheva: Ben-Gurion University Press.

Hütteroth, Wolf D.

1975   "The Pattern of Settlement in Palestine in the Sixteenth Century." In *Studies on
               Palestine during the Ottoman Period*, edited by Moshe Ma'oz, pp. 3–10. Jerusalem:
               Magnes Press.

Hütteroth, Wolf D., and Kamal Abdulfattah

1977   *Historical Geography of Palestine, Transjordan and Southern Syria in the Late 16th
               Century.* Erlanger geographische Arbeiten, Sonderband 5. Erlangen: Fränkischen
               Geographischen Gesellschaft in Kommission bei Palm & Enke.

Israel, Yigael M.

2007   The Black Gaza Ware from the Ottoman Period. Ph.D. dissertation, Ben Gurion
               University. [in Hebrew]

Johnson, Douglas L.

1969   *The Nature of Nomadism: A Comparative Study of Pastoral Migrations in Southwestern
               Asia and Northern Africa.* University of Chicago, Department of Geography Research
               Paper 118. Chicago: University of Chicago.

Khazanov, Anatoly M.

1984   *Nomads and the Outside World.* Cambridge Studies in Social Anthropology 44.
               Cambridge: Cambridge University Press.

Kozloff, B.

1972/73   "A Brief Note on the Lithic Industries of Sinai." *Museum Ha'aretz Yearbook* 15/16:
               35–49.

1981   "Pastoral Nomadism in Sinai: An Ethnoarchaeological Study." *Production pastorales
               et société: Bulletin d'écologie et d'anthropologie des sociétés pastorales* 8: 19–24.

Kraemer, Caspar J.

1958   *Excavations at Nessana,* Volume 3: *Non-Literary Papyri.* Princeton: Princeton
               University Press.

Kupper, Jean-Robert

1957   *Les nomades en Mésopotamie au temps des rois de Mari.* Bibliothèque de la Faculté
               de philosophie et lettres de l'Université de Liège 142. Paris: Les Belles Lettres.

Lender, Yeshayahu

1990   *Archaeological Survey of Israel: Map of Har Nafha (196) 12-01.* Jerusalem: Israel
               Antiquities Authority.

Levy, Thomas E., and Augustin F. C. Holl

2002   "Migrations, Ethnogenesis, and Settlement Dynamics: Israelites in Iron Age Canaan
               and Shuwa-Arabs in the Chad Basin." *Journal of Anthropological Archaeology* 21:
               83–118.

Lewis, Norman N.
    1987   *Nomads and Settlers in Syria and Jordan, 1800–1980.* Cambridge Middle East Library. Cambridge: Cambridge University.

Luke, John T.
    1965   Pastoralism and Politics in the Mari Period: A Re-examination of the Character and Political Significance of the Major West Semitic Tribal Groups on the Middle Euphrates, ca. 1828–1758 B.C. Ph.D. dissertation, University of Michigan.

Marfoe, Leon
    1979   "The Integrative Transformation: Patterns of Sociopolitical Organization in Southern Syria." *Bulletin of the American Schools of Oriental Research* 234: 1–42.

Marx, Emanuel
    1967   *Bedouin of the Negev.* New York: Praeger.

Matthews, Victor H.
    1978   *Pastoral Nomadism in the Mari Kingdom (ca. 1830–1760 B.C.).* American Schools of Oriental Research, Dissertation Series 3. Cambridge: American Schools of Oriental Research.

Mayerson, Philip
    1960   *The Ancient Agricultural Regime of Nessana and the Central Negev.* London: British School of Archaeology in Jerusalem.
    1975   "Observations on the 'Nilus' *Narrationes*: Evidence for an Unknown Christian Sect?" *Journal of the American Research Center in Egypt* 12: 51–74.
    1980   "The Ammonius Narrative: Bedouin and Blemmye Attacks in Sinai." In *The Bible World: Essays in Honor of Cyrus H. Gordon*, edited by Gary Rendsburg, Ruth Adler, Milton Arfa, and Nathan H. Winter, pp. 133–48. New York: Ktav.
    1990   "Toward a Comparative Study of a Frontier." *Israel Exploration Journal* 40: 267–79.
    1994   *Monks, Martyrs, Soldiers, and Saracens: Papers on the Near East in Late Antiquity (1962–1993).* Jerusalem: Israel Exploration Society.

Meshel, Zeev
    1980   "Desert Kits in Sinai." In *Sinai in Antiquity: Researches in the History and Archaeology of the Peninsula*, edited by Zeev Meshel and Israel Finkelstein, pp. 265–88. Tel Aviv: Hakkibutz Hameuchad Publishing. [in Hebrew]

Na'aman, Nadav
    1986   "Habiru and the Hebrews: Transfer of a Social Term to the Literary Sphere." *Journal of Near Eastern Studies* 45: 271–88.

Nahlieli, Dov
    2007   "Settlement Patterns in the Late Byzantine and Early Islamic Periods in the Negev, Israel." In *On the Fringe of Society: Archaeological and Ethnoarchaeological Perspectives on Pastoral and Agricultural Societies*, edited by Benjamin A. Saidel and Eveline van der Steen, pp. 79–86. British Archaeological Reports, International Series 1657. Oxford: Archaeopress.

Negev, Avraham
    1986   *The Late Hellenistic and Early Roman Pottery of Nabatean Oboda: Final Report.* Qedem 22; Publications of the Institute of Archaeology. Jerusalem: Hebrew University.

Nevo, Yehuda D.
    1985   *Sede Boqer and the Central Negev in the 7–8th Centuries A.D.* Jerusalem: Israel Publication Services.

1991   *Pagans and Herders: A Re-examination of the Negev Runoff Cultivation Systems in the Byzantine and Early Arab Periods.* New Sources for the History of the Byzantine and Early Arab Periods 1. Jerusalem: Israel Publication Services.

Parker, S. Thomas

1986   *Romans and Saracens: A History of the Arabian Frontier.* American Schools of Oriental Research, Dissertation Series 6. Winona Lake: Eisenbrauns.

1987   "Peasants, Pastoralists, and Pax Romana: A Different View." *Bulletin of the American Schools of Oriental Research* 265: 35–51.

Porat, Naomi

1989   "Petrography of Pottery from Southern Israel and Sinai." In *L'Urbanisation de la Palestine à l'âge du Bronze ancien,* edited by Pierre de Miroschedji, pp. 169–88. British Archaeological Reports, International Series 527. Oxford: British Archaeological Reports.

Pratico, Gary

1985   "Nelson Glueck's 1938–1940 Excavations at Tell el-Kheleifeh: A Reappraisal." *Bulletin of the American Schools of Oriental Research* 259: 1–32.

Redford, Donald B.

1992   *Egypt, Canaan, and Israel in Ancient Times.* Princeton: Princeton University Press.

Ronen, Abraham

1970   "Flint Implements from South Sinai: Preliminary Report." *Palestine Exploration Quarterly* 102: 30–41.

Rosen, Arlene M.

2007   *Civilizing Climate: Social Responses to Climate Change in the Ancient Near East.* Lanham: AltaMira Press.

Rosen, Steven A.

1987a   "Byzantine Nomadism in the Negev: Results from the Emergency Survey." *Journal of Field Archaeology* 14: 29–42.

1987b   "Demographic Trends in the Negev Highlands: Preliminary Results from the Emergency Survey." *Bulletin of the American Schools of Oriental Research* 266: 45–58.

1991   "Paradigms and Politics in the Terminal Pleistocene Archaeology of the Levant." In *Perspectives on the Past: Theoretical Biases in Mediterranean Hunter-Gatherer Research,* edited by Geoffrey A. Clark, pp. 307–21. Philadelphia: University of Pennsylvania Press.

1992   "Nomads in Archaeology: A Response to Finkelstein and Perevolotsky." *Bulletin of the American Schools of Oriental Research* 287: 75–85.

1994   *Archaeological Survey of Israel: Map of Makhtesh Ramon (204).* Archaeological Survey of Israel. Jerusalem: Israel Antiquities Authority.

1993   "A Roman Period Pastoral Tent Camp in the Negev, Israel." *Journal of Field Archaeology* 20: 441–51.

1997   *Lithics after the Stone Age: A Handbook of Stone Tools from the Levant.* Walnut Creek: AltaMira Press.

2002   "The Evolution of Pastoral Nomadic Systems in the Southern Levantine Periphery." In *In Quest of Ancient Settlements and Landscapes: Archaeological Studies in Honour of Ram Gophna,* edited by Edwin van den Brink and Eli Yannai, pp. 23–44. Tel Aviv: Ramot Publishing, Tel Aviv University.

2003   "Early Multi-Resource Nomadism: Excavations at the Camel Site in the Central Negev." *Antiquity* 77: 750–61.

2007   "The Nabateans as Pastoral Nomads: An Archaeological Perspective." In *The World of the Nabataeans* (Volume 2 of the International Conference, "The World of the Herods and the Nabataeans," at the British Museum, 17–19 April 2001), edited by

Konstantinos D. Politis, pp. 345–74. Oriens et occidens 15; Alte Geschichte. Stuttgart: Steiner Verlag.

In press   "Desert Chronologies and Periodization Systems." In *Culture, Chronology, and the Chalcolithic*, edited by Yorke Rowan and Jaimie Lovell. London: Council for British Research in the Levant.

Rosen, Steven A., and Gideon Avni

1993   "The Edge of Empire: The Archaeology of Pastoral Nomads in the Southern Negev Highlands in Late Antiquity." *Biblical Archaeologist* 56: 189–99.

1997   *The 'Oded Sites: Investigations of Two Early Islamic Pastoral Camps South of the Ramon Crater*. Beer-Sheva 11, Studies by the Department of Bible and Ancient Near East. Beersheva: Ben-Gurion University Press.

Rosen, Steven A.; Fanny Bocquentin; Yoav Avni; and Naomi Porat

2007   "Investigations at Ramat Saharonim: A Desert Neolithic Sacred Precinct in the Central Negev." *Bulletin of the American Schools of Oriental Research* 346: 1–27.

Rosen, Steven A.; Sorin Hermon; Jacob Vardi; and Yael Abadi

2006   "The Chipped Stone Assemblage from Be'er Resisim in the Negev Highlands: A Preliminary Study." In *Confronting the Past: Archaeological and Historical Essays on Ancient Israel in Honor of William G. Dever*, edited by Seymour Gitin, J. Edward Wright, and J. P. Dessel, pp. 133–44. Winona Lake: Eisenbrauns.

Rosen, Steven A., and Benjamin A. Saidel

In press   "The Camel and the Tent." *Journal of Near Eastern Studies*.

Rosen, Steven A.; Arkady B. Savinetsky; Yosef Plakht; Nina K. Kisseleva; Bulat F. Khassanov; Andrey M. Pereladov; and Mordecai Haiman

2005   "Dung in the Desert: Preliminary Results of the Negev Holocene Ecology Project." *Current Anthropology* 46: 317–27.

Rothenberg, Beno

1972a   "An Archaeological Survey in Southern Sinai 1967–1972." *The Haa'retz Museum Bulletin* 14: 89–99.

1972b   "Sinai Exploration III." *Museum Haaretz Yearbook* 15/16: 16–34.

1972c   *Were these King Solomon's Mines? Excavations in the Timna Valley*. New Aspects of Archaeology. London: Stein & Day.

Rothenberg, Beno, and Jonathan Glass

1992   "The Beginnings and Development of Early Metallurgy and the Settlement and Chronology of the Western Arabah from the Chalcolithic Period to the Early Bronze IV." *Levant* 24: 141–57.

Rowton, Michael B.

1974   "Enclosed Nomadism." *Journal of the Economic and Social History of the Orient* 17: 1–30.

1977   "Dimorphic Structure and the Parasocial Element." *Journal of Near Eastern Studies* 36: 181–98.

Saidel, Benjamin A.

2001   "Ethnoarchaeological Investigations of Abandoned Tent Camps in Southern Jordan." *Near Eastern Archaeology* 64: 150–57.

2008   "The Bedouin Tent: An Ethno-Archaeological Portal to Antiquity or a Modern Construct?" In *The Archaeology of Mobility: Old World and New World Nomadism*, edited by Hans Barnard and Willeke Z. Wendrich, pp. 465–86. Cotsen Advanced Seminars 4. Los Angeles: Cotsen Institute of Archaeology, University of California.

Segal, Irina, and I. Roman
    1999   "Chemical and Metallurgical Studies of Copper Ingots from Horbat 'En Ziq and
                    Horbat Be'er Resisim." In *Early Settlement in the Negev Highlands*, by Rudolph
                    Cohen, pp. 22*–37*. Israel Antiquities Reports 6. Jerusalem: Israel Antiquities
                    Reports.

Segal, Irina, and Steven A. Rosen
    2005   "Copper Among the Nomads: Early Bronze Age Copper Objects from the Camel Site,
                    Central Negev, Israel." *Institute of Archaeometallurgical Studies* 25: 3–8.

Sharon, Moshe
    1975   "The Political Role of the Bedouins in Palestine in the Sixteenth and Seventeenth
                    Centuries." In *Studies on Palestine during the Ottoman Period*, edited by Moshe
                    Ma'oz, pp. 11–30. Jerusalem: Magnes Press.

Simms, Steven R.
    1988   "The Archaeological Structure of a Bedouin Camp." *Journal of Archaeological
                    Science* 15: 197–211.

van der Steen, Eveline
    1995   "Aspects of Nomadism and Settlement in the Central Jordan Valley." *Palestine
                    Exploration Quarterly* 127: 141–58.
    2006   "Tribal Power in the Ottoman Empire." *Near Eastern Archaeology* 69: 27–44.

Vardi, Jacob
    2005   The Analysis of the Lithic Assemblage from Ein Ziq, An Early Bronze IV (2300–
                    2000 BCE) Site in the Negev Highlands. M.A. thesis, Ben-Gurion University. [in
                    Hebrew]

Yekutieli, Yuval
    1998   The Early Bronze Age I of North Sinai — Social, Economic, and Spatial Aspects.
                    Ph.D. dissertation, Ben Gurion University. [in Hebrew]

Zarins, Juris
    1990   "Early Pastoral Nomadism and Settlement of Lower Mesopotamia." *Bulletin of the
                    American Schools of Oriental Research* 280: 31–65.
    1992   "Pastoral Nomadism in Arabia: Ethnoarchaeology and the Archaeological Record
                    — A Case Study." In *Pastoralism in the Levant: Archaeological Materials in
                    Anthropological Perspective*, edited by Ofer Bar-Yosef and Anatoly M. Khazanov,
                    pp. 219–40. Monographs in World Archaeology 10. Madison: Prehistory Press.

Zeevi, Dror
    1996   *An Ottoman Century: The District of Jerusalem in the 1600s.* State University of New
                    York Series in Medieval Middle East History. Albany: State University of New York
                    Press.

5

PITCHING CAMP: ETHNOARCHAEOLOGICAL INVESTIGATIONS OF INHABITED TENT CAMPS IN THE WADI HISMA, JORDAN

BENJAMIN ADAM SAIDEL, EAST CAROLINA UNIVERSITY

INTRODUCTION

This research builds upon previous studies of abandoned pastoral nomad encampments in the southern Levant. Among these are ethnoarchaeological investigations carried out at abandoned Bedouin tent camps in order to determine whether these types of habitations leave archaeological signatures after the tents are taken down and the site is abandoned (e.g., Banning and Köhler-Rollefson 1986, 1992; Simms 1988). The site plans presented in many of these studies demonstrate that encampments of individual black tents do leave behind archaeological remains associated with the structure of the site (Banning and Köhler-Rollefson 1992; Simms 1988). The archaeological signature of black tents is shaped by land-use patterns and local topography (Saidel 2001). Other studies pertinent to the present research describe the characteristics of abandoned Bedouin settlement systems in the southern Levant (e.g., Avni 1992; Banning and Köhler-Rollefson 1986; Palmer and Daly 2006).

The focus of this study is on inhabited tent camps located at the western end of the Wadi Hisma in southern Jordan (figs. 5.1–2), with the aim of determining the range of variation in the size and layout of tents at modern Bedouin campsites. This research represents a methodological departure from previous ethnoarchaeological investigations in that it uses Google Earth as a coarse-grain tool for collecting ethnoarchaeological information.[1] Specifically, the program is used to generate ethnoarchaeological data in order to address five issues: first, to determine the locations of these tent camps in the landscape; second, to document the number of tents at each site; third, to record the arrangement of tents at each location; fourth, to ascertain variations in the size of black tents; and fifth, to document the presence and size of animal pens at both occupied and presumably abandoned tent camps. The initial implications of this research for ethnography and ethnoarchaeology are considered below. Ultimately, data derived from this analysis will be used to provide insights that eventually aid in the excavation of abandoned Bedouin encampments dating to the Ottoman and British Mandate periods in the southern Levant.

---

[1] An essay focusing on the use of Google Earth as a research tool for ethnoarchaeological investigations has recently been submitted for publication.

SURVEY UNIVERSE

The area selected for this research was based upon the availability in Google Earth of a high-resolution satellite photograph of southern Jordan (figs. 5.1–2). The photograph chosen covers portions of the Ma'an plateau, the Ras en Naqab escarpment, and the western end of the Wadi Hisma.[2] The survey universe is limited to the western end of Wadi Hisma, the northern and eastern boundaries of which are delimited by the Ras en Naqab escarpment and Judaiyid basin, respectively. The western and southern limits of the survey area are demarcated by the satellite image coverage (fig. 5.2). Major topographic features in this part of the Wadi Hisma include the Wadi Judaiyid, Wadi Ras en Naqab, and Jebel Jill. The landscape ranges in elevation from 1000 to 1300 m and is covered with Irano-Turanian steppe vegetation (e.g., Henry 1995: 16, fig. 1.5, 1.7). Significant landmarks in the western part of the survey universe include a north–south road, Highway 15, and the community of Dabet Hanoot.

Black tents and animal pens were identified in Google Earth by scrolling through the survey universe at an "eye elevation" ranging from 1.01 to 1.39 km.[3] Also visible in the photograph are circular and square patches of sediments that vary in color from light brown to black. Based upon the author's previous fieldwork elsewhere in southern Jordan (Saidel 2001), these discolorations are interpreted as dung deposits associated with disused animal pens (fig. 5.3). Motor vehicles and water tanks were identified at a few tent camps. Measurements of the length and width of tents, pens, structures, and other features were made in square meters using the Google Earth "ruler tool" (fig. 5.4).

CONTEMPORARY SETTLEMENT PATTERNS

Studies conducted from the late 1970s through the early 1980s indicate that some portions of Bedouin society in Jordan continued to dwell in tents on a seasonal or year-round basis (e.g., Abu Jaber, Gharaibeh, and Hill 1987:16;[4] Layne 1987, 1994: xiii–xiv, 52–78). The presence of black tents in the Wadi Hisma in the satellite photo of 24 December 2003 demonstrates that this type of shelter remained in use, presumably on a seasonal basis, at least until this date. A total of thirty-one tent camps were recorded within the survey area, the majority situated on interfluves and wadi terraces (fig. 5.5). The largest concentration of these camps is located in the vicinity of the Wadi Judaiyid and Wadi Ras en Naqab (figs. 5.2, 5.6). Five tent sites are located in the community of Dabet Hanoot, most pitched at the southern end of the town. These tents are often erected next to enclosed walled compounds. A few tent camps are situated in other topographic settings (fig. 5.5).

The majority of encampments comprise either one or two tents; however, there are campsites that contain as many as three to four tents (table 5.1). An anomaly is Site 404 which contains nine tents that are strung out along Wadi Ras en Naqab (fig. 5.7). At those sites containing more than two tents, the majority of them are arranged in a linear pattern (e.g., fig. 5.7). At one tent camp these shelters are positioned in a staggered pattern such that one tent is not directly behind the other (fig. 5.8). The long axis of these shelters is oriented in one

---

[2] The image of southern Jordan used in this study was photographed by DigitalGlobe's QuickBird satellite on 24 December 2003 (cat. no.1010010002941A00).

[3] The term "eye elevation" refers to "the elevation of your viewpoint" in Google Earth (http://earth.google.com/userguide/v4/tutorials/navigating.html).

[4] Abu Jaber, Gharaibeh, and Hill's report was published a decade after the completion of fieldwork (1987: vi).

of three directions, east–southeast–west–northwest (3%), north–south (36%), and northeast–southwest (61%). Presumably, those structures with their long axis in either a north–south or northeast–southwest direction are situated to take advantage of the sunlight and the circulation of air (e.g., Avni 1992: 245; Jabbur 1995: 252).

The average size of the tents in this portion of Wadi Hisma is 65.60 sq. m in size, with a standard deviation of 33.74 m (table 5.1). The space inside these shelters is similar to the size of the homes and compounds built by the Jordanian government for other Bedouin. For example, in Umm Saihum the government sponsored compounds, including both roofed and unroofed space, measured 62.4 sq. m in size (Bienkowski and Chlebik 1991: 178, n. 9). In another example from the village of Mu'addi, the cinder block homes built for the Bedouin measured 62 sq. m in size (Layne 1987: 350). In contrast, the size of the tents pitched in Dabet Hanoot are in some instances larger, and in some smaller, than those buildings situated in this community (table 5.2). The average size of the tents in the survey universe may be attributed to a number of factors, such as the affordability of tents and access to cheap mechanical transportation which would be necessary to move these large shelters (e.g., Chatty 1996: 110). Perhaps the size of these tents represents a desire to match the size of their state sponsored homes.

Animal pens are present at nineteen of the thirty-one campsites. The average size of these corrals is 35.55 sq. m with a standard deviation of 27.27 sq. m. Pens are positioned in two locations, either abutting a tent or situated away from it. Without ground-truthing it is not possible to determine if the animal pens continue underneath the shelter of the tent. There are examples from Jordan, however, where animal pens are partially covered by a tent (e.g., Saidel 2001: 154, Site 12; Palmer and Daly 2006: 111, fig. 5.5). Given the decline in herding camels, the presence of these pens is most likely evidence for the herding of sheep and/or goat (e.g., Abu Jaber, Gharaibeh and Hill 1987: 42–44).[5]

Seasonal patterns of the historic Bedouin in the Wadi Hisma have changed as a result of the introduction of mechanized transportation and towed water tanks (e.g., Henry 1992: 137–38). Vehicles are present only at three of the thirty-one campsites in the survey universe. Individual vehicles are parked at Sites 413 and 414 and two vehicles at Site 408. Given the gender roles in Bedouin society, the mechanized transport at these three sites may represent evidence for the presence of men (e.g., Abu-Lughod 1984: 10; Chatty 1978: 406–08 and 1996: 106–08). For instance, regarding the integration of the truck into Bedouin society, Chatty (1978: 408) observes the following gender pattern:

> [W]omen had little, if any, contact with the household truck. They took no part in decorating, cleaning, or mechanical repair and upkeep of the vehicles, whereas they had themselves once decorated the camels with hand-woven tassels and ropes.

The presence of vehicles at three tent camps may be an indicator of economic activity or "wealth" (e.g., Abu Jaber, Gharaibeh, and Hill 1987: 46). The frequency of vehicles present at the campsites in this part of the Wadi Hisma is broadly similar to that in the Badia (Abu Jaber, Gharaibeh, and Hill 1987: 46):

> ...[I]t is found that close to 10 per-cent of the surveyed families own some kind of a mechanical vehicle such as a car, pick-up, or tractor, and this type of ownership is more prevalent in the south Badia than in its northern counterpart.

---

[5] For a discussion of animal husbandry among the Bedouin of the Badia in Jordan, see Abu Jaber, Gharaibeh, and Hill 1987: 42–44, 46–51; and Lancaster and Lancaster 1991.

At the time the satellite photograph was taken, vehicles were not present at the tent camps in the survey universe in which towed water tanks were located, namely, Sites 404, 406, and 411.

Based on the size of Bedouin households in the Sharrah and Rum Districts in Jordan (Abu Jaber, Gharaibeh, and Hill 1987: 135, table 4), population estimates can be generated for each category of tent camp in the survey universe, as well as the total number of individuals accommodated in this type of shelter. Accordingly, campsites comprising one tent have an estimated population of six people; the largest encampment, comprising nine tents, has an estimated population of fifty-four people (table 5.3). The total estimated number of individuals living in black tents in this part of the Wadi Hisma is 359. This estimate is significant if the inhabitants of these shelters migrate on a seasonal basis from the community of Dabet Hanoot, as the population of this community numbered 628 as of 10 December 1994 (Hashemite Kingdom of Jordan Department of Statistics 1994). This would demonstrate that there is variation, presumably seasonal, in the types of shelters used by the population in this region of Jordan.

HISTORIC SETTLEMENT PATTERNS

The data from Google Earth provides information for studying changes in the nature of Bedouin tents and tent camps from the nineteenth through the beginning of the twenty-first century. Taken as a whole, the size of the black tents in the survey universe tends to be larger than that of many of the contemporaneous Bedouin tents located in other parts of Arabia, Egypt, and the southern Levant (table 5.4). The size of the black tents recorded in this part of the Wadi Hisma is also larger than many tents from the nineteenth and early twentieth centuries (tables 5.1–2, 5.4).

The number and layout of tents at campsites in the Wadi Hisma are by and large different from those at nineteenth- and early twentieth-century campsites. Of the thirty-one sites in the survey universe, the majority contained one or two tents, with only one — Site 404 — comprising more than four tents (table 5.1). In contrast, travel accounts and ethnographies from the beginning of nineteenth century indicate that the number of tents at Bedouin encampments ranged from ten to as many as 800 (e.g., Burckhardt 1831/1967: 33). By the beginning of the twentieth century, Rwala tent camps fell into three broad categories: those comprising fewer than ten tents (designated *ferîz* in Arabic); those with ten–twenty-nine tents (designated *neğe* in Arabic); and those exceeding thirty tents (designated *nezel* in Arabic) (Musil 1928: 77). The diminution in the number of tents at Bedouin campsites in the survey universe reflects the sedentarization of this population within the modern nation of Jordan (e.g., Abu Jaber, Gharaibeh, and Hill 1987).

Concomitant with the sedentarization of the Bedouin are changes in the layout of tent camps. Within the survey universe, tents are arranged in linear alignments. In contrast, historical sources and travelogs from the nineteenth through the twentieth centuries describe variations in the layout of tents at Bedouin campsites, depending upon the size of the camping group and the time of year: they could be arranged in a circle, rectangle, triangle, or individual or multiple rows (e.g., Burckhardt 1831/1967: 33; Conder 1887: 339; Jaussen 1908: 76). According to Musil (1928: 180), layout was influenced by animal husbandry and security: Bedouin who raised sheep and goats tended to arrange their tents in the shape of an ellipse, whereas those who herded camels pitched their tents in parallel lines; in areas in which there was no threat of physical attack, tents were scattered or arranged in parallel rows, whereas when the Rwala were expecting an attack, tents were grouped together to form larger concentrations, although Musil does not specify shape (1928: 77, 149–622).

Acknowledging the gulf in time between Musil's observations and the present study, it is nevertheless possible that the linear alignment of black tents in the survey universe reflects the current secure economic and political conditions in the Hashemite Kingdom of Jordan. Another explanation, and one that is not mutually exclusive with the above, is that the size and layout of tent camps is also affected by local topography.

RAMIFICATIONS FOR ETHNOARCHAEOLOGY

The data collected from the Google Earth image provide insights into subjects related to seasonality, site history, and contemporaneity of tent camps. For instance, the presence of abandoned tent camps in specific topographical locations has been used by ethnoarchaeologists as one line of evidence to determine seasonality: those in sheltered locations, such as wadi terraces, are interpreted as evidence of winter occupation, and those in exposed locations as representing summer occupation (e.g., Avni 1992: 245; Banning and Köhler-Rollefeson 1986: 160, 1992: 189; Palmer and Daly 2006: 104, 121–22). This study showns, however, that both abandoned and inhabited tent camps are situated in sheltered locations, such as wadi terraces, and in seemingly more exposed locations, such as interfluves (fig. 5.11). Based on the settlement patterns revealed in this image, there is no reason to assume that the location of tent camps on wadi terraces and on topographical features immediately above them represents evidence for two different seasons of occupation.

Pedestrian surveys can identify locations that have been repeatedly reused for pitching tent camps (e.g., Saidel 2001: 155). Google Earth, however, provides a better perspective for determining whether tents are pitched on top of previously abandoned encampments, as indicated by the faded dung deposits and/or the outlines of rectangular tents visible at fourteen of the thirty-one inhabited campsites. At Site 428, for example, a corral lies partially on top of a disused animal pen (fig. 5.4). Deposits of dung not only demarcate the presence of disused animal pens, but also outline the perimeter of the rectangular tents at Sites 406, 414, and 415 (see fig. 5.12). Furthermore, the presence of disused animal pens adjacent to pitched tents provides an indication that select locations were systematically used for erecting tent camps. This is illustrated at Site 412, where there is a concentration of deserted pens to the north and west of these shelters (fig. 5.10). The locations of the abandoned pens and the inhabited tents suggest that there are shifting residential patterns at this site. From an archaeological perspective, pastoral sites with multiple occupations from the same chronological period would most likely provide more material culture than tent camps that were inhabited for one or two seasons (e.g., Rosen 1993: 448–49; Rosen and Avni 1997: 63, n. 3).

The reuse of campgrounds over specific periods of time — say, the nineteenth or twentieth century — raises the methodological issue of establishing the contemporaneity of various deserted tents at an abandoned campground (e.g., Banning and Köhler-Rollefeson 1992: 189, fig. 4; Saidel 2001: 154–55, Site 35 plan). How does one determine whether the tents at a given site represent contemporaneous use of multiple tents or repeated reuse of the location by a smaller group accommodated in an individual tent? The problem of establishing contemporaneity is illustrated in an observation made by Blunt (1879: 305):

> The Mehéd camp covers several miles of ground, and the tents are scattered about, in groups of ten or a dozen, at intervals of a least a quarter of a mile, so that it is impossible to make even a guess at the whole number.

Within the survey universe the problem of establishing contemporaneity is represented by Site 404, which contains nine tents strung out in a southwest to northeast direction along the

Wadi Ras en Naqab (fig. 5.7). This encampment measures 469 m in length and the minimum and maximum distance between tents is 9.17 and 91.20 m, respectively. Given these distances, establishing contemporaneity could be problematic in that the tents are not stratigraphically connected. This issue is troublesome, considering that historic Bedouin tent camps exhibit more variation in size than the encampments recorded by ethnoarchaeologists (see Banning and Köhler-Rollefeson 1992; Musil 1928: 77; Saidel 2001). One method that might partially resolve this issue is to use aerial photographs prior to excavation in order to identify alignments of structures that correspond to the layouts of Bedouin tent camps from the recent past. The lack of Bedouin tents in linear alignments or other identifiable patterns could be interpreted as evidence for the presence of individual tent camps such as those abandoned sites situated in the upper portions of the Wadi Judaiyid (fig. 5.6).

From an ethnoarchaeological perspective, the sedentarization of modern pastoral nomads is often marked by the transition from the use of goat-hair tents to structures made of durable materials (e.g., Bienkowski and Chlebik 1991; Cribb 1991: 154–60; Daker 1984; Layne 1994: 55–59). Although many Bedouin have permanent dwellings, it is not uncommon for them to pitch black tents behind their homes and/or use them on a seasonal basis (e.g., Bienkowski and Chlebik 1991: 163, fig. 22; Layne 1987, 1994: 61–62). At the southern end of Dabet Hanoot, for example, a number of black tents are pitched next to permanent structures. This behavior pattern, as it is recorded in the ethnoarchaeological literature, occurs within the social and political context of modern nation-states (e.g., Bienkowski and Chlebik 1991; Cribb 1991: 154–60; Daker 1984; Layne 1994: 55–59). Information contained in ethnohistorical sources, however, demonstrates that the combined use of tents and durable shelters has also occurred within tribal societies, as seen in Burckhardt's (1831/1967: 402) observations regarding the nature of the shelters used in the village of Ayme:

> Ayme is no longer in the district of Kerek, its Sheikh being now under the command of the Sheikh of Djebal, whose residence is at Tafyle. One half of the inhabitants live under tents, and every house has a tent pitched upon its terrace, where the people pass the mornings and evenings, and sleep.

At the time of Burckhardt's journey along the eastern bank of the Jordan River, the areas to the south of Salt were under the control of tribal leaders rather than Ottoman officials (Rogan 1999: 18, 31–32; van der Steen 2007: 93–94). Therefore, the behavioral pattern of pitching tents behind structures made of durable materials cannot be solely attributed to contact with, or subjugation to, state-level societies.

Finally, this research provides yet another line of evidence that should put to rest the ill-founded notion that Bedouin campsites cannot be identified in the archaeological record, a premise that has been most forcefully argued by Finkelstein and Perevolotsky (1990: 68):

> In the desert areas the opposite is true: groups that practice subsistence economy based on hunting and gathering or on animal husbandry — and migrate in search of food, water, and good pasture — do not leave traceable remains.

Given that the outlines of abandoned rectangular tents are visible in satellite photographs (e.g., fig. 5.12), it is obvious that these remains can be located by pedestrian survey (e.g., Avni 1992; Banning and Köhler-Rollefson 1986, 1992).[6]

---

[6] In July 2007, the author and Tali Erickson-Gini excavated the remains of a Bedouin tent camp at the site of Nahal Be'erotayim West in the Negev Desert. The remains of this tent camp are tentatively dated to the late nineteenth–early twentieth century A.D. This site was identified in the course of a pedestrian survey of the Be'erotayim area, (map 156).

CONCLUSIONS

The study of occupied tent camps in the Wadi Hisma demonstrates that the majority of campsites comprise either one or two tents. The sizes of these tents seem to be larger than most of the black tents documented in the ethnographic and ethnoarchaeological sources (table 5.4). Although this is speculative, the relatively large size of the tents in the Wadi Hisma may reflect a desire to use tensile structures of similar size to state-sponsored houses. The Google Earth image used in this study shows the contemporaneous presence of tent camps on both interfluves and wadi terraces, demonstrating that there is no reason to assume that their location on wadi terraces and on topographical features immediately above them represent evidence for two different seasons of occupation. Lastly, this study demonstrates that although there is continuity in the use of the black tent, the size of this shelter and the layout of contemporary tent camps have changed since the nineteenth century.

Table 5.1. Number of tents at sites in survey area

Number Tents per Campsite	Number of Campsites	Average Size of Tent	Standard Deviation
1	16	73.62	30.74
2	9	59.98	37.36
3	4	52.56	30.71
4	1	87.52	26.76
9	1	71.24	33.52

Table 5.2. Size in square meters of tents and structures
situated in the community of Dabet Hanoot

Site	Size of Tent in Square Meters	Size of Structures in Square Meters
421	67.30	50.52
422	29.33 57.75	47.74
423	45.00	104.58 (structure) 44.72 (roofless structure) 6.39 (small structure)
424	27.98	79.00
425	82.65	111.00

Table 5.3. Population estimates for tent camps in the survey universe
based on fieldwork results in Abu Jaber, Gharaibeh, and Hill 1987: 135, table 4

Number of Tents per Campsite	Estimated Population per Campsite	Number of Campsites	Total Population per Campsite Category
1	6	16	101
2	12	9	108
3	18	4	72
4	24	1	24
9	54	1	54
		Total	359

Table 5.4. Sizes of Bedouin tents from selected sources

Location and/or Tribe	Tent Size	Reference
Petra, Jordan	60 m	Simms 1988: 202
Petra, Jordan, "Main Tent"	51.5 sq. m	Bienkowski and Chlebik 1991: 169, table 4
Petra, Jordan, "Second Tent"	18.4 sq. m	Bienkowski and Chlebik 1991: 169, table 4
'Ammarîn Bedouin, Beidha, "Typical Size of Tent"	27 m	Banning and Köhler-Rollefson 1992: 193
'Ammarîn Bedouin, Beidha, Camp 37	48 m	Banning and Köhler-Rollefson 1992: 190, fig. 5
'Ammarîn Bedouin, Beidha, Camp 35, Tent Area 1	33 m	Banning and Köhler-Rollefson 1992: 189, fig. 4
'Ammarîn Bedouin, Beidha, Camp 35, Tent Area 2	48 m	Banning and Köhler-Rollefson 1992: 189, fig. 4
Disi and southern Jordan, 23 Tents	43 m, STDEV 22 m	Cataldi and Pizziolo 1988: 15
Wadi Arabah, Jordan	18 m	Abu Jaber, Gharaibeh, and Hill 1987: 16
Al-Talib Tent, al-'Ardah, Jordan	40 sq. m	Layne 1987: 357, fig. 7.3
Sarahin Bedouin, southern Negev Highlands, Israel	24–45 m	Avni 1992: 245
Egypt, Eastern Desert (Ma'aza Bedouin)	32 m	Hobbs 1989: 51
Wadi Fatima, Saudi Arabia	40 m	Katakura 1977: 73

Jabbur, one-room tent with one pole	4–5 m long	Jabbur 1995: 242–43
Rwala tent, without main pole (*harbus*)	4–6 × 2.5–3 m	Musil 1928: 72
Rwala tent with one main pole (*katba*)	12 × 3.5 m	Musil 1928: 72
Rwala tent for children or "the poorest inhabitants of the camp" (*tuzz*)	4 × 2 m	Musil 1928: 72
"Small" tent of T'aamireh and Jâhlîn	10 ft long	Conder 1887: 339
"Average" tent of T'aamireh and Jâhlîn	20–25 ft long	Conder 1887: 339
"Large" tent of T'aamireh and Jâhlîn	40 ft long	Conder 1887: 339
Ahl el Shemal Bedouin ("two middle posts")	25–30 × 10 ft	Burckhardt 1831/1967: 42

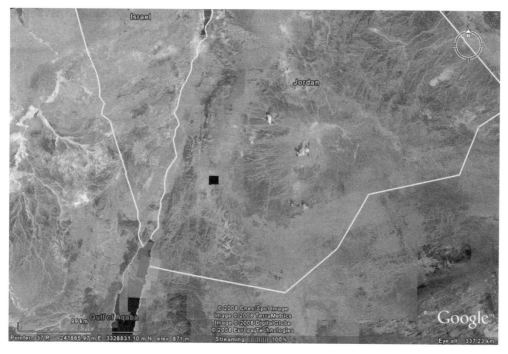

Figure 5.1. Map from Google Earth showing location of survey universe area,
black box, in Southern Jordan

Figure 5.2. Survey universe and location of community of Dabet Hanout

Figure 5.3. Five animal pens at Bedouin tent camp located in Jebel Thurga, Jordan. Notice animal pen in foreground has fence enclosing this space, while other pens do not have fencing, suggesting that these corrals are no longer in use

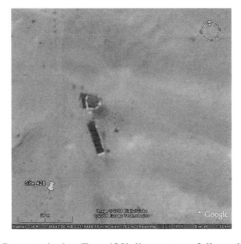

Figure 5.4. Pen attached to Tent 428b lies on top of disused animal pen

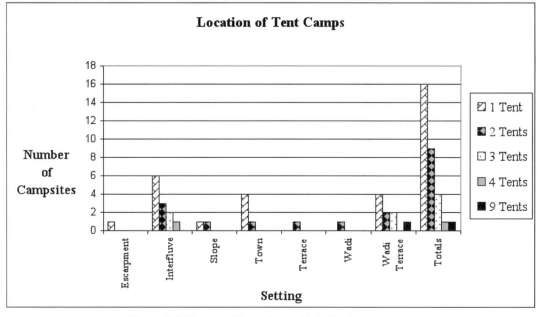

Figure 5.5. Topographic settings of inhabited tent camps

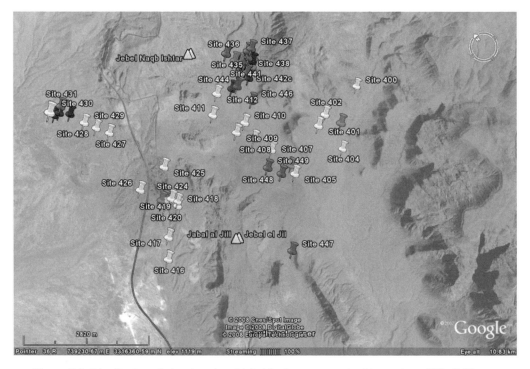

Figure 5.6. Distribution of abandoned and inhabited tent camps in this portion of Wadi Hisma. Inhabited tent camps demarcated by white pins, abandoned campsites represented by gray pins

Figure 5.7. Tents of Site 404 spread out along the Wadi Ras en Naqab

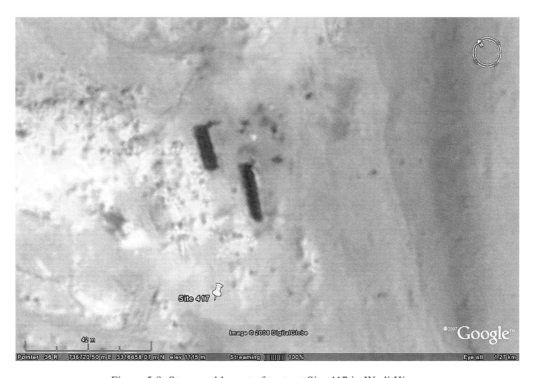

Figure 5.8. Staggered layout of tents at Site 417 in Wadi Hisma

BENJAMIN ADAM SAIDEL

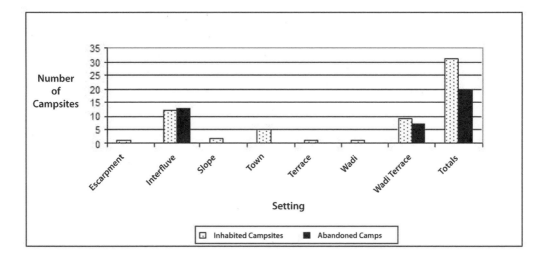

Figure 5.9. Topographical settings of abandoned and inhabited tent camps

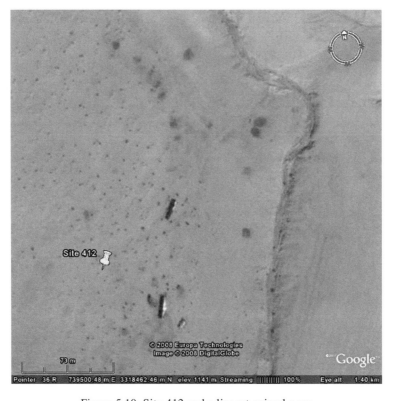

Figure 5.10. Site 412 and adjacent animal pens

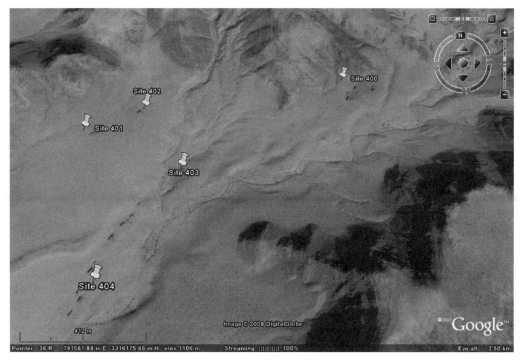

Figure 5.11. Tent camps located on interfluves and on wadi terraces along Wadi Ras en Naqab

Figure 5.12. Deposits of dung at Sites 414 and 451 demarcated the location of abandoned rectangular tents. Lines demarcate the long axis of these abandoned shelters

BIBLIOGRAPHY

Abu Jaber, Kamel S.; Fawzi A. Gharaibeh; and Allen Hill

    1987   *The Badia of Jordan: The Process of Change.* Amman: University of Jordan.

Abu-Lughod, Lila

    1984   "Change and Egyptian Bedouins." *Cultural Survival Quarterly* 8: 6–10.

Avni, Gideon

    1992   "Survey of Deserted Bedouin Campsites in the Negev Highlands and Its Implications for Archaeological Research." In *Pastoralism in the Levant: Archaeological Materials in Anthropological Perspectives*, edited by Ofer Bar-Yosef and Anatoly M. Khazanov, pp. 241–54. Monographs in World Archaeology 10. Madison: Prehistory Press.

Banning, E. B., and Isle Köhler-Rollefson

    1986   "Ethnoarchaeological Survey in the Beda Area, Southern Jordan." *Zeitschrift des deutschen Palästina-Vereins* 102: 152–70.

    1992   "Ethnographic Lessons for the Pastoral Past: Camp Locations and Material Remains near Beidha, Southern Jordan." In *Pastoralism in the Levant: Archaeological Materials in Anthropological Perspectives*, edited by Ofer Bar-Yosef and Anatoly M. Khazanov, pp. 181–204. Monographs in World Archaeology 10. Madison: Prehistory Press.

Bienkowski, Piotr, and Basia Chlebik

    1991   "Changing Places: Architecture and Spatial Organization of the Bedul in Petra." *Levant* 23: 147–80.

Blunt, Anne

    1879   *Bedouin Tribes of the Euphrates.* New York: Harper & Brothers.

Burckhardt, John Lewis

    1822   *Travels in Syria and the Holy Land.* London: John Murray.

    1831 (1967) *Notes on the Bedouins and Wahabys: Collected During His Travels in the East.* New York: Johnson Reprint Corporation.

Cataldi, Giancarlo, and Giorgio Pizziolo

    1988   "Territory and Tents in Southern Jordan." In *Environmental Design: Journal of the Islamic Environmental Design Research Centre* 1–2: 10–23.

Chatty, Dawn

    1978   "Changing Sex Roles in Bedouin Society in Syria and Lebanon." In *Women in the Muslim World,* edited by Lois Beck and Nikki Keddie, pp. 399–415. Cambridge: Harvard University.

    1996   *Mobile Pastoralists: Development Planning and Social Change in Oman.* New York: Columbia University.

Conder, Claude R.

    1887   *Tent Work in Palestine: A Record of Discovery and Adventure.* London: Richard Bentley & Son.

Cribb, Roger

    1991   *Nomads in Archaeology.* Cambridge: Cambridge University.

Daker, Naoras

    1984   "Contribution à l'évolution de l'habitat Bédouin en Syrie." In *Nomades et Sédentaires: Perspectives ethnoarchéologiques,* edited by Olivier Aurenche, pp. 51–79. Lyon: Maison de l'Orient Méditerranéen.

Finkelstein, Israel, and Avi Perevolotsky

    1990   "Processes of Sedentarization and Nomadization in the History of the Negev and Sinai." *Bulletin of the American Schools of Oriental Research* 279: 67–88.

Hashemite Kingdom of Jordan, Department of Statistics
1994   "Population (by Sex), Number of Households, Housing Units and Buildings AQABA Governorate by Administrative Division, as of 10/12/1994." [accessed 12 June 2008]

Henry, Donald O.
1992   "Seasonal Movements of Fourth Millennium Pastoral Nomads in Wadi Hisma." *Studies in the History and Archaeology of Jordan* 4: 137–41.
1995   *Prehistoric Cultural Ecology and Evolution.* New York: Plenum.

Hobbs, Joseph John
1989   *Bedouin Life in the Egyptian Wilderness.* Austin: University of Texas.

Jabbur, Jibrail S.
1995   *The Bedouins and the Desert: Aspects of Nomadic Life in the Arab East.* Albany: State University of New York.

Jaussen, Antonin
1908   *Coutumes des Arabes au pays de Moab.* Paris: J. Gabalda.

Katakura, Motoko
1977   *Bedouin Village: A Study of a Saudi Arabian People in Transition.* Tokyo: University of Tokyo.

Lancaster, William, and Fidelity Lancaster
1991   "Limitations on Sheep and Goat Herding in the Eastern Badia of Jordan: An Ethno-Archaeological Enquiry." *Levant* 23: 125–38.

Layne, Linda L.
1987   "Village-Bedouin: Patterns of Change from Mobility to Sedentism in Jordan." In *Method and Theory for Activity Area Research: An Ethnoarchaeological Approach,* edited by Susan Kent, pp. 345–73. New York: Columbia University.
1994   *Home and Homeland: The Dialogics of Tribal and National Identities in Jordan.* Princeton: Princeton University.

Musil, Alois
1928   *The Manners and Customs of the Rwala Bedouins.* American Geographical Society, Oriental Explorations and Studies 6. New York: American Geographical Society.

Palmer, Carol, and Patrick Daly
2006   "Jouma's Tent: Bedouin and Digital Archaeology." In *Digital Archaeology: Bridging Method and Theory,* edited by Thomas L. Evans and Patrick Daly, pp. 97–127. London and New York: Routledge.

Rogan, Eugene
1999   *Frontiers of the State in the Late Ottoman Empire: Transjordan, 1850–1921.* Cambridge: Cambridge University.

Rosen, Steven A.
1993   "A Roman Period Pastoral Tent Camp in the Negev, Israel." *Journal of Field Archaeology* 20: 441–51.

Rosen, Steven A., and Gideon Avni
1997   *The 'Oded Sites: Investigations of Two Early Islamic Pastoral Camps South of the Ramon Crater.* Beersheva 11, Studies by the Department of Bible and Ancient Near East. Beersheva: Ben-Gurion University.

Saidel, Benjamin Adam
2001   "Ethnoarchaeological Investigations of Abandoned Tent Camps in Southern Jordan." *Near Eastern Archaeology* 64/3:150–57.

Simms, Steven R.

    1988   "The Archaeological Structure of a Bedouin Camp." *Journal of Archaeological Science* 15: 197–211.

van der Steen, Eveline

    2007   "Town and Countryside of the Kerak Plateau." In *On the Fringe of Society: Archaeological and Ethnoarchaeological Perspectives on Pastoral and Agricultural Societies*, edited by Benjamin A. Saidel and Eveline J. van der Steen, pp. 93–98. British Archaeological Reports International Series 1657. Oxford: Archaeopress.

6

TRIBAL SOCIETIES IN THE NINETEENTH CENTURY: A MODEL

EVELINE VAN DER STEEN

In this paper I investigate the possibilities of the ethnohistory and ethnography of the nineteenth century A.D. as potential models for the history and archaeology of the ancient Near East. Written sources of the ancient Near East, from the Middle Bronze Age onward, suggest that society in the region has been tribally organized from a very early period onward. These sources include descriptions in Akkadian texts that document the ascendancy of the Amorite tribes into some of the most powerful states of the Middle Bronze Age, the Mari archives (Fleming 2004), Egyptian sources about the Shasu and Sutu, and not forgetting the various stories in the Old Testament about the tribal organization of Israel.

How we define a tribe, its political organization and social and economic structure, in this historical context is more difficult to detect from these sources. Definitions of tribal societies abound in the anthropological literature. Many of these are ultimately based on Elman Service's definition (1971), but there are fundamental "regional" differences in definitions of what constitutes a tribe. These not only often refer to the minimum and maximum size of a tribe, its economy, and other characteristics largely dependent on the geographical and ecological context, but also to social or political organization, and other fundamental issues.

WHAT IS A TRIBE?

The history of the anthropological research on tribalism has been extensively dealt with in Parkinson 2002. The definition I give below applies to the Near East only and reflects the social and political organization of nineteenth-century tribal societies in the Near East.

- A segmentary social structure based on an accepted patrilineal lineage system,[1] consisting of families and clans bonded by a system of sodalities or social networks that crosscut the clan system. The different clans may recognize one communal apical ancestor. This system does not so much represent actual kinship and descent relations, but can be reconstructed and manipulated for social and political purposes with the consent of the members.

- A strong and formalized sense of group responsibility and group loyalty: individual actions reflect on the whole group, and the group is responsible for the welfare of the individual.

- Leadership of the tribe is maintained through a combination of ascribed and achieved qualities. In most studies the emphasis is on achieved qualities, and the leader is de-

---

[1] In other societies matrilineal systems occur, but not in Near Eastern societies, as far as I know. The matrilineal bond plays a role in the maintenance of honor within a tribe, as pointed out by Lancaster (1981: 44–45).

picted as a "first among equals." In Near Eastern tribes leadership is hereditary within a leading clan and family from which the leader is chosen. Changes of the leading clan (or leading tribe within a confederation) are major political events that frequently lead to bloodshed and political turmoil.

• Social interaction within and between tribes is strongly determined by the concept of "honor." (Abu-Lughod 1986: *passim*; Eickelman 1989: 153; Lancaster 1981: 43–45). This is also reflected in the second point (above): the individual is responsible for maintaining the honor of the group and vice versa.

This definition of tribe describes its social organization. It does, however, also have consequences for the political and economic organization of society.

WHY THE NINTEENTH CENTURY?

The time from the Napoleonic invasion of Egypt to the First World War, roughly the nineteenth century, was a period of social, political, and economic turmoil that proved to be the end of an era in the Levant. The primary reason for examining the nineteenth-century tribes is that it was the last period in which the major tribes and tribal confederations of the region, such as the Anaze, the Adwan, the Beni Sakhr, the Shammar, were in actual political control in the Levant. These tribes had their territorial borders and power structures, intertribal hierarchies, and conflicts. They created and maintained alliances and confederations and, on several occasions, complex state-like power structures that can throw light on the concept of the tribal state.

The Ottoman administration had little to no authority in these tribal regions. The last Ottoman governor in the region who had any actual power was Achmed Jezzar ("the Butcher"), Pasha of Acco and on several occasions of Damascus. He had been appointed by the government to restore order in the Palestinian region after an uprising, and he did so, but at a heavy cost: he left the countryside depleted; the less subservient tribes simply moved out of the area and out of his reach and wreaked havoc farther to the south and east (Browne 1806: 422; Buckingham 1825: 5; Cohen 1973: 107–08, 163–64). After Jezzar's death, the various tribal groups in the region took control again.

The Wahabi uprising, followed by the Egyptian rule of Muhammad Ali and Ibrahim Pasha, transformed the country for a short period and thoroughly upset the sociopolitical structure of the Ottoman dominions. Travelers in Jordan and the Arabian Peninsula, such as Seetzen (1854–59), Burckhardt (1822, 1829, 1830), and Buckingham (1822, 1825) reported regular clashes and actual wars between the Wahabi and their opponents, both the Turks and the opposing tribes. The Egyptian pashas beat the Wahabis and maintained a tight control over the region. Robinson and Smith (1841: 156) report that even the tribes of the Beni Sakhr and the Howeitat in Jordan paid taxes to the Egyptian government.

However, after the Egyptian defeat at the hands of the British, the region fell back into its former state of relative anarchy. Anarchy, that is, as far as Ottoman rule was concerned. The region had a political configuration of its own, with power once again in the hands of various powerful tribes and families, each with their own territory, and answering to laws that were universally known and recognized.

The main areas of interaction between the Ottoman government and the tribal south were the ports of trade with the Mediterranean and Europe, such as Gaza, Acco, Jaffa, Saida, Beirut, and Tripoli, and the yearly pilgrimage to Mecca and Medina. The government was responsible for the safety of the Hajj routes for the pilgrims, which went through various tribal territories. The government paid the tribes *surra*, protection money, to stop them from attacking the pilgrims — which amounted to permission to cross their territory. This was an old practice, and a considerable source of income for the tribes.

Ever since the Napoleonic invasion, the Ottoman sultans realized that in order to keep their empire and compete with the European powers, they had to reform, get rid of corruption, and take control, both in the cities and also in more peripheral territories. The Tanzimat, a series of reforms in administration, land use, and political organization, instigated by Sultan Abdulmajed I and continued by Abdel Aziz (1839–1876), began to make itself felt shortly after the withdrawal of the Egyptian forces (Findley 1986). The initial effect of these measures was limited, and especially in peripheral areas such as the Hauran and southern Transjordan, it took a long time before they had any effect.

In these peripheral areas power was shared and contested between the main tribes, the Beni Sakhr, the Adwan, the Howeitat in the south, and the various tribes of the Anaze confederation in the north and east. Tribal towns such as Nablus, Hebron, and Kerak also continued to resist Ottoman power until the end of the century. A comparable situation existed in the Arabian Peninsula, where a power struggle between the Ibn Sa'ud and the Ibn Rashid led to the creation of several independent emirates.

Nevertheless, the Tanzimat began to gain ground in Jordan and Palestine. In 1867, at the request of the local farmers, the Ottoman armies invaded the Belqa, with the support of the Beni Hassan (Oppenheim 1943: 179; Wood 1869, quoted in Shryock 1997: 260). They defeated the Adwan and abolished the practice of *Khawa* (protection fees) (Shryock 1997: 77). In the 1880s the Hauran and Jaulan came under the control of the Damascus government. Schumacher (1886: 25) describes the Hauran as "wheat country" and the Jaulan as "grazing country." It would take until the very end of the century, however, before the government managed to get a grip on the south. The Kerak Plateau was controlled from Kerak by the independent Majali family. When, finally, an Ottoman government was established in Kerak in 1893, the Majali stayed in actual power, alongside the Ottomans, and even today they are one of the most powerful families in the country.

So around the turn of the century the Ottoman empire had re-established its control over much of the region and the tribes. However, the World War turned everything upside down again. The Bedouin tribes saw their power curbed by a more efficient Ottoman administration, and their camel-based economy weakened by the coming of the railways. Many sided with the foreign powers against the Turkish empire. There were several uprisings, one of which was led by Hussayn, supreme Sharif, and his four sons. The British supported this revolt in an effort to undermine the authority of the Ottomans. The involvement of the Bedouin and other tribes in the war has been described by T. E. Lawrence in *The Seven Pillars of Wisdom* (1926/1962). The war divided the tribes of the region into two camps and changed the political map forever. Afterward, the Western powers divided the region among themselves, with little regard for tribal territories and sensitivities. The sons of Hussayn were made rulers of states under mandate of France and England, and they rewarded the tribes that had supported them with wealth and positions of power.

Other tribes retreated into the desert, and the farming tribes welcomed the new security. The creation of the State of Israel and the cultivation of the Negev was the final blow to the tribes' political and economic organization, albeit not to their existence as tribes. Tribal societies remain an important source of influence in the region. Tribal affiliation is an important part of the social networks, and election results are decided by tribal loyalty, rather than political ideals (Shryock 1997: 146, 278, 324–26). Concepts of honor have not changed significantly, nor has the concept of group responsibility. Within the state structure, the tribal organization has found a new form.

My second reason for choosing the nineteenth century as an ethnohistoric model is that it has by far the largest corpus of sources describing tribal society. Napoleon's expeditions brought a large number of scientists, historians, and geologists in their train. They described and mapped the region and triggered both the curiosity of Western scholars and the greed of adventurers.

The eighteenth-century Danish expedition that included Carsten Niebuhr was an exception; now came a stream of scientific expeditions and individual adventurers exploring the East. Most of these focused on the Holy Land and Egypt. Jordan remained largely terra incognita, and Arabia was only slowly being discovered.

Many of these travelers published accounts of their travels, in one form or another. For the Holy Land alone there are over 5,000 sources from the nineteenth century (Ben-Arieh 1979: 11–18). The scope and the quality of these accounts vary widely, and we have to take this into account when we study these sources. Most travelers and explorers, certainly in the earlier period, had other axes to grind, and considered their encounters with the local tribes as a nuisance at best (van der Steen, forthcoming). But others lived among the tribes, spoke the language, and got to know them well.

At the beginning of the nineteenth century, John Lewis Burckhardt (1822) and Ulrich Jasper Seetzen (1854–59) were the first two Westerners to travel in Jordan since antiquity. They did so to perfect their disguises as Arabs to be able to explore the interior of Africa. Neither reached their goal, both dying before they could travel into Africa. However, whilst living as Arabs in the Levant, they became very familiar with Arab society east of the Jordan and described it in detail. Other travelers, such as Irby and Mangles (1868), Robinson (1856; Robinson and Smith 1841), and Palmer (1871), were more interested in finding and describing antiquities. They considered dealings with the tribes a necessary evil, an attitude that is reflected in their accounts. Nevertheless, their observations, however biased, are valuable because they throw light on the role of the tribes in society, and on the power structures that they found so obstructive and irritating.

Finally, Alois Musil (1907–08, 1927, 1928a–b), at the end of the nineteenth century, belonged to a new generation of travelers who were genuinely interested in the customs and habits of the local population. He lived with the Rwala Bedouin and was the first to use photography extensively as a tool in his research. His publications on the tribes of the region are invaluable because he observed and recorded the beginning of the end of tribal hegemony in the region. The accounts of Lawrence of Arabia, which marked the end itself, have already been mentioned.

Two case studies illustrate the interaction between government and tribal society, and the concept of tribal state formation, respectively. The first is taken from nineteenth-century Palestine and concerns one of the most colorful tribal leaders in the region: Akila Agha.

AKILA AGHA[2]

Akila was the youngest son of an Egyptian mercenary, who had wandered into Palestine in the eighteenth century in the service of Suleiman Pasha. Akila served as commander in the Egyptian army of Ibrahim Pasha. In 1834 he deserted and joined the *fellahin* revolt. After the defeat of Ibrahim, Akila went to serve a local Nazareth ruler. He also started to collect his own band of followers, men who, like him, were unemployed and uprooted by the chaos that followed the defeat of the Egyptians. However, in 1845, after a conflict with the Ottoman governor, he fled with his men to the east side of the Jordan, where he received hospitality from the Beni Sakhr. He allied himself to the Beni Sakhr through marriage and, with his followers, started robbing the region. His power and influence became so great that two years later the Pasha of Acco summoned him back and made him leader of a band of seventy-five mercenaries from the Hawara and Henadi, two tribes of Egyptian origin (see Burckhardt 1830: 226). He based himself in Abelin, a village in the Galilee, and in a very short time gained control over the Galilee, partly by force, partly through the voluntary submission of the local population. Officially he was still in the service of the government but, de facto, he was an independent leader. The government, in no position to defeat him, made him an army colonel.

At this time William Lynch met him. Lynch had launched an expedition to travel down the Jordan by boat. He describes Akila on their first meeting at the house of the American consul in Acco as "a great border sheikh of the Arabs." Lynch recognized the usefulness of a man who controlled the west side of the Jordan and was allied to the Beni Sakhr on the east side, and he hired Akila as a guide for his whole journey. He greatly admired the sheikh, calling him "a magnificent savage" and "the Achilles of our camp" (Lynch 1849: 127, 195). Lynch was well aware that Akila had been, and on occasion still was, a notorious raider, although while with the Lynch party he was more busy making alliances. Lynch suspected him of wanting to unite the tribes in the region to throw off the (already nominal) Turkish rule and start his own sovereignty (Lynch 1849: 360). Later reports, among others that of Hepworth Dixon and Finn, suggest that he may have made serious attempts in that direction. At the very least, relations between Akila and the Ottoman government were always strained, neither one trusting the other.

In 1852 the government, in whose service he still officially acted, ordered Akila to protect northern Palestine against an uprising in the Hauran. Afterward, on an accusation of defecting, they arrested him and imprisoned him in Bulgaria. But a year later, after a spectacular escape, he returned to Palestine. His men, in the meantime, had been conscripted by the government for the Crimean War. When they heard of his return they deserted and returned to his service. The government, facing a lack of officers, was forced to employ him again, to patrol the countryside and keep the roads safe for travelers. Occasionally, Akila also served as a tax collector, apparently for the more difficult regions, in which capacity he visited Kerak.

In 1855 Mary Eliza Rogers met Saleh Agha, Akila's brother, and she describes the brothers as "the most powerful and formidable people in the Pashalic of Akka" (Rogers 1989: 178). Akila's power continued to increase, alarming the government, so that in 1857 they set a Kurdish army against him. In the battle that followed on the ancient battlefield of Hattin, Akila, supported by his old allies the Beni Sakhr, won a glorious victory.

---

[2] Sources for the history of Akila Agha and the Henadi are: Finn 1878: 411–33; Hepworth Dixon 1885: 109–16; Lynch 1849; Macalister and Masterman 1906; Oppenheim 1943: 30–34.

In 1864, another Bedouin revolt broke out in reaction to the reforms of the Tanzimat. According to Hepworth Dixon (1885: 37, 74), Akila was one of the main instigators of this rebellion. Other sources, such as Stewart MacAlister (1906: part 5, pp. 221–25), state that Akila was originally entrusted by the government to impose the Tanzimat measures but fell out with the Kaimakam (governor) of Akko. Akila moved to Kerak. He returned briefly to Palestine but the story repeated itself: the governor of Nablus tried to arrest him, but he escaped and went to live in Salt. Later he returned to Galilee, but never regained his former power. He died in 1870 and was buried in his former stronghold of Abelin.

Akila's leadership developed from that of a commander in the Turkish army to leader of a predatory band of Egyptian immigrants, to sheikh of a powerful tribe in control of the whole region of the Galilee. Most of his strategies were based on personal, achieved qualities. His original command of the Hawara band may have been at least partly the result of his family relationship as son to a Hawara commander. But after that, he was on his own. Akila was both a fearless fighter and a clever politician. He had personal courage and charisma, and very cleverly manipulated the political situation, becoming a powerful tribal sheikh in the Galilee. When Lynch met him, in 1848, he controlled the region west of the Jordan, was a famous raider, and saw himself as a tribal sheikh. His diplomacy was that of a tribal leader too: he created alliances with the tribes surrounding him, partly by marriage (he married a Beni Sakhr woman, and later also one of the new Henadi immigrants). At the same time, his political connections included European powers, particularly the French, according to various accounts. The Prince of Wales had given him a "fine revolver" (Hepworth Dixon 1885: 113–14).

Akila's relationships with the Ottoman government remained ambiguous. For much of his working life Akila was officially in the service of the government. At the same time he posed as an independent tribal sheikh, allied himself to the enemies of the government, the Beni Sakhr, and, with their help, beat an army of Kurds sent by the government to defeat him. He was also well known as a raider, and his code of honor was that of the Bedouin. The government could not afford to let him out of its sight, so it continued to offer him positions in the army, or give him commissions, which Akila duly fulfilled, or pretended to fulfill, at the same time keeping to his own agenda. After Akila's death the Henadi continued to harass the area for a while, but without their leader they were easily beaten and absorbed into the mosaic of tribes and clans in the area.

The case of Akila Agha illustrates the sudden rise of small and aggressive polities in a tribal society in a period of weak control, and their dependence on the leadership of one man. Had he lived earlier, longer before the end of the Ottoman empire, his tale could well have grown into a tribal epic, on the scale of the Sirat Delhemmeh, or even the Sirat Antar, epic accounts of the adventures of Arabian heroes.

THE EMIRATE OF IBN RASHID[3]

The second case study is that of the emirate of Ibn Rashid, in the Nejd in the Arabian Peninsula, which has a number of characteristics of the tribal state. The emirate of Ibn Rashid emerged from the tribal confederation of the Shammar, who inhabited the double chain of granite mountains named after them: Jebel Shammar. In earlier periods one section of the

---

[3] Main sources for the history of the Ibn Rashid emirate are: Blunt 1881; Doughty 1921; Euting 1914; Musil 1928a–b; Palgrave 1866; al-Rasheed 1991 with references; and Wallin 1979.

Shammar had moved north to Mesopotamia in search of pasture. These northern Shammar lived as pastoralists and farmers and were notorious raiders (Burckhardt 1830: 17). The two sections remained in contact, and every year a major trade caravan traveled north from Hayil to the northern Shammar.

The southern Shammar confederation consisted of four independent tribes, each with its own tribal leader: the Sinjara, the Abde, the Aslam, and the Tuman. These were subdivided into clans or subtribes, several of which are mentioned by travelers such as Wallin and Burckhardt. Among the Shammar lived the Beni Tamim, who inhabited the Jebel before the Shammar and had allied themselves to them. They were farmers and had their own villages in the Shammar territories.

In 1836, a change of power took place in the Abde leadership. Abdallah Ibn Rashid challenged the sheikh of the tribe, who was his cousin. Abdallah was exiled and found refuge with the Ibn Saud family in Riadh. The Ibn Saud were leaders of the Wahabi and ruled most of the peninsula. Abdallah won the support of Faisal Ibn Saud by helping him to save his throne, and he returned to Jebel Shammar to claim the Abde leadership. Eventually, with the help of a band of supporters, he overthrew his cousin. Abdallah was an ambitious man, and he immediately started to expand the power of the Abde.

At the same time, the Arabian Peninsula was in political turmoil, with the Wahabi, the Egyptians of Muhammad Ali, and the Ottoman empire fighting for control. The Shammar felt the danger of being caught in the middle of it and looked for a strong leader. Abdallah and his Abde were successful raiders, who gave the Shammar a feeling of confidence and power. In a relatively short period of time, he managed to rally not only the Abde behind him, but also the other Shammar tribes, the Sinjara, the Aslam, and the Tuman. They joined in the raids he organized and gradually adopted his leadership. Thus Abdallah changed the structure of the confederation, which now had a paramount sheikh, something they had not had before.

Abdallah died in 1847. He was succeeded by his son Talal, with the support of the tribes. Talal continued to forge the confederation into a more state-like structure. He also adopted the title of amir. He was still sheikh of the Abda, but this new title reflected his leadership over the whole confederation.

Hayil was traditionally the home village of the Abde tribe. Talal now turned it into his power base. He finished the Barzan palace and he encouraged international trade, concentrating it in the town. His liberal attitude encouraged not only Shiite Muslims, but also Jews and Christians, to settle and trade in Hayil. He rebuilt settlements that had been destroyed during the war and expanded his dominions, partly by conquest, although his liberal politics and the prosperity and peace of his government brought other tribes and towns to ally themselves to the Ibn Rashid. This process was facilitated by the tyrannical politics of the Wahabi. In a world where political power was based on alliances, tribes and towns could choose their protectors by simply paying or withholding tribute, and many preferred the Rashidi leaders.

Succession was now firmly established within the Rashid family, but apart from that, there were no rules to determine who would be the new amir. The succession of Talal became a bloody affair. His brother and successor Mitab was murdered within a year by Talal's eldest son, Bandar. Many members of the family left Hayil and were offered refuge in Riyadh.

Another brother of Talal's, Mohammad, was a successful caravan leader between Hayil and Iraq. Trade with the Iraqi Shammar was an important asset of the emirate in which both the settled population and the Bedouin were involved, either as producers and consumers of the trade goods, or as providers of camels. Because of his popularity among the Bedouin as well as the settled population, when Muhammad killed Bandar and pronounced himself amir, he had the support of both. He killed most of the possible contenders to his throne, practically all the male members of the family, a cruel, but within the context of the political situation, hardly surprising measure.

Mohammad's rule was the longest in the history of the Shammar emirate, lasting from 1869 to 1897, when he died of natural causes. It was also the period of the greatest expansion of the emirate. Its domain included most of Nejd, including the Saudi territory with the capital Riyadh, and to the north it extended toward Jauf. Even Palmyra paid tribute to the Rashidis. Under Talal and Muhammad the oasis of Hayil grew into one of the largest trade centers of the region.

Under the successors of Mohammad the emirate began to show the early signs of disintegration. The conquered territories never became integrated. They constituted a sphere of influence, a commonwealth rather than a unified state. International political developments did not favor the consolidation of the expanded emirate. In 1902 the Saudis recaptured Riyadh and regained the support of a number of tribes in the region between Riyadh and Hayil. At the same time, the tribes in the north, around Jauf, were being courted by the ruling family of the Rwala, the Ibn Sha'alan, to persuade them to desert the Shammar and put themselves under the protection of the Ibn Sha'alan.

For a short time, power in the ruling family of the Ibn Rashid was usurped by the Obeid branch, descended from the brother of the first leader, Abdallah, who commanded the support of a majority of the Shammar. During their reign the emirate lost several more districts. The original ruling branch of the Ibn Rashid tried to regain their power and a bloody struggle followed, as a result of which the Abde (the tribe to which the ruling family belonged) and the Sinjara put themselves under the protection of the Ibn Sha'alan.

The Great War further divided the emirate which, together with the continuing war with the Saudis and declining revenues from trade and the Hajj, eventually brought about the end. The Rashidis were thrown back on Hayil, deserted by most of the tribes. In 1921 they were expelled, and that was the end of their emirate.

THE EMIRATE OF IBN RASHID AS A TRIBAL STATE

The emirate of Ibn Rashid developed from a tribal confederation with no overall leadership, to what can be defined as a "tribal state." It had a ruling dynasty and a developed administration concentrated in the Barzan palace, a capital that served as a service center for the population and a focus of power for the rulers and administration. It also had a standing army that managed to maintain law and order (according to Wallin [1979: 68], in Abdallah's time, "one may go from one end of their land to another, bearing his gold on his head, without being troubled with any questions").

At the same time, the tribal structure of society was maintained, actively used and manipulated by the rulers to organize their administration. The tribal territories remained intact and the tribes retained a high degree of autonomy in their economy, their social organization, and judiciary system. They could either give or refuse their support to the rulers, who would persuade them with presents and privileges. This interaction of features, characteristic for a state, and incorporating and exploiting elements that are typical for a tribal society, is what constitutes a "tribal state" or "tribal kingdom" (LaBianca 1999).

It is often assumed that the transformation from a tribal society into a higher level of integration and political organization is induced by external pressure (LaBianca 1999; al-Rasheed 1991: 48). In the case of the Shammar, the pressure came from three sides: the Wahabis, represented by the house of Ibn Sa'ud, the Egyptian army, and the Ottoman empire, all three of which strived for control of the region. The Shammar felt the pressure, and when a strong leader appeared on the horizon, they rallied behind him.

Also instrumental in the forging of a tribal state is the ascendancy of a strong leader at the right moment. Abdallah Ibn Rashid was such a leader. His success was based on a combination of personal courage, charisma, and political shrewdness at a turning point in history.[4] Originally, Abdallah's main asset was his military success, particularly in raids in which the other tribes were invited to take part — in return for a part in the booty. These raids and battles did much to cement the confederation. But he was also known for "his intrepidity and manliness, his strict justice, often inclining to severity, his unflinching adherence to his word and promise, of a breach of which he was never known to have rendered himself guilty; and, above all, to his unsurpassed hospitality and benevolence towards the poor, of whom, it was a well-known thing, none ever went unhelped from his door" (Wallin 1979: 68).

Bedouin tribes had no professional armies. Every man capable of carrying arms would take them up in raids and wars, afterward returning to his daily duties. Abdallah created a standing army, consisting largely of his followers, slaves, townsmen, and deserters from the Egyptian army. They functioned as permanent "peace-keeping forces" in the subjected domains and were sent on expeditions in the countryside to control the Bedouin and prevent their raiding. If and when tribesmen joined the forces, they did so for a raid or battle only, afterward returning to their tents.

Even though Hayil had been the place of residence for the Abda leaders for a long time, it was Abdallah who turned it into a center of power for the emirate. Euting, who visited the town in 1885, describes the various sectors: the Persian quarter, where Persian traders lived, and where he lodged with his companions; and a Slave quarter, which housed the 1,000 slaves that belonged to the emir (Euting 1914: vol. 1, 178–80). Numerous foreign traders lived in the town. International trade was actively concentrated in the town by the Rashidi rulers. Some three-hours' walk from Hayil was a much larger village, Kafar, which belonged to the Beni Tamim. Kafar was the main local market for basic supplies such as dates and cereals, which were exchanged for cattle, but was rarely visited by traveling tradesmen, who generally went to Hayil.

The decline in trade toward the end of the emirate, when most of the trade routes were diverted to Riyadh, had a major impact not only on the prosperity of the town but also on the loyalty of the tribes (Musil 1928b: 244). It has been shown above that the disintegration came when the tribes, one by one, deserted the ruling family and the confederation.

CONCLUSION

These case studies may throw light on events and processes in the early history of the Near East. The rapid rise and decline of small states and polities in periods of weak or absent overall government, and the role of the various tribal societies in these processes, may be highlighted and clarified by the events surrounding the rise of Akila Agha or the history of the Ibn Rashid emirate.

---

[4] Winder (1965: 101–05), largely basing himself on the historian Dari Ibn Rashid, gives an extensive description of the take-over of Ha'il by Ibn Rashid.

It is tempting to draw parallels between these nineteenth-century events and episodes from the history of the region. An obvious example is the kingdom of Mari, which seems to have intriguing parallels with the Ibn Rashid emirate, particularly according to the lucid analysis of Daniel Fleming (2004). However, exactly because it is so tempting, we need to be aware of the traps of drawing such parallels. The emirate of Ibn Rashid, with its combination of state elements and tribal structure, was a product of the nineteenth century. Its development was determined by nineteenth-century power relations and influenced by nineteenth-century technology and nineteenth-century religious ideas, all of which were very different from those of the Middle Bronze Age.

Nevertheless, the parallels should not be ignored: but they have to be treated with caution, used not so much as a model or a template with which to explain our ancient sources, but rather as a means to make sense of them. There is much in the underlying structure of subrecent and ancient societies that our historical sources show to be the same: the kinship structure and the role of the individual within it; the relation with territory; territorial competition; economic responses to seasonal and ecological vicissitudes; intertribal power structures and tribal autonomy within a hierarchical structure. The history of the Ibn Rashid emirate shows how a tribal state can function in practice, within one specific context. Different contexts would generate a different "set" of tribal and state elements, but the combination would still qualify as a tribal state.

The same approach can be applied to the case of Akila Agha. The concept of a "strong man," defying the existing powers with a small band of followers and creating an independent polity has been repeated in history over and over. David, king of Israel, and Idrimi of Alalakh are good examples. Both the stories of David and of Idrimi have been heavily edited and turned into heroic epics in which the elements of historic truth and the flights of heroic fancy have become intertwined.[5]

We may never unravel these elements or discover the historic truth about Bronze or Iron Age "heroes," but the history of Akila does throw light on the personality it takes to create a "strong man" and how they can shape and change society in a tribally organized environment.

---

[5] This form of hero-worshipping has remained common. William Palgrave (1866: 84) recorded stories about Abdallah Ibn Rashid, some twenty years after his death, that involved miraculous rescues by animals, and superhuman prowess, stories that had been "borrowed" from existing hero epics, and "applied" to the history of Abdallah, thus demonstrating how oral traditions can create heroes in a very short time.

BIBLIOGRAPHY

Abu-Lughod, Lila
    1986   *Veiled Sentiments: Honor and Poetry in a Bedouin Society*. Berkeley: University of California Press.

Ben-Arieh, Yehoshua
    1979   *The Rediscovery of the Holy Land in the Nineteenth Century*. Jerusalem: Magnes Press.

Blunt, Anne
    1881   *A Pilgrimage to Nejd, the Cradle of the Arab Race: A Visit to the Court of the Arab Emir, and "Our Persian Campaign."* 2 volumes. London: J. Murray.

Browne, William George
    1806   *Travels in Africa, Egypt, and Syria from the Year 1792 to 1798*. 2nd edition. London: Cadell & Davies, and Longman, Hurst, Rees & Orme.

Buckingham, James Silk
    1822   *Travels in Palestine Through the Countries of Bashan and Gilead, East of the River Jordan, Including a Visit to the Cities of Geraza and Gamala in the Decapolis*. 2 volumes. London: Longman, Rees, Hurst, Orme & Brown.
    1825   *Travels Among the Arab Tribes Inhabiting the Countries East of Syria and Palestine*. London: Longman, Rees, Hurst, Orme, Brown and Green.

Burckhardt, John Lewis
    1822   *Travels in Syria and the Holy Land*. London: J. Murray.
    1829   *Travels in Arabia, Comprehending an Account of Those Territories in the Hadjaz Which the Mohammedans Regard as Sacred*. 2 volumes. London: Henry Colburn.
    1830   *Notes on the Bedouins and Wahábys, Collected During His Travels in the East*. London: Colburn & Bentley.

Cohen, Amnon
    1973   *Palestine in the 18th Century: Patterns of Government and Administration*. Uriel Heyd Memorial Series. Jerusalem: Magness Press.

Doughty, Charles Montagu
    1921   *Travels in Arabia Deserta*. 2nd edition. New York: Boni and Liveright.

Eickelman, Dale F.
    1989   *The Middle East: An Anthropological Approach*. 2nd edition. Englewood Cliffs: Prentice-Hall.

Euting, Julius
    1914   *Tagbuch einer Reise in Inner-Arabien*. 2 volumes. Leiden: E. J. Brill.

Findley, Carter V.
    1986   "The Evolution of the System of Provincial Administration as Viewed from the Center." In *Palestine in the Late Ottoman Period: Political, Social, and Economic Transformation*, edited by David Kushner, pp. 3–29. Leiden: Brill.

Finn, James
    1878   *Stirring Times, or Records from Jerusalem Consular Chronicles of 1853 to 1856*. 2 volumes. London: C. Kegan Paul.

Fleming, Daniel E.
    2004   *Democracy's Ancient Ancestors: Mari and Early Collective Governance*. Cambridge: Cambridge University Press.

Hepworth Dixon, William
    1885   *The Holy Land*. London: Bickers & Son.

Irby, Charles Leonard, and James Mangles
  1868   *Travels in Egypt and Nubia, Syria, and the Holy Land, Including a Journey Round the Dead Sea, and Through the Country East of the Jordan.* New edition. London: John Murray.

LaBianca, Øystein S.
  1999   "Salient Features of Iron Age Tribal Kingdoms." In *Ancient Ammon*, edited by Burton MacDonald and Randall W. Younker, pp. 19–23. Studies in the History and Culture of the Ancient Near East 17. Leiden: Brill.

Lancaster, William
  1981   *The Rwala Bedouin Today.* Changing Cultures. Cambridge: Cambridge University Press.

Lawrence, T. E.
  1962   *Seven Pillars of Wisdom: A Triumph.* Reprint of 1926 original. Penguin Modern Classics 1696. London: Penguin Books.

Lynch, William Francis
  1849   *Narrative of the United States' Expedition to the River Jordan and the Dead Sea.* New and corrected edition. Philadelphia: Lea & Blanchard.

Macalister, R. A. S., and E. W. G. Masterman
  1906   "Occasional Papers on the Modern Inhabitants of Palestine." *Palestine Exploration Fund Quarterly Statement* 33–50: 110–14, 221–25, 286–91.

Musil, Alois
  1907–08   *Arabia Petraea.* 3 volumes. Vienna: Alfred Hölder.
  1927   *Arabia Deserta: A Topographical Itinerary.* 2 volumes. American Geographical Society, Oriental Explorations and Studies 2. New York: American Geographical Society.
  1928a   *The Manners and Customs of the Rwala Bedouins.* Oriental Explorations and Studies 6. New York: American Geographical Society.
  1928b   *Northern Nejd: A Topographical Itinerary.* American Geographical Society of New York, Oriental Explorations and Studies 5. New York: American Geographical Society.

Oppenheim, Max von
  1943   *Die Beduinen*, Volume 2: *Die Beduinenstämme in Palästina, Transjordanien, Sinai, Hedjaz.* Leipzig: Harrassowitz.

Palgrave, William Gifford
  1866   *Narrative of a Year's Journey Through Central and Eastern Arabia (1862–1863).* 2 volumes. 3rd edition. London: MacMillan & Co.

Palmer, Edward Henry
  1871   *The Desert of the Exodus: Journeys on Foot in the Wilderness of the Forty Years' Wanderings.* 2 volumes. Cambridge: Deighton, Bell, & Co.

Parkinson, Willam A., editor
  2002   *The Archaeology of Tribal Societies.* Archaeological Series 15. Ann Arbor: International Monographs in Prehistory.

al-Rasheed, Madawi
  1991   *Politics in an Arabian Oasis: The Rashidis of Saudi Arabia.* Society and Culture in the Modern Middle East. London: Tauris.

Robinson, Edward
  1856   *Later Biblical Researches in Palestine and in the Adjacent Regions: A Journal of Travels in the Year 1852.* London: John Murray.

Robinson, Edward, and Eli Smith

    1841   *Biblical Researches in Palestine, Mount Sinai, and Arabia Petraea: A Journal of Travels in the Year 1838*. 3 volumes. London: J. Murray

Rogers, Mary Eliza

    1989   *Domestic Life in Palestine*. Reprint of 1862 original. Kegan Paul International Paperbacks. London: Kegan Paul International.

Schumacher, Gottlieb

    1886   *Across the Jordan: Being an Exploration and Survey of Part of Hauran and Jaulan*. London: Bentley & Son.

Seetzen, Ulrich Jasper

    1854–59   *Reisen durch Syrien, Palästina, Phönizien, die Trans-Jordan Länder, Arabia-Petraea und Unter-Ägypten*. Berlin: G. Reimer.

Service, Elman R.

    1971   *Primitive Social Organization: An Evolutionary Perspective*. 2nd edition. Studies in Anthropology. New York: Random House.

Shryock, Andrew

    1997   *Nationalism and the Genealogical Imagination: Oral History and Textual Authority in Tribal Jordan*. Comparative Studies on Muslim Societies 23. Berkeley: University of California Press.

van der Steen, Eveline

    Forthcoming   "British Travellers in the Levant." In *The Ancient Levant*, edited by Katherine Wright, Kathryn Piquette, and Tina Paphitis.

Wallin, Georg August

    1979   *Travels in Arabia (1845 and 1848)*. Reprint of 1859 original. Arabia Past and Present Series 9. Cambridge: Oleander Press.

Winder, R. Bayly

    1965   *Saudi Arabia in the Nineteenth Century*. London: MacMillan.

7

SPECIFIC CHARACTERISTICS OF CHALCOLITHIC AND BRONZE AGE PASTORALISM IN THE NEAR EAST

ANATOLY M. KHAZANOV, UNIVERSITY OF WISCONSIN-MADISON

Despite a rather widespread opinion, pure pastoral nomadism, in all probability, was a rather late development in the Near East, and early pastoralists had to be quite different from their later counterparts. In fact, pastoralist economies embrace a large variety of different types and forms, ranging from a mixed economy to herdsman husbandry (often called transhumance in anthropological literature) and semi-sedentary pastoralism (agro-pastoralism), and ultimately to semi-nomadic pastoralism and pure pastoral nomadism as the most specialized form, which is characterized by the absence of agriculture, even as a supplementary and secondary activity (Khazanov 1994: 17–25). This is not an armchair classification. To a large extent, it is based on traditional criteria of pastoralists themselves. Thus, the Arabs differentiated between pure nomadic camel-breeders, sheep-breeders who were often semi-nomads, semi-sedentary pastoralists, and cultivators (Musil 1928: 44–45; Dickson 1951: 108–11; Coon 1976: 198–99).

Inasmuch as pastoral nomadism still lacks a generally accepted definition, I have to start with arguing my own understanding of this form of pastoralism. Some scholars pay particular attention to mobility and use the term "nomadism" very broadly. They consider to be nomads such economically different groups as wandering hunters and gatherers, mounted hunters (the Great Plains Indians of North America), all kinds of pastoralists, some ethno-professional groups like the Roma (Gypsies), the "sea nomads" of Southeast Asia, and even certain categories of workers in contemporary societies (the so-called industrial mobility). Others perceive pastoral nomadism as a socio-economic system and write about "the pastoral mode of production." Still others perceive it primarily in cultural terms of a specific way of living, lifestyle, world view, value system, et cetera.

These definitions, however, neglect or underestimate the economic side of nomadism which, in my opinion, is its most important aspect. Above all other characteristics, extensive mobile pastoralism is a specific type of food-producing economy that implies two opposites: between animal husbandry and cultivation, and between mobility and sedentism. The size and importance of cultivation in pastoralist societies, along with ecological factors, determines the degree of their mobility and may serve as a criterion for different varieties of pastoralism.

In this case, pastoral nomadism may be perceived as being based on the following main characteristics: (1) Pastoralism is the predominant form of economic activity; cultivation is either absent altogether or plays a very insignificant role. In the latter case it is small scale, occasional, and opportunistic. (2) Pastoralism has an extensive character connected with the maintenance of grazing or browsing herds all year round on natural pastures, without stables and without laying in fodder for livestock. (3) The pastoralist economy requires mobility within the boundaries of specific grazing territories, or else between such territories. (4) All, or at least the majority of the population, participates in these periodic migrations. (5) The traditional pastoralist economy was aimed at the requirements of subsistence. It was never profit oriented in a modern capitalist sense, although it was often considerably exchange-oriented. (6) Social organization of pastoral nomads is based on kinship, and, in the case of the nomads of the Eurasian steppes and the Near and Middle East, also on various segmentary systems and genealogies, whether real or spurious. (7) Pastoral nomadism implies certain cultural characteristics connected with its mobile way of life, sociopolitical peculiarities, and some other factors.

Any specialization implies dependency, and pastoral nomadism is no exception. It was an innovative solution for assimilating certain, previously underexploited ecological zones. The emergence of pastoralism, and later of pastoral nomadism, was a crucial moment in the spreading of food-producing economies in the arid and semi-arid zones of the oikumene, because for a very long time they had an advantage there over all other types of economic activity.

However, the shortcomings of pastoral nomadism are also quite evident. First, its specialization was principally different from that of industrial and even of traditional farming and urban societies. Since the internal division of labor within pastoral nomadic societies was undeveloped, their very existence implied division of labor between societies with different economies.

Second, unlike many types of farming which had the potential for diachronic technological development, in pastoral nomadism, once its formation was complete, the reproduction of similar and highly specialized forms prevailed. Its ecological parameters significantly limited the capabilities for economic growth through technological innovation; they also placed very serious obstacles to the intensification of production. Thus, even temporary maximization of the number of livestock could be achieved mainly by increasing the production base through territorial expansion.

Third, pastoral nomadism as an economic system was characterized by constant instability. It was based on a balance between three variables: the availability of natural resources (such as vegetation and water), the number of livestock, and the size of the population, all of which were constantly oscillating. The situation was further complicated because these oscillations were not synchronic, as each of the variables was determined by factors both temporary and permanent, regular and irregular. The simplest and best-known case of temporary imbalance was periodic mass loss of livestock and consequent famine due to various natural calamities and epizootic diseases. In other cases, stock numbers sometimes outgrew the carrying capacities of available pastures. It was just such cyclical fluctuations that maintained the long-term balance in the pastoral nomadic economy, however ruinous they might be in the short run. In other words, the balance was not static but dynamic.

Under these conditions, pastoral nomadic economies were never self-sufficient and could never be so. An integral part of nomadic ideologies was the antithesis between nomadic and sedentary ways of life, which to some extent reflected the differences in actual conditions of existence. On a symbolic level this antithesis played an integrating function within nomadic societies and a differentiating one regarding the sedentary world. Moreover, it created a negative view of the sedentary way of life. Nevertheless, pastoral nomadic societies always needed sedentary farming and urban societies for their efficient functioning and their very existence. Cereals and other farm products always formed an important part of their dietary systems. A diet of animal products alone, without any vegetable supplements, in principle cannot be healthy and balanced. Besides, meat is expensive, and its calorific yield is lower than that of grain; the Near Eastern pastoral nomads consume very little of it (Marx 1992: 256). In addition, the nomads also procured a substantial part of their material culture from sedentary territories.

The dependence of pastoral nomadic societies on the sedentary ones was noticed already by Ibn Khaldun:

> The desert civilization is inferior to urban civilization, because not all the necessities of civilization are to be found among the people of the desert .... While they [the Bedouin] need cities for their necessities of life, the urban population needs [the Bedouin] for convenience and luxuries. Thus, as long as they live in the desert and have not acquired royal authority and control of the cities, the Bedouin need the inhabitants of the latter (Ibn Khaldun 1967: 122).

Thus, pastoral nomads in the Near East, just like in other regions, always had to adapt not only to a specific natural environment but also to an external sociopolitical and cultural environment. The economic dependence of nomads on sedentary societies, and their various modes of adaptation to them, carried corresponding cultural implications. As the nomadic economy had to be supplemented with products of cultivation and crafts from external sources, so did nomadic culture need sedentary culture as a course, a component, and a model for comparison, borrowing, imitation, or rejection. Moreover, for efficient and long-term functioning pastoral nomads not only needed sedentary societies but complex and stratified ones capable of producing a regular surplus product and possessing mechanisms for its extraction, distribution, and redistribution.

The nomads understood very well certain social and military advantages of their way of life. At the same time, they also comprehended that their culture was less complex, rich, and refined than that of their sedentary counterparts. Their attitudes toward the latter had some similarities with the attitude toward the Western culture of many in the Third World: experiencing its irresistible glamor but, being outside its socioeconomic sphere, they reject it in principle, but strive to borrow and to benefit from some of its achievements. Interrelations of the pastoral nomads with sedentary societies ranged from direct exchange, trade mediation, and other related services, to becoming mercenaries, and to raiding, looting, blackmailing, occasional or more or less institutionalized subsidies and payments, regular tribute extraction, and direct conquests and subjugations.

It is no wonder then that pure nomads are recorded only in few regions of pastoralism (northern Eurasia, High Inner Asia, the Eurasian steppes, Arabia, the Sahara), and even in those regions pastoral nomadism usually co-existed with other forms of pastoralism. Semi-nomadic pastoralism was and is much more widespread throughout the world than pure pastoral nomadism. However, cultivation without irrigation is a risky endeavor in the dry zones and often results in overexploitation of productive ecosystems.

Be that as it may, not infrequently the paucity of the archaeological record and textual sources at our disposal poses many difficulties in the identification of exact historical and prehistorical pastoralist forms. Perhaps this is one of the reasons why archaeologists often prefer to use liberally generic terms like "pastoralism" or "pastoral nomadism," although in and of themselves these terms are too imprecise and unspecific.

Thus, Cribb (1991: 16) insists that the search for a fully nomadic society should be abandoned in favor of an approach which recognizes nomadic tendencies manifested in varying degrees in a wide range of societies and communities. To make pastoral nomadism, or pastoralism in general, an all-encompassing and ill-defined category may be convenient for some scholars because of the nature of archaeological sources, but this will hardly advance a better understanding of prehistoric pastoralism. In this case, the difference between cultivating and pastoralist societies, and specifics of the latter, become blurred. The elimination of the problem does not equal its solution.

Another danger is an excessive reliance on ethnographic models and analogies, because sometimes they may be misleading. Archaeologists studying the pastoralists of the Chalcolithic and Bronze Ages in the Near East (and in the Eurasian steppes as well) sometimes perceive them in the image of pastoral nomads of the early Iron Age and even of later historical periods. In the Near East, they perceive them in the image of the Bedouin. This is a certain anachronism that does not take into account significant differences between those pastoralisms which cannot be reduced only to chronology. Ethnographic materials may serve as parallels and as comparative data in our models of prehistoric and early historic past, but they should not be taken as direct analogies for archaeological reconstructions. The application of ethnographic parallels and analogies to early pastoral systems requires particular care in the Near and Middle East given the variety of systems found ethnographically even within the same environmental zones.

No wonder that the origin of specialized types of pastoralism, and especially of pastoral nomadism, is still one of the most difficult and disputed questions in the general study of mobile pastoralism. In most cases, scholars have to rely upon archaeological materials, which are often ambiguous and open to different interpretations. One can only hope that further investigations will be able to solve this question both by accumulating new data and by refining the methods of interpretation. Recently, some works pursuing this goal have been published, but these are still inconclusive (e.g., Bar-Yosef and Khazanov 1992; Barnard and Wendrich 2008; Cribb 1991; Harris 1996; Sadr 1991). As a result, while some scholars insist that pastoral nomadism in the ancient Near East emerged as early as the Neolithic (Cauvin 2000: 21–22), others, including myself, tend to view this hypothesis with skepticism.

Sherratt (1981, 1983) has provided serious arguments in support of his hypothesis that secondary products of sheep, goats, and cattle, including milk, hair, wool, traction, and pack transport, began to be utilized intensively only in the fifth and fourth millennia B.C. Only after that development could the early pastoralism begin to resemble the forms known to history, or used in ethnographic parallels. Still, this resemblance remained incomplete and sketchy.

Actually, many varieties of pastoralism were not completely divergent from cultivation, while pure pastoral nomadism without cultivation as a supplementary economic activity was not only a rare but also a late development. Attempts to prove its existence in the Eurasian steppes as early as the Chalcolithic and Bronze Age periods turned out to be unconvincing, and I strongly suspect that this is also true for the Near East. There is no reason to look upon the biblical Israelites, Amorites, Sutaeans, Arameans, and others as pure pastoral nomads, like the later Bedouin.

In my opinion, specialized forms of pastoral nomadism based on mounted animals (horses and camels) emerged only in the second half of the second and, especially, in the beginning of the first millennium B.C., although the use of those animals for traction and carrying loads, and as additional sources of meat and milk products had started much earlier (e.g., Sherratt 2003; Zarins 1989, and many others). In the Near East, horses were mainly used for military purposes: for chariot-driving and, later, for riding, and also for sports and hunting. Their possession had high prestige value, and they were important in military campaigns, but their meat and milk were not used for food. It was dromedaries that drastically increased the pastoralist mobility, opened new avenues of communication, including trade and natural resource exploitation, and allowed utilization of remote pastures, especially in the vast desert areas of the Arabian Peninsula and Sahara.

However, camel herds cannot be pastured together with small stock because they have a different pattern of movements and their feeding requirements are quite different from those of sheep and goats. A healthy camel's diet needs desert plants rich in salt. The laws of ecology in this respect are more immutable than many human laws. This state of affairs in itself had determined many characteristics of pastoralism in the Near East. The boundaries between pure pastoral nomadism and other forms of mobile pastoralism there appear to be more clear-cut than in many other regions.

Therefore, grazing territories available to the early sheep and goat pastoralists were more limited (Levy, Adams, and Muniz 2004: 71). To the best of my knowledge, so far no detailed estimate of carrying capacity of the pastureland has been made with regard to particular regions of the Near East, such as the Negev, Sinai, or Syrian steppe. Were it done, we would have a better comprehension of the maximal number of stock that those pastoralists had been able to maintain, especially if climatic fluctuations were also taken into account. Still, it is indicative that in the beginning of the twentieth century the Bedouin population of the Negev did not exceed a few thousand people. Their population explosion after the establishment of the State of Israel was mainly connected with extra-pastoralist factors. There are simply not enough pastures in Southwest Asia to practice a large-scale pastoralist economy without long-distance migrations, which are impossible without camels and horses.

One can only surmise that the Chalcolithic and Bronze Age pastoralists were few in number. The only pack and transport, and, perhaps, also riding animals at their disposal might be donkeys. It is true that a donkey can carry up to 100 kilograms, which is two to three times less than a camel can carry, but camels move faster and need less frequent feeding and watering (Davis 1987: 166). Across the world donkeys are transport animals of cultivators and semi-sedentary or semi-nomadic groups, like the *shawiyah* of the Arabs, but never of pure pastoral nomads. Donkeys are ill-suited for long-distance migrations. True Bedouin, or other nomads, do not ride donkeys; in their societies donkeys have very low status. The only exception that I know are the Air Tuareg, who occasionally use donkeys in certain areas with rough terrain.

For these reasons, the Chalcolithic and Bronze Age pastoralists were hardly able to move more than thirty kilometers from sources of water. Even working camels can go as far as 1,000 kilometers without water during the cool season, and in the summer they can go without drinking for eight to ten days (Gauthier-Pilters and Dagg 1981: 50–53). However, sheep have to be watered every four to five days even in cold weather. This allows them to graze in a radius of 20 miles from the water source. In warm weather, they require water every day and can graze no more than 10 or 12 miles from a well or other water source (Mitchell 1971: 70).

Correspondingly, the size of herds of the early pastoralists should be smaller, too. Besides, there is no convincing evidence that the donkey became widespread throughout the Near and Middle East much earlier than by the third (Davis 1987: 152; Ovadia 1992; cf., however, Epstein 1985) or the fourth millennium B.C. (Eliot Braun, pers. comm.).

I would also add that without riding animals and mounted warfare, the early pastoralists should lack a military advantage over their settled neighbors. Nomadic conquests and their consequences always attracted great attention. However, a related question has not been sufficiently addressed: why the pastoral nomads, with their limited human and economic resources, were, for centuries and even millennia, so strong in military respects? Each individual case certainly depended on many circumstances and deserves a special study, but in general terms the answer seems to be connected with the undeveloped division of labor and wide social participation, which provided the nomads with the edge in the military realm.

With but few exceptions, in sedentary states war was a specialized and professionalized sphere of activities. On the contrary, in pastoral nomadic societies, every male commoner was a warrior, most of them mounted ones. It is just these circumstances that allowed the nomads, despite their small number, to mobilize sufficiently large armies. Moreover, their specific way of life, among other things, implied the availability of a large number of horses and camels, and almost natural military training. In terms of individual skills, only the European knights and the Middle Eastern mamluks were a match to nomadic warriors; but the training and military equipment of the latter reflected many nomadic military traditions.

Things should be quite different in the Chalcolithic and Bronze Ages. Pastoralists of those periods did not have any military advantage over sedentary populations. Besides, they were smaller in number. Indeed, raiding and harassment cannot be excluded, but the cultivators could always reciprocate and do the same. Prior to the first millennium B.C., large-scale military invasions and conquests by pastoralists as explanatory hypotheses seem rather dubious. This circumstance should be taken into serious account in all discussions on the reasons for political changes in the ancient Near East, including the disintegration and collapse of some states and the ascent of others. In my opinion, the role of Chalcolitic and Bronze Age pastoralists in these processes should not be overestimated. In this regard they were also different from their later counterparts.

Remarkably, contrary to the Bedouin, in the early medieval period, contemporary writers disregarded small stock pastoralists even more than the rural population. Those pastoralists were always militarily weak and mostly dominated by sedentary people (Franz 2005: 65, 67). Until recently, the situation remained basically the same. In the Near and Middle East, mobility has long been a distinguishing criterion in tribal ranking. The "noble" status of tribes was connected to their range of movement and mobility, and to raising camels in the interior of the deserts. The herding of sheep and goats was considered an activity carried out by "inferior" tribal groups that had to stay near agricultural lands (Chatty 1996: 195–96, n. 7; Eickelman 1998: 78).

In all, I suspect that there had been few, if any, pure pastoral nomads in the Near East until the first millennium B.C. The majority had to supplement stock-raising with cultivation, procurement of natural resources, specialized production of secondary products (such as wool-production in the Assyrian steppes from the third millennium B.C.), intermediary exchange and trade, or other occupations, even more so than pastoralists in later periods. Their dependence on sedentary agricultural and urban groups and societies should also be even greater than in the later periods.

Ethnographic data on the pastoral nomads in Southwest Asia indicate that a family of five needs thirty to fifty head of small stock, or even more, in addition to a few animals for transportation and riding, which are also used as milk animals. Only in that case would they be capable of regularly selling or exchanging some pastoral products for agricultural ones and to lead a relatively well-to-do life by local standards. These circumstances made early pastoralism even less self-sustainable than its latter varieties. One may also wonder whether the subsistence economy of early pastoralists was always capable of producing regular surplus for exchange and trade on a scale that would compensate for the disadvantages of their specialization. The frequent movements of pastoralists out of the dry zones might be dictated by the necessity to obtain food and other products in the areas of cultivation. Their presence within the settled zone is a well-established fact (Rowton 1974, 1977). Actually, the overlap of farming and pastoral zones and their joint utilization, which has been recorded by scholars in modern times (e.g., in the countries of the Fertile Crescent, or in Arabia on the borders with Syria, and in Qasim) might be even more characteristic of the early pastoralism (Betts and Russel 2000: 31–32). These circumstances might also imply specific forms of political integration and socioeconomic structure; some of them could be quite different from those practiced since the first millennium B.C.

However, the migrations of pastoralists in the Near East in the third and second millennia B.C., as a rule, consisted of slow, gradual, and by no means centralized movement — sometimes infiltration, rather than rapid conquest — the more so because pastoralists there were the immediate neighbors of cultivated regions. One may assume that often not entire tribes (I use this term only tentatively because their existence cannot be taken for granted, and must be proven in any individual case), but their individual segments or other smaller groups were involved in such migrations (Klengel 1972: 37). In any case, migrations of pastoralists into cultivated areas might often result in their complete or partial sedentarization.

In many cases, we still cannot discriminate with certainty between seasonal camps, which were left by independent groups of mobile pastoralists, and those that belonged to groups who practiced a settlement-based transhumance (herdsman husbandry), in which only a part of the population carried out more or less specialized pastoral occupation. There is the risk that archaeological data on specialized segments of society (e.g., settlement-based transhumance and/or seasonally migrating shepherds) may be mistaken for a higher taxonomic unit, particularly if some cultural specifics are involved.

Many years ago, during my fieldwork among the groups that practiced transhumance in Central Asia and the Caucasus, I noticed that material culture of their shepherds, while they were away from permanent settlements, had many peculiarities in dwellings, dress, or utensils. At that time my knowledge of the early pastoralists in the Near East was next to nothing. Still, an idea crossed my mind that if future archaeologists, in addition to permanent settlements, study seasonal camps of those shepherds, without having any ethnographic information about them, they may well come to a conclusion that they are dealing with different ethno-cultural groups.

It is possible that in many cases Chalcolithic and Bronze Age pastoralist groups did not constitute separate societies, but rather were more or less specialized but integrated parts of larger agrarian-urban societies within a shared kinship idiom, sociopolitical organization, or other institutions. In any case, their interrelations with those societies might be quite different from interrelations maintained by the Bedouin in later historical periods. One may wonder whether even ideological opposition and symbolic dichotomy between nomadic and sedentary ways of life existed at that time at all.

BIBLIOGRAPHY

Bar-Yosef, Ofer, and Anatoly M. Khazanov, editors
1992   *Pastoralism in the Levant: Archaeological Materials in Anthropological Perspectives.* Monographs in World Archaeology 10. Madison: Prehistoric Press.

Barnard, Hans, and Willeke Z. Wendrich, editors
2008   *The Archaeology of Mobility: Old World and New World Nomadism.* Cotsen Advanced Seminars 4. Los Angeles: Cotsen Institute of Archaeology, University of California.

Betts, Allison V. G., and Kenneth W. Russell
2000   "Prehistoric and Historic Pastoral Strategies in the Syrian Steppe." In *The Transformation of Nomadic Society in the Arab East*, edited by Martha Mundy and Basim Musallam, pp. 24–32. Cambridge: Cambridge University Press.

Cauvin, Jaques
2000   "The Emergence of Agriculture, Animal Husbandry and Pastoral Nomadism in the Near East." In *The Transformation of Nomadic Society in the Arab East,* edited by Martha Mundy and Basim Musallam, pp. 17–23. Cambridge: Cambridge University Press.

Chatty, Dawn
1996   *Mobile Pastoralists: Development Planning and Social Change in Oman.* New York: Columbia University Press.

Coon, Carleton S.
1976   *Caravan: The Story of the Middle East.* New York: Huntington.

Cribb, Roger
1991   *Nomads in Archaeology.* New Studies in Archaeology. Cambridge: Cambridge University Press.

Davis, Simon J. M.
1987   *The Archaeology of Animals.* New Haven: Yale University Press.

Dickson, Harold R. P.
1951   *The Arab of the Desert: A Glimpse into Badawin Life in Kuwait and Sa'udi Arabia.* 2nd edition. London: George Allen & Unwin.

Eickelman, Dale F.
1998   *The Middle East and Central Asia: An Anthropological Approach.* 3rd edition. Upper Saddle River: Prentice-Hall.

Epstein, Claire
1985   "Laden Animal Figurines from Chalcolithic Period in Palestine." *Bulletin of the American Schools of Oriental Research* 258: 53–62.

Franz, Kurt
2005   "Resources and Organizational Power: Some Thoughts on Nomadism in History." In *Shifts and Drifts in Nomad-Sedentary Relations*, edited by Stefan Leder and Bernhard Streck, pp. 55–77. Nomaden und Sesshafte 2. Wiesbaden: Reichert Verlag.

Gauthier-Pilters, Hilde, and Anne I. Dagg
1981   *The Camel, Its Evolution, Ecology, Behavior, and Relationship to Man.* Chicago: University of Chicago Press.

Harris, David R., editor
1996   *The Origins and Spread of Agriculture and Pastoralism in Eurasia.* Washington, D.C.: Smithsonian Institution Press.

Ibn Khaldun
1967   *The Muqaddimah: An Introduction to History.* Translated from the Arabic by F. Rosental. Abridged and edited by N. J. Dawood. London: Routledge and Kegan Paul.

Khazanov, Anatoly M.
  1994   *Nomads and the Outside World.* 2nd edition. Madison: University of Wisconsin Press.

Klengel, Horst
  1972   *Zwischen Zelt und Palast: Die Begegnung von Nomaden und Sesshaften im alten Vorderasien.* Leipzig: Koehler & Amelang.

Levy, Thomas E.; Russel B. Adams; and Adolfo Munz
  2004   "Archaeology and the Shasu Nomads: Recent Excavations in the Jabal Hamrat Fidan, Jordan." In *Le-David Maskil: A Birthday Tribute for David Noel Freedman,* edited by Richard Elliott Friedman and William H. C. Propp, pp. 63–89. Biblical and Judaic Studies 9. Winona Lake: Eisenbrauns.

Marx, Emanuel
  1992   "Are There Pastoral Nomads in the Middle East?" In *Pastoralism in the Levant, Archaeological Materials in Anthropological Perspectives,* edited by Ofer Bar-Yosef and Anatoly M. Khazanov, pp. 255–60. Monographs in World Archaeology 10. Madison: Prehistoric Press.

Mitchell, W. A.
  1971   "Movement and Pastoral Nomadism: A Tentative Model." *Rocky Mountain Social Science Journal* 8: 63–71.

Musil, Alois
  1928   *The Manners and Customs of the Rwala Bedouins.* Oriental Explorations and Studies 6. New York: American Geographical Society.

Ovadia, Eran
  1992   "The Domestication of the Ass and Pack Transport by Animals: A Case of Technological Change." In *Pastoralism in the Levant: Archaeological Materials in Anthropological Perspectives,* edited by Ofer Bar-Yosef and Anatoly M. Khazanov, pp. 19–28. Monographs in World Archaeology 10. Madison: Prehistoric Press.

Rowton, Michel B.
  1974   "Enclosed Nomadism." *Journal of the Economic and Social History of the Orient* 17: 1–30.
  1977   "Dimorphic Structure and the Parasocial Element." *Journal of Near Eastern Studies* 36: 181–98.

Sadr, Karim
  1991   *The Development of Nomadism in Ancient Northeast Africa.* Philadelphia: University of Pennsylvania Press.

Sherratt, Andrew
  1981   "Plough and Pastoralism: Aspects of the Secondary Products Revolution." In *Patterns of the Past: Studies in Honour of David Clarke,* edited by Ian Hodder, Glynn L. Isaac, and Norman Hammond, pp. 90–104. Cambridge: Cambridge University Press.
  1983   "The Secondary Exploitation of Animals in the Old World." *World Archaeology* 15: 90–104.
  2003   "The Horse and the Wheel: The Dialectics of Change in the Circum-Pontic Regions and Adjacent Areas, 4500–1500 BC." In *Prehistoric Steppe Adaptation and the Horse,* edited by Marsha Levine, Colin Renfrew, and Katherine V. Boyle, pp. 233–68. McDonald Institute Monographs. Cambridge: McDonald Institute for Archaeological Research.

Zarins, Juris
  1989   "Pastoralism in Southwest Asia: The Second Millennium BC." In *The Walking Larder: Patterns of Domestication, Pastoralism, and Predation,* edited by Juliet Clutton-Brock, pp. 127–55. London: Unwin Hyman.

8

PREHISTORIC MOBILE PASTORALISTS IN SOUTH-CENTRAL AND SOUTHWESTERN IRAN

ABBAS ALIZADEH, UNIVERSITY OF CHICAGO

Many scholars consider pastoral nomadism as a late development (e.g., Bobek 1962; Garthwaite 1983; Lattimore 1951; Lees and Bates 1974), and nomads as essentially different and subservient to settled farming communities and urban centers (Cribb 1991: 14; Khazanov 1984, among others). For example, William Sumner (1986; see also Miroschedji 2003) considers the Proto-Elamite period (ca. 3000–2700 B.C.) as representing a tribal nomadic society, an adaptation that in Fars replaced the town/village settled farming economy. As I have argued elsewhere (Alizadeh 2006), specialized mobile pastoralism began much earlier in the fifth millennium B.C., was not limited to the Kur River Basin, and did not replace the farming economy, but the two modes of production were combined. From at least the fifth millennium B.C. on, the lowlands and highlands are to be understood not separately and in isolation, but as parts of an interacting system that successfully combined both regions' resources, providing a context within which the most durable political system in the ancient Near East, that is, the Elamite state, developed.

As just mentioned, pastoral nomads are usually viewed as being integrated into agrarian societies (Rowton 1973a–b, 1974, 1980; see also Irons 1979: 371; Lattimore 1962: 487; Zagarell 1982: 109), living on the margin of these societies, and dependent on them for their needed grains. Most scholars (e.g., Irons 1979; Khazanov, this volume; Krader 1979; Zagarell 1989: 300) also believe that state formation among the nomads is a secondary process, and that the military superiority of the historically known nomadic tribes was only made possible with the domestication of the horse and camel. Such views of nomads are probably true for the vast steppes of Central Asia, eastern Iran, the Negev, Arabia, the steppes of northwestern Mesopotamia and eastern Syria, and the Sahara, for example. But in regions with high population density, fertile alluvial plains, and intermontane valleys, such as lowland Susiana, highland Fars, and, to a lesser degree, Kerman (ancient Marhashi[?]) (Carter and Stolper 1984: 11; Steinkeller 1982, 2007), such views of nomads cannot be supported. In southwestern and south-central Iran, the trajectory of sociopolitical development may have been different.

It is the central theme of this paper that in southwestern and south-central Iran, settled farming villages were fully integrated into the nomadic pastoral economy and that farming villages became direct economic dependencies of the pastoral confederacies.[1] Another aim of this paper is to show that in many regions of Iran, separation of mobile pastoralism and settled farming is a false dichotomy and that they are two sides of the same coin (for similar view on the Mesopotamian social landscape, see Adams 1974). Furthermore, I believe that a

---

[1] For eastern Iran, see Lamberg-Karlovsky and Tosi 1989; for a generally high nomadic-sedentist interaction in the Middle East as opposed to Central Asia, see Patai 1951 and Bacon 1954.

diachronic analysis of the archaeology and history of southwestern and south-central Iranian plateau suggests the important role of the region's mobile pastoralists in state formation, and that the history of Elam may be better understood from the perspective of the highland nomads, who acted as the political force behind interactions between Mesopotamia and western Iran.

THE NOMADIC PASTORAL ECONOMY

Nomadic tribes loom large throughout Iranian history (Beck 1986, 2003; Garthwaite 1983; Lambton 1953). Prior to the establishment by Reza Shah of a nation-state with a centralized administration, there existed a number of mobile tribes in Iran (Sykes 1930), of which the most numerous, most powerful, and most sociopolitically complex were the Qashqai and the Bakhtiyari. The Qashqai occupied the southeastern Zagros Mountains in the northwestern and central regions of Fars province (Beck 1986, 2003), while the Bakhtiyari occupied the central Zagros Mountains and eastern part of Khuzestan (Garthwaite 1983).

In many ways, these mobile tribes differ fundamentally from similar tribes in the Middle East. First, despite their biannual migrations, they spend only a fraction of the year on the move. In their summer pastures in high altitudes, the Qashqai and the Bakhtiyari occupy regions that consist of both small fertile valleys and lands not suitable for grain agriculture and are thus sparsely populated. At elevations between 1500–2500 m above sea level, these fertile intermontane plains vary in area from 20 to 60 square km. In their winter pastures in Fars and lowland Khuzestan, the Qashqai and Bakhtiyari tribes stay put for several months in heavily populated and agriculturally rich areas. The Bakhtiyari and Qashqai khans used to reside in the middle of some of the intermontane valleys in relatively modest fortified centers surrounded by tents and a few small villages. The ruined remnants of most of these fortified centers can still be seen in many regions in Iran.

The Qashqai and Bakhtiyari also owned permanent and semi-permanent villages with solid architecture in both their summer and, especially, winter territories, in close proximity to the settled farmers and urban centers (Beck1986: 187; Garrod 1946; Garthwaite 1983: 30; Lambton 1953: 289). In addition to villages with solid architecture, they also owned large tracts of agricultural lands. In both summer and winter territories, the nomads would secure the crops in their own villages or in makeshift storage bins (Black-Michaud 1974: 221; Garthwaite 1983: 21, 40; Hole 1978: 152; Lambton 1953: 283; Stack 1882: 68, 100; Stark 1934: 160; Varjavand 1967: 14–20). By farming in both the highlands and lowlands, therefore, the nomads not only took full advantage of their environment, but they also solved the difficult problem of transporting large quantities of grain while migrating. Numerous nomadic people practice some farming, but in southwestern and south-central Iran it is much more widespread, more productive, and less risky. In general, the practice of farming allows for a greater independence and flexibility in adapting to various environmental and political calamities that are inherent in the pastoral mode of production and way of life (Spooner 1972).

SOCIOPOLITICAL STRUCTURE

The abundance of natural resources and regular social and economic interaction with settled farming communities have contributed to the sociopolitical structure of these two tribal confederations. Compared to other pastoral nomadic tribes in Iran such as the Komachi of Kerman (Bradburd 1994), or the Yamut Turkmen of northeastern Iran (Irons 1971, 1994), the Qashqai and the Bakhtiyari had developed a relatively complex social and political system that at times was only one level below the state, one may even say a state within a state (Barth 1961: 128–29; Beck 1986: 35, 52; Garthwaite 1983; Oberling 1974: 195). The military prowess of the two tribal confederations was clearly demonstrated when, in the 1920s and 1930s during the reign of Reza Shah, government troops with airplanes, artillery, and machine guns could not easily overwhelm and subdue these Zagros nomadic tribes, who were armed with only some World War I rifles, sling shots, and rocks. The built-in military superiority of the Zagros pastoralist tribes should be considered as another factor in their sociopolitical development. Studies suggest that the military advantage of nomadic groups alone can lead to extortion that in turn may lead to warrior-client interaction and subsequently to stratification and increased social complexity (Sáenz 1991). Because of the economic and demographic power of these confederacies and of those that preceded them, their strategic locations, and their relatively complex political hierarchy, they were feared by the state. This, of course, does not mean that various states in Iran were unable to control nomads and to extend state administration to include the nomadic regions. While highly centralized nation-states with modern technology would not tolerate autonomous areas in their territories, prior to the rise of the nation-states in the Middle East the cost of maintaining troops and administrative offices in tribal nomadic regions far exceeded its benefit (see Irons 1979: 372).

In agricultural regions pastoralists were, of course, numerically inferior to the settled farming communities; but even in the absence of horses, camels, and firearms this numerical inferiority does not necessarily translate into a military one in southwestern and south-central Iran. In the absence of state organizations, or in situations where organized military response cannot be immediate, fleet-footed mobile tribesmen can bring a settled regional population to submission by sheer harassment. It is easy to imagine the vulnerability of farmers during or immediately after the harvest; a small band of nomads could easily set fire to the harvest and disappear without a trace into the nearby mountains; similarly, flocks of sheep and goats sent by farmers to the nearby hills could easily be stolen. This type of hostility need not be routine; the threat of violence and the possibility of losing livelihood would create a strong strategic advantage for the nomads. Such intimidating strategy could be successful even within a decentralized state society.

The environmental features in southwestern and south-central Iran also create a context in which pastoral nomads can easily switch from mobile pastoralism to settled farming and vice versa. Barth (1961: 16–17) has shown how relatively easy it is for a pastoral nomad of Fars to become sedentary, and that this sedentarization does not necessarily develop into sedentism. The reverse, however, is difficult, if not practically impossible. Settled farmers with no tribal nomadic membership cannot simply become nomads, as some archaeologists like to think when a region seems to be suddenly depopulated. Most traditional village farmers in the Middle East own a few sheep and goats and perhaps a cow or two. In addition to the major problem of lacking the right to use pasture lands that belong to nomadic tribes, pastoral nomadism as a viable subsistence economy requires some sixty to one hundred animals, which is clearly beyond the reach of most settled farmers.

Farming by the rank-and-file Zagros nomads provided insurance against environmental calamities, but for the nomadic chiefs it had political advantage. The most important impediment to political and economic aspirations of nomadic chiefs lies in the special mode of nomadic production, over which the khans had little control or room for variation and expansion. This limitation would make it difficult for the khans to exercise tight political and economic control over their fluid subjects. It is therefore imperative, perhaps also visceral, for the nomadic khans to expand the nomadic production and demography bases to include farming and settled farmers. Once the khans have solved this problem through the acquisition of land and the integration of farming into pastoral economy as a much more secure and manageable source of surplus, they would then be in a position to use coercion that is necessary for the development and maintenance of state organizations.

Because this imperative is born out of the pastoral mode of subsistence and facilitated by a resource-rich environment, there is good reason to maintain that this same problem also existed for the early Zagros nomadic chiefs, as the nature of nomadic production with its limitations remains the same, regardless of sociopolitical changes and ethnic replacements that occurred in the region.

PREHISTORIC MOBILE PASTORALISM

With this short overview of some fundamental features of the two contemporary Zagros pastoral confederations, we may now turn our attention to a brief account of the archaeology and history of Mesopotamia and Iran before we address its implications. Ubaid 0 is the earliest phase of prehistoric settlement of southern Mesopotamia (table 8.1). From the beginning of this phase in the early sixth millennium until the end of the Ubaid 2–3 phases, Susiana and southern Mesopotamia shared a similar repertoire of material culture. By the beginning of the fifth millennium, the Ubaid and Middle Susiana cultures diverged and expanded beyond their old boundaries. Middle Susiana expanded into the central Zagros and Fars, and Ubaid into northern Mesopotamia, Syria, and southeastern Anatolia.

This trend continued until the end of the fourth millennium when a number of regional rival centers developed and vied for regional supremacy. The Akkadian dynasty unified the region, but was overthrown by the highlanders. After another period of political fragmentation, the Ur III dynasty once again unified the region only to be overthrown again by the highlanders. The same fate befell the Old Babylonian, the Kassite, the Neo-Assyrian, and the Neo-Babylonian dynasties. This basic trend of unification and fragmentation continued until the sixth century B.C. when Mesopotamia became part of the Achaemenid empire, with its homeland in highland Fars.

The events in lowland Susiana and the Zagros Mountains were vastly different. Lowland Susiana, in the province of Khuzestan, is often referred to as an extension of the Mesopotamian plain (figs. 8.1–2). This is, of course, true geologically and to some extent environmentally; both regions consist of flat alluvial fertile land with major rivers. Nevertheless, there are some major differences between the two regions that may have contributed to their specific long-term trajectories of cultural development. Lowland Susiana is much smaller in area and much closer to the mountains than southern Mesopotamia; the entire width of the plain can be crossed on foot in less than a day. The center of the plain used to be crisscrossed by many small natural streams that could be easily tapped for small-scale irrigation. In the upper Susiana plain, the pebbly soil is fed by underground springs and a high water table from the seepage of the Karkheh and the Dez, which made the area ideal for both pasture and low-risk dry farming (Adams 1962).

In the eastern sector of the plain, before the area was cut by numerous wadis that today mark the landscape, seasonal floodwaters were distributed widely across the area, making the practice of recessional farming possible. This area used to be the heart of the winter territories of some Bakhtiyari tribes, and compared with the lands on the west bank of the Karun, both ancient and modern-day settlements here are rare (Alizadeh et al. 2004). Lowland Susiana is also surrounded from the north, east, and southeast by a number of intermontane valleys with fertile soil and excellent winter pastures (figs. 8.1–2).

With this short introduction, we can now turn to the archaeology of the region. After its initial settlement in the seventh millennium B.C., the site of Chogha Mish grew to about 15 ha and became the largest site in the region in the Late Middle Susiana period (Ubaid 3) around 5200 B.C. (Alizadeh 2008b; Delougaz and Kantor 1996). By the end of the sixth millennium B.C., presumably because of a violent event that resulted in the destruction of its monumental building, Chogha Mish and a number of its satellites were abandoned for several generations. The first phase of Chogha Mish abandonment seems to have been a turning point in the region. After Chogha Mish was abandoned, Susa, on the opposite side of the plain, was settled and became the largest population center in Susiana, replacing Chogha Mish. During this phase (Late Susiana 2/Susa 1) there was a drop in the number of settlements, and Susa's contemporary settlements consisted of small villages scattered on the plain. The number of sites began to decrease steadily until the end of the fifth millennium B.C., when Susiana reached its lowest level of prehistoric population (table 8.1).

The demise of Chogha Mish in the early fifth millennium B.C. may have been the result of the initial conflict of interest between the pastoralist and farming communities of the region, as there was no contemporary nearby population center in the area that could have posed a serious danger to Chogha Mish. I mentioned before that eastern Khuzestan, where Chogha Mish is located, has been used by a large number of the Bakhtiyari tribes as their winter grounds. If this pattern, which is dictated by the region's geographical and geological features, obtained in late prehistoric times, then the unprecedented population growth in this region around the turn of the sixth millennium B.C. may have created increasing demands for more land to be brought under cultivation,[2] which in turn would have reduced vital resources such as pasture and fuel (wood/trees) and would hinder the movement of herds.[3] Or, Chogha Mish was abandoned because of major unresolved issues between the farming and pastoralist sectors of the society. Both these scenarios demand archaeological evidence for the existence of prehistoric nomads.

The abandonment of Chogha Mish around 5000 B.C. roughly corresponds with the appearance of the ancient nomadic cemeteries of Hakalan and Parchineh and with the diffusion of the specific early fifth-millennium B.C. black-on-buff pottery of southwestern Iran into highland Fars, the central Zagros region, and surprisingly enough into the Central plateau. Because I am interpreting these events as connected with the region's prehistoric pastoral nomads, we should now consider this evidence.

A series of surface surveys and limited excavations were conducted by Henry T. Wright (Wright 1984, 1979; Wright and Carter 2003; Wright and Redding 1979) in some Zagros intermontane plains as well as in the small marginal plains surrounding Susiana (Zagarell 1982). These highland valleys have always been part of the territories of the historically known pastoral nomads of the region and usually contained a modest mudbrick fortification with a few small villages scattered throughout (Zagarell 1982). Wright and his colleagues discovered a similar settlement pattern that may be classified as exhibiting a two-tiered settlement hierarchy.

---

[2] There is no evidence of irrigation canals in prehistoric Susiana. This implies dry farming which requires much more land under cultivation than in canal irrigation agriculture.

[3] See Hole 1978: 157 for the modern-day observations in Lurestan.

While the archaeological evidence from these surveys and limited excavations may be ambiguous, Vanden-Berghe's discoveries of a large number of isolated highland cemeteries are less controversial (fig. 8.3). Apart from numerous cemeteries dating from the fourth to the first millennia B.C. (Vanden-Berghe 1970, 1973a–c), in the early 1970s Vanden-Berghe discovered two fifth-millennium B.C. cemeteries of Hakalan and Parchineh in northern Deh Luran (Vanden-Berghe 1975, 1987; see also Haerinck and Overlaet 1996 for the final report).

In both cemeteries, pottery vessels were the most abundant objects. The pottery found in these tombs exhibit several regional styles with parallels in Mesopotamia, the central Zagros, highland Fars, and lowland Susiana. Other objects consisted of stone and copper mace-heads, stone vessels and tools, stone and shell beads, and seventeen stamp seals. The obvious continuum of the material richness of the tombs at both cemeteries is an indication of at least a level of socioeconomic differentiation, perhaps a ranked society. At this level of social evolution, the society that is represented in these cemeteries does not seem to have been much different from that of the contemporary lowlands.

The archaeological discoveries just mentioned are not the only lines of archaeological evidence we have to bear on the existence of prehistoric mobile pastoralists in highland Iran. In 2001, we selected a fifth-millennium B.C. site in the eastern part of Susiana for excavation (Alizadeh 2008a; Alizadeh et al. 2004). Known locally as Dar Khazineh (KS-1626) the site seemed to be a settlement of the fifth millennium with Late Susiana 1 and 2 ceramics. In this part of the Susiana plain, both prehistoric and historical sites are buried under some two meters of alluvial deposits (Alizadeh 2008a; Alizadeh et al. 2004). As a result, sites in this area are only visible in the exposed sections of the wadis that have sliced the plain. At the site of Dar Khazineh, we could see from the exposed sections that under some two meters of alluvial deposits the cultural layers continued down to the bed of the wadi. When we eventually cleared the sections, we realized that the depth of the mound ranged only from 30 cm to about 180 cm and that in some parts of the mound there was no cultural deposit at all. Excavations in our main trench revealed a peculiar depositional pattern not reported before from any other sites on the plain. Clayish and sandy sediments ranging from 5 to 10 cm thick were sandwiched between thin lenses of cultural deposits. We found no solid architecture except fragments of badly preserved pisé partition walls whose faces were usually burnt, similar to some contemporary fireplaces of the Bakhtiyari; we also found postholes, traces of ash, and fire pits. Excavations at other parts of the site revealed a single burial with grinding stone implements and a copper pin as well as a stone pavement similar to that from the nomadic site of Kalleh Nisar and to those that the nomads usually use in and around their tents to keep supplies and bedding dry (Vanden-Berghe 1970, 1973a; see also Hole 1978: 151 for the ethnographic evidence). The most revealing evidence of the ephemeral nature of the site was the fact that the surfaces on which such remains were found consisted of alluvial deposits. Thus, when, in the main area of excavation, we factored out the alluvial levels from the cultural lenses, we were left with just over 30 cm of deposit for perhaps the entire duration of the fifth millennium B.C. We believe that this type of stratigraphy can happen when a site lacks solid architecture and is repeatedly occupied (in winter) and left exposed to the elements for several months (in mid-spring and summer).

Earlier I mentioned that the ceramics of the Late Susiana 1 phase penetrated into highland Fars and the central Zagros area. This easily distinguished black-on-buff pottery was also found as far as the Central plateau (fig. 8.1). Here, side by side with the black-on-red Cheshmeh Ali pottery, genuine Late Susiana 1 black-on-buff ceramics were found on at least six mounds (Kaboli 2000). If the appearance of the typical southwestern ceramics in the

Central plateau had anything to do with trade in copper ore and semi-precious stones (lapis and turquoise), Zagros mobile pastoralists would have been in the best position to take advantage of it. Taken together, I propose the lines of evidence just described as strong archaeological clues for the existence of prehistoric nomadic groups in both the highlands and lowlands.

Having discussed the evidence of the ancient mobile pastoralists in prehistoric times, I now return to lowland Susiana. After the abandonment of Chogha Mish, Susa and its much smaller satellites enjoyed relative peace and prosperity until the end of the fifth millennium B.C., when Susa shrank to about 5 ha and the millennia-old tradition of painted pottery disappeared. By the middle of the fourth millennium, Susa grew again to about 20–25 ha and Chogha Mish was reoccupied with an area of about 17 ha; once again southern Mesopotamia and Susiana shared not merely a similar but an almost identical repertoire of material culture. By the end of the fourth millennium B.C., Susa again shrank to about 10 ha and Chogha Mish and most of its satellites were once again abandoned (for site size estimations, see Johnson 1973). The outcome of the fourth-millennium events in Susiana was drastically different from that in southern Mesopotamia, where major population centers developed into local polities and consolidated their hinterlands, while Susiana became almost completely depopulated.

The following period is known as Susa 3 or the Proto-Elamite period (Alden 1982, 1987; Miroschedji 2003). Despite the almost empty landscape, Susiana appears to be the center of a truly international exchange network system that included Fars, Kerman, Sistan, and the western Central plateau (Lamberg-Karlovsky and Tosi 1989). The pottery of this period later developed strong similarities with those from the central Zagros area, Deh Luran (Neely and Wright 1994), and the Hamrin and Diyala regions (see Haerinck 1986; Carter 1986), all primary nomadic regions in historical periods.

The evidence of an unprecedented network of exchange that was recorded in the Proto-Elamite script with its center at Susa is in sharp contrast to the settlement pattern in the lowlands and highland Fars. John Alden (1982, 1987) once suggested that during the Proto-Elamite period, Susa was a port of trade with Mesopotamia and the highlands. While this may well be the case, the forces of the production and the administrative hierarchy presiding over it remains to be addressed. Given the long-term cultural development in southwestern Iran as outlined here, a pastorally based polity could be the most likely force capable of producing sheep, goats and their products, and man-power, as well as conducting or controlling inter-regional trade. But we still have to account for the bulk of grains as listed in the tablets (Dahl 2005). As mentioned before, it is perfectly possible for the Zagros mobile pastoralists to engage in cereal farming without being attached to fixed settlements. It is, therefore, logical to assume that the large quantities of grains recorded in the Proto-Elamite tablets from Susa were produced by the Zagros agro-pastoralists.

The Proto-Elamite period coincides with the rise of Early Dynastic states in Mesopotamia. These, and later the Akkadian and Ur III states, intermittently controlled lowland Susiana, while the nascent Elamite polities were consolidating in the highlands. The highlanders eventually overthrew the Akkadian and Ur III empires, but it was not until the fourteenth century B.C. that a truly national Elamite state emerged that effectively united both the lowlands and highlands. For the first time, the Elamites used their own language and script, invested heavily in large-scale irrigation projects, and erected monumental buildings throughout their territories. Nevertheless, the known Elamite texts are highly laconic and rarely contain details and historical information. Furthermore, in the Elamite world there is no evidence of poetry, hymns, mythology, legends, chronicles, or law codes, to name a few urban cultural productions. The absence of these important urban activities in Elamite centers does not, of course, mean their absence from the Elamite society, in which oral tradition must have prevailed, just as in any non-urban, particularly pastoral society.

SUMMARY

In summary, I argue that the lowlands and highlands are to be understood not separately and in isolation, but as parts of an interacting adaptive system that successfully combined both regions' resources. I also hypothesize that the political hierarchy of that system was drawn from the highlands.

Mesopotamian sources make it clear that from at least the beginning of historical periods, it was the various highland, not lowland, polities who had both hostile and non-hostile contact with Mesopotamian states. Nevertheless, the only model for primary state formation in southwestern Iran has lowland Susiana as the locus of this development (Johnson 1973; Wright and Johnson 1975). Yet, the long-term pattern of cultural and political development in western Iran, and the fact that the landscape of Mesopotamian contact with the east was populated with highland polities, means that there is no overwhelming theoretical reason the problem of state formation in western Iran should not be investigated in the highlands.

Starting in the third millennium B.C., Susiana as a region became the bone of contention between the highlands and southern Mesopotamian states. Susiana was important for the Zagros nomads, both as the ideal pasture grounds and as the largest and most fertile contiguous region in Iran. Control of Susiana with its human and natural resources was necessary for the highland polities to expand their military and political control in the region and beyond. Once the unification of the Zagros highlands and Susiana lowlands was achieved, the relentless struggle for the control of lowland Mesopotamia began in earnest. This struggle lasted until 538 B.C. when lowland Mesopotamia and highland Iran were finally integrated under the Persian Achaemenids.

DATE B.C.	SUSIANA	FARS	CENTRAL PLATEAU	MESOPOTAMIA
1000–500	Late Elamite	Shogha/Teimuran	Iron II/III	Neo-Babylonian
1500–1000	Mid-Elamite	Kaftari/Qale	Iron I	Kassite
1900–1550	Old Elamite (Sukkalmah)	Kaftari Kaftari	Late Bronze	Old Babylonian
2100–1900	Old Elamite (Shimashki)	Kaftari		Isin/Larsa
2350–2100	Old Elamite (Awan)	*Gap*	Middle Bronze	Ur III Akkadian
2600–2350	? (Early Dynastic)	*Gap*		Early Dynastic
3000–2600	Proto-Elamite	Late Banesh	Early Bronze	
3900–3000	Susa II (Uruk)	Lapui/Early Banesh		Uruk
4000–3900	Terminal Susa I	Lapui	Late Plateau	Terminal Ubaid
4500–4000	Late Susiana 2 (Susa I)	Bakun A		Ubaid 4
4800–4500	Late Susiana 1	Gap/Bakun B2	Middle Plateau	
5400–4800	Late Middle Susiana	Bakun B2	(Cheshme Ali)	Ubaid 3
5600–5400	Early Middle Susiana	Bakun B1	Early Plateau	Ubaid 2
5800–5600	Early Susiana			Ubaid 1
			Archaic Plateau	
		Jari B		Ubaid 0
6100–5800	Archaic Susiana 3			Hassuna
6300–6100	Archaic Susiana 2	Mushki		Jarmo
6500–6300	Archaic Susiana 1			
		Arsanjan Cave Site		
6700–6500	Archaic Susiana 0			

Table 8.1. Relative chronology of ancient sites in Southwest Asia

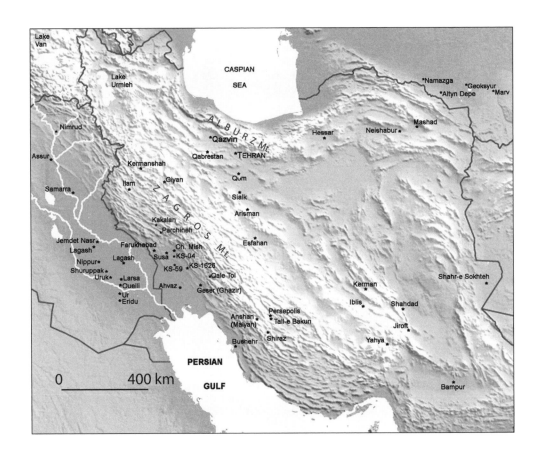

Figure 8.1. Map of Southwest Asia

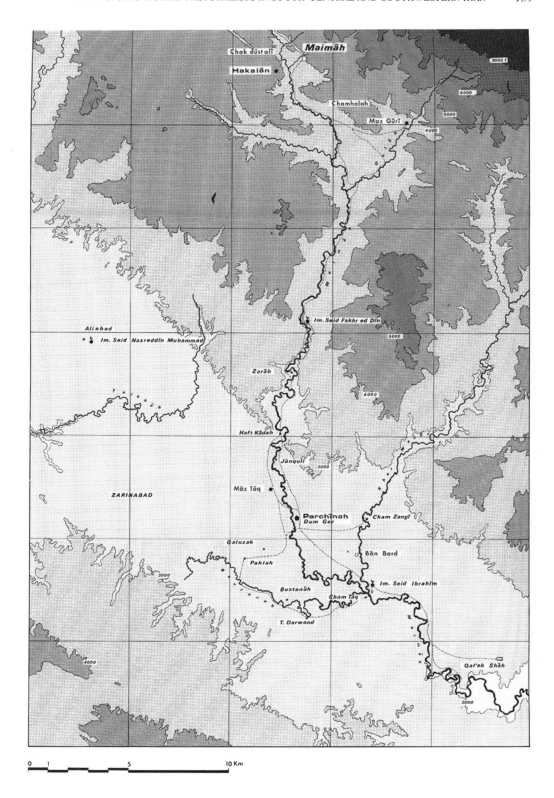

Figure 8.2. Map of Deh Luran (Pusht-e Kuh) showing the locations of Hakalan and Parchineh
(with author's permission)

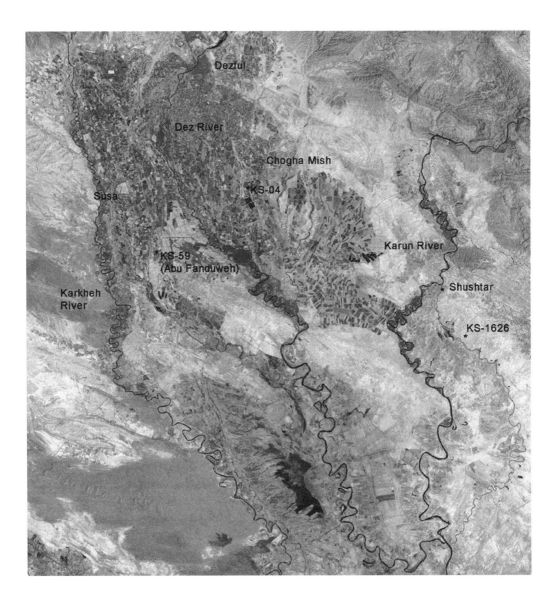

Figure 8.3. Satellite image of Lowland Susiana

BIBLIOGRAPHY

Adams, Robert McC.

1962   "Agriculture and Urban Life in Early Southwestern Iran." *Science* 136: 109–22.

1968   "Early Civilizations, Subsistence, and Environment." In *Man in Adaptation: The Biosocial Background*, edited by Yehudi A. Cohen, pp. 363–77. Chicago: Aldine.

1974   "The Mesopotamian Social Landscape: A View from the Frontier." In *Reconstructing Complex Societies: An Archaeological Colloquium*, edited by Charlotte B. Moore, pp. 1–20. Supplement to the Bulletin of the American Schools of Oriental Research 20. Cambridge: American Schools of Oriental Research.

Alden, John R.

1982   "Trade and Politics in Proto-Elamite Iran." *Current Anthropology* 23: 613–40.

1987   "The Susa III Period." In *The Archaeology of Western Iran: Settlement and Society from Prehistory to the Islamic Conquest*, edited by Frank Hole, pp. 157–70. Smithsonian Series in Archaeological Inquiry. Washington, D.C.: Smithsonian Institution Press.

Alizadeh, Abbas

2006   *The Origins of State Organizations in Prehistoric Highland Fars, Southern Iran: Excavations at Tall-e Bakun*. Oriental Institute Publications 128. Chicago: The Oriental Institute.

2008a   "Archaeology and the Question of Mobile Pastoralism in Late Prehistory." In *The Archaeology of Mobility: Old World and New World Nomadism*, edited by Hans Barnard and Willeke Z. Wendrich, pp. 78–114. Cotsen Advanced Seminars 4. Los Angeles: Cotsen Institute of Archaeology, University of California.

2008b   *Chogha Mish*, Volume 2: *The Development of a Prehistoric Regional Center in Lowland Susiana, Southwestern Iran: Final Report on the Last Six Seasons of Excavations, 1972–1978*. Oriental Institute Publications 130. Chicago: The Oriental Institute.

Alizadeh, Abbas; Nicholas Kouchoukos; Tony Wilkinson; Andrew Bauer; and Marjan Mashkour

2004   "Preliminary Report on the Joint Iranian-American Landscape and Geomorphological Reconnaissance in the Susiana Plain, September–October 2002." *Paléorient* 30: 69–88.

Bacon, Elizabeth

1954   "Types of Pastoral Nomadism in Central and Southwest Asia." *Southwestern Journal of Anthropology* 10: 44–68.

Barth, Fredrik

1961   *Nomads of South Persia: The Basseri Tribe of the Khamseh Confederacy*. London: Allen & Unwin.

Beck, Lois

1986   *The Qashqa'i of Iran*. New Haven: Yale University Press.

2003   "Qashqa'i Nomadic Pastoralists and Their Use of Land." In *Yeki bud, Yeki nabud: Essays on the Archaeology of Iran in Honor of William M. Sumner*, edited by Naomi F. Miller and Kamyar Abdi, pp. 289–304. Cotsen Institute of Archaeology Monograph 48. Los Angeles: Cotsen Institute of Archaeology, University of California.

Black-Michaud, Jacob

1974   "An Ethnographic and Ecological Survey of Luristan, Western Persia: Modernization in a Nomadic Pastoral Society." *Middle Eastern Studies* 10: 211–28.

Bobek, Hans

1962   "The Main Stages in Socio-Economic Evolution from a Geographical Point of View." In *Readings in Cultural Geography*, edited by Philip L. Wagner and Marvin W. Mikesell, pp. 218–47. Chicago: University of Chicago Press.

Bradburd, Daniel
    1994   "Historical Bases of the Political Economy of Kermani Pastoralists: Tribal and
                World Markets in the Nineteenth and Early Twentieth Centuries." In *Pastoralists at
                the Periphery,* edited by Claudia Chang and Harold A. Koster, pp. 42–61. Tucson:
                University of Arizona Press.

Carter, Elizabeth
    1986   "The Piedmont and the Pusht-I Kuh in the Early Third Millennium BC." In *Préhistoire
                de la Mésopotamie: La Mésopotamie préhistorique et l'exploration récente du Djebel
                Hamrin* (Paris, 17–19 December 1984), edited by Jean-Louis Huot, pp. 73–83. Paris:
                Éditions du Centre National de la Recherche Scientifique.

Carter, Elizabeth, and Matthew W. Stolper
    1984   *Elam: Surveys of Political History and Archaeology.* University of California
                Publications, Near Eastern Studies 25. Berkeley: University of California Press.

Cribb, Roger
    1991   *Nomads in Archaeology.* New Studies in Archaeology. Cambridge: Cambridge
                University Press.

Dahl, Jacob
    2005   "Animal Husbandry in Susa during the Proto-Elamite Period." *Studi Micenei ed
                Egeo-Anatolici* 47: 81–134.

Delougaz, Pinhas, and Helene J. Kantor
    1996   *Chogha Mish,* Volume 1: *The First Five Seasons of Excavations 1961–1971.* Edited
                by Abbas Alizadeh. Oriental Institute Publications 101. Chicago: The Oriental
                Institute.

Garrod, Oliver
    1946   "The Qashqai Tribe of Fars." *Journal of the Royal Central Asiatic Society* 33:
                293–306.

Garthwaite, Gene R.
    1983   *Khans and Shahs: A Documentary Analysis of the Bakhtyari in Iran.* Cambridge:
                Cambridge University Press.

Haerinck, Ernie
    1986   "The Chronology of Luristan, Pusht-I Kuh in the Late Fourth and First Half of the
                Third Millennium BC." In *Préhistoire de la Mésopotamie: La Mésopotamie préhisto-
                rique et l'exploration récente du Djebel Hamrin* (Paris, 17–19 December 1984), edited
                by Jean-Louis Huot, pp. 55–72. Paris: Éditions du Centre National de la Recherche
                Scientifique.

Haerinck, Ernie, and Bruno Overlaet
    1996   *The Chalcolithic Period Parchinah and Hakalān: Belgian Archaeological Mission in
                Iran: The Excavations in Luristan, Pusht-i Kuh (1965–1979).* Luristan Excavation
                Documents 1. Brussels: Royal Museum of Art and History.

Hole, Frank
    1978   "Pastoral Nomadism in Western Iran." In *Explorations in Ethnoarchaeology,* edited
                by Richard A. Gould, pp. 127–67. School of American Research Advanced Seminar
                Series. Albuquerque: University of New Mexico Press.

Irons, William
    1971   "Variation in Political Stratification among the Yamut Turkmen." *Anthropological
                Quarterly* 44: 143–56.
    1979   "Political Stratification among Pastoral Nomads." In *Pastoral Production and
                Society/Production pastorale et société* (Proceedings of the International Meeting
                on Nomadic Pastoralism in Paris, 1–3 December 1976), edited by Equipe écologie et

anthropologie des sociétés pastorales, pp. 361–74. Cambridge: Cambridge University Press.

1994   "Why Are the Yamut Not More Stratified?" In *Pastoralists at the Periphery: Herders in a Capitalist World,* edited by Claudia Chang and Harold A. Koster, pp. 175–96. Tucson: University of Arizona Press.

Johnson, Gregory A.

1973   *Local Exchange and Early State Development in Southwestern Iran.* Anthropological Papers 51. Ann Arbor: Museum of Anthropology, University of Michigan.

Kaboli, Mir Abedin

2000   *Archaeological Survey at Qomrud.* Tehran: Iranian Cultural Heritage Organization. [in Persian]

Khazanov, Anatoly M.

1984   *Nomads and the Outside World.* Cambridge Studies in Social Anthropology 44. Cambridge: Cambridge University Press.

Krader, Lawrence

1979   "The Origin of the State among the Nomads of Asia." In *Pastoral Production and Society/Production pastorale et société* (Proceedings of the International Meeting on Nomadic Pastoralism in Paris, 1–3 December 1976), edited by Equipe écologie et anthropologie des sociétés pastorales, pp. 221–34. Cambridge: Cambridge University Press.

Lamberg-Karlovsky, Carl C., and Maurizio Tosi

1989   "The Proto-Elamite Community at Tepe Yahya: Tools of Administration and Social Order." In *South Asian Archaeology 1985: Papers from the Eighth International Conference of South Asian Archaeologists in Western Europe* (Denmark, 1–5 July 1985), edited by Karen Frifelt and Per Sørenson, pp. 104–13. Occasional Papers of the Scandanavian Institute of Asian Studies 4. London: Cruzon Press.

Lambton, Ann K. S.

1953   *Landlord and Peasant in Persia: A Study of Land Tenure and Land Revenue Administration.* London: Oxford University Press.

Lattimore, Owen

1951   *Inner Asian Frontiers of China.* 2nd edition. American Geographical Society of New York Research Series 21. New York: Capitol Publishing.

1962   *Studies in Frontier History: Collected Papers, 1928–1958.* London: Oxford University Press.

Lees, Susan, and Daniel G. Bates

1974   "The Origins of Specialized Nomadic Population: A Systemic Model." *American Antiquity* 39: 187–93.

Miroschedji, Pierre de

2003   "Susa and the Highlands: Major Trends in the History of Elamite Civilization." In *Yeki bud, Yeki nabud: Essays on the Archaeology of Iran in Honor of William M. Sumner*, edited by Naomi F. Miller and Kamyar Abdi, pp. 17–38. Cotsen Institute of Archaeology Monograph 48. Los Angeles: Cotsen Institute of Archaeology, University of California.

Neely, James A., and Henry T. Wright

1994   *Early Settlement and Irrigation on the Deh Luran Plain: Village and Early State Socities in Southwestern Iran.* Technical Report of the University of Michigan, Museum of Anthropology 26. Ann Arbor: University of Michigan Press.

Oberling, Pierre

1974   *The Qashqai Nomads of Fars.* Near and Middle East Monographs 6. The Hauge: Mouton.

Patai, Raphael
 1951   "Nomadism: Middle Eastern and Central Asian." *Southwest Journal of Anthropology*
      7: 401–14.

Rowton, Michael B.
 1973a   "Autonomy and Nomadism in Western Asia." *Orientalia* 42: 247–58.
 1973b   "Urban Autonomy in a Nomadic Environment." *Journal of Near Eastern Studies* 32:
      201–15.
 1974   "Enclosed Nomadism." *Journal of Economic and Social History of the Orient* 17:
      1–30.
 1980   "Pastoralism and the Periphery in Evolutionary Perspective." In *L'archéologie de
      l'Iraq du début de l'époque néolithique à 333 avant notre ère*, pp. 291–301. Colloque
      Internationaux du Centre National de la Recherche Scientifique 580. Paris: Éditions
      du Centre National de la Recherche Scientifique.

Sáenz, Candelario
 1991   "Lords of the Waste: Predation, Pastoral Production, and the Process of Stratification
      among the Eastern Twaregs." In *Chiefdoms: Power, Economy, and Ideology*, edited
      by Timothy K. Earle, pp. 100–18. School of American Research Advanced Seminar
      Series. Cambridge: Cambridge University Press.

Spooner, Brian
 1972   "Iranian Desert." In *Population Growth: Anthropological Implications*, edited by
      Brian Spooner, pp. 245–68. Cambridge: M.I.T. Press.

Stack, Edward
 1882   *Six Months in Persia*. 2 volumes. New York: G. P. Putnam's Sons.

Stark, Freya
 1934   *The Valleys of the Assassins and Other Persian Travels*. London: John Murray.

Steinkeller, Piotr
 1982   "The Question of Marhasi: A Contribution to the Historical Geography of Iran in the
      Third Millennium B.C." *Zeitschrift für Assyriologie* 72: 237–65.
 2007   "New Light on Šimaški and Its Rulers." *Zeitschrift für Assyriologie* 97: 215–32.

Stolper, Matthew W.
 1982   "On the Dynasty of Simaski and the Early Sukkalmahs." *Zeitschrift für Assyriologie*
      72: 42–67.

Sumner, William M.
 1986   "Proto-Elamite Civilization in Fars." In *Ǧamdat Nasr: Period or Regional Style?*
      (Papers given at a Symposium, Tübingen, November 1983), edited by Uwe Finkbeiner
      and Wolfgang Rölling, pp. 199–211. Beihefte zum Tübinger Atlas des Vorderen
      Orients, Reihe B, Geisteswissenschaften 62. Wiesbaden: Ludwig Reichert.

Sykes, Percy Molesworth
 1930   *A History of Persia*. 2 volumes. 3rd edition. London: MacMillan.

Vanden-Berghe, Louis
 1970   "La nécropole de Kalleh Nisar." *Archéologia* 32: 64–73.
 1973a   "Excavations in Luristan, Kalleh Nisar." *Bulletin of the Asia Institute* 3: 25–56.
 1973b   "Le Lurestan avant l'âge du Bronze: Le nécropole de Hakalan." In *Proceedings of the
      Second Annual Symposium on Archaeological Research in Iran*, pp. 66–79. Tehran:
      Iranbastan Museum.
 1973c   "Le Luristan avant l'âge du Bronze: La nécropole de Hakalan." *Archéologia* 57:
      49–58.
 1975   "Luristan. La nécropole de Dum-Gar-Parchinah." *Archéologia* 79: 46–61.

1987   "Luristan, Pusht-i-Kuh au chalcolithique moyen (les nécropoles de Parchinah et Hakalān)." In *Préhistoire de la Mésopotamie: La Mésopotamie préhistorique et l'exploration récente du Djebel Hamrin* (Paris, 17–19 December 1984), edited by Jean-Louis Huot, pp. 91–106. Colloque international du Centre National de la Recherche Scientifique. Paris: Éditions du Centre National de la Recherche Scientifique.

Varjavand, Parviz
1967   *Bamadi, Tayefe-i as Bakhtiari*. Tehran: Tehran University. [in Persian]

Wright, Henry T.
1981   *An Early Town on the Deh Luran Plain: Excavations at Tepe Farukhabad*. Memoirs of the Museum of Anthropology 13. Ann Arbor: Museum of Anthropology, University of Michigan.

1984   "Prestate Political Formation." In *On the Evolution of Complex Societies: Essays in Honor of Harry Hoijer, 1982*, edited by Timothy Earle, pp. 41–78. Other Realities 6. Malibu: Undena Publications.

Wright, Henry T., editor
1979   *Archaeological Investigations in Northeastern Xuzestan, 1976*. University of Michigan Technical Reports 10; Research Reports in Archaeology 5; Survey Report, Iranian Center for Archaeological Research 1. Ann Arbor: Museum of Anthropology, University of Michigan.

Wright, Henry T., and Elizabeth Carter
2003   "Archaeological Survey on the Western Ram Hormuz Plain." In *Yeki bud, Yeki nabud: Essays on the Archaeology of Iran in Honor of William M. Sumner*, edited by Naomi F. Miller and Kamyar Abdi, pp. 61–82. Cotsen Institute of Archaeology Monograph 48. Los Angeles: Cotsen Institute of Archaeology, University of California.

Wright, Henry T., and Gregory Johnson
1975   "Population, Exchange, and Early State Formation in Southwestern Iran." *American Anthropologist* 77: 267–89.

Wright, Henry T., and Richard Redding
1979   "Test Excavations at Tappeh Sabz 'Ali Zabarjad." In *Archaeological Investigations in Northeastern Xuzestan, 1976*, edited by Henry T. Wright, pp. 38–42. University of Michigan Technical Reports 10; Research Reports in Archaeology 5; Survey Report, Iranian Center for Archaeological Research 1. Ann Arbor: Museum of Anthropology, University of Michigan.

Zagarell, Allen
1982   *The Prehistory of the Northeast Bahtiyari Mountains, Iran: The Rise of a Highland Way of Life*. Beihefte zum Tübinger Atlas des Vorderen Orients, Reihe B, Geisteswissenschaften 42. Wiesbaden: Ludwig Reichert.

1989   "Pastoralism and the Early State in Greater Mesopotamia." In *Archaeological Thought in America*, edited by Carl C. Lamberg-Karlovsky, pp. 280–301. Cambridge: Cambridge University Press.

9

PASTORAL NOMADS AND IRON AGE METAL PRODUCTION IN ANCIENT EDOM

THOMAS E. LEVY, UNIVERSITY OF CALIFORNIA, SAN DIEGO

INTRODUCTION

Most scholars working on the problem of the archaeology and history of Iron Age Edom, its heartland being in present-day southern Jordan, are in agreement that a kind of "nomadic imperative" has operated in the evolution of complex societies in this region since the second millennium B.C. until the early twentieth century A.D. (Bienkowski 1992; Bienkowski and van der Steen 2001; Kitchen 1992; Knauf-Belleri 1995; LaBianca 1999; LaBianca and Younker 1995; Levy 2002; Levy 2004; MacDonald 2000; Porter 2004). This means that there is general recognition that during the course of the past three millennia, the socioeconomic structure of nomadism has provided an important, if not special, adaptive advantage to life in this semi-arid and arid region of the southern Levant. However, there is a tendency among these researchers to disagree about the social evolutionary trajectory that the Iron Age nomadic communities of this region, generally referred to as "Edomites," took to achieve increasingly complex levels of social organization to the tipping point of being recognized in historical sources as a "kingdom" or in anthropological circles as an archaic state (cf. Feinman and Marcus 1998). In this paper, I explore three interrelated anthropological processes in conjunction with the most recent Iron Age archaeological fieldwork in southern Jordan to help bring the scholarly community into closer agreement on the role of nomadism in the formation of complex societies in the arid zone of Edom. These models include:

1) Ethnogenesis rooted in the works of G. Emberling (Emberling 1997; Emberling and Yoffee 1999), A. Faust (Faust 2006), myself (Levy and Holl 2002), and others.

2) Political ecology where access to natural resources plays an important role in structuring the political and economic life of societies. The political ecology model was developed by anthropologists such as J. Cole and E. R. Wolf (Cole and Wolf 1999) based on the earlier cultural ecology model of J. Steward (Steward 1968), R. Rappaport (Rappaport 1969), and others where the material conditions of society, especially how food and other basic resources are procured, help structure society. The political ecology model has evolved further through application in other fields including political science and geography.

3) What we refer to here as an "oscillating tribal segmentary social system" model. The latter model builds on the work of R. Tapper (Tapper 1990), T. Earle (Earle 1991a; Earle 1991b; Earle 1987), M. Sahlins (Sahlins 1968), and others. This multivariate model used to explain the rise of social complexity in Iron Age Edom is illustrated in figure 9.1.

NOMADIC CONTEXT

In his magisterial synthesis, *Nomads and the Outside World* (Khazanov 1994: 274), when considering nomads and their emergence as pre-industrial "nomadic states" in the Near East, Anatoly Khazanov says "It is indicative that the first states in pre-Islamic Arabia primarily emerged on the peripheries of the peninsula where nomads were the immediate neighbours of richer and more developed countries. Amongst these states were those of the Kidarites, the Nabateans, the Kindites, the Himyarites and the Lakmids." While the nomadic states alluded to by Khazanov emerged mostly in the Classical and Byzantine periods, this observation raises two important issues concerning the role of nomads in the evolution of complex societies during the Iron Age (ca. 1200–500 B.C.) in Arabia's northwestern neighboring area — the southern Levant. First, is the notion of nomadic societies playing an active role in secondary state formation along the periphery of the Arabian Peninsula from at least the fourth century B.C. and hence a cyclical process of "nomadic state" formation in the arid zones of the ancient Near East. And second, is the distinction of "pre-Islamic Arabia" and the implied role of Islam in later state formation in the region. While the rich ethnographic and historical record of the Middle East can and should serve as a source of analogy in building models of prehistory and ancient history, it is important to beware of the complexities of using ethnographic analogy (including ethnoarchaeological and ethnohistorical sources) in attempting understand historical processes that occurred thousands of years ago. As I. Hodder (Hodder 1982: 12) suggests, the use of analogy can be dangerous when scholars assume a "deterministic uniformitarianism" — where archaeologists assume that societies and cultures similar in some aspects are uniformly similar in all other aspects. To help alleviate the abuse of analogy in archaeological research, I suggest a four-tier model of analogy in archaeology that includes: (1) simple direct analogy, (2) "cautionary tales," (3) processual analogy, and (4) cognitive analogy (see Holl and Levy 1993). Simple direct analogies deal with site-formation processes, "action" or "experimental archaeology." "Cautionary tales" are case studies that refute archaeological claims by showing the variation of interpretations offered by ethnoarchaeological and ethnohistorical research. Processual analogies stress the dynamic relationship between social and economic aspects of culture and the environment as the foundation for understanding the processes of culture change. "Cognitive analogies" are an alternative to materialist processual analogy and look to ideology as an active organization force in societies that result in symbolic ethnoarchaeological research that runs the risk of cultural relativism that cannot be directly applied to ancient cultures (Hodder 1982; Miller and Tilley 1984). For ancient Edom, P. Bienkowski and E. van der Steen (Bienkowski and van der Steen 2001) have presented very original research that uses ethnohistorical data concerning the local nineteenth- and early twentieth-century A.D. Bedouin nomadic communities of Transjordan and Arabia to reconstruct the nature of ancient Iron Age society in Edom. Although not stated explicitly, they attempt to cull the following processual analogies to transcend their ethnographic case study (ibid., p. 35): (1) territory and movement, (2) trade, (3) interaction with a gateway town, (4) relationship to central government, and (5) relationship to an imperial power. However, the veil of assumed civilization core-dominance theories (Frank and Gills 1996; Wallerstein 1974) covers the Iron Age archaeological data as interpreted by this ethnohistorically informed model. It assumes that the Edomite "state" emerged under the influence of a (singular) gateway town, a deterministic relationship with a central government, as well as an imperial power.

In this paper, Iron Age state formation in one of the southern Levant's most peripheral regions — Edom, which borders the northwestern Arabian Peninsula — I examine data from Iron

Age Edom from the interdisciplinary perspective of archaeology, history, and anthropology in the context of the multivariate model noted above (fig. 9.1). Earlier interpretations of the rise of social complexity and the Iron Age "state" in Edom have assumed this occurred under the direct influence of the Assyrian empire in the seventh and eighth centuries B.C. (Bennett 1992; Bennett and Bienkowski 1995; Bienkowski 2000; Bienkowski 2001; Bienkowski and van der Steen 2001; Crowell 2004; Porter 2004; Whiting 2007). However, as shown by G. Stein (Stein 1999: 16), core civilization dominance models are inherently weak since they minimize the roles of polities of social groups on the periphery of these core regions because they assume consistent core dominance, core control over an asymmetric exchange system, and the causal primacy of long-distance interaction in structuring the political economy on the periphery. Accordingly, these assumptions "remove or minimize the roles of polities or social groups in the periphery, local production and local exchange, and internal dynamics of developmental change." To date, the discussions of the rise of Iron Age complex societies in Edom have been presented mostly based on a number of assumptions that force the archaeological data into models that determine the trajectory that led nomadic peoples in Edom to evolve into increasingly complex social formations during the Iron Age sequence as dependent on Assyrian core civilization. Some of these assumptions include the following:

1) A late date for the beginning of the Iron Age in Edom, during the seventh and early eighth centuries B.C.

2) The centrality of seventh- and eighth-century Assyrian core civilization dominance in the promotion of nomad clients in Edom into a small dependent state on the periphery of Assyria whose success depended on paying tribute to the core civilization.

3) Over-reliance on nineteenth- and twentieth-century ethnographic data as the main analogical source for cultural model-building and examination of the Iron Age archaeological record of Edom that are also grounded in core civilization dominance (Ottoman and British) on the south Levantine periphery.

In this paper, rather than begin with assumptions concerning the development of Iron Age societies in Edom, we start with an examination of the environmental context of Edom and the Iron Age archaeological record of the region based on the most recent archaeological fieldwork. By working from the archaeological data, it should be possible to discover various material correlates for social organization and production that existed in Iron Age Edom and then examine these patterns in light of the historical record and anthropological models concerning local south Levantine nomad ethnographic research.

SOCIAL COLLAPSE AT THE END OF THE LATE BRONZE AGE: ENVIRONMENTAL AND SOCIAL CONTEXT TO THE RISE OF COMPLEX LEVANTINE IRON AGE SOCIETIES

At the end of the second millennium B.C. (Late Bronze IIb period), the core civilizations of the eastern Mediterranean underwent a social and environmental crisis that led to their collapse (Chew 2001). The major civilization collapse included the Mycenaeans on mainland Greece (Tainter 2006; van Andel, Zangger, and Demitrack 1990; Wright 1968), the Hittites in Anatolia (Drews 1993), and a short crisis in Egypt at the end of the thirteenth century that brought the Nineteenth Dynasty to an end (Mazar 1992: 288) and ultimately brought an end to the Egyptian New Kingdom. One of the results of the collapse of these empires was the disruption of trade around the eastern Mediterranean, with the island of Cyprus and its highly successful Late Bronze metal industry being decimated. As is shown below, the interruption of the Cypriot copper trade along with poorer climatic conditions helped set in place a number of opportunities for sociopolitical development for the local peoples of the southern Levant.

The core area of ancient Edom extends in the north from the Wadi al-Hasa, along the Wadi Arabah on the west, the desert plateau on the east, and the Wadi Hisma in the south which borders the Hijaz Desert of the Arabian Peninsula. During some phases of occupation during the Iron Age, the area of Edom may have extended westward across the Wadi Arabah into the region that makes up part of the southern Negev Desert (Royal Jordanian Geographic Centre 2001; Rainey and Notley 2006). The core area of Edom includes approximately 12,000 sq. km with four major phytogeographic zones including: (1) a narrow band (ca. 20 × 110 km, or 2,200 sq. km) of Mediterranean vegetation that receives over 450 mm of average annual rainfall (AAR) and 800 plant species; (2) a sinuous semi-arid band (ca. 45 × 170 km, or 5,450 sq. km) of Irano-Turano vegetation that engulfs the limited ridge of Mediterranean environment where there are approximately 250–450 mm AAR and approximately 300 plant species; (3) the Saharo-Arabian desert zone that includes ca. 4,350 sq. km of territory characterized by 150–24 mm AAR and some 300 plant species; and (4) restricted areas of Sudanian vegetation composed mostly of Acacia trees and other thorn species, dwarf shrubs, and African grasses (Danin 1983); the Sudanian environment is found in pseudo-savanna in wadi beds, cliffs and rock formations, oases, and in the Dead Sea Rift, as well as a variety of secondary habitats outside the rift (Shmida and Aronson 1986). In general, these phytogeographic zones in Edom constitute two main geomorphologic units: the highlands dominated by the semi-arid and Mediterranean zones, and the lowlands that consist primarily of Saharo-Arabian and Sudanian vegetation. In examining the impact of the environment on human occupation, it is important to review the paleoenvironmental evidence for the Late Bronze–Iron Age for any evidence of climatic change and its influence on culture change at this time.

In a recent synthesis of south Levantine paleoenvironmental data, Arlene Rosen (Rosen 2007: 42–43) suggests that it is significant that the social and political events surrounding the development of the first secondary states in the southern Levant during the Iron Age occurred when rainfall conditions seem to have been drier than those at present. In addition to the sociopolitical opportunities due to Late Bronze Age civilization collapse in the eastern Mediterranean, poor climatic conditions also set in at the end of the Late Bronze Age (Late Bronze IIb, ca. 1300–1200 B.C.) that may have contributed to the collapse of the major eastern Mediterranean civilizations at this time. Thus, Iron Age complex societies emerged and crystallized in Israel, Philistia, Ammon, Moab, Edom, and other regions under a rainfall regime that was even less beneficial for dry farming than that of today evidenced in speleotherm data (Bar-Matthews and Ayalon 2004), paleo-limnology studies (Enzel et al. 2003), geomorphology (Rosen 1986), and other paleoenvironmental datasets. The net impression is that climatic conditions were drier than today. As Rosen (ibid., p. 143) points out, during the Iron Age the southern Levantine societies had to contend with feeding increasingly large populations. If the Chalcolithic period (ca. 4500–3600 B.C.) represents the first "population explosion" in the southern Levant, the Iron Age is the second major growth spurt in human population in the region. To cope with the poorer climatic conditions, a wide range of new agro-technologies were employed, from the adoption of widespread agricultural terracing and cistern construction in the highlands of Canaan (Hopkins 1985; Hopkins 1993) to the adoption of innovative systems of production and trade in Edom. As suggested here, we need to search for a multivariate model that takes into account social, political, and environmental variables to explain the rise of Early Iron Age complex societies in the southern Levant in general and for Edom in particular. In summary, the collapse of Late Bronze Age civilizations in the eastern Mediterranean may represent a unique situation in the history of the region. Not just one major power declined, whose place was quickly filled by another ancient "superpower," but rather, at the end of the thirteenth century B.C. there was a complete disruption of all core-civilization authority in the eastern Mediterranean that led to a power vacuum that the region had not witnessed since the formative prehistoric periods when the first chiefdoms emerged during the late fifth millennium B.C. (Levy 2006; Levy 2007). This paper does not attempt to investigate the reasons Late Bronze Age civilizations in the eastern Mediterranean collapsed, as the notion of societal collapse is a study in its own right (Burton 2004; Diamond 2005; Tainter 1988; Yoffee and Cowgill 1988). As shown by the paleoenvironmental data discussed here, the socioeconomic collapse of Late Bronze Age civilizations was also accompanied by a general decrease in rainfall and deterioration of the climatic conditions that required new agro-technology strategies, and as is suggested here, new social organizations to cope with these social opportunities and environmental constraints. The power vacuum enabled new ethnic groups to converge on the southern Levant (modern Israel, Palestine, Jordan, southern Lebanon, Syria, and the Sinai Peninsula) such as the Sea Peoples (Stager 1985a; Stager 2003) and nomadic tribes from the Arabian Peninsula and perhaps other neighboring regions.

THE IRON AGE ARCHAEOLOGICAL CONTEXT IN EDOM

Recent large-scale Iron Age archaeological research in Edom has focused primarily in the lowland zone, especially in the copper-ore-rich Faynan district. The recent research provides new archaeological and radiometric dating evidence that demonstrates that the Iron Age history of Edom extends much earlier than previous researchers assumed. The new data are important because they situate the Iron Age history of the lowlands of Edom in the late eleventh through ninth centuries B.C. — approximately 300 years earlier than previous researchers have assumed (Bienkowski and van der Steen 2001; Dever 2003; Porter 2004). While not denying an important Late Iron Age (sixth–eighth centuries B.C.) Edomite archaeological landscape identified by earlier researchers at sites on the highland plateau — such as Busayra (thought to be the capital of biblical Edom; Balla and Bienkowski 2002), Tawilan (Bennett and Bienkowski 1995), Umm al-Biyara (Bennett 1966a; Bennett 1966b), and other sites (Hart 1987; Hart 1989) — the new data effectively remove the assumption that the beginning of Edomite state formation was a result of some kind of vassal relationship with Assyrian core civilization from the search for the emergence of complex society in Iron Age Edom. It is important to summarize these new archaeological data so that the alternative multivariate model noted above can be implemented.

Since 2002, the University of California, San Diego (UCSD), and the Department of Antiquities of Jordan (DOAJ) have carried out five major campaigns ending in 2007 that focused on Iron Age problems. The aim of the UCSD-DOAJ Iron Age research in Faynan has been to complete the first phase of a deep-time study of the role of mining and metallurgy on the evolution of societies from the Pre-Pottery Neolithic B period (ca. 7500–6,000 B.C.), characterized by autonomous village settlement to the Iron Age (ca. 1200–500 B.C.) when the first historic state-level societies emerged in the region. Earlier non-systematic archaeological research was carried out in the lowlands of Edom by A. Musil (Musil 1907), G. S. Blake, N. Glueck (Glueck 1935; Glueck 1938; Glueck 1940), F. Frank (Frank 1934), R. G. Head, G. Horsfield, and D. Kirkbride (Albright 1934: 16). Large prehistoric sites were recorded near the western entrance to the Faynan district along the Wadi Fidan by T. Raikes (Raikes 1980) in the late 1970s. In the 1980s and early 1990s, the German Mining Museum, under A. Hauptmann (Hauptmann 2000; Hauptmann 2007), carried out a number of archaeometallurgical surveys and test excavations in the Faynan district. Working in northern Edom, B. MacDonald (MacDonald and Amr 1992) systematically surveyed many of the wadi segments that drain the highlands of Edom and debouch into the Wadi Arabah (wadis Numeira, Hasa, Matsus, Umm Jufna, Feifa, Umruq, Khanazir, el-Tilah, el-Dahal, al-Hassiya, al-Guwayb, and Wadi Fidan). Working in the center of the Faynan district along the Wadi Faynan, G. Barker, D. Gilbertson, and D. Mattingly carried out a landscape survey that retrieved Iron Age material related to a general study of archaeology and desertification in the region (Barker 2001; Barker et al. 1998; Barker et al. 1999; Barker et al. 1997; Barker et al. 2008). However, the UCSD-DOAJ Edom Lowlands Project represents the first large-scale interdisciplinary research project to focus specifically on the Iron Age landscape of this part of the southern Levant accompanied by large-scale excavations and surveys.

The first systematic full-coverage pedestrian survey carried out by the UCSD team was conducted in 1998 along the Wadi Fidan (Levy et al. 2001). In terms of the twenty-four Iron Age sites recorded, at the time of the survey it was not possible to distinguish any chronological sub-phasing as no stratified excavations had taken place in the lowland region. Thus, surface sherds collected from sites were dated to the "Iron I–II" period. The most significant observation concerning the Iron Age settlement pattern along the Wadi Fidan (ca. 500 m on both sides of the drainage) was the paucity of agricultural installations (one) and settlements (one), and the large number of cemeteries (seven) and metallurgical processing sites (four). Of the metallurgical sites, we should also add an eighth site to this tally because the 2007 excavations at the site of Khirbet Hamra Ifdan (Levy et al. 2002) showed that most of the massive black slag mounds visible on the site surface date to the Iron Age and not the Early Bronze Age.

The UCSD-DOAJ surveys in the Edom lowlands indicate, as noted long ago by Nelson Glueck (1940), that there were two major copper-smelting sites in the region — the largest center being Khirbet en-Nahas (KEN, ca. 10 ha; fig. 9.4) on the Wadi al-Guwayb, a secondary center at Khirbet al-Jariyeh (KAJ, ca. 3 ha; fig. 9.5), and a number of smaller sites at Khirbet Hamra Ifdan on the Wadi Fidan (Levy et al. 2002) and other isolated sites along the main Wadi Faynan drainage and secondary wadis in the area first identified by the German Mining Museum (Hauptmann 2000; 2007). There are also several small defensive "watch tower" (Rujm Hamra Ifdan) and "caravanserai" sites (Khirbet Hamra Ifdan), as well as tent encampments dating to the Iron Age in the lowlands, but none of these reflect permanent settlement.

While Khirbet en-Nahas and Khirbet al-Jariyeh have widespread stone-built architecture visible on the surface (figs. 9.4–5), preliminary studies of the faunal assemblages from the UCSD-DOAJ excavations at Khirbet en-Nahas (Levy et al. 2005) and Khirbet al-Jariyeh do not show evidence of year-round occupation at these metal production sites (Muniz and Levy n.d.). This is in sharp contrast to Pre-Pottery Neolithic sites in the region such as Tel Tifdan (Twiss) and the Early Bronze III metal production manufactory at Khirbet Hamra Ifdan (Muniz 2006) that show strong evidence of year-round occupation. In summarizing the Iron Age settlement pattern data for the lowlands of Edom there a number of large-scale metal production sites, numerous mines, campsites (Homan 2002), smaller sites with a variety of functions (figs. 9.2–3), and a substantial number of cemeteries.

The most recent 2006 excavations the KEN metal-production center have revealed, for the first time, industrial-scale metal production in the tenth and ninth centuries B.C. This has been demonstrated in Area M at the site where an approximately 6 m deep section through industrial slag has been dated with twenty new high-precision radiocarbon dates processed at the Oxford Radiocarbon Accelerator Lab. Approximately 3 m of tenth-century B.C. and 3 m of ninth-century B.C. industrial-scale production were recorded. This was published recently in the Proceedings of the National Academy of Science (Levy et al. 2008). Following C. Costin's (Costin 1991) models of craft production and society, the mode of copper production indicated by these data from KEN is a clear indicator that Iron Age IIa metal production in Faynan was organized by a complex society during this approximately 200-year period. Recent Iron Age ceramic analysis at KEN (Smith and Levy 2008) demonstrates that most of the seventh- to sixth-century pottery assemblages in the highlands of Edom (and linked to Edomite ethnicity), have their roots in the ninth- through tenth-century B.C. forms present in the lowlands. The implication is that the formation of Edomite identity was much earlier than that suggested by Porter (2004), who stresses the formation of an elite Edomite identity during the eighth and seventh centuries B.C. based on: (1) encouraging the shift *from* pastoral nomadic subsistence practices *to* sedentary ones; (2) promotion of a unified cult under Qos as evidenced on epigraphic finds; (3) the construction of a political and administrative center at Busayra; (4) the redistribution of prestige objects to loyal subjects; and (5) the territorial expansion of the Edomite polity. While elite Edomite identity may have crystallized in the eighth–seventh centuries, the new data from the Edom lowlands indicates that this process started much earlier and that following Tapper (1990: 65), it was the ability of Edomite elites — already in the tenth century B.C. — to instill the hope of material gain for themselves and/ or their society though new production opportunities in metallurgy (beyond pastoralism), that led to the emergence of complex societies (Edomite chiefdom confederacy) as early as the tenth century B.C.

The general impression of the Iron Age settlement pattern in this Saharo-Arabian desert zone is of a non-sedentary population in close association with mining and metallurgical sites. The only Iron Age cemetery to have been sampled in the lowlands of Edom is the site of Wadi Fidan 40 (Levy, Adams, and Muniz 2004; Levy, Adams, and Shafiq 1999) located at the western entrance to the Faynan copper-ore district on the edge of the Wadi Arabah. As mortuary sites are perhaps the best source of information on ethnicity in the archaeological record (Faust 2004; Rakita et al. 2005), and the role of ethnogenesis in the rise of complex societies in Edom is be discussed below, the following is a brief overview of this Iron Age cemetery.

The Wadi Fidan 40 cemetery was first systematically excavated in 1997 when sixty-two graves were excavated (Levy et al. 1999), followed by two emergency excavations in 2003 that revealed fifty-two graves and in 2004, 173 graves, giving a total of 287 excavated graves. The cemetery is situated on a Pleistocene conglomerate terrace that overlooks the Wadi Arabah and marks the entrance to the copper-ore-rich Faynan district (fig. 9.6). The UCSD-DOAJ surveys in the Edom lowlands identified seven Iron Age cemeteries along the Wadi Fidan, four along the Wadi al-Guwayb, and nine on the banks of the Wadi al-Jariyeh. There are also isolated rock cairns, such as those excavated at the Early Bronze Age site of Wadi Fidan 4, that represent Iron Age tombs. Given the large number of Iron Age cemeteries in the lowland region, the unusually well-preserved grave sample from Wadi Fidan 40 is especially important in terms of identifying the Iron Age human population in the area. Here only a brief summary is presented.

The core area of the cemetery extends over an area of 0.69 hectare (6,900 sq. m). Based on the recently excavated grave sample of ca. twenty-five graves per 25 sq. m excavation unit, it is possible that within the cemetery core area there are nearly 7,000 graves present. This estimate is based on the more recent 2003–2004 excavations and is considerably higher than the 1997 excavations estimate (Levy et al. 1999). The reason for this is that the 1997 sample exposed only those graves that had grave-circle features visible on the site surface, whereas in 2003–2004 we re-excavated all the excavation squares (as well as opening new units), revealing a much more dense packing of graves than previously imagined (fig. 9.6).

By the end of the 2004 excavation season it was clear that a range of different style burial monuments were present in the cemetery including large grave circles above cists, isolated stone-lined cists, square platforms, extensive (over 5 m in diameter) grave circles, concentric grave circles with standing stones (fig. 9.7), and other mortuary structures. At present, the full assemblage of graves and their contents is being studied (Beherec n.d.).

Most of the graves seem to have been disturbed in antiquity, probably during the Iron Age. In spite of these disturbances, a wide range of burial offerings were found with the bulk of the non-secondary burial population. It seems that cists were specifically designed for the individual dead depending on their size. Thus, infants and children are found in small cist graves and adults in full-size units that accommodate their extended or semi-crouched burial position. Some of the offerings include beads, necklaces, copper and iron jewelry (bracelets, anklets, finger and toe rings), wooden vessels, shrouds (of linen and animal skins), pomegranates, and other objects (Levy et al. 1999). The most recent excavations revealed an important assemblage of carved anthropomorphic standing stones that range from 25 to 90 cm in height and consist mostly of individuals with protrusions indicating shoulders, noses, and ears (fig. 9.8) (Levy et al. 2005a). These anthropomorphic standing stones are unique to the Edom lowlands and may be an important cultural/ethnic marker of the Iron Age population buried at this site. Preliminary spatial analyses suggests clustering of graves in family units with some social ranking based on remaining grave-good inclusions (Goldstein 1981) and energy expenditure in burial monument construction (Binford 1971; Levy and Alon 1982). The lack of ceramic grave offerings, the projection of social wealth on female burials, the presence of wooden-bowl burial gifts, and the absence of Iron Age habitation villages along the Wadi Fidan, Wadi al-Guwayb, and Wadi al-Jariyeh, especially in close proximity to the massive cemetery at Wadi Fidan 40, suggests the buried population was part of a nomadic community. High precision radiocarbon dates (Levy et al. 2005) from short-life pomegranate seeds found inside four tombs from different parts of the cemetery show that it was in use from the late eleventh through ninth centuries B.C. with peak usage during the tenth century.

In summary, the recent archaeological surveys and excavations in the Edom lowlands indicate a landscape where sites related to mining, metallurgy, and mortuary sites dominate the Iron Age archaeological record. The paucity of Iron Age villages, with the exception of Barqa el-Hetiye (Fritz 1994), a small ninth-century B.C. copper-working settlement located in the dune area some 6 km south of the main Wadi Faynan drainage (and possibly Tel Faynan usually linked to Biblical Punon), coupled with widespread cemetery evidence that may indicate territorial markers, suggests the presence of a large nomadic population interacting with the lowlands throughout the Iron Age. The presence of a large tenth-century B.C. fortress at Khirbet en-Nahas contemporary with industrial-scale copper production and a re-organized ninth-century B.C. production center with widespread construction activities must be evaluated in connection the ceramic assemblage at the site. As shown in the first in-depth study of the ceramics from the site (Smith and Levy 2008), while the archaeological strata where these artifacts come from have been securely dated with high precision radiocarbon dates, the assemblage is locally produced and stylistically similar to the Late Iron Age (IA IIc, seventh and eighth centuries B.C.) ceramic assemblages defined at the highland sites and labeled "Edomite" (Hart 1986; Hart 1987; Hart 1989; Hart and Knauf 1986; Oakshott 1978; Oakshott 1983). While there is a problem in linking pottery with people, as shown in many ethnoarchaeological studies (Dever 1995; Jones 1997; Killebrew 2005; Redmount 1995; Small 1997), potting traditions may indeed reflect the identity of the makers (David and Kramer 2001; Holl and Levy 1993; Kramer 1985; Sengupta, Roychoudhury, and Som 2006). Given these constraints, if the material cultural assemblage of the seventh- through eighth-century B.C. highland sites such as Busayra, Umm al-Biyara, Tawilan, and others are taken to be "Edomite," the development of these traditions can be traced in the archaeological record of the lowlands of Edom during the eleventh through ninth centuries B.C. This means that the majority of the Iron Age archaeological evidence from the Edom lowlands, with the exception of some trade items, indicates an especially active "Edomite" population in the lowlands during the tenth through ninth centuries and probably earlier. More limited eighth- through seventh-century "Edomite" activity is evidenced by a variety of sites such as the large enclosure at Rujm Hamra Ifdan (Smith, Levy, and Najjar n.d.), several smelting sites and mines (Hauptmann 2007), and some newly discovered forts overlooking the Wadi al-Guwayb (Ben Yosef, Levy, and Najjar 2008). Thus, the centrality of a nomadic population interacting with mining, metallurgy, and trade against the background of fortified sites throughout the Iron IIa–c sequence is evident.

ETHNOGENESIS

To attempt to identify some of the underlying forces that may have led to the emergence of Iron Age complex societies in Edom — whether we refer to them as complex chiefdoms, chieftaincies, Levantine Iron Age kingdoms, small secondary states, or nomadic states — we may productively investigate this through the processual lens of ethnogenesis. Iron Age historical records suggest that societies in Edom were organized along patrilineal decent principles (Schloen 2001) where kinship remained a central factor in alliance formation (Stager 1985). This suggests the importance of ethnic identity in the formation of these complex polities in Iron Age Edom. Following De Vos (De Vos 1995) ethnicity can be defined as "self-perceived inclusion of those who hold in common a set of traditions not shared by others with whom they are in contact." These include a number of traditions such as: "Folk" religious beliefs and practices, language, aesthetic cultural patterns (such as tastes in food, dance tradition, styles of clothing, and definitions of physical beauty), a sense of historical continuity, common ancestry, or place of origin, territoriality, and economic specialization. The group's actual history often trails off into legend or mythology, which includes some concept of an unbroken biological-genetic generational continuity to the group. While endogamy is usual, there are ways to initiate outsiders into the ethnic group so that the group's sense of generational continuity is not upset. Many of these attributes of ethnicity have material correlates in the archaeological record. The processes in which ethnic identity are formed can be subsumed under the notion of "ethnogenesis."

The *Macmillan Dictionary of Anthropology* defines ethnogenesis as "the construction of group identity and resuscitation or persistence of cultural features of a people undergoing rapid and radical change. It may also be used to refer to a new ethnic system emerging out of an amalgamation of other groups" (1986: 97). For T. Patterson, "ethnogenesis is the historical creation of a people with a sense of their collective identity..." (1991: 31). From a social evolutionary perspective, G. Emberling (Emberling 1997: 308), links the formation of ethnic identities with the emergence of states and suggests "that ethnogenesis is closely connected with state formation processes and with state control, arguing the creation of new ethnic identities emerges when a state or empire conquers independent groups. In A. Faust's 2006 work on Israelite ethnogenesis (see also Levy and Holl 2002) he follows Emberling in seeing ethnicity as a form of *resistance*, especially among social groups interacting with state-level societies. I agree with this, but add that the formation and strengthening of ethnic identities can also occur through a wide range of what C. Renfrew and J. Cherry refer to as processes of "*peer-polity interaction*" or competitive social interactions on the local scale within and between band, tribe (or segmentary society), and chiefdom organizations — as well as archaic states. Thus, the catalyst for ethnogenesis must be a multivariate process that occurs, for example, as a result of conflict when a state or empire conquers independent groups or these groups compete against each other for resources. Patterson (1991: 31) suggests that cultural transformation or new ethnicities may result from *hybridization, fusion, or even replacement by state-imposed forms*; alternatively, ethnogenesis may emerge due to resistance or attempts to assert tradition. Thus, the activity of a central government can both "impose" an identity on a group of people, even if they did not have this identity before, as well as promote the emergence of a new ethnic identity as a form of resistance to its activities. Agreeing with Emberling (Emberling 1997; Emberling and Yoffee 1999) and Faust (Faust 2006), I suggest that *resistance* to "the other" — whatever the level of social organization (tribe, chiefdom, chieftaincy, confederacy, "protostate," "nomadic state," "secondary state") — is one of the key factors that promotes ethnogenesis in Iron Age Edom and ultimately complex society.

SOME HISTORICAL BACKGROUND
IN LIGHT OF NEW RADIOCARBON DATES

As discussed here and elsewhere (Hauptmann 2007; Higham et al. 2005; Levy et al. 2004; Levy et al. 2005b), archaeological and radiocarbon data show that the Iron Age of the Edom lowlands begins as early as the eleventh century B.C. and has a floret of metal production during the tenth and ninth centuries B.C. There is also limited evidence of Iron Age activity in this region during the eighth and seventh centuries B.C. While some scholars have taken issue with the early dating of the Iron Age occupation in the lowland region (Finkelstein 2005; Levy and Najjar 2006b; Levy, Najjar, and Higham 2007b; van der Steen and Bienkowski 2006) these critics have been countered with hard archaeological and radiometric data demonstrating the long Iron Age occupation of Edom (Levy, Higham, and Najjar 2006; Levy and Najjar 2006b; Levy, Najjar, and Higham 2007a; Levy et al. 2008a). While eighth–seventh-century B.C. settlement data are limited in the lowlands, at this time the highlands experienced an expansion of settlement with a central site located at Busayra (Balla and Bienkowski 2002), numerous villages and defensive sites such as Umm al-Biyara (Bennett 1966a; Bennett 1966b), Sela (Dalley and Goguel 1997), and other locales. Thus, in light of the new archaeological data from the lowlands of Edom, the search for historical sources linked to Edom can confidently span the eleventh through seventh centuries B.C. and probably several centuries on both sides of this block of time.

While there are local Edomite signet seals, seal impressions, inked ostraca, and graffiti dating from the eighth through seventh centuries B.C. found in late Iron Age levels at the port site of Tell el-Kheleifeh, highland sites in Edom (Crowell 2004; DiVito 1993; Naveh 1982;

Porter 2004), and some locales in Israel, textual data from the formative period of Iron Age Edom comes mostly from Egypt, with some glimmers of history in various "layers" of the Hebrew Bible (Levy 2008a, 2008b). To date, no evidence of Late Bronze Age mining, metallurgy, or occupation has been found in the Faynan district, however, 106 km to the south at Timna, in the other main copper-ore district of the Wadi Arabah, there is evidence of Egyptian activities in the region during the Nineteenth and Twentieth Dynasties as evidenced by several cartouches of pharaohs from Seti I through Ramesses IV, ca. 1300–1150 B.C. (Rothenberg 1972), and an Egyptian Late Bronze Age shrine or temple (Rothenberg 1988). The presence of "Midianite" or "Quwayra ware" pottery has led Rothenberg (Rothenberg 1999) and Bartlett (Bartlett 1989: 74–75) to suggest that the population at Timna was composed of Egyptians, local inhabitants (Edomites?), and others (Midianites?) — including prisoners and slaves who were forced to work the mines for the Egyptians. As noted above, the Iron Age archaeological settlement pattern data for the lowlands of Edom indicate a non-sedentary nomadic population that we may assume relied on herding as one important component of their economy. K. Kitchen's 1992 summary of Late Bronze Age to early Iron Age textual data from Egypt support this interpretation where Edom is referred to as *Seir* and inhabited by "clans" (*whȝywt*) ruled by "chiefs" (*wrw*). This is portrayed in the Papyrus Anastasi VI that uses the term "Edom" and states, "we have finished with allowing the Shasu clansfolk of Edom to pass the fort of Merneptah that is in Succoth, to the pools of Pi-Atum of Merneptah that are in Succoth, to keep them alive and to keep alive their livestock..." (Gardiner 1937: 76–77; translations in Pritchard 1969: 259′, with notes in Caminos 1954: 293). The later text from the reign of Ramesses III (ca. 1184–1153 B.C.), known as the Papyrus Harris I, also portrays a pastoral nomadic population in Edom and the shifting nature of relations between the Egyptian state and these northeastern nomads: "I destroyed the Seirites, the clans of the Shasu, I pillaged their tents, with their people, their property and their livestock with limit..." (Erichsen 1933: 93; translations in Pritchard 1969: 262:I). While it is clear that the Late Bronze–early Iron Age Egyptian state referred to the pastoral nomadic population of Seir/Edom as "Shasu," we do not yet know what these people actually referred to themselves as. It is against this historical background that the Wadi Fidan 40 cemetery has been linked to the Shasu population mentioned in these Egyptian texts (Levy, Adams, and Muniz 2004; Levy, Adams, and Shafiq 1999). Based on the radiocarbon dates from this cemetery (Levy et al. 2005a), its peak use was during the tenth century B.C. Taken together, these data indicate the presence of a very large nomadic population during the tenth century B.C. in the lowlands of Edom. Based on the scholarly consensus on the centrality of nomadism as an important "deep-time" adaptive mechanism for populations residing in the region of Edom (Bienkowski and van der Steen 2001; LaBianca and Younker 1995; Levy 2004), an important variable for understanding the rise of the "nomadic state" in Iron Age Edom is the structural underpinnings of the Middle East tribal system from a processual perspective. For some discussion of issues concerning Iron Age Edom, metal production, and the Hebrew Bible, see Bartlett 1989; Bienkowski 1995; Edelman 1995; Finkelstein 2005; Knauf-Belleri 1995; Knauf and Lenzen 1987; Levy 2002; Levy 2004; Levy 2008; Levy and Najjar 2006a; Levy and Najjar 2007; Na'aman 2004; and Whiting 2007.

OSCILLATING TRIBAL SEGMENTARY SYSTEM

In discussing the emergence of "tribal kingdoms" in the Iron Age of Transjordan, some scholars see the role of nomadism in the rise of these complex polities (LaBianca 1999;

LaBianca and Younker 1995). Part of the problem may be an over-reliance on late nine-teenth- and twentieth-century A.D. ethnographic and ethnohistorical research that results in a static picture of the nomadic and semi-nomadic Bedouin Arab tribes of the region. Similar assumptions have been made in other parts of the Middle East, such as Iran, in L. Helfgott's (Helfgott 1980) study of the Qajjar state. As pointed out by Khazanov (Khazanov 1994), while pastoralism is a key component of nomadic societies, their relationship with neighboring polities — mostly settled — opens up a wide range of other economic pursuits by nomadic peoples. Rather than focus on the notion of herds and herding as the central variable for pro-moting change in nomadic people's social organization through time, it may be more useful to spotlight some aspects of the segmentary lineage model that underlies tribal genealogy and kinship structure. The sementary lineage system has been defined as a particular form of higher order descent group organization ... a part of a wider system of kinship in specific societies and part of kinship analysis in cultural systems (Baştuğ 1998: 95). The segmentary lineage system model was conceived by Evans Pritchard in the 1940s, and like all general models, has been both embraced and critiqued as not applicable in some areas of the Middle East (Munson 1989) or of little value. Without delving into this long-standing anthropological controversy, most scholars find value in the focus on the principle of "segmentation" that structures this principle in tribal societies — especially those nomadic societies in the Middle East. This was first clarified by E. L. Peters, who worked with camel-herding tribes of Cyrenaica (Peters 1967) and showed the segmentary linage model to be more of a tribal ideology than an in-dicator of behavior. In a general discussion of the "segmentary tribe," Sahlins (1968: 20) portrays it as the basic structural building blocks that enable chiefdoms to emerge where at the lower end of social complexity tribes are inherently decentralized, and at the higher end, chiefdoms (still organized along kinship and decent) work toward integration of the segmen-tary system at its highest levels. With the establishment of chiefdoms, segmentary tribes are consolidated into more complex social organizations with more developed ritual, ideology, and economic structures. Without assuming a teleological "social evolutionary step-ladder" of band-tribe-chiefdom-state (Yoffee 1998), it is the segmentary principle (Eickelman 1981: 131–38) embedded in tribal societies that allows them to evolve and devolve, to adapt to changes in both the natural and cultural environments and oscillate between small decentral-ized tribes to complex chiefdoms, to chiefly confederacies and back. According to T. Barfield (Barfield 1993: 75), the patrilineal lineage model is exemplified in the Bedouin Arab tribal systems of the Middle East where "within the tribe, the relationship between each lineage or clan rested in theory on segmentary opposition, that is, they were expected to support or oppose one another based on their degree of relatedness." This process of social fusion and fission provides nomadic tribal societies with an adaptive mechanism which, along with the principle of social "resistance" in ethnogenesis and the notion of political ecology, may help explain the rise of Iron Age complex societies in Edom.

POLITICAL ECOLOGY

As noted above, political ecology aims at understanding how access to natural resources plays a critical role in structuring the political and economic life of societies, especially how food and other basic resources are procured. One of the guiding studies for political ecology research is Piers Blaikie's 1985 *The Political Economy of Soil Erosion*, which examined how land degradation in sub-Saharan Africa was linked to colonial land appropriation, rather than over-use by local traditional farmers. As an analytical tool for archaeologists, political ecology can help (a) clarify decisions that communities make about their natural environment in the context of their changing political environment, economic pressure, and cultural context; (b) explore how unequal relations among societies in a research area affect the natural environment; and (c) investigate how unequal sociocultural relations affect the environment.

SUMMARY

In the context of a distinctive civilization collapse of all eastern Mediterranean ancient "superpowers" at the end of the Late Bronze Age, and increasingly aridity, nomadic peoples residing in the southern Levantine desert zone and the Hijaz region in northwest Arabia took advantage of a power vacuum created by the collapse of world (eastern Mediterranean) markets and colonial projects. For the southern Levant, one of the most significant impacts was the collapse of Cyprus as the main supplier of Late Bronze Age copper for the region. During the Iron I–IIa periods, new social groups converged on Canaan (such as the Sea Peoples) and Transjordan that gradually evolved into distinct ethnic groups such as the Philistines, Israelites, Moabites, and Edomites. New archaeological data from the lowlands of Edom show a relatively rapid process for the formation of a local complex chiefdom already in the tenth century B.C. that was nomadic in both practice and ideology, but in the context of the political ecology of the region increased their production strategies beyond animal husbandry to include sophisticated mining, metallurgy, and control of the copper trade to boost their economies and dominate neighboring peoples. The prominence of mining and metallurgical activities in the Faynan district created a highly specialized Iron Age industrial landscape infused with local nomadic Edomites who formed part of a complex chiefdom. Through processes of fusion and fission related to the dictates of carrying out metal-production activities in this Saharo-Arabian desert zone in an environment with less rainfall than today, the Edomites carried out metal production activities in the cool fall months and winters, and moved up to the highlands in the summer months. A burial with tenth-century B.C. gold jewelry found at Tawilan and stylistically similar to samples found at KEN and the WFD 40 cemetery may be an indicator of such lowland-highland interaction (Levy et al. 2005a; Ogden 1995). By developing a highly successful metal industry in the tenth century B.C., it is possible the Edomites attracted the interest of neighboring polities such as Israel early in the century, and perhaps at the end of the tenth century B.C. the Egyptians, as evidenced by ornaments dating from the time of Siamun and Sheshonq (Shishak) I found in a securely dated context in a metal-production building at Khirbet en-Nahas. As suggested by the ethnogenesis model above (Faust 2006; Levy and Holl 2002; Levy 2008a, 2008b), Edomite resistance to neighboring polities such as the Israelite, as well as the Egyptian state, may have been another key factor in stimulating the expansion of eleventh–ninth-century B.C. copper production and their social and ethnic identity as an expanding chieftaincy at this time.

The following summary points can be made concerning the data that indicate the formation of the Edomite chiefly confederacy that begins in the tenth century B.C. and peaks in the ninth century B.C.:

- High-precision radiocarbon dates demonstrate the deep-time history of Iron Age Edom, from at least the twelfth through ninth centuries B.C. (Higham et al. 2005; Levy et al. 2004; Levy et al. 2005b). Most recently, a new sequence of high-precision radiocarbon dates from the first controlled excavations of a slag mound at Khirbet en-Nahas demonstrates intensive industrial-scale metal production during the tenth and ninth centuries B.C. (Levy et al. 2008). The mining and smelting activities associated with these archaeometallurgical data indicate that complex societies were responsible for industrial-scale metal production during these centuries. While it is not yet possible to identify who controlled metal production in Faynan during these centuries, the dominance of local "Edomite" pottery from the excavation samples indicates the centrality of the local population in metal production at this time (Smith and Levy 2008). When these data are linked to archaeological materials such as Qurayra ware, Egyptian scarabs and amulets, Cypro-Phoenician ware, black burnished juglets, and other ceramic types, there is evidence of interaction between a number of different ethnic groups at KEN, including Edomites, Phoenicians, Israelites, Egyptians, and "Midianites" (see Levy et al. 2004; Rothenberg 1998; Rothenberg and Glass 1983) during the Iron Age from production and other sites in the Faynan district of the Edom lowlands. The establishment of a radiocarbon-based chronology from stratified excavations in southern Jordan adds some 300 more years to the Iron Age chronology of Edom (Levy et al. 2008). This new framework requires that researchers re-engage the Hebrew Bible and other historical datasets concerning pre-eighth-century B.C. Edom to test and model the nature of socioeconomic change at this time.

- Excavations in the Iron Age WFD 40 cemetery indicate the presence of a large nomadic population in Edom lowlands with economic specialization in pastoralism, but possibly mining and metallurgy. Chemical analyses of human remains will be carried out to test the hypotheses that this population was involved in the industrial-scale metal production in the Faynan region. There is potential for such studies for human and animal remains in Faynan and the Negev Desert (see Grattan, Gilbertson, and Hunt 2007; Grattan, Huxley, and Pyatt 2003; Hunt et al. 2004; Pyatt et al. 2000; Pyatt and Grattan 2001; Pyatt 1999). This research is being planned with geochemist Yigal Erel from the Institute of Earth Sciences, Hebrew University of Jerusalem. Contamination of the environment with toxic metals (e.g., lead, cadmium, copper) has been a worldwide problem since the Industrial Revolution. However, there is ample evidence that the global pollution by metals started a long time before then, as shown by J. Grattan and others (Grattan, Gilbertson, and Hunt 2007). Among other issues, our research will trace through the Iron Age how humans have been polluted from metal production and how this may have related to the rise of ranked societies at this time in the southern Levant.

- Although studies of the Wadi Fidan 40 cemetery have been preliminary (Beherec in progress; Levy, Adams, and Shafiq 1999; Levy et al. 2005a), the layout of the circular and cist grave mortuary structures shows no centralized burial monuments and probably reflects a segmentary society social organization. The burial patterns reflect local "Folk" religious beliefs and practices. Based on historical Egyptian data, the Egyptians referred to these people as "Shasu" nomads (Avishur 2007; Kitchen 1992; Levy and Najjar 2006a). At this time, we do not know by what name this population referred to themselves. However, based on numerous studies of the Hebrew Bible, the name "Edomites" is most likely.

- The typical decorated painted ceramic wares from Iron Age Edom, sometimes referred to as Busayra ware, were typically ascribed by earlier researchers as dating only to the seventh century B.C. or later. However, new studies of this material found at sites in Israel have pushed the dating of this ware back to the eighth century B.C.

(Singer-Avitz 2004). Our recent excavations at Iron Age sites in the lowlands of Edom demonstrate Busayra ware is also found in tenth- and ninth-century B.C. stratified sequences. Taken together, the new data imply long-term development of *aesthetic cultural patterns* between the lowlands and highlands of Edom providing a possible indicator of Edomite ethnicity and the process of ethnogenesis.

- Twelfth- through ninth-century Edomite identity was shaped by local peer-polity interaction (Renfrew 1986; Renfrew and Cherry 1986) and resistance to neighboring social groups — as well as rejuvenated by Egyptian state expansionary projects in the Twenty-first and Twenty-second Dynasties. While Egypt was unable to reinstitute its Late Bronze Age-style colonization of Palestine, the pharaoh Shoshenq I was keen to disrupt the socioeconomic order that David and his son Solomon had established. The recent excavations and analyses of a mound of industrial copper slag at KEN document a major disruption in production at the end of the tenth century B.C. that may be attributed to the Shoshenq I campaign (Levy et al. 2008). Due to processes of oscillations in core civilization power during the Twenty-first and Twenty-second Egyptian Dynasties, they were unable to reinstate the colonial model, probably due to what Gil Stein (Stein 1999) refers to as the "Distance Parity Model." With the dissipation of core civilization influence from both Mesopotamia and Egypt at this time, peer-polity interaction between Edom, Israel, Moab, Philistia, and other small local complex societies became a major platform for the negotiation of power.

- Early *resistance to neighboring peer polities* and conflict within Shasu segmentary society of Iron Age Edom led to processes of fission within Seir/Edom. Soleb temple and Amarah inscriptions "*Yhw* (in) in the land of the Shasu." Dates from late fifteenth century B.C. suggesting the "tetragrammaton" name of the Israelite god "Yahweh." Biblical tradition suggests that Yahweh came "forth from Se'ir" and originated in Edom (see Redford 1992: 273, who calls them the Shasu/Israel group), thus early Israel may have been one of the Shasu clans.

- As outlined here, and as especially articulated in Faust's work for ancient Israel, different processes of ethnogenesis were followed for the different ethnic groups in southern Jordan/Hijaz, Northwest Arabia, that is, Midianites, Edomites, Israelites. This is an extremely fertile problem area for future investigation.

- Language — Development of the Edomite script may represent the tail-end of ethnogenesis among elite groups in Edomite society (Porter 2004).

- Finally, maintenance of Edomite ethnicity in the Neo-Assyrian period (seventh–sixth centuries B.C.) led to resistance and negotiation with a core civilization, effecting social changes that went well beyond those caused by peer polity interaction.

In conclusion, the "oscillating tribal segmentary social system" model discussed here can help explain how, in a marginal desert environment under the push and pull of neighboring polities and ancient core civilizations, nomadic peoples could adapt and grow into a small secondary state-level society. By focusing on three interrelated processes — ethnogenesis, political ecology, and the oscillating tribal segmentary social system — we are on the road to understanding how social evolution in the late second and first millennia could occur. Much more work needs to be done that is rooted in archaeological field research and scientific approaches to the Iron Age archaeological record of the southern Levant.

ACKNOWLEDGMENTS

Many thanks to Jeff Szuchman and Gil Stein for inviting me to participate in this Oriental Institute seminar and Anatoly Khazanov for suggesting my name to the University of Chicago organizers. I would also like to thank my students and colleagues who are part of the UCSD Edom Lowlands Regional Archaeology Project (ELRAP): Mohammad Najjar, Neil Smith, Erez Ben-Yosef, Yoav Arbel, Marc Beherec, Adolfo Muniz, Kyle Knabb, Aaron Gidding, Caroline Hebron, Alina Levy, Lisa Tauxe, Mohammad Dafala, and the Bedouin workers from the Faynan district who have helped with our different expeditions. Special thanks to Dr. Fawwaz al-Khraysheh, Director General of the Department of Antiquities of Jordan, for his long-term support of the ELRAP project. Funding for this research was provided by National Geographic Society Committee for Research and Exploration GRANT #8095-06, California Institute of Telecommunications and Information Technology(Calit2), National Science Foundation, co-PI with Prof. Lisa Tauxe, Scripps Institution of Oceanography, UCSD, Grant Number 0636051, and private donors.

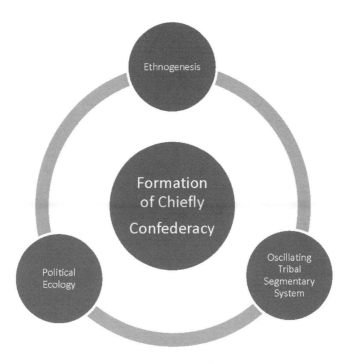

Figure 9.1. Model for the formation of a chiefly confederacy

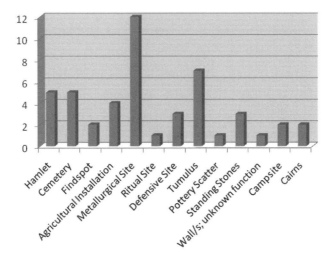

Figure 9.2. Histogram of Iron Age sites by function along the Wadi Fidan, 1998 and 2004 surveys (Levy et al. 2001) (note: 2004 data published here for the first time)

Iron Age Site Distribution by Function for Wadi al-Jariya
n=62

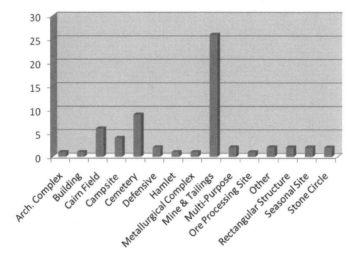

Figure 9.3. Iron Age archaeological sites along the Wadi al-Jariyeh, 2002, 2007 surveys. Note the spike in copper-mining sites (for 2002 survey data, see Levy et al. 2003)

Figure 9.4. Aerial view of Iron Age (ca. eleventh–ninth century B.C.) copper-production center at Khirbet en-Nahas, Jordan (photo courtesey of UCSD Levantine Archaeology Laboratory)

Figure 9.5. Overview of Khirbet al-Jariyeh, a secondary center of copper
production in the Edom Lowlands (photo by T. E. Levy)

Figure 9.6. Overview of 2004 excavations in Iron Age cemetery at Wadi Fidan 40, looking north.
Note that the Wadi Arabah is visible in the upper left corner. Most graves are characterized by stone-
lined cists that are excavated ca. 80–100 cm below the surface. The location of the cists was then
marked by a circle (average 1.20 cm diameter) of Dolorite wadi cobbles (photo by T. E. Levy)

Figure 9.7. Overview of grave circle marking the location of a sub-surface cist grave (Area C, Grave 712). This is an unusual example in that it has a well-preserved standing stone in the center of the grave surrounded by a smaller circle of stones (photo by T. E. Levy)

Figure 9.8. Dolerite anthropomorphic standing stone with carved shoulders and elongated nose found on the surface of the Wadi Fidan 40 Iron Age cemetery, Area A (Basket 3233), Scale = 20 cm (photo courtesy of the UCSD Levantine Archaeology Laboratory)

BIBLIOGRAPHY

Albright, W. F.
1934 "Sounding at Ader, a Bronze Age city of Moab." *Bulletin of the American Schools of Oriental Research* 53:13–18.

Avishur, Isaac
2007 "Edom." In *Encyclopaedia Judaica*. 2nd edition. Volume 6, pp. 369–77. Jerusalem: Keter.

Balla, Márta, and Piotr Bienkowski
2002 *Busayra: Excavations by Crystal-M. Bennett, 1971–1980*. British Academy Monographs in Archaeology 13. Oxford: Oxford University Press.

Bar-Matthews, Miryam, and Avner Ayalon
2004 "Speleotherms as Palaeoclimate Indicators: A Case Study from Soreq Cave Located in the Eastern Mediterranean Region, Israel." In *Past Climate Variability through Europe and Africa*, edited by R. Battarbee, F. Gasse, and C. E. Stickley, pp. 363–91. Dordrecht, The Netherlands: Springer.

Barfield, Thomas J.
1993 *The Nomadic Alternative*. Englewood Cliffs: Prentice-Hall.

Barker, Graeme W.
2001 "A Tale of Two Deserts: Contrasting Desertification Histories on Rome's Desert Frontiers." *World Archaeology* 33: 488–507.

Barker, G. W.; R. Adams; O. H. Creighton; D. D. Gilbertson; J. P. Grattan; C. O. Hunt; D. J. Mattingly; S. J. McLaren; H. A. Mohamed; P. Newson; T. E. G. Reynolds; and D. C. Thomas
1998 "Environment and Land Use in Wadi Faynan, Southern Jordan: The Second Season of Geoarchaeology and Landscape Archaeology (1997)." *Levant* 30: 5–25.

Barker, G. W.; R. B. Adams; O. H. Creighton; D. Crook; D. D. Gilbertson; J. P. Grattan; C. O. Hunt; D. J. Mattingly; S. J. McLaren; H. A. Mohammed; P. Newson; C. Palmer; B. Pyatt; T. E. G. Reynolds; and R. Tomber
1999 "Environment and Land Use in the Wadi Faynan, Southern Jordan: the Third Season of Geoarchaeology and Landscape Archaeology (1998)." *Levant* 31: 255–92.

Barker, G. W.; O. H. Creighton; D. D. Gilbertson; C. O. Hunt; D. J. Mattingly; S. J. McLaren; and D. C. Thomas
1997 "The Wadi Faynan Project, Southern Jordan: A Preliminary Report on Geomorphology and Landscape Archaeology." *Levant* 29: 19–40.

Barker, G.; D. Gilbertson; and D. Mattingly, eds.
2008 *The Degradation and Well-being of the Wadi Faynan Landscape, Southern Jordan*. Oxford: David Brown Book Company.

Bartlett, John R.
1989 *Edom and the Edomites*. Journal for the Study of the Old Testament Supplement Series 77. Sheffield: Journal for the Study of the Old Testament Press.

Baştuğ, Sharon
1998 "The Segmentary Lineage System: A Reappraisal." In *Changing Nomads in a Changing World*, edited by J. Ginat and A. Khazanov, pp. 94-123. Brighton: Sussex Academic Press.

Beherec, Marc A.
In progress *Nomads in Transition: Mortuary Archaeology in the Lowlands of Edom (Jordan)*. San Diego: University of California Press.

Bennett, Crystal M.
1966a "Fouilles d'Umm el-Biyara: Rapport préliminaire." *Revue Biblique* 73: 372–403.

1966b   "Umm el-Biyara." *Revue Biblique* 73: 400–01, pl. 22b.

1992   "Neo-Assyrian Influence in Transjordan." In *Studies in the History and Archaeology of Jordan*, edited by A. Haddidi, Volume 1, pp. 181–87. Amman: Department of Antiquities, Jordan.

Bennett, Crystal M., and Piotr Bienkowski

1995   *Excavations at Tawilan in Southern Jordan*. Oxford: The British Institute at Amman for Archaeology and History and Oxford University Press.

Bienkowski, Piotr, editor

1992   *Early Edom and Moab: The Beginning of the Iron Age in Southern Jordan*. Sheffield Archaeological Monographs 7. Sheffield: J. R. Collis.

Bienkowski, Piotr

1995   "The Edomites: The Archaeological Evidence from Transjordan." In *You Shall Not Abhor an Edomite for He Is Your Brother: Edom and Seir in History and Tradition*, edited by D. V. Edelman, pp. 41–92. Archaeological and Biblical Studies 3. Atlanta: Scholars Press.

2000   "Transjordan and Assyria." In *The Archaeology of Jordan and Beyond: Essays in Honor of James A. Sauer*, edited by L. E. Stager, J. A. Greene, and M. D. Coogan, pp. 44–58. Studies in the Archaeology and History of the Levant 1. Winona Lake: Eisenbrauns.

2001   "Iron Age Settlement in Edom: A Revised Framework." In *The World of the Aramaeans*, Volume 2: *Studies in History and Archaeology in Honour of Paul-Eugène Dion*, edited by P. M. M. Daviau, J. W. Wevers, and M. Weigl, pp. 257–69. Journal for the Study of the Old Testament Supplement Series 325. Sheffield: Sheffield Academic Press.

Bienkowski, Piotr, and Eveline van der Steen

2001   "Tribes, Trade, and Towns: A New Framework for the Late Iron Age in Southern Jordan and the Negev." *Bulletin of the American Schools of Oriental Research* 323: 21–47.

Binford, Lewis R.

1971   "Mortuary Practices: Their Study and Potential." In *Approaches to the Social Dimensions of Mortuary Practices*, edited by J. A. Brown, pp. 6–29. Memoirs of the Society for American Archaeology 25. Washington, D.C.: The Society for American Archaeology.

Burton, Margie M.

2004   "Collapse, Continuity, and Transformation: Tracking Protohistoric Social Change through Ceramic Analysis; Case Studies of Late 5th–Early 4th Millennium Societies in the Southern Levant." Ph.D. dissertation, University of California, San Diego.

Caminos, Ricardo A.

1954   *Late-Egyptian Miscellanies*. London: Oxford University Press.

Chew, Sing C.

2001   *World Ecological Degradation: Accumulation, Urbanization and Deforestation, 3000 B.C.–A.D. 2000*. Walnut Creek: AltaMira.

Cole, John W., and Eric R. Wolf

1999   *The Hidden Frontier: Ecology and Ethnicity in an Alpine Valley*. Berkeley: University of California Press.

Costin, Cathy L.

1991   "Craft Specialization: Issues in Defining, Documenting, and Explaining the Organization of Production." *Archaeological Method and Theory* 3: 1–56.

Crowell, B. L.
  2004   On the Margins of History: Social Change and Political Development in Iron Age
              Edom. Ph.D. dissertation, University of Michigan.

Dalley, Stephanie, and Anne Goguel
  1997   "The Sela-Sculpture: A Neo-Babylonian Rock Relief in Southern Jordan." *Annual of
              the Department of Antiquities of Jordan* 41: 169–76.

Danin, Avinoam
  1983   *Desert Vegetation of Israel and Sinai.* Jerusalem: Cana.

David, Nicholas, and Carol Kramer
  2001   *Ethnoarchaeology in Action.* New York: Cambridge University Press.

De Vos, George A.
  1995   "Ethnic Pluralism: Conflict and Accommodation." In *Ethnic Identity*, edited by
              L. Romanucci-Ross and G. A. De Vos, pp. 15–47. Walnut Creek: AltaMira.

Dever, William G.
  1995   "Ceramics, Ethnicity, and the Question of Israel's Origins." *Biblical Archaeologist*
              58: 200–13.
  2003   *Who Were the Israelites, and Where Did They Come From?* Grand Rapids: Eerdmans.

Diamond, Jared M.
  2005   *Collapse: How Societies Choose to Fail or Succeed.* New York: Viking.

DiVito, Robert A.
  1993   "The Tell el-Kheleifeh Inscriptions." In *Nelson Glueck's 1938–1940 Excavations
              at Tell el-Kheleifeh — A Reappraisal*, edited by G. D. Pratico, pp. 51–63. Atlanta:
              Scholars Press.

Drews, Robert
  1993   *The End of the Bronze Age: Changes in Warfare and the Catastrophe ca. 1200 B.C.*
              Princeton: Princeton University Press.

Earle, Timothy K.
  1987   "Chiefdoms in Archaeological and Ethnohistorical Perspective." *Annual Review of
              Anthropology* 16: 279–308.

Earle, Timothy K., editor
  1991a   *Chiefdoms: Power, Economy and Ideology.* New York: School of American
              Research.
  1991b   "The Evolution of Chiefdoms." In *Chiefdoms: Power, Economy, and Ideology*, edited
              by T. Earle, pp. 1–15. Cambridge: Cambridge University Press.

Edelman, Diana V., editor
  1995   *You Shall Not Abhor An Edomite for He Is Your Brother: Edom and Seir in History
              and Tradition.* Archaeology and Biblical Studies 3. Atlanta: Scholars Press.

Eickelman, Dale F.
  1981   *The Middle East: An Anthropological Approach.* 2nd edition. Prentice-Hall Series in
              Anthropology. Englewood Cliffs: Prentice-Hall.

Emberling, Geoff
  1997   "Ethnicity in Complex Societies, Archaeological Perspectives." *Journal of
              Archaeological Research* 5: 295–344.

Emberling, Geoff, and Norman Yoffee
  1999   "Thinking about Ethnicity in Mesopotamian Archaeology and History." In *Fluchtpunkt
              Uruk: Archäologische Einheit aus methodologischer Vielfalt; Schriften für Hans Jörg
              Nissen*, edited by H. Kühne, R. Bernbeck, and K. Bartl, pp. 272–81. Rahden: Leidorf.

Enzel, Yehouda; Revital Bookman; David Sharon; Haim Gvirtzman; Uri Dayan; Baruch Ziv; and Mordechai Stein
    2003   "Late Holocene Climates of the Near East Deduced from Dead Sea Level Variations and Modern Regional Winter Rainfall." *Quaternary Research* 60: 263–73.

Erichsen, W. C.
    1933   *Papyrus Harris I: Hieroglyphische Transkription*. Bibliotheca aegyptiaca 5. Brussels: Édition de la Fondation égyptologique Reine Élisabeth.

Faust, Avi
    2004   "'Mortuary Practices, Society and Ideology': The Lack of Iron I Burials in the Highlands in Context." *Israel Exploration Journal* 54: 174–90.
    2006   *Israel's Ethnogenesis: Settlement, Interaction, Expansion and Resistance*. Approaches to Anthropological Archaeology. London: Equinox.

Feinman, Gary M., and Joyce Marcus, editors
    1998   *Archaic States*. Santa Fe: School of American Research Press.

Finkelstein, Israel
    2005   "Khirbet en-Nahas, Edom and Biblical History." *Tel Aviv* 32: 119–25.

Frank, Andre Gunder, and Barry K. Gills, editors
    1996   *The World System: Five Hundred Years or Five Thousand?* London: Routledge.

Frank, Fritz
    1934   "Aus der Araba I: Reiseberichte." *Zeitschrift des deutschen Palästina-Vereins* 57: 191–280.

Fritz, V.
    1994   "Vorbericht über die Grabungen in Barqa el-Hetiye im Gebiet von Fenan, Wadi el-Araba (Jordanien) 1990." *Zeitschrift des deutschen Palästina-Vereins* 110/2: 125–50.

Gardiner, Alan H.
    1937   *Late-Egyptian Miscellanies*. Bibliotheca aegyptiaca 7. Brussels: Édition de la Fondation égyptologique Reine Élisabeth.

Glueck, Nelson
    1935   "Explorations in Eastern Palestine, II." In *Annual of the American Schools of Oriental Research*, Volume 15, pp. 1–288. New Haven: American Schools of Oriental Research.
    1938   "The First Campaign at Tell el-Kheleifeh (Ezion-Geber)." *Annual American Schools of Oriental Research* 71: 3–17.
    1940   *The Other Side of the Jordan*. New Haven: American Schools of Oriental Research.

Goldstein, Lynne G.
    1981   "One-Dimensional Archaeology and Multi-Dimensional People: Spatial Organization and Mortuary Analysis." In *The Archaeology of Death*, edited by R. Chapman, I. Kinnes, and K. Randsborg, pp. 53–69. Cambridge: Cambridge University Press.

Grattan, John P.; D. D. Gilbertson; and Chris O. Hunt
    2007   "The Local and Global Dimensions of Metalliferous Pollution Derived from a Reconstruction of an Eight Thousand Year Record of Copper Smelting and Mining at a Desert-Mountain Frontier in Southern Jordan." *Journal of Archaeological Science* 34: 83–110.

Grattan, J. P.; S. I. Huxley; and F. B. Pyatt
    2003   "Modern Bedouin Exposures to Copper Contamination: An Imperial Legacy?" *Ecotoxicology and Environmental Safety* 55: 108–15.

Hart, S.
    1986   "Some Preliminary Thoughts on Settlement in Southern Jordan." *Levant* 18: 51–58.

1987   "The Edom Survey Project, 1984–85: The Iron Age." In *Studies in the History and Archaeology of Jordan*, Volume 3, ddited by A. Hadidi, pp. 287–90. Amman: Department of Antiquities.

1989   The Archaeology of the Land of Edom. Ph.D. dissertation, Macquarie University.

Hart, S., and E. A. Knauf
1986   "Wadi Feinan Iron Age Pottery." *Newsletter of the Institute of Archaeology and Anthropology, Yarmouk University* 1: 9–10.

Hauptmann, Andreas
2000   *Zur frühen Metallurgie des Kupfers in Fenan (Jordanien).* Beiheft 11: *Der Anschnitt.* Veröffentlichungen aus dem Deutschen Bergbau-Museum 87. Bochum: Deutsches Bergbau-Museum.

2007   *The Archaeometallurgy of Copper: Evidence from Faynan, Jordan.* New York: Springer.

Helfgott, Leonard M.
1980   "The Structural Foundations of the National Minority Problem in Revolutionary Iran." *Iranian Studies* 13: 195–214.

Higham, T.; J. van der Plicht; C. Bronk Ramsey; H. J. Bruins; M. Robinson; and T. E. Levy
2005   "Radiocarbon Dating of the Khirbat-en Nahas Site (Jordan) and Bayesian Modeling of the Results." In *The Bible and Radiocarbon Dating: Archaeology, Text and Science*, edited by T. E. Levy and T. Higham, pp. 164–78. London: Equinox.

Hodder, Ian
1982   *Symbols in Action: Ethnoarchaeological Studies of Material Culture.* Cambridge: Cambridge University Press.

Holl, Augustin F. C., and Thomas E. Levy
1993   "From the Nile Valley to the Chad Basin: Ethnoarchaeology of Shuwa Arab Settlements." *Biblical Archaeologist* 16: 166–79.

Homan, Michael M.
2002   *To Your Tents, O Israel! The Terminology, Function, Form, and Symbolism of Tents in the Hebrew Bible and the Ancient Near East.* Culture and History of the Ancient Near East 12. Leiden: Brill.

Hopkins, David C.
1985   *The Highlands of Canaan: Agricultural Life in the Early Iron Age.* Sheffield: Almond.

1993   "Pastoralists in Late Bronze Age Palestine: Which Way Did They Go?" *Biblical Archaeologist* 56: 200–11.

Hunt, C. O.; H. A. Elrishi; D. D. Gilbertson; J. Grattan; S. McLaren; F. B. Pyatt; G. Rushworth; and G. W. Barker
2004   "Early-Holocene Environments in the Wadi Faynan, Jordan." *The Holocene* 14: 933–42.

Jones, Sian
1997   *The Archaeology of Ethnicity: Constructing Identities in the Past and Present.* London and New York: Routledge.

Khazanov, Anatoly M.
1994   *Nomads and the Outside World.* 2nd edition. Madison: The University of Wisconsin Press.

Killebrew, Ann E.
2005   *Biblical Peoples and Ethnicity: An Archaeological Study of Egyptians, Canaanites, Philistines, and Early Israel, 1300–1100 B.C.E.* Atlanta: Society of Biblical Literature.

Kitchen, Kenneth A.
  1992   "The Egyptian Evidence on Ancient Jordan." In *Early Edom and Moab: The Beginning
                of the Iron Age in Southern Jordan*, edited by P. Bienkowski, pp. 21–34. Monograph
                7. Sheffield: J. R. Collis.

Knauf-Belleri, E. A.
  1995   "Edom: The Social and Economic History." In *You Shall Not Abhor an Edomite
                for He Is Your Brother: Edom and Seir in History and Tradition*, edited by D. V.
                Edelman, pp. 93–117. Archaeological and Biblical Studies 3. Atlanta: Scholars Press.

Knauf, E. A., and C. Lenzen
  1987   "Edomite Copper Industry." In *Studies in the History and Archaeology of Jordan* 3,
                edited by A. Haddidi, pp. 83–88. Amman: Department of Antiquities, Jordan.

Kramer, Carol
  1985   "Ceramic Ethnoarchaeology." *Annual Review of Anthropology* 14: 77–102.

LaBianca, Øystein S.
  1999   "Salient Features of Iron Age Tribal Kingdoms." In *Ancient Ammon*, edited by
                B. MacDonald and R. W. Younker, pp. 19–23. Studies in the History and Culture of
                the Ancient Near East 17. Boston: Brill.

LaBianca, Øystein S., and R. W. Younker
  1995   "The Kingdoms of Ammon, Moab and Edom: The Archaeology of Society in Late
                Bronze/Iron Age Transjordan (ca. 1400–500 BCE)." In *The Archaeology of Society in
                the Holy Land*, edited by Thomas E. Levy, pp. 399–415. London: Leicester University
                Press.

Levy, Thomas E.
  2002   "Tribes, Metallurgy, and Edom in Iron Age Jordan." *American Center of Oriental
                Research Newsletter* 14: 3–5.
  2004   "Some Theoretical Issues Concerning the Rise of the Edomite Kingdom: Searching
                for 'Pre-Modern Identities.'" In *Studies in the History and Archaeology of Jordan*,
                edited by F. al-Khraysheh, Volume 8, pp. 63–89 . Amman: Department of Antiquities,
                Jordan.
  2006   "Archaeology, Anthropology and Cult: Exploring Religion in Formative Middle
                Range Societies." In *Archaeology, Anthropology and Cult: The Sanctuary at Gilat,
                Israel*, edited by T. E. Levy, pp. 3–33. London: Equinox.
  2007   *Journey to the Copper Age: Archaeology in the Holy Land*. San Diego: San Diego
                Museum of Man.
  2008a   "'You Shall Make for Yourself No Molten Gods' Some Thoughts on Archaeology and
                Edomite Ethnic Identity." In *Sacred History, Sacred Literature: Essays on Ancient
                Israel, the Bible, and Religion in Honor of R. E. Friedman on His 60th Birthday*, ed-
                ited by S. Dolansky, pp. 239–55. Winona Lake: Eisenbrauns.
  2008b   "Ethnic Identity in Biblical Edom, Israel and Midian: Some Insights from Mortuary
                Contexts in the Lowlands of Edom." In *Exploring the Longue Durée: Essays in Honor
                of Lawrence E. Stager*, edited by D. Schloen, pp. 251–61. Winona Lake: Eisenbrauns.

Levy, Thomas E.; R. B. Adams; J. D. Anderson; N. Najjar; N. Smith; Y. Arbel; L. Soderbaum; and M.
Muniz
  2003   "An Iron Age Landscape in the Edomite Lowlands: Archaeological Surveys along the
                Wadi al-Guwayb and Wadi al-Jariyeh, Jabal Hamrat Fidan, Jordan, 2002." *Annual of
                the Department of Antiquities Jordan* 47: 247–77.

Levy, Thomas E.; R. B. Adams; A. Hauptmann; M. Prange; S. Schmitt-Strecker; and M. Najjar
  2002   "Early Bronze Age Metallurgy: A Newly Discovered Copper Manufactory in Southern
                Jordan." *Antiquity* 76: 425–37.

Levy, Thomas E.; R. B. Adams; and A. Muniz
    2004   "Archaeology and the Shasu Nomads: Recent Excavations in the Jabal Hamrat Fidan, Jordan." In *Le-David Maskil: A Birthday Tribute for David Noel Freedman*, edited by W. H. C. Propp and R. E. Friedman, pp. 63–89. Winona Lake: Eisenbrauns.

Levy, Thomas E.; R. B. Adams; M. Najjar; A. Hauptmann; J. A. Anderson; B. Brandl; M. Robinson; and T. Higham
    2004   "Reassessing the Chronology of Biblical Edom: New Excavations and 14-C dates from Khirbat en-Nahas (Jordan)." *Antiquity* 78: 863–76.

Levy, Thomas E.; R. B. Adams; and R. Shafiq
    1999   "The Jabal Hamrat Fidan Project: Excavations at the Wadi Fidan 40 Cemetery, Jordan (1997)." *Levant* 31: 293–308.

Levy, Thomas E.; R. B. Adams; A. J. Witten; J. Anderson; Y. Arbel; S. Kuah; J. Moreno; A. Lo; and M. Waggoner
    2001   "Early Metallurgy, Interaction, and Social Change: The Jabal Hamrat Fidan (Jordan) Research Design and 1998 Archaeological Survey: Preliminary Report." *Annual of the Department of Antiquities of Jordan* 45: 159–87.

Levy, Thomas E., and D. Alon
    1982   "The Chalcolithic Mortuary Site Near Mezad Aluf, Northern Negev Desert: A Preliminary Study." *Bulletin of the American Schools of Oriental Research* 248: 37–59.

Levy, Thomas E.; T. Higham; C. Bronk-Ramsey; N. G. Smith; E. Ben Yosef; M. Robinson; S. Munger; K. Knabb; J. Schultz; M. Najjar; and L. Tauxe
    2008   "High Precision Radiocarbon Dating and Historical Biblical Archaeology in Southern Jordan." *Proceedings of the National Academy of Science.*
    n.d.   "King Solomon's Mines? High Precision Radiocarbon Dating and the New Biblical Archaeology."

Levy, Thomas E.; T. Higham; and M. Najjar
    2006   "Response to van der Steen and Bienkowski." *Antiquity* 80: 3–5.

Levy, Thomas E., and Augustin F. C. Holl
    2002   "Migrations, Ethnogenesis, and Settlement Dynamics: Israelites in Iron Age Canaan and Shuwa-Arabs in the Chad Basin." *Journal of Anthropological Archaeology* 21: 83–118.

Levy, Thomas E., and M. Najjar
    2006a   "Edom and Copper: The Emergence of Ancient Israel's Rival." *Biblical Archaeology Review* 32: 24–35, 70.
    2006b   "Some Thoughts on Khirbat en-Nahas, Edom, Biblical History and Anthropology: A Response to Israel Finkelstein." *Tel Aviv* 33: 107–22.

Levy, Thomas E., and M. Najjar
    2007   "Ancient Metal Production and Social Change in Southern Jordan: The Edom Lowlands Regional Archaeology Project and Hope for a UNESCO World Heritage Site in Faynan." In *Crossing Jordan: North American Contributions to the Archaeology of Jordan*, edited by T. E. Levy, M. Daviau, R. W. Younker, and M. Shaer, pp. 97–105. London: Equinox.

Levy, Thomas E.; M. Najjar; and T. Higham
    2007a   "Iron Age Complex Societies, Radiocarbon Dates, and Edom: Working with Data and Debates." *Antiguo Oriente* 5: 13–34.
    2007b   "Iron Age Complex Societies, Radiocarbon Dates and Edom: Working with the Data and Debates." *Antiguo Oriente* 5: 13–34.

Levy, Thomas E.; M. Najjar; A. Muniz; S. Malena; E. Monroe; M. Beherec; N. G. Smith; T. Higham; S. Munger; and K. Maes

2005a   "Iron Age Burial in the Lowlands of Edom: The 2004 Excavations at Wadi Fidan 40, Jordan." *Annual of the Department of Antiquities Jordan* 49: 443–87.

Levy, Thomas E.; M. Najjar; J. van der Plicht; N. G. Smith; H. J. Bruins; and T. Higham
2005b   "Lowland Edom and the High and Low Chronologies: Edomite State Formation, the Bible and Recent Archaeological Research in Southern Jordan." In *The Bible and Radiocarbon Dating: Archaeology, Text and Science*, edited by T. E. Levy and T. Higham, pp. 129–63. London: Equinox.

Levy, Thomas E.; T. Higham; C. Bronk Ramsey; N. G. Smith; E. Ben-Yosef; M. Robinson; S. Munnger; K. Knabb; J. Schulze; M. Najjar; and L. Tauxe
2008   "High-precision Radiocarbon Dating and Historical Biblical Archaeology in Southern Jordan." *Proceedings of the National Academy of Sciences* 105: 16460–65.

MacDonald, Burton
2000   *"East of the Jordan": Territories and Sites of the Hebrew Scriptures*. Boston: American Schools of Oriental Research.

MacDonald, Burton, and Khairieh Amr
1992   *The Southern Ghors and Northeast 'Arabah Archaeological Survey*. Sheffield Archaeological Monographs 5. Sheffield: J. R. Collis.

Mazar, Amihai
1992   *Archaeology of the Land of the Bible, 10,000–586 B.C.E.* New York: Doubleday.

Miller, Daniel, and Christopher Tilley, editors
1984   *Ideology, Power and Prehistory*. New Directions in Archaeology. Cambridge: Cambridge University Press.

Muniz, Adolfo A., and Thomas E. Levy
n.d.   "Preliminary Analyses of the Faunal Remains from Khirbat en-Nahas, 2002 Season, Jordan." San Diego: UCSD Levantine Archaeology Laboratory.

Muniz, Adolfo A.
2006   "Feeding the Periphery: Modeling Early Bronze Age Economics and the Cultural Landscape of the Faynan District, Southern Jordan." Ph.D. dissertation, University of California, San Diego.

Munson, H. J.
1989   "On the Irrelevance of the Segmentary Lineage Model in the Moroccan Rif." *American Anthropologist* 91: 386–400.

Musil, Alois
1907   *Arabia Petraea*. Volume 1: *Moab: Topograhischere Reisebericht*. Volume 2. *Edom: Topographischere Reisebericht*. Vienna: Alfred Holder.

Na'aman, N.
2004   "Sources and Composition in the Biblical History of Edom." In *Sefer Moshe: The Moshe Weinfeld Jubilee Volume; Studies in the Bible and the Ancient Near East, Qumran, and Post-Biblical Judaism*, edited by C. Cohen, A. Hurvitz, and S. M. Paul, pp. 313–20. Winona Lake: Eisenbrauns.

Naveh, Joseph
1982   *Early History of the Alphabet: An Introduction to West Semitic Epigraphy and Palaeography*. Jerusalem: Magnes Press.

Oakshott, M. F.
1978   "A Study of the Iron Age II Pottery of East Jordan" with special reference to unpublished material from Edom. Ph.D. dissertation, University of London.
1983   "The Edomite Pottery." In *Midian, Moab and Edom: The History and Archaeology of Late Bronze and Iron Age Jordan and North-West Arabia*, edited by J. F. A. Sawyer and D. J. A. Clines. Sheffield: Journal for the Study of the Old Testament Press.

Ogden, J.
1995   "The Gold Jewellery." In *Excavations at Tawilan in Southern Jordan*, edited by C. M. Bennett, Volume 8, pp. 69–78. London: British Academy Monographs in Archaeology.

Patterson, Thomas Carl
1991   *The Inca Empire: The Formation and Disintegration of a Pre-Capitalist State*. New York: Berg.

Peters, E. L.
1967   "Some Structural Aspects of the Feud among the Camel-Herding Bedouin of Cyrenaica." *Africa* 37: 261–82.

Blaikie, Piers
1985   *The Political Economy of Soil Erosion*. London: Methuen.

Porter, B. W.
2004   "Authority, Polity, and Tenuous Elites in Iron Age Edom (Jordan)." *Oxford Journal of Archaeology* 23: 373–95.

Pritchard, James B.
1969   *Ancient Near Eastern Texts Relating to the Old Testament*. 3rd edition. Princeton: Princeton University Press.

Pyatt, F. B.; G. Gilmore; J. P. Grattan; C. O. Hunt; and S. McLaren
2000   "An Imperial Legacy? An Exploration of the Environmental Impact of Ancient Metal Mining and Smelting in Southern Jordan." *Journal of Archaeological Science* 27: 771–78.

Pyatt, F. B., and J. P. Grattan
2001   Some Consequences of Ancient Mining Activities on the Health of Ancient and Modern Human Populations. *Journal of Public Health Medicine* 23: 235–36.

Pyatt, F. B.; P. Birch; D. D. Gilbertson; J. P. Grattan; and D. J. Mattingley
1999   King Solomon's Miners: Starvation and Bioaccumulation? An Environmental Archaeological Investigation in Southern Jordan. *Ecotoxicology and Environmental Safety* 43: 305–08.

Raikes, T.
1980   "Notes on Some Neolithic and Later Sites in Wadi Araba and the Dead Sea Valley." *Levant* 12: 40–60.

Rainey, Anson F., and R. Steven Notley
2006   *The Sacred Bridge: Carta's Atlas of the Biblical World*. Jerusalem: Carta.

Rakita, G. F. M.; J. E. Buikstra; L. A. Beck; and S. R. Williams, editors
2005   *Interacting with the Dead: Perspectives on Mortuary Archaeology for the New Millennium*. Gainesville: University Press of Florida.

Rappaport, Roy A.
1969   *Pigs for the Ancestors: Ritual in the Ecology of a New Guinea People*. New Haven: Yale University Press.

Redmount, C. A.
1995   "Ethnicity, Pottery, and the Hyksos at Tell El-Maskhuta in the Egyptian Delta." *Biblical Archaeologist* 58: 182–90.

Renfrew, Colin
1986   "Introduction: Peer Polity Interaction and Socio-Political Change." In *Peer Polity Interaction and Socio-Political Change*, edited by C. Renfrew and J. F. Cherry, pp. 1–18. Cambridge: Cambridge University Press.

Renfrew, Colin, and J. F. Cherry, editors
    1986   *Peer Polity Interaction and Socio-Political Change*. Cambridge: Cambridge
                University Press.

Rosen, Arlene Miller
    1986   "Environmental Change and Settlement at Tel Lachish, Israel." *Bulletin of the
                American Schools of Oriental Research* 263: 55–60.

    2007   *Civilizing Climate: Social Response to Climate Change in the Ancient Near East*.
                Lanham: AltaMira.

Rothenberg, Benno
    1972   *Timna: Valley of the Biblical Copper Mines*. London: Thames & Hudson.

    1988   *The Egyptian Mining Temple at Timna*. London: Institute for Archaeometallurgical
                Studies and Institute of Archaeology, Thames & Hudson.

    1998   "Who Were the 'Midianite' Copper Miners of the Arabah?" *Der Anschnitt* 8:
                197–212.

    1999   "Archaeo-metallurgical Researches in the Southern Arabah 1959–1990. Part 2:
                Egyptian New Kingdom (Ramesside) to Early Islam." *Palestine Exploration
                Quarterly* 131: 149–75.

Rothenberg, B., and J. Glass
    1983   "The Midianite Pottery." In *Midian, Moab and Edom*, edited by J. F. A. Sawyer and
                D. J. A. Clines, pp. 65–124. Journal for the Study of the Old Testament Supplement
                Series 24. Sheffield: JSOT Press.

Royal Jordanian Geographic Centre
    2001   *Jordanian School Atlas*. 1st edition. Amman: Royal Jordanian Geographic Centre.

Sahlins, Marshall David
    1968   *Tribesmen*. New Jersey: Prentice-Hall.

Schloen, David
    2001   *The House of the Father as Fact and Symbol: Patrimonialism in Ugarit and the
                Ancient Near East*. Winona Lake: Eisenbrauns.

Sengupta, Gautam; Suchira Roychoudhury; and Sujit Som, editors
    2006   *Past and Present: Ethnoarchaeology in India*. New Delhi: Pragati.

Shmida, A., and J. A. Aronson
    1986   "Sudanian Elements in the Flora of Israel." *Annals of the Missouri Botanical Garden*
                73: 1–28.

Singer-Avitz, L.
    2004   "'Busayra Painted Ware' at Tel Beersheba." *Tel Aviv* 31: 80–89.

Small, D. B.
    1997   "Group Identification and Ethnicity in the Construction of the Early State of Israel:
                From the Outside Looking In." In *The Archaeology of Israel: Constructing the Past,
                Interpreting the Present*, edited by N. A. Silberman and D. B. Small, pp. 271–88.
                Sheffield: Journal for the Study of the Old Testament Supplement.

Smith, N. G., and Thomas E. Levy
    2008   "The Iron Age Pottery from Khirbat en-Nahas, Jordan: A Preliminary Study." *Bulletin
                of the American Schools of Oriental Research* 353: 1–51.

Stager, Lawrence E.
    1985   "The Archaeology of the Family in Ancient Israel." *Bulletin of the American Schools
                of Oriental Research* 260: 1–35.

    1985a   "Merenptah, Israel and Sea Peoples: New Light on an Old Relief." *Eretz-Israel* 18:
                56–64.

2003   "The Impact of the Sea Peoples (1185–1050 BCE)." In *The Archaeology of Society in the Holy Land*, edited by T. E. Levy, pp. 332–48. London: Continuum.

Stein, Gil J.
1999   *Rethinking World-Systems: Diasporas, Colonies, and Interaction in Uruk Mesopotamia*. Tucson: The University of Arizona Press.

Steward, J. H.
1968   "Cultural Ecology." In *International Encyclopedia of the Social Sciences*. 19 vols. edited by D. L. Sills, pp. 337–44. New York: Macmillan.

Tainter, Joseph A.
1988   *The Collapse of Complex Societies*. Cambridge: Cambridge University Press.
2006   "Archaeology of Overshoot and Collapse." *Annual Review of Anthropology* 35: 59–74.

Tapper, R.
1990   "Anthropologists, Historians, and Tribespeople on Tribe and State Formation in the Middle East." In *Tribes and State Formation in the Middle East*, edited by P. S. Khoury and J. Kostiner, pp. 48–73. Berkeley: University of California Press.

Twiss, K. C.
2007   "The Zooarchaeology of Tel Tif'dan (Wadi Fidan 001), Southern Jordan." *Paleoorient* 33: 127–45.

van Andel, T. H.; E. Zangger; and A. Demitrack
1990   "Land Use and Soil Erosion in Prehistoric and Historic Greece." *Journal of Field Archaeology* 17: 379–96.

van der Steen, Eveline, and Piotr Bienkowski
2006   "Radiocarbon Dates from Khirbat en-Nahas: A Methodological Critique." *Antiquity* 80: 1–3.

Wallerstein, Immanuel M.
1974   *The Modern World-System*. Volume 1: *Capitalist Agriculture and the Origins of the European World-Economy in the Sixteenth Century*. Studies in Social Discontinuity. San Diego: Academic Press.

Whiting, Charlotte M.
2007   *Complexity and Diversity in the Late Iron Age Southern Levant: The Investigation of "Edomite" Archaeology and Scholarly Discourse*. BAR International Series 1672. Oxford: Archaeopress.

Wright, H. E.
1968   "Climatic Change in Mycenaean Greece." *Antiquity* 42: 123–27.

Yoffee, Norman
1998   "Conclusion: A Mass in Celebration of the Conference." In *The Archaeology of Society in the Holy Land*, edited by T. E. Levy, pp. 542–48. London: Leicester University Press.

Yoffee, Norman, and George L. Cowgill, editors
1988   *The Collapse of Ancient States and Civilizations*. Tucson: University of Arizona Press.

10

WHO LIVED IN THE THIRD-MILLENNIUM "ROUND CITIES" OF NORTHERN SYRIA?

BERTILLE LYONNET, CENTRE NATIONAL DE LA RECHERCHE SCIENTIFIQUE, PARIS

INTRODUCTION: PROBLEMATIC AND AIMS

Excavations and texts found in the alluvium plain of southern Mesopotamia have led to models for cities and society that deeply influenced research made later in other areas of Mesopotamia. In these models, cities evolved from villages and are large, mostly irregular, fortified settlements made of the (haphazard) aggregation of houses, workshops, temples, shrines, and palaces built over many centuries (Stone 2007), while society was based on sedentarism and irrigated agriculture. Texts show that at some point these sedentary peoples came into conflict with nomads, usually labeled as Amorites, coming from the northwest, who finally took over at the very beginning of the second millennium.[1]

With this model in mind, it is not very surprising that archaeological work done later on in northern Syria, especially on the main mounds, was interpreted in the same way: major settlements are also considered there as cities with large populations ruled by kings, the major economic activity is said to be agriculture, eventually improved by irrigation canals, and society is considered to be mostly sedentary.

But northern Mesopotamia and central Syria differ greatly from southern Mesopotamia, both in landscape and in climate, and it is possible to distinguish two major geographical areas:

1. An area with sufficient rain for dry agriculture, above the isohyet of 300 mm rainfall, and where many tells are still visible; it is situated mainly in the west and northeast,[2] at the foot of the mountains.

2. A semi-arid zone under the isohyet of 300 mm rainfall, not suitable for agriculture without serious risks and with much fewer traces of settlement; it is situated mainly in the center, but includes also part (southwest) of the Upper Khabur (fig. 10.1).

Curiously, it is in this semi-arid zone that flow most of the perennial rivers — the Euphrates, the Balikh, and the Khabur. Along these narrow ribbons of water, irrigation is possible in small areas but in very restricted conditions; therefore, it is not possible to compare them with the alluvial southern plain. Most of this territory is otherwise just a huge steppe

---

[1] Semitic/Amorite names are mentioned in very early texts from the third millennium, see for instance Sollberger and Kupper 1971: 60, n. 2, about the added name "Lumma" to E'annatum, third king of the Lagash Dynasty, and about his nephew's and grandmother's names. This has recently been first reasserted by Marchesi (2006: 1–28), who linked

"his Tidnean name" (name of an Amorite tribe) to E'annatum; but he finally rejected it (ibid., p. 126).

[2] The northern part of the arch of the Fertile Crescent is mostly in modern Turkey and is not considered here.

incised by temporary wadis, the home of wild onagers and gazelles, but also an excellent pastureland for sheep and goats at certain periods of the year.

Obviously, the way of life that developed in this semi-arid zone is not necessarily the same as in southern Mesopotamia. In fact, the predominance of nomads and/or pastoralists in this area has long been evidenced in texts and sources from the third millennium until present times (Lyonnet 2001). These more or less mobile groups were first seen by the epigraphers as constant opponents (Rowton 1973; Kupper 1982), or at best as the main basis for the wealth of the cities because of their flocks, until it was discovered that the kings themselves belonged to the same nomadic tribes (Charpin and Durand 1986), and that nomadism and pastoralism had played a far more important role in the local societies than previously supposed (Durand 2004).

As do many ethnographic studies, these texts show several degrees of mobility and constant change of status and kinships within these groups, including moments of full sedentarism until they returned to mobile life again. Many reasons for these constant changes can be advanced, either political, economic, and/or climatic, and it is not easy to trace them in the absence of precise textual data. Many of these tribes, or at least part of them, spent/spend some months close to wadis or rivers during the winter where they dealt/deal with the plowing of the fields and small irrigation work to grow cereals, both for themselves and for their herds (Yedid 1984; D'hont 1994).

Though all this is known, nomads or pastoralists are most of the time still considered in an extreme way — totally illiterate tent dwellers dealing exclusively with animal husbandry — so that any new text or inscription, architectural, or agricultural feature has to be the hallmark of sedentary people without any connections to nomads except for fighting or eventually controlling them. Rare are those like F. Hole (1991), A. Porter (2002, 2004), or myself (Lyonnet 1998, 2001, 2004) who see traces of these mobile groups in the ruins they excavate in northern Mesopotamia or in the new documents they find.

On the basis of the results from a survey, I had pointed out a repeated cultural fracture at different periods along a line placed slightly higher up than the 300 mm isohyet (fig. 10.2) and proposed that the area to its southwest was linked to the steppe, and therefore a domain for pastoralists and/or nomads (Lyonnet 1996). Concerning the third millennium, this led me to understand the contemporary villages and *Kranzhügel* (or "round cities") of this semi-arid zone as due to semi-mobile pastoralists (Lyonnet 1998, 2004). In my proposal, these people are considered as integrated into a complex socioeconomic system and would have moved seasonally from the best suited areas for the cultivation of barley (mostly the river valleys) to the steppe plateau where their flocks could have pastured. In this system, villages are mainly used as storage places with numerous silos,[3] and only a few of them offered houses not necessarily used all the year around,[4] while most of the population — numerous according to the number of cemeteries found in the area (Lyonnet 2004) — probably lived in light shelters or tents, traces of which have not yet been discovered. Finally, the largest circular settlements are considered not as "cities" for a sedentary population, since only a few families could have lived there, but rather as places of gathering for these pastoral groups. They could have been used for different purposes: politics/justice/protection because of the possible residence for the sheikh of the tribe; religious because of temples for rituals; economic because of silos and empty places for the exchange of products.

---

[3] Sites like Tell Khazne, Tell 'Atij, Tell Raq'ai, Tell Kerma, etc.

[4] Sites like Tell Bderi, Tell Kneidig, Tell Melebiya, Tell Rad Shaqrah.

One of the main problems raised by many colleagues against this proposal is the size and the plan of some of these round cities, considered far too sophisticated to be due to mobile groups. It is the aim of this article to try to answer this important question.

Recent excavations have brought to light more data on round cities and it is now clear that they appear at two different times during the third millennium, first around 2900 B.C. in northern Mesopotamia and again around 2400 B.C. in central Syria,[5] and that they lasted for some centuries. Reconsidering three of these sites at different periods, Mari at the time when it was founded and during the first centuries that follow (Ville I, around 2900–2500 B.C.), Beydar at the time of the tablets that were discovered (around 2400 B.C.), and Al-Rawda before its abandonment (near the end of the third millennium), I will try, on the basis of the information given by their main excavators, to argue further for my interpretation: instead of being cities or even capitals conceived by and for a sedentary population, they were founded and inhabited by tribal groups dealing mainly with animal husbandry, part of whom lived most of the time in the surrounding steppe, but who were nevertheless able to produce grain and to build, including eventually some monumental constructions.

Though connected by a long tradition, each of these round cities at these different times of the third millennium presents a different image. This is possibly due to a variation in the mobile/sedentary status of the population at each of these different periods, or to historical events: different issues to explain these differences are raised in the conclusion.

URBANIZATION IN NORTHERN SYRIA AND THE ODD CASE OF THE ROUND CITIES

In northern Mesopotamia, it is during the Late Uruk period that the first urbanization process[6] is thought to have started. This ended rather abruptly for still unknown reasons and seems to have been followed by a short period of dark age. Few excavated large sites, except Brak, give an uninterrupted sequence from the fourth to the third millennium, and up to now there has not been enough information to understand what happened. It is only several centuries later, slightly before the middle of the millennium, that a second phase of urbanization is detected, contemporary with the Early Dynastic III of Southern Mesopotamia (Akkermans and Schwartz 2003: 233–87).

Curiously though, it is between these two urban phases, somewhere during the Early Jezirah I and/or II period[7] that a whole set of new circular settlements made their first appearance. These are usually known as *Kranzhügel* because most of them consist of a circular mound surrounded by a ring. Because they are being excavated, the best known are Tell Chuera, Tell Beydar, and Mari,[8] but there are about a dozen of them (see fig. 10.2). Their size is mostly much larger than the usual size of settlements in this area.[9] Other smaller

---

[5] Sites like Al-Rawda, Sheirat, Umm el-Marra.

[6] In Syria, no major city other than Habuba Kabira is known for this period. But it now seems that Brak and Hamoukar, like Gawra, extended to "city" sizes on local grounds already at the beginning of the Uruk Period or Late Chalcolithic 2–3 (beginning of the fourth millennium). Unfortunately, there is no comparable information in southern Mesopotamia at that time. How different the organization of those northern

settlements is from that of the city-states of third millennium is difficult to determine, for rare are the sites that have been excavated on a sufficient scale.

[7] Contemporary with Early Dynastic I or II.

[8] Margueron (2004: 66–67) refutes the idea that Mari is a *Kranzhügel* and dates the other *Kranzhügel* to a slightly later phase.

[9] Diameter of Chuera: 900 m, Beydar: 430 m, Mari: 1900 m, Malhat ed-Deru: 620 m.

contemporary sites,[10] such as Khazne, Rad Shaqrah, or Hassek, are also circular in shape though they do not present this ring.

Besides their architecture, another odd feature of all these circular sites is that they are exclusively situated in the semi-arid zone of northern Mesopotamia, where previous sedentary occupation was extremely rare (Hole 2002; Hole and Kouchoukos in press). Finally, it should be stressed that the cultural zone to which they belong is distinct from the area where "Ninevite 5" pottery dominates, since only a few sherds of this type of pottery have been found there (Lyonnet 1996; Ur and Wilkinson 2008). Though pots and peoples rarely match, this distinction, added to all the other differences mentioned above, could also be a sign of a different ethnic group from that of the Ninevite area. We consider that question in the conclusion, but let us first consider three of these round cities more precisely.

THE CASE OF MARI

Mari is the only round city that has been excavated enough to give some information on the period of its foundation (Ville I) (Margueron 2004: 49–123), even though it is known mainly through small soundings. It is also the only circular site known along the Euphrates[11] and this position in the river valley has led some researchers to doubt that it was one of the *Kranzhügel* because all the others are in the steppe, even if along wadis or depressions favorable for the collection of temporary water. However, the site is not close to the river but at some distance on the Holocene terrace; we return to the implications of this position below. The site has been extremely damaged and only part of it still stands, but the undisputable circularity of the inner city,[12] as well as the existence of the ring outside are, I think, sufficient features to correlate it with the other round cities (fig. 10.3).

According to J. Margueron Mari was founded as a new town on virgin territory in the beginning of the third millennium.[13] The outer ring was established at the same time and consists mainly of a huge heap of earth over a core made of a stone (gypsum) wall surmounted with mudbricks. No repair of this exterior ring has been done during the entire period I, said to have lasted about 250 years.[14] Though considered as a protection, it is not seen as a real defensive rampart at that time, and Margueron thinks that it mainly played a role against flooding from the Euphrates. The space between the ring and the town itself (300 m) was free of any structure.

The inner town (diameter 1,200 m) is enclosed by a real rampart of mudbricks on a stone base, with rectangular towers and doors. No repair was made on the inner rampart during the course of period I. From one excavated door, one street goes north probably to the center of the town, and several other streets are supposed to also converge there from the other doors.

---

[10] The same circular architecture also appears in northern Iraq (Hamrin) at Tell Gubba, Tell Razuk, Tell Maddhur, and Tell Soleima; see Forest 1996: 201–04.

[11] Margueron (2004: 67) mentions a similar site at Tell Mohasan, a small distance from Mari, but the plan he refers to in Geyer and Monchambert (2003: 132) does not seem to be circular.

[12] Even if the inner rampart is a juxtaposition of short linear sections.

[13] The foundation of Mari is dated between 2950 and 2860 B.C. (Early Dynastic I) by thermoluminescence and radiocarbon data, but ceramics are rather considered as belonging to the Early Dynastic II period (Margueron 2004: 8–9, 57–59). The end of period I is not yet precisely dated but it should be either late within the Early Dynastic II or at the beginning of Early Dynastic III (see nn. 14 and 15). Ville II starts during the Early Dynastaic III period (thermoluminescence date around 2550–2500 B.C.).

[14] It probably lasted longer.

Several excavations and soundings into different parts of the site show, for Ville I, a succession of different levels. Each phase presents a totally new arrangement even within one small area, and it is not yet possible to establish connections between the different areas:

- In the west (Ishtar temple area), from bottom to top, one large building has been discovered, made of bricks (only a few left) on large stone (gypsum) foundations (of the same kind as the wall inside the outer ring); it contains several small square rooms and one larger rectangular room but its function is unknown. It is followed by what seems to be a stone platform, then by small mudbrick multi-room houses and, finally, at the end of Ville I, by three large stone-vaulted tombs that apparently contained rich material but have been disturbed.

- In the same zone (area L), five levels were excavated with craft installations (metallurgy and pottery kilns) associated with modest architecture. In one of the levels, impressions of wooden wheels from a cart and two equid skeletons have been discovered. The upper level gave tombs with a very rich material and cylinder seals, one of which is dated to the late Early Dynastic II period.[15]

- In the north (area B), eight levels have been noticed, each showing thin straight or curvilinear walls and tombs. Unfortunately, the sounding was not large enough to understand the architecture.

- Under the palace, the first level encountered on virgin soil is that of six tombs[16] deprived of funerary material, built in bricks and compared to those of Kheit Qasim in the Hamrin (Iraq): they are deposited over a layer of earth said to have been laid artificially on virgin soil.[17] Over this level of tombs, circular hearths and layers of ash have been discovered. In the following phases, the area served for metallurgy, evidenced by the presence of a large hearth and installations associated with poor architectural remains. Several layers of decay follow until the appearance of another craft installation with a pottery kiln, hearths, and tombs. All this is finally covered by 1 m of both decay and leveling done before the reconstruction of Ville II; because of the presence of tombs, Margueron thinks that it is houses that had probably been leveled.[18]

- To the east of the palace (area H), nine different floor levels were found, eight of which are associated with small mudbrick architecture and two hearths, probably houses.

- Under the Ninhursag temple, a wide wall in mudbricks could be part of a platform 2.2 m high.

To sum up, the city of Mari Ville I does not present any proof of real urban organization (Margueron 2004: 103), except for the general shape and street plan. No system of collecting water (sewer or drain) is visible. Only one important building (said to be probably an administrative building) and platforms (one of which is mentioned as possibly a religious building) have been found, but the rest of the architecture is said to be modest, and the houses are small

[15] This information appears only on p. 296 under the legend of fig. 285 (Margueron 2004). The author considers that it means that Ville I lasted longer than said earlier.

[16] The tombs are said to be probably part of a cemetery.

[17] In a recent lecture, Margueron proposed that the earth comes from the digging of the canal bringing water into the town (*canal de dérivation*).

[18] Since tombs are said to be under the floors of houses.

and often rebuilt and/or restored. Furthermore, the architecture seems very varied. It is difficult to have complete plans of the houses but one is said to have a very small central space, while several others have only one standardized rectangular room surrounded by a courtyard with small utility rooms around it. The author compares this architecture to houses at Tell Arad in southern Levant or to others at Tell Mohammed Arab in northern Iraq (Margueron 2004: 105). Tombs are also of various kinds and present diverse degrees of wealth. The richest and largest are apparently all in the last level of Ville I. Finally, ceramics also combine different traditions: some, like "Grey Polished Ware" and "Scarlet Ware," are imported from Mesopotamia, others, like "Metallic" and "Ninevite Ware" from northern Mesopotamia, while the local ceramics seem to mainly consist of hole-mouth cooking ware with crescent-shape lugs and of rather coarse ware (Margueron 2004: 105, legend of fig. 76).

All these data do not fit well with the capital city that Margueron claims it to be. Rather than an administrative place, the large building could just as well be a collective storage bin, since only two doorways have been found. The very modest architecture of the houses, their constant repair and rebuilding, and the comparison proposed by Margueron himself with Arad, could rather make them temporary dwellings for mobile groups, living there only in winter time. This does not mean that during the course of Ville I some of them would not have settled longer. This could well have been the case at the end of this period around what can be considered as the tombs of ancestors (for such tombs, see Peltenburg 1999; Porter 2002).

Nevertheless, Margueron has vigorously rejected this idea of mobile groups arguing that the main building presents a degree of skill too high to have been built by semi-mobile groups even in the course of sedentarization (Margueron 2004: 103) and that metallurgical activities could not have been managed by such people, though there are several examples of such connections (Levy, this volume; Mouton 1999; Kohl 2007: 149–50).

Because he defends the idea of a city on a Mesopotamian model, he also considers that, being huge in size, Mari was inhabited by a large sedentary population. This statement implies a series of other postulates dealing with regional water management, and especially the construction of three major canals (Margueron 2004: 68–82):

- Water was needed inside the city, both for everyday life and for trade (harbor) and, since there is no evidence of wells and the Euphrates is too far away, therefore a by-channel, or derivation canal (*canal de dérivation*) was built that passed through the city itself.

- Irrigated agriculture was necessary to feed the people, and therefore an irrigation canal was built on the Holocene terrace.

- Trade was the vital concern of this capital city, and to favor communications both with the north and with Mesopotamia, therefore a navigation canal 120 km long was built on the opposite (left) bank of the Euphrates, with its head about 20 km up the mouth of the Khabur and its end in the Baghouz area.

Mentions of boats and of canals do exist in the Mari texts of the eighteenth century B.C., but for the moment nothing in them allows one to say that a canal and a harbor were located within the city itself or to correlate the mentioned irrigation channels — the dimensions of which are unknown — with the ruins still visible on the surface of the Holocene terrace.

Each of the canals proposed by Margueron is a huge enterprise and the first two would have dangerously threatened the city. The depth of the derivation canal needed for boats to enter the city would have made it a gateway both for the annual floods of the Euphrates and for human invaders, as mentioned by the author himself (Margueron 2004: 69). Dikes would have been necessary but none has ever been found. As for the irrigation canal, it is over 100 m wide and can be followed at least 17 km along the Holocene terrace but would have been much longer depending on where its head was. Not only does it present the same problem as the derivation canal (gateway for the annual floods), but also, as stressed by B. Geyer (Geyer and Monchambert 2003: 70–74), irrigation on this terrace without draining causes an accumulation of salt which ultimately puts any cultivation in danger. Furthermore, the necessity of such a huge irrigation canal has to be questioned since it has been established by the Mari texts that only winter crops were produced in the early second millennium,[19] so that water would have been needed only during late winter and early spring (Geyer and Monchambert 2003: 111, 194–95; Margueron 2004: 37, 81), when it rains the most and when the level of the Euphrates is at its highest. Simple small channels with elevating machines, such as shadufs,[20] would have been able then to provide enough water for the fields.

Finally, all attempts to date these canals have failed to show any trace going back to the third millennium. No section in what is considered to be a trace of the derivation canal has been excavated, and no sites dating to the third or early second millennium have been found along the irrigation canal (Margueron 2004: 37, 81). Only three sherds collected on the surface of a canal or of a secondary branch are dated to the Middle Bronze Age (Geyer and Monchambert 2003: 194).

The navigation canal, Nahr Dawrin, is 120 km in length and is sometimes dug within the rock of the above plateau. If really made during the course of Ville I, it would have been a colossal work, unique in the ancient Middle East for that period. Its position on the other side of the river, correlated to the fact that neither its head nor its end are directly across from Mari, makes it difficult to believe that it was done under and for Mari's control. Only three sites dating to a phase earlier than Islamic have been identified in a survey made along the canal and, as said by S. Berthier, they could be the ruins of a seasonal occupation (Berthier 2001: 163).[21] Later dates have a much more secure basis. Its construction could be due to the Assyrians in relation either to Tell Shekh Hamad/Dur-Katlimmu (Ergenzinger and Kühne 1991), because of the existence close to it of a canal on the right bank of the Khabur joining the Nahr Dawrin, or to Tell Masaïkh/Kar Assurnasirpal because it stands right above the city. But it could also date as late as the Islamic period since only Islamic sherds have been found in the four sections made at different places along the canal (Berthier 2001: 36, 52, 63). Furthermore, the height of the water flowing in the canal is said not to have exceeded 1 m, making the Nahr Dawrin not navigable for boats.

To sum up, there is no proof for any of the assumptions that Mari I, when founded as a *Kranzhügel*, was a capital city on the same model as those of southern Mesopotamia. This statement rests only on the a priori idea advanced by the excavator, "if we exclude the irrigation and navigation canals, we are condemned not to understand the foundation of Mari"

---

[19] We do not have botanical or textual information about crops during the third millennium. Since summer crops are known only during the Islamic period, it is supposed that the situation during third millennium was the same as that of the Mari texts.

[20] Margueron (2004: fig. 28) notes that such machines are attested on cylinder seals of the third millennium.

[21] In Geyer and Monchambert (2003: 212, n. 73), only one site, Diban 4 (site number 84) is said to be Early or Middle Bronze Age, but the data concerning this site (page 91) mention that ceramic is rare and the date Early Bronze Age or Middle Bronze is followed by a question mark.

(translated from Margueron 2004: 76). But, as I try to show, there are other possibilities for understanding the position of this settlement. If we see it as a central place for the gathering of mobile groups living there only part of the year, or as a place where only part of the tribe lived all year around while the rest wandered in the steppe around, there is no need for such huge water management; simple irrigation with elevating machines would have been sufficient to grow enough barley for the members of the tribe and their sheep. Mari would then have fitted naturally in its environment.

THE CASE OF BEYDAR

Situated along the Wadi Aaoueij, on the east of the Khabur River, Beydar is the eastern most *Kranzhügel*. Because of its location within the Khabur triangle, where most of the ecosystem is that of rain-fed agriculture, Beydar is usually correlated to the cultural area where Ninevite 5 pottery developed. However, as mentioned above, this has been denied by a survey showing that sites southwest of a line going approximately from Tell Brak to Ras-el Aïn were rather linked to the settlements of the semi-arid zone (Lyonnet 1996, 2004), and recently confirmed by another survey (Ur and Wilkinson 2008).

The date of the foundation of Beydar as a *Kranzhügel* is not yet precisely established, but is considered by its main excavator, Marc Lebeau, to be more or less contemporary to that of Mari (Lebeau 1997; Lebeau and Milano 2003; Lebeau and Rova 2003). Its architecture (exterior levee rather than rampart, empty space between the levee and the city itself, interior rampart with towers and doors) is also very similar to that of Mari (fig. 10.4). The survey done on the site before it was excavated shows that it was not established on virgin land, since previous occupations are attested (Lyonnet 2000: table 4, site number 15).[22] The excavations have not yet reached on a large scale the beginnings of the site in the early third millennium. I therefore concentrate on the period of the tablets found at the site and dated to the Early Jezira IIIb, or late Early Dynastic III.[23] This corresponds to Mari Ville II, famous for its successive palaces and temples, and to the period of Palace G at Ebla a little before its destruction by Sargon, or by Mari according to latest developments (Archi and Biga 2003). This period is that of the second urbanization phase of northern Mesopotamia mentioned earlier, and cuneiform texts have been found at the major sites, including at Beydar itself.

The site is considered as an important city, now identified almost certainly with ancient Nabada (Sallaberger 1998), but it was not the capital of an independent realm since it depended on the regional state of Nagar, modern Tell Brak. Even if not very large in size,[24] its "urban" character is often stated because of the presence of 216 written documents (tablets and sealings) (Lebeau 2004), proving the existence of an administration. The existence of a large imposing building on the acropolis (palace of the ruler), of four temples, as well as a rampart around the interior city, have led both the excavators and the epigraphers of the site toward this interpretation (e.g., Sallaberger 2007).

The most important subject of the first discovered archives is the production and administration of grain (Sallaberger 1996), a fact that shows the importance of agriculture and the

---

[22] Halaf occupation there is said to be possible, Ubaid seems not very important, but Late Chalcolithic/"Uruk period" is attested in four of the nine zones.

[23] Lebeau (2004) gives radiocarbon dates between 2475 and 2380 cal. B.C.

[24] As Sallaberger and Ur (2004: n. 23) note, its size is estimated differently by several authors: Lebeau: 29 ha (*sic*), Lyonnet: 14.5 ha, and Sallaberger and Ur: 17 ha, since the space between the exterior ring and the inner city is not thought to have been inhabited.

existence of settled villages around Bedyar. At least twelve, if not twenty-two "settlements" were administered by Nabada. On the basis of the texts, the population of the site has been tentatively estimated at 1,500 persons, though this figure is said to probably also include the villages immediately around (Sallaberger and Ur 2004).

The area where Beydar is located has been the focus of many recent rescue and/or regular excavations. All the excavated sites are small in size but many are surrounded by impressive ramparts. Most contain large bins for the storage of cereals, and some are exclusively focused on this activity, which confirms the practice of agriculture in this area. This has also been interpreted by most of the excavators to mean that these sites were settlements for sedentary populations (see references in Lyonnet 2004). Nevertheless, this and other data coming from the architecture, from the texts, and from archaeological research also present many aspects that do not fit well with the supposed urbanization and sedentary system.

As far as the architecture of Beydar is concerned, the excavations have shown that the inner town is mainly occupied by large official buildings (fig. 10.5) — the Official Block/palace, temples, and storage buildings. This does not leave much space for a dense quarter of houses and for a dense population in the city itself (Sallaberger and Ur 2004). To this must be added the odd presence of a large sheepfold close to the palace (Pruss and Sallaberger 2003–04). The space between the two ramparts is said to be a ditch excavated in the Early Jezira II period and re-dug in the Early Jezira IIIa, where water stayed for a long time, and therefore not suitable for houses (Lebeau 2006). As already mentioned, houses are also absent, or of very small size, in many of the small sites within the cultural limit mentioned earlier (see Lyonnet 2004).

Texts do underline the importance of grain, but a recent study of the area has pointed out an excessive degree of surplus production compared to the size of the sites, and also mentions the necessity of importation of labor for work in the fields, which implies mobile groups around (Ur and Wilkinson 2008). Furthermore, texts also stress the very high significance of animal husbandry administered by the palace, especially a considerable number of sheep and goats, and a special kind of equid — a hybrid between an ass and onager — able to draw carts or wagons. They also show the importance of secondary products like wool and tanned skins (Van Lerberghe 1996; Sallaberger 2004). As a matter of fact, grain is often mentioned as fodder for the animals (Milano 2004). This husbandry activity has been confirmed, as mentioned above, by the presence of a sheepfold close to the palace but also by paleozoological and paleobotanical research showing the immense growth of sheep-raising at the beginning of the third millennium in this area (McCorriston 1995, 1998).[25] Finally, a study of the place names related to the area and mentioned in the Ebla texts shows that many of them are formed on the basis of personal names, a characteristic also found during the Old Babylonian period and considered as a testimony for the existence of tribal groups in the area (Archi 1998).

These data, combined with ethnographic examples, rather tend to show that we here see a system of semi-sedentary (or semi-mobile) life. The sites and their ramparts would play the role of protection and storage for the grain, wool, and skins, as well as for the herds at certain times of the year, while the largest settlements — especially the *Kranzhügel* — would also be the place of the "house/palace" of the "sheikh" of the area, of temples, and a central point for diverse gatherings including trade.[26] The very small number of houses discovered altogether

---

[25] The date for the specialization of sheep-raising is now advanced to the beginning of the fourth millennium; see McMahon and Oates 2007.

[26] Similar "cities" have been described in the nineteenth century; see Ha'il in Arabia in van der Steen, this volume.

in the area, combined with the amount of sheep and goats to look after, the amount of grain
to be cultivated, and the construction of some huge settlements (especially the *Kranzhügel*),
all point to the necessary existence of "invisible nomads" living mostly in the steppe. Either
only part of them had settled and practiced agriculture, or they all settled in the winter to raise
enough grain for their herds and for themselves. Anyhow, there is no reason to oppose the two
groups who were all part of the same tribe(s). Ramparts could have been raised to prevent
razzias between different tribal groups.

However, it is not possible to deny that the management of animal husbandry had reached
by then a very sophisticated level, and, if there are many examples of ramparts and megalithic constructions associated with mobile life in the archaeological literature (for instance,
Braemer, Échallier, and Taraqji 2004; Mouton 1997), it is more difficult to find traces of an
administrative system, or of palaces.

THE CASE OF AL-RAWDA

Al-Rawda is not a *Kranzhügel* and is located in the west of the semi-arid zone of northern
Syria, about midway between the Euphrates and Ebla (Castel et al. 2004, 2005; Castel and
Peltenburg 2007). The area is considered by its main excavator, Corinne Castel, as the limit
for sedentary life since no settlement has been found eastward. However, a temporary wadi
and enough arable land in the *fayda*,[27] would have allowed people to settle there at different
periods.

Al-Rawda is not very large, about 11 ha *intra muros*,[28] circular in plan, and surrounded by
a rampart. It was founded as a new town at the end of Early Bronze III or early Early Bronze
IV (ca. 2400 B.C.)Its duration was rather short, being abandoned at the end of Early Bronze
IV (end of the third millennium). Previous occupations on the spot cannot be excluded, but as
yet there is no evidence for earlier strata. Up to now, the excavations have mainly concerned
the last period before abandonment at the end of the third millennium and this is the period
I deal with here.

The rampart, made of mudbricks on a stone foundation, is impressive, with rectangular
towers and five doors, one of which at least is said to be monumental (Gondet and Castel
2004). Two ditches and a dike on its exterior are also considered defensive features (Castel
and Peltenburg 2007). The excavations have established that fortifications did not exist in
the very beginning and were erected only in a later phase. Nevertheless, within a short period
of time the rampart was rebuilt once (Castel et al. 2005). Before the rampart was erected, at
least two levels with ashes and stone structures have been observed.

Inside the city, a geomagnetic survey has revealed a dense net of ruins and streets (Gondet
and Castel 2004), though there is no clue to distinguish the different phases of their construction. At least four wide radial streets go from the doors to the central part and three others
are concentric, the inner one apparently surrounding a central oval area. These streets seem
to have existed from the beginning to the end.[29]

---

[27] Local term for the arable land along a wadi in a
dry area.

[28] Approximately 15–16 ha with the ramparts.

[29] The streets are linked with the doors in the rampart.
It is therefore premature, I believe, to say that they
existed before the rampart was erected.

A temple *in-antis* preceded by a large courtyard has been excavated in the northeast. Two phases are attested, each with several reconstructions. Before this temple, two previous buildings existed with the same plan (Castel et al. 2005). In a room near the entrance, a dressed stone baetyl has been discovered (Castel and Peltenburg 2007). Two other temples *in-antis* have been detected in other areas of the settlement by the geomagnetic survey.

Three complete houses (fig. 10.6) have been excavated in the southwest section of the settlement (Castel et al. 2005). They are said to have been built in mudbrick — though there is no longer trace of them — on a stone foundation. They are dated to the last period of occupation, but present several levels: two major stages of occupation separated by a phase of abandonment have been identified in two of them, and repair is visible within the last stage. Their plan is almost the same, and consists mainly of two aligned rectangular rooms, usually communicating, and opening on a courtyard. One of these rooms was used as a dwelling (20–35 sq. m) and the other was devoted to storage (slightly less than 20 sq. m). Though they are not very wide, traces left by central pillars to hold the roof are visible. Eventually, small annexes were attached around the courtyard. The material found on the floor consists of jars, spindle whorls, mortars, and polishers. The largest house with its courtyard covered an area of 150 sq. m. Almost no botanic remains were found in the houses, and the paleobotanic study was therefore made on samples coming from the pre-rampart ash level. They contained mainly barley and up to 70 percent of wild species. A very small percentage of wheat, vine, olive, pistachio, and legumes is also attested (Castel et al. 2005).

The excavations done in the oval central area did not confirm the density of constructions visible on the geomagnetic survey but showed several buildings, the function of which is not yet clear, although they are apparently not of a palatial type (Castel et al. 2005). The regularity of the inner structure of the settlement is assumed to be a preconceived plan of urbanism, and only a sedentary population "significant" in number could have been responsible for it (Gondet and Castel 2004).

Here again, however, several features can be interpreted otherwise. First, the small size of the living space of the houses does not seem to support a significant population. Furthermore, their plan is closer to the long houses with central pillars dating to the beginning of the second millennium at Khirbet el-Umbashi (Braemer, Échallier, and Taraqji 2004: 141–60), a site linked to semi-mobile groups, or to that of contemporary Bedouin houses (Daker 1984; Jarno 1984), than to multi-room houses usual for sedentary populations. The noticed traces of abandonments and repairs within a short period of time could just as well be due to temporary life in the settlement, while the total absence of mudbricks over the stone foundation leaves open the possibility of the existence of a light superstructure (thorn bushes, or tent?), as in Mleiha two thousand years ago (Mouton 1999). The existence within the main temple of a cultic place with a baetyl, a feature considered typical, though not exclusively, of mobile groups, is also a sign that could be interpreted as a testimony for the presence of these groups in the "town."

Outside the city, on the nearby plateau, a necropolis with at least three different types of tombs (a majority of shaft tombs with collective burials, a few stone cists surrounded by a stone circle, and one tumulus) has been partly excavated. It is considered to be the cemetery of the city.

An intensive survey around the settlement has shown a dense occupation of the area. At least eight other sites are contemporary with Al-Rawda and are said to be occupied either by sedentary (site RW 11) or by semi-nomadic (site RW 6) peoples. Ten kites, several circular constructions in stones, and tombs of the same three types as those identified in the necropolis have also been identified. Several water-management systems (dikes, ponds, walls, etc.) and terraces made in order to control and/or to retain the flow of temporary water, both for irrigation and for the herds, have been noticed. Though no element can date them, most are considered to be related to the settlement of Al-Rawda (Castel et al. 2005). According to Castel, the survey around the city shows a hierarchy of settlements specialized either in agriculture (rain-fed or irrigated) or in pastoralism (Castel et al. 2005).

Though in the case of Al-Rawda the existence of mobile groups is not denied and sometimes even stressed, the water-management system, irrigation, and construction of terraces for the fields are all linked to a sedentary population different from the mobile pastoralists. However, many examples of such constructions are known to be the work of nomads, like in Jawa (Helms 1981), Khirbet el-Umbashi (Braemer, Échallier, and Taraqji 2004: 48–51), or near Hama (Yedid 1984).

To sum up, the general picture that stems from the different articles written about Al-Rawda is that of an area inhabited mostly by pastoralists — eventually identified as the Benjaminites of the Mari texts (Castel et al. 2004) or the Ib'al of the Ebla texts (Castel and Peltenburg 2007) — within which was inserted a "town" with a different population, said to have lived there year-round (Gondet and Castel 2004; Castel et al. 2005). This settlement is considered the result of an expansion of sedentary peoples, maybe under Ebla's control, in order to exploit the local resources of the nomads, especially wool, at a time when textile production was highly prized. It is also proposed that the site played a role as a kind of caravanserai in the interregional trade. Only recently, the possibility that pastoralists could have played a much more important role in this urban process has also been raised (Castel and Peltenburg 2007).

As shown by my remarks, there is no reason to differentiate the "round city" from the rest of the area. Once again, we are most probably dealing here with a population partly mobile and partly semi-mobile, but belonging to the same tribal system, and together responsible for the erection of Al-Rawda, the necropolis, kites, circular sheep-shelters, and the surrounding hydraulic systems.

CONCLUSION

These three examples of round cities, though dating to different phases of the third millennium, share many similar features and can be considered as belonging to a same tradition. Rather than cities on a Mesopotamian model, with a dense population living in large houses and depending mainly on agriculture, these settlements can be interpreted as places of gathering for semi-mobile populations dealing mainly with animal husbandry, but able also to raise their own crops (and eventually good metallurgists as well).

Even at the time when they are closest to the Mesopotamian image of the town, that is, when there is use of writing[30] and when a large house/palace is found in them, most of the evidence underlines that their major activity is that of sheep-herders. And even then, these "towns" are almost empty of houses, while most buildings in them consist of temples, of storage areas, and eventually of some large tombs that can be linked to the ancestors of the group.

---

[30] Writing is one of the ten criteria retained by Childe (1950) to characterize urban civilization, and these criteria are still more or less used by many authors.

A similar process of "urbanization" appears also in the Levant during the course of the third millennium. There too, small fortified towns appear and disappear very quickly, depending on the sedentarizing stage of the population of the area and on its participation in interregional trade (Nicolle 1999).

If their pastoralist way of life is now better ascertained, is it possible to say who lived in these round cities? Or to say it otherwise, do we have evidence as to their "ethnos?" This is far more delicate and there is no sure proof for what follows. It is, of course, tempting to relate these settlements to the Amorites mentioned in the early texts. We could, for that matter, relate them to the interpretations given by some of the epigraphers about E'annatum of Lagash (see n. 1): even if there is still uncertainty for the explanation of his "Tidnean name," we do have evidence of relations between northern and southern Mesopotamia at that time, since this king claims that, from the Anta-Sura of Nin-Girsu (or the northern frontier of his realm, according to J.-M. Durand's personal communication), he repelled Mari's assaults (Sollberger and Kupper 1971: 59). Instead of being assaults of an army, could it be attempts of the Mari nomads to enter the area with their flocks, a situation that is better known when later kings were compelled to build a wall against these northern nomads?

Even if antagonistic, these relations could perhaps explain the introduction in northern Mesopotamia of cuneiform writing, of southern-style seals, and of "palaces" for the main local rulers (more probably the previous sheikhs), albeit with many adaptations to the local aspects of life. Unfortunately, if the dates of E'annatum (twenty-fifth century B.C.) seem to fit more or less with the first testimonies of writing in Syria, they postpone the introduction of the southern style of seals[31] so that this explanation is not totally satisfactory.

We must also admit that we lack information as to a local formation stage for these round settlements. Nothing similar is known during the fourth millennium in northern Syria, nor in western Syria, the supposed homeland of the Amorites. However, possibilities for their origin should be searched for "in the North." As we know, the end of the Uruk expansion in northern Mesopotamia and Anatolia was marked by the intrusion, from Transcaucasia, of a new population linked to the Kura-Araxes culture. This population is characterized both by its semi-mobile herders[32] and by its highly qualified metallurgists (Courcier 2007), as shown by the discoveries made in Arslantepe (Frangipane and Palumbi 2007). Traces left by this migration can be followed from Arslantepe to the Levant over a rather long period of time (Greenberg 2007).[33]

It is usually supposed that newcomers, when entering a territory, push away the local population, especially in the case of mobile groups. This could eventually be an explanation for an eastward movement of the Amorites. But very similar types of tombs and weapons to those of Arslantepe have also been found all along the Euphrates, so that part of these Transcaucasian groups (and other Anatolian populations) probably also settled in the semi-arid zone of northern Syria.

In the study made by Marchesi (2006: 10), Tid(a)num is related to the semitic word for bison/buffalo. This animal has been considered by some as the totem of the Tidnum tribes,

---

[31] The intrusion of south Mesopotamian style of seals at Beydar is dated to the late Early Jezira II/early Early Jezira IIIa period by E. Rova (2008), before E'annatum's reign.

[32] Transcaucasian groups are more cattle herders than sheep herders.

[33] Some sherds of this culture were recently identified by me among the ceramics of Qal'at Seman, near Aleppo.

and as an eponym for Hammurabi's ancestors or for the primordial kings of the Assyrian King List, as well as some Amorite clans. The term is also often used for Amorite personal names. But no such animal ever existed in the semi-arid zone of northern Mesopotamia and it probably could not have lived either in the Levant mountains. On the other hand, it is well known in the piedmont zone of the Caucasus.

In conclusion, the population we are dealing with in the semi-arid zone of northern Mesopotamia during the third millennium is probably a mixture of different "ethnic" groups coming from different geographical horizons, but all sharing the same mobile way of life. Their skills, religious beliefs, language, and architectural traditions were certainly different originally. It is probably their mixture that made the appearance of these round cities in northern Syria possible. The language they ultimately spoke and wrote, and the ancestors they ultimately claim, do not necessarily have to be related to their original ethnos.

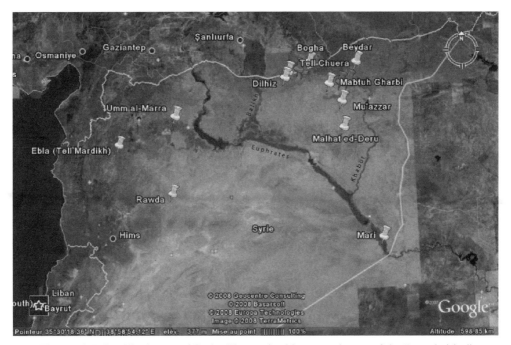

Figure 10.1. Satellite image of Syria. The semi-arid zone and most of the "round cities" mentioned in this article

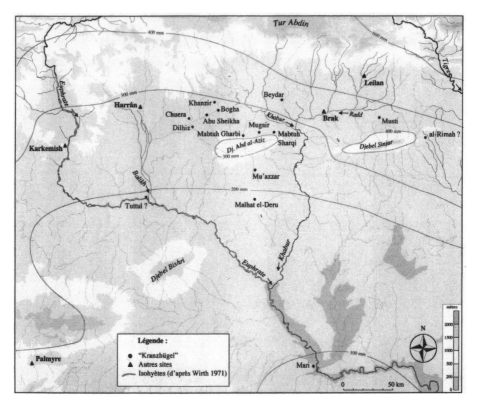

Figure 10.2. The modern isohyet curves and the *Kranzhügel* sites. Note that the 300 mm line was probably higher up toward the northeast during the third millennium because Tell Beydar is the easternmost *Kranzhügel*

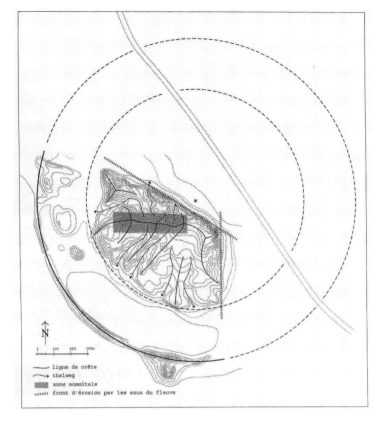

Figure 10.3. Mari, general plan of the actual mound (from Margueron 2004: fig. 23, p. 66)

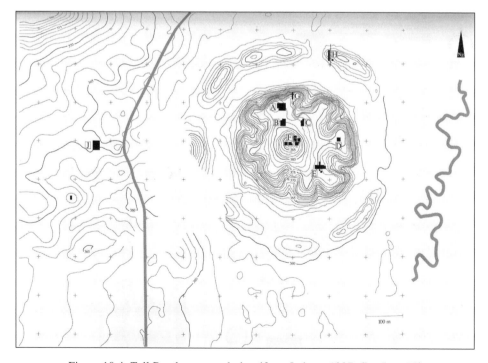

Figure 10.4. Tell Beydar, general plan (from Lebeau 1997: fig. 5, p. 15)

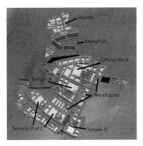

Figure 10.5. Tell Beydar, buildings in the inner city (from Tell Beydar/Nabada, The Resurrection of a Bronze Age City in the Syrian Jezirah, 2006, brochure accessible on the Internet site of Tell Beydar)

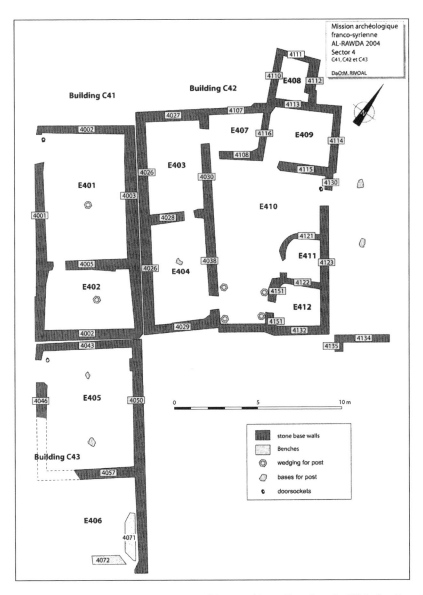

Figure 10.6. Al-Rawda, plan of the excavated houses (from Castel et al. 2005: fig. 7, p. 68)

BIBLIOGRAPHY

Akkermans, Peter M. M. G., and Glenn M. Schwartz

2003   *The Archaeology of Syria: From Complex Hunter-Gatherers to Early Urban Societies
            (ca. 16,000–300 BC)*. Cambridge World Archeology. Cambridge: Cambridge
            University Press.

Archi, Alfonso

1998   "The Regional State of Nagar According to the Texts of Ebla." In *About Subartu:
            Studies Devoted to Upper Mesopotamia*, edited by Marc Lebeau, pp. 1–15. Subartu
            4. Brussels: Brepols.

Archi, Alfonso, and Maria Giovanna Biga

2003   "A Victory over Mari and the Fall of Ebla." *Journal of Cuneiform Studies* 55:
            1–44.

Berthier, Sophie

2001   "Étude archéologique." In *Le peuplement rural et aménagements hydro-agricoles
            de la moyenne vallée de l'Euphrate, fin du 7e–15e siècle*, edited by Sophie Berthier,
            pp. 29–264. Publications de l' Institut Français d'études Arabes de Damas 191.
            Damascus: Institut Français d'études Arabes de Damas.

Braemer, Frank; Jean-Claude Échallier; and Ahmad Taraqji

2004   *Khirbet al Umbashi: Villages et campements de pasteurs dans le "désert Noir"
            (Syrie) à l'âge du Bronze; Travaux mission conjointe franco-syrienne 1991–1996*.
            Bibliothèque Archéologique et Historique 171. Beirut: Institut Français du Proche-
            Orient.

Castel, Corinne; Dorothée Archambault; Olivier Barge; Thomas Boudier; P. Courbon; A. Cuny; S.
Gondet; L. Herveux; F. Isnard; L. Martin; J.-Y. Montchambert; B. Moulin; and S. Sanz

2005   "Rapport préliminaire sur les activités de la mission archéologique franco-syrienne
            dans la micro-région d'Al-Rawda (Shamiyeh): Deuxième et troisième campagnes
            (2003 et 2004)." *Akkadica* 126: 51–95.

Castel, Corinne; Nazir Awad; Olivier Barge; Thomas Boudier; A. Cuny; L. Delattre; F. Joannès; B.
Moulin; and S. Sanz

2004   "Rapport préliminaire sur les activités de la première mission archéologique franco-
            syrienne dans la micro-région d'al-Rawda (Syrie intérieure): La campagne de 2002."
            Akkadica 125: 27–77.

Castel, Corinne, and Edgar Peltenburg

2007   "Urbanism on the Margins: Third Millennium BC Al-Rawda in the Arid Zone of
            Syria." *Antiquity* 81: 601–16.

Charpin, Dominique, and Jean-Marie Durand

1986   "Fils de Sim'al: Les origines tribales des rois de Mari." *Revue d'Assyriologie et
            d'Archéologie orientale* 80: 141–83.

Childe, Gordon

1950   "The Urban Revolution." *Town Planning Review* 21: 3–17.

Courcier, Antoine

2007   "La métallurgie dans les pays du Caucase au Chalcolithique et au début de l'Age
            du Bronze: Bilan des études et perspectives nouvelles." In *Les cultures du Caucase
            (VIe–IIIe millénaires avant notre ère): Leurs relations avec le Proche-Orient*, edited
            by Bertille Lyonnet, pp. 198–231. Paris: Éditions Recherche sur les Civilisations.

D'hont, Olivier

1994   *Vie quotidienne des 'Agedat: Techniques et occupation de l'espace sur le moyen
            Euphrate*. Publications de l' Institut Français d'Études Arabes de Damas 147.
            Damascus: Institut Français d'Études Arabes de Damas.

Daker, Naoras
1984   "Contribution à l'étude de l'évolution de l'habitat bédouin en Syrie." In *Nomades et sédentaires: Perspectives ethnoarchéologiques*, edited by Olivier Aurenche, pp. 51–79. Éditions Recherche sur les Civilisations Mémoire 40; Centre Jean Palerne 4. Paris: Éditions Recherche sur les Civilisations.

Durand, Jean-Marie
2004   "Peuplement et sociétés à l'époque amorrite: (1) Les clans bensim'alites." In *Nomades et sédentaires dans le Proche-Orient ancien* (Compte rendu de la 46ᵉ Rencontre Assyriologique Internationale, Paris, 10–13 July 2000), edited by Christophe Nicolle, pp. 111–97. Amurru 3. Paris: Éditions Recherches sur les Civilisations.

Ergenzinger, Peter J., and Hartmut Kühne
1991   "Ein regionales Bewässerungssystem am Habur." In *Die Rezente Umwelt von Tall Seh Hamad und Daten zur Umweltrekonstruktion der assyrischen Stadt Dur-katlimmu*, edited by Hartmut Kühne, pp. 163–90. Berichte der Ausgrabung Tall Seh Hama/Dur-katlimmu 1. Berlin: D. Reimer.

Forest, Jean-Daniel
1996   *Mésopotamie: L'apparition de l'état, 7ᵉ–3ᵉ millénaires*. Grandes civilisations. Paris: Paris-Méditerranée.

Frangipane, Marcella, and Giulio Palumbi
2007   "Red-Black Ware, Pastoralism, Trade, and Anatolian-Transcaucasian Interactions in the 4th–3rd Millennium BC." In *Les cultures du Caucase (VIᵉ–IIIᵉ millénaires avant notre ère): Leurs relations avec le Proche-Orient*, edited by Bertille Lyonnet, pp. 232–55. Paris: Éditions Recherche sur les Civilisations.

Geyer, Bernard, and Jean-Yves Monchambert, editors
2003   *La basse vallée de l'Euphrate syrien: Du Néolithique à l'avènement de l'Islam: Géographie, archéologie et histoire*. 2 volumes. Bibliothèque Archéologique et Historique 166; Mission archéologique de Mari 6. Beirut: Institut Français d'Archéologie du Proche-Orient.

Gondet, Sébastien, and Corinne Castel
2004   "Prospection géophysique à Al-Rawda et urbanisme en Syrie au Bronze ancien." *Paléorient* 30: 93–110.

Greenberg, Raphael
2007   "Transcaucasian Colors: Khirbet Kerak Ware at Khirbet Kerak (Tel Bet Yerah)." In *Les cultures du Caucase (VIᵉ–IIIᵉ millénaires avant notre ère): Leurs relations avec le Proche-Orient*, edited by Bertille Lyonnet, pp. 257–68. Paris: Éditions Recherche sur les Civilisations.

Helms, Svend W.
1981   *Jawa, Lost City of the Black Desert*, London: Methuen.

Hole, Frank
1991   "Middle Khabur Settlements and Agriculture in the Ninivite 5 Period." *Bulletin of the Canadian Society for Mesopotamian Studies* 21: 17–29.
2002   "Intermittent Settlement in the Jebel Abd al-Aziz Region, The Syrian Jezira." *Cultural Heritage and Interpretations. Documents d'Archéologie Syrienne*: 139–52.

Hole, Frank, and Nicholas Kouchoukos
In Press "Preliminary Report on the Archaeological Survey in the Western Khabur Basin, 1994." *Annales Archéologiques Arabes Syriennes*.

Jarno, Roland
1984   "Tente et maison: Le jeu annuel de la sédentarisation à Qdeir (Syrie)." In *Nomades et sédentaires: Perspectives ethnoarchéologiques*, edited by Olivier Aurenche, pp.

191–229. Éditions Recherche sur les Civilisations Mémoire 40; Centre Jean Palerne 4. Paris: Éditions Recherche sur les Civilisations.

Kohl, Philip L.

2007   *The Making of Bronze Age Eurasia*. Cambridge World Archaeology. Cambridge: Cambridge University Press.

Kupper, Jean Robert

1982   *Les nomades en Mésopotamie au temps des rois de Mari*. 3rd edition. Bibliothèque de la Faculté de Philosophie et Lettres de l'Université de Liège 142. Paris: Les Belles Lettres.

Lebeau, Marc

1997   "La situation géographique, la topographie et les périodes d'occupation de Tell Beydar." In *Tell Beydar, Three Seasons of Excavations (1992–1994): A Preliminary Report*, edited by Marc Lebeau and Antoine Suleiman, pp. 7–19. Subartu 3. Brussels: Brepols.

2004   "Le contexte archéologique et stratigraphique des documents épigraphiques découverts en 1996 et 2002." In *Third Millennium Cuneiform Texts from Beydar (Seasons 1996–2002)*, edited by Lucio Milano, Walther Sallaberger, Philippe Talon, and Karel Van Lerberghe, pp. 1–11. Subartu 12. Brussels: Brepols.

2006   "Tell Beydar/Nabada: La résurrection d'une cité du Bronze ancien en Syrie orientale." Conférence présentée aux MRAH (17-12-2006). http://www.beydar.com/pdf/nabada-conf-fr.pdf.

Lebeau, Marc, and Lucio Milano

2003   "Radiocarbon Determinations for Tell Beydar." In *Tell Beydar, the 1995–1999 Seasons of Excavations: A Preliminary Report*, edited by Marc Lebeau and Antoine Suleiman, pp. 15–20. Subartu 10. Brussels: Brepols.

Lebeau, Marc, and Elena Rova

2003   "Periodisation at Tell Beydar." In *Tell Beydar, the 1995–1999 Seasons of Excavations: A Preliminary Report*, edited by Marc Lebeau and Antoine Suleiman, pp. 6–14. Subartu 10. Brussels: Brepols.

Lyonnet, Bertille

1996   "La prospection archéologique de la partie occidentale du Haut-Khabur (Syrie du N.E.): Méthodes, résultats et questions autour de l'occupation aux IIIe et IIe millénaires avant notre ère." In *Mari, Ebla, et les Hourrites: Dix ans de travaux* (Actes du colloque international, Paris, May 1993), Part 1, edited by Jean-Marie Durand, pp. 363–76. Amurru 1. Paris: Éditions Recherche sur les Civilisations.

1998   "Le peuplement de la Djéziré occidentale au début du 3e millénaire, villes circulaires et pastoralisme: questions et hypothèses." In *About Subartu: Studies Devoted to Upper Mesopotamia*, edited by Marc Lebeau, pp. 179–93. Subartu 4. Brussels: Brepols.

2000   "Objectifs de la prospection, méthodologie et résultats généraux." In *Prospection archéologique du Haut-Khabur occidental (Syrie du N.E.)*, Volume 1, edited by Bertille Lyonnet, pp. 5–73. Bibliothèque Archéologique et Historique 155. Beirut: Institut Français d'archéologie du Proche-Orient.

2001   "L'occupation des marges arides de la Djéziré. Pastoralisme et nomadisme aux débuts du 3e et du 2e millénaire." In *Conquête de la steppe et appropriation des terres sur les marges arides du Croissant fertile*, edited by Bernard Geyer, pp. 15–26. Travaux de la Maison de l'Orient 36. Lyon: Maison de l'Orient.

2004   "Le nomadisme et l'archéologie: Problèmes d'identification; Le cas de la partie occidentale de la Djéziré aux 3e et début du 2e millénaire avant notre ère." In *Nomades et sédentaires dans le Proche-Orient ancien* (Compte rendu de la 46e Rencontre Assyriologique Internationale, Paris, 10–13 July 2000), edited by Christophe Nicolle, pp. 25–49. Amurru 3. Paris: Éditions Recherches sur les Civilisations.

Marchesi, Gianni

    2006   *LUMMA in the Onomasticon and Literature of Ancient Mesopotamia*. History of the Ancient Near East, Studies 10. Padua: Sargon.

Margueron, Jean-Claude

    2004   *Mari, métropole de l'Euphrate au IIIe et au début du IIe millénaire av. J.-C*. Paris: Picard/Éditions Recherche sur les Civilisations.

McCorriston, Joy

    1995   "Preliminary Archaeobotanical Analysis in the Middle Habur Valley, Syria, and Studies of Socioeconomic Change in the Early Third Millennium BC." *Bulletin of the Canadian Society for Mesopotamian Studies* 29: 33–46.

    1998   "Landscape and Human Environment Interaction in the Middle Khabur Drainage from the Neolithic Period to the Bronze Age." *Bulletin of the Canadian Society for Mesopotamian Studies* 33/*Travaux de la Maison de l'Orient* 28: 43–53.

McMahon, Augusta, and Joan Oates

    2007   "Excavations at Tell Brak 2006–2007." *Iraq* 69: 145–71.

Milano, Lucio

    2004   "Inscribed Bullae and Other Documents Mainly from the Area North of the Official Block, Texts 173–211." In *Third Millennium Cuneiform Texts from Tell Beydar: Seasons 1996–2002*, edited by Lucio Milano, Walther Sallaberger, Philippe Talon, and Karel Van Lerberghe, pp. 23–30. Subartu 12. Brussels: Brepols.

Mouton, Michel

    1997   "Les tours funéraires d'Arabie, *Nefesh* monumentales." *Syria* 74: 81–98.

    1999   "Ethnoarchéologie et sédentarisation: Évolution de l'architecture domestique à Mleiha (Sharja, Emirats Arabes Unis)." In *Habitat et Société* (Actes des 19e Rencontres internationales d'Archéologie et d'Histoire d'Antibes, 22–24 October 1998), edited by Frank Braemer, Serge Cleuziou, and Anick Coudart, pp. 109–30. Antibes: Association pour la promotion et la diffusion des connaissances archéologiques.

Nicolle, Christophe

    1999   *L'époque des premiers bourgs fortifiés: Pertinence de l'existence d'un processus d'urbanisation dans le Levant sud au troisième millénaire*. Bibliothèque Archéologique et Historique 156. Beirut: Institut Français d'archéologie du Proche-Orient.

Peltenburg, Edgar

    1999   "The Living and the Ancestors: Early Bronze Age Mortuary Practices at Jerablus Tahtani." In *Archaeology of the Upper Syrian Euphrates, The Tishrin Dam Area* (Proceedings of the International Symposium in Barcelona, 28–30 January 1998), edited by Gregorio del Olmo Lete and Juan-Luis Montero-Fenollós, pp. 427–42. Aula Orientalis, Supplementa 15. Barcelona: Editorial Ausa.

Porter, Anne

    2002   "The Dynamics of Death: Ancestors, Pastoralism and the Origins of a Third Millennium City in Syria." *Bulletin of the American Schools of Oriental Research* 325: 1–36.

    2004   "The Urban Nomad: Countering the Old Clichés." In *Nomades et sédentaires dans le Proche-Orient ancien* (Compte rendu de la 46e Rencontre Assyriologique Internationale, Paris, 10–13 July 2000), edited by Christophe Nicolle, pp. 69–74. Amurru 3. Paris: Éditions Recherches sur les Civilisations.

Pruss, Alexander, and Walther Sallaberger

    2003–04   "Tierhaltung in Nabada/Tell Beydar und die Bilderwelt der Terrakotten als Spiegel von Wirtschaft und Umwelt." *Archiv für Orientforschung* 50: 293–307.

Rova, Elena
  2008   "Seal Impressions from Tell Beydar (2002–2006 Seasons)." In *Beydar Studies* 1,
                  edited by Marc Lebeau and Antoine Suleiman, pp. 63–194. Subartu 21. Brussels:
                  Brepols.

Rowton, Michael B.
  1973   "Autonomy and Nomadism in Western Asia." *Orientalia* 42: 247–58.

Sallaberger, Walther
  1996   "Grain Accounts: Personal Lists and Expenditure Documents." In *Administrative
                  Documents from Tell Beydar*, edited by Farouk Ismail, Walther Sallaberger, Philippe
                  Tallon, and Karel Van Lerberghe, pp. 89–106. Subartu 2. Brussels: Brepols.
  1998   "Der antike Name von Tell Beydar: Nabada (Na-ba_4-da^{ki}/Na-ba-ti-um^{ki})." *Nouvelles
                  Assyriologiques Brèves et Utilitaires* 130: 122–25.
  2004   "A Note on the Sheep and Goat Flocks: Introduction to Texts 151–167." In *Third
                  Millennium Cuneiform Texts from Tell Beydar: Seasons 1996–2002*, edited by Lucio
                  Milano, Walther Sallaberger, Philippe Talon, and Karel Van Lerberghe, pp. 13–21.
                  Subartu 12. Brussels: Brepols.
  2007   "From Urban Culture to Nomadism: A History of Upper Mesopotamia in the Late
                  Third Millennium." In *Sociétés humaines et changement climatique à la fin du troi-
                  sième millénaire: Une crise a-t-elle eu lieu en haute Mésopotamie?* (Actes du collo-
                  que de Lyon, 5–8 December 2005), edited by Catherine Kuzucuoglu and Catherine
                  Marro, pp. 417–56. Varia Anatolica 19. Istanbul: Institut français d'études anato-
                  lienne Georges-Dumézil.

Sallaberger, Walther, and Jason Ur
  2004   "Tell Beydar/Nabada in its Regional Setting." In *Third Millennium Cuneiform Texts
                  from Tell Beydar: Seasons 1996–2002*, edited by Lucio Milano, Farouk Ismail,
                  Walther Sallaberger, Philippe Talon, and Karel Van Lerberghe, pp. 51–71. Subartu
                  12. Brussels: Brepols.

Sollberger, Edmond, and Jean-Robert Kupper
  1971   *Inscriptions royales sumériennes et akkadiennes*. Littératures anciennes du Proche-
                  Orient 3. Paris: Éditions du Cerf.

Stone, Elizabeth
  2007   "The Mesopotamian Urban Experience." In *Settlement and Society: Essays Dedicated
                  to Robert McCormick Adams*, edited by Elizabeth C. Stone, pp. 213–34. Ideas,
                  Debates, and Perspectives 3. Los Angeles: Cotsen Institute of Archaeology, University
                  of California; Chicago: The Oriental Institute.

Ur, Jason, and Tony J. Wilkinson
  2008   "Settlement and Economic Landscapes of Tell Beydar and its Hinterland." In *Beydar
                  Studies* 1, edited Marc Lebeau and Antoine Suleiman, pp. 305–27. Subartu 21.
                  Brussels: Brepols.

Van Lerberghe, Karel
  1996   "The Livestock." In *Administrative Documents from Tell Beydar* (*Seasons 1993–
                  1995*), edited by Farouk Ismail, Walther Sallaberger, Philippe Tallon, and Karel Van
                  Lerberghe, pp. 107–17. Subartu 2. Brussels: Brepols.

Yedid, H.
  1984   "Crise et regression du système pastoral bédouin nomade des hauts plateaux du nord-
                  est de la ville de Hama (Syrie)." In *Nomades et sédentaires: Perspectives ethnoar-
                  chéologiques*, edited by Olivier Aurenche, pp. 19–50. Éditions Recherche sur les
                  civilisations, Mémoire 40; Centre Jean Palerne 4. Paris: Éditions Recherche sur les
                  Civilisations.

11

BEYOND DIMORPHISM: IDEOLOGIES AND MATERIALITIES OF KINSHIP AS TIME-SPACE DISTANCIATION[1]

ANNE PORTER, UNIVERSITY OF SOUTHERN CALIFORNIA

In 1974, Susan Lees and Daniel Bates argued that the introduction of canal irrigation in southern Mesopotamia gave rise to specialized pastoralism at the expense of mixed farming strategies. Canal irrigation had higher labor needs than rain-fed farming, needs incompatible with the exigencies of both small-scale domestic, or sedentary (as Stein 2004 calls it) herding and cereal cropping; and as well it reconfigured the space available for pasturing animals (Lees and Bates 1974: 189). Household units therefore chose to pursue one subsistence strategy or the other, and those who pursued herding were forced to graze their herds farther away from the core irrigated zones, and, therefore, farther away from their social group. The reduction of land open to pasture because it was now irrigated, the greater population densities supported by irrigation, and the redistribution of population centers all contributed to the increasing physical marginalization of animal husbandry, and once households made their subsistence choice and became nomads they become "politically discrete and potentially predatory" (Lees and Bates 1974: 191) after only a very few generations. For although initially pastoralists would have had kin ties to the sedentary farmers with whom they exchanged goods, distance and mobility, fragmentation and dispersal, served to sever those social bonds.

This brief summary encapsulates why it is that, despite geographic contiguity and well-understood economic symbiosis, archaeologists still believe nomads to be essentially alien to urban and agricultural society in the Near East of the third and second millennia B.C., even after the shifts in consciousness brought by processual and especially post-processual paradigms. Whether or not one agrees with Bates and Lee's depiction of the origins of specialized pastoralism, the fundamental ideas that the only available choice was one strategy or the other; that social integration is only maintained by personal presence; and that pastoralists have no affective, that is, social and/or emotional, ties beyond the boundaries of their own immediate group, have proved very powerful in our reconstructions of pastoralism in the past, perpetuating this pervasive idea of an innate, an endemic, separation, if not outright hostility between the sedentary/urban world and nomads. Sometimes the debt to Bates and Lees is explicit (Abdi 2003; McCorriston 1997: 526), sometime it is only implicit in an unexamined intellectual inheritance of the discipline (such as Archi 2006: 99), but in either case it is based on understandings that are no longer theoretically nor empirically valid for the following reasons:

- it is an understanding derived from our own unreflexive positioning in creating and then viewing the "other," having long ago identified with, and privileged, the cultivation-based, urban world;

---

[1] This paper was prepared while a visiting fellow at the Institute for the Study of the Ancient World, New York University.

- at the same time it derives from anthropological understandings of kinship as determined only by blood and as therefore bounded and ultimately exclusionary, views no
  longer sustainable within anthropology itself;

- it is deterministic, for while pastoralism no doubt has certain characteristics and constraints, these do not necessitate any inevitable outcomes;

- it takes insufficient account of issues of "time-space distanciation."

While there are many histories that go into the first point, such as colonialism, historical
materialism, and the role of anthropological analogy in archaeology, and a vast amount of
recent work to elucidate the second point, it is the last two that are the focus of this paper.
What is of essential interest about pastoralism is not so much the mechanics of animal husbandry, but what the mechanics of animal husbandry often (but by no means necessarily)
lead to, that is, mobility. It is in mobility that the fundamental questions lie because mobility
brings constraints, ones obviously to do with time and space, but also to do with organization. Explanatory interest therefore is vested in the effects of mobility on social, political,
and economic life.

Although there are of course others, the key constraints on which this paper focuses are
those of fragmentation and dispersal, for these are the factors that are assumed to result in
that essential separation and disaffection between pastoralist and farmers that so thoroughly
undergirds the perspectives of Near Eastern studies. But separation is not an *inevitable* result
of fragmentation and dispersal for it may be countered by the stretching/shrinking of time and
space — distanciation as Anthony Giddens (1981) terms it. I suggest there is evidence that
indicates time and space was transcended in the ancient Near East, certainly in the third and
second millennia B.C., by an intricate mesh of social structures, political ideologies, religious
beliefs, rituals, and other practices, that, whether consciously intended or not, had the effect of
binding disparate, and distant, components of the sociopolitical entity into one. This complex
of structure, thought, and practice was constitutive of ideologies of kinship — not kinship as
pre-existing in actual connections through birth, although they are both present and implicit,
but kinship as created and incorporative of networks of social relations no matter actual birth
relations.

I discuss here two examples of the invocation of social networks as time-space distanciation. It must be stated categorically that these two examples are in no way adduced to prove
each other; rather they are simply parallel, and independent, phenomena. They do, however,
serve to elucidate each other when placed in apposition, for our sources in neither instance are
complete. The first is a second-millennium illustration as found in the Mari texts: the meaning and significance of the place called Der. The second belongs to the third millennium, and
consists of archaeological investigations at two sites that I propose are closely connected:
Tell Banat and Tell Chuera.

DER

Meaning "encampment" (Durand and Guichard 1997: 39–40), the various attestations
of Der seem to indicate that at least four separate locations bear this name. There is a Der on
the Balikh, one near Mari, one to the east of the Tigris, and one in the land of Apum, but as
Apum itself is apparently attested in two different regions (Charpin 2003), it is unclear to
which Apum this Der belongs. This might mean nothing more than the fact that there are a lot

of pastoral encampments that people encountered as they went about the kingdom's business, although if that were all there was to it, four hundred such places might be expected, not just four, and they would be attested not only in the Old Babylonian period but in all periods. But that is not all there is to it in fact. The multiple sites of Der are associated, albeit sometimes at a distance, with the multiple locales of Simalites, the pastoralist peoples from whom Zimri-Lim, the king at Mari, claims descent (Charpin and Durand 1986).

As well as Mari itself, the archives from which have provided unprecedented information documenting their activities (Durand 1997, 1998, 2000; Fleming 2004; Heimpel 2003), the Simalites constitute a number of diverse political entities, among whom the Yamutbal (cf. Durand 1992: 116) may be counted, and I would suggest, Ida-Maraṣ.[2] Located in the western Khabur, Ida-Maraṣ is more generally understood as a group of independent city states, probably relics of the third-millennium system, that by very definition, therefore, lie outside the mobile socioeconomic and political affiliation of Simalites and Yaminites seen in the Mari letters. But if at Mari the use of the word "Hana" designates the mobile section of Zimri-Lim's Simalite descent group (Fleming 2004), then its use by a king of the Ida-Maraṣ confederacy in recognizing the "abiding bond" between Hana and Ida-Maraṣ (Guichard 2002: 126, lines 10–11) perhaps represents a similar connection. The simple fact that Ida-Maraṣ is located in the dry-farming zone we associate with cultivation-based cities should not blind us to the presence of a pastoralist component associated specifically with these centers (Lyonnet 1998, 2004, and this volume; Porter 2007) evident in the texts (see Durand 2004: 130; and cf. Heimpel 2003: 30–31), especially if there has been a period of climatic degradation affecting agricultural productivity as Weiss and others have argued (Ristvet and Weiss 2005; Weiss et al. 1993[3]). And as well, the pre-Sargonic Beydar texts certainly show that multicomponent polities, by which I mean here both the devolved construction of the Nagar state and its reliance on cereal cultivation, mobile pastoralism, and stock breeding, existed in this very region in the third millennium (Ismail et al. 1996; Milano et al. 2004), the supposed peak of agricultural output.

Common identification as Simalite is no guarantee of either congruity in political organization or any necessary political allegiance, however. This is one reason why the word "tribe" should be avoided — it implies a certain political form in addition to the kin connection that the reality on the ground indicates is far more complicated and diverse than can be encompassed by a single term. Moreover, descent group identification and membership of any one polity are hardly synonymous categories, even if those polities are based on kinship ideologies. In very basic, even simplistic, terms, at the time of the Mari letters Ida-Maraṣ is a confederacy of multiple and highly competitive leaders based in towns (such as Heimpel 2003: 418, no. 27 20), who only seem to act in unity in reference to an outside entity (such as Durand 1998: 8, no. 442; Fleming 2004: 126), while Mari represents the intersection of city, steppe, and riverbank farmlands under a single king.

The Yamutbal, however, are something else again. They have two distinct locations according to attestations in the Mari texts and other sources, one in the north around Jebel Sinjar, and one in the far south (where the name is rendered Emutbala [Steinkeller 2004: 30]), in the

[2] Mari scholars generally consider Ida-Maraṣ to have only "affiliations" with Simalites (Fleming 2004: 126).

[3] In Porter 2007, I incorrectly characterize Weiss et al. 1993 as claiming that a catastrophic event brought about climate change at the end of the third millennium B.C., when in fact they argue that the causes of the change are unclear.

region between Larsa and Maškan Šapir, with histories that have been assumed as independent, but which might equally have been closely intertwined. For within this general duplication of the name Yamutbal there is a much more specific pattern: six town names — Harusanum, Kaspanum, Lakusir, Rasum, Razama, and Tilla (Charpin 2003: 14) — are to be found in both. This is in fact part of a much more widespread phenomenon of duplicated nomenclature practiced at this time, called "mirrored toponyms" by Charpin (2003) and Durand (1992: 109ff.), that has been argued as evidence of the passage of Amorites (Charpin and Durand 1986) from the west, across the north, and then down to the south (Charpin 2003). There is, though, no sure evidence of directionality or temporal distinction to these duplications (Charpin 2003: 19) in the Mari texts, and other explanations are equally feasible. In the case of the northern Yamutbal, Durand suggests that because they have both king and a center of power, Andarig, some of that group settled permanently in the area of the Jebel Sinjar, while the rest continued onward as tribal pastoralists, eventually coming to settle in the south (Durand 2004: 133). But the situation in both north and south may equally well parallel that of Mari, with mobile and sedentary components alike integral parts of the same polity. Perhaps the Yamutbal originated in one of these two places then went to the other, leaving some members behind, perhaps both areas were always incorporated in the seasonal movements of this group as they searched for pasture. Thereafter, either relations between the two components of the group were severed, if only because of time and distance, or they were continued through some combination of the following three factors: kinship connections, territorial connections, or political connections. While there is no external evidence of which I am aware that might prove an original political continuity between Yamutbal and Emutbala, the simple *absence* of any documentation of a continued polity is not conclusive, in that by the time of our sources for the northern Yamutbal, the Mari texts, a political connection might no longer exist for control of the southern Emutbala has been usurped by the Elamite Kudur-mabuk (Frayne 1990; Porter n.d.; Steinkeller 2004).[4] Such an event might very well have brought any unity between the two areas to an end (cf. Durand 1998: 214ff.; idem 2004: 133, n. 134), and this would have taken place before the time of Samsi-Addu. But a postulated political continuity may be imagined in several ways — a shared rule as we see for Kudur-mabuk himself and also for Samsi-Addu, both of whom gave far distant cities to their sons,[5] or as two independent leaderships nevertheless linked by idioms of kinship.

In the absence of these six town names in both north and south there would in fact be no reason to suppose any particular, or current, connection between Yamutbal and Emutbala, but their presence demands explanation. There is something more concrete going on here than replication because of simple historical memory or wholesale process of emigration. The shared name of Yamutbal in and of itself offers a clue, for it signifies, and would be understood as,

---

[4] Attribution of an ethnicity or even political affiliation to Kudur-mabuk is not without its problems, because although linguistically his name is Elamite (Steinkeller 2004: 30–31), he is called in his son's royal inscriptions (Frayne 1990: 206) "Father of the Amorites," a title taken by many to indicate actual Amorite ethnicity. Neither element of this duality should be taken too literally, however, for while the latter may be a purely political designation, the former may be the result of a number of situations, not least of which was a close association between the eastern highlands and the Tidnum group who are labeled Mardu/Amorite. Nevertheless, other circumstantial evidence suggests Kudur-mabuk may actually have been an Elamite. For further discussion of this issue, evidence for Kudur-mabuk's usurpation, and an alternative interpretation of the meaning of "Amorite," see Porter n.d., chapter four.

[5] Although Steinkeller 2004 argues that the kingdoms of Samsi-Addu and Kudur-mabuk are quite different, I conclude (Porter n.d.) that they are in fact very similar.

a conception of common descent affiliation, and such affiliation brings with it sets of rights and obligations. For Emutbala is located in the heartland of the southern Mesopotamian zone of irrigated agriculture, with very limited potential for pastoralist exploitation. While the assumption then might be that the Emutbala were no longer pastoralists, there is no a priori reason why this should be the case; certainly the invocation of kinship would give access to pasturage in the north, all things being equal — that is, if there were no adverse climatic or political conditions that would force seasonal movement in other directions or tend to exclusionary kinship practices. And here is where the mirrored toponyms assume specific meaning and function; they themselves may be thought of as geographic representations of ideologies of kinship and descent. Replicating place names is the replication of social identity; it is the invocation of a shared past and a future history that reinforces the mutual obligations that members of the same descent group share.

If access to the northern pastures were interrupted for some reason, the Emutbala might move eastward, toward the traditional pastoralist zones of the Zagros foothills. But here there is evidence of a second Ida-Maraṣ, and one might wonder if this attestation indicates the traditional grazing lands of the pastoralist components of the towns of the Khabur region that are incorporated under this rubric (fig. 11.1). On the face of it this does not make sense because the western Khabur south of the Jebel Abd al Aziz would surely be Ida-Maraṣ's main grazing area. But in the geography of the Mari texts and other sources there is a puzzling gap, for information about this area is conspicuous by its absence. Durand (2004: 131) understands this to be because it is particularly inhospitable, full of bandits, lions, and malaria,[6] yet this is the area where some of the great *Kranzhügel* sites of the third millennium such as Malhat ed-Deru (Kouchoukos 1998: 386–87; McClellan and Porter 1995) are to be found. Something has happened to change the habitability of this land, usually assumed to be climatic degradation. But for whatever reason, this area seems off-limits; it is far to the east that we see other indications of Simalite presence in the replication of Ida-Maraṣ.

It is far to the east too that we find the location of the third Der, in addition to the one on the Balikh, and the one near Mari. The locations of these three Ders is not coincidental, but, I suggest, specifically related to Simalite social structures, political ideologies, religious beliefs, and rituals in the practice of time-space distanciation; transcending fracture in the maintenance of political integrity and establishing both territorial relations and boundaries for three very differently organized entities: Mari, Yamutbal, and most diffuse of all, Ida-Maraṣ. All three political entities incorporated key towns where administrative functions were most obviously located[7] — the city of Mari goes without saying, but also Andarig for the northern Yamutbal, and Larsa and Maškan Šapir for the southern Emutbala. In Ida-Maraṣ, Ašnakkum and Ašlakka are prominent. All three political entities had significant mobile components, although because of their varying population distributions, geographic locations, and political organizations, the problems, and possibilities, wrought by this, were different. Yet in all cases, a ritual site, bearing the same name, figured large in their ideo-political lives.

---

[6] Malaria would imply water or at the least a humid climate, which would then suggest that human habitation was possible; while one of the explanations for the third-millennium presence in this area is a possible climate spike that subsequently evaporated, there is little doubt in my mind (and see Lyonnet, this volume) that pastoralism was a key subsistence component in the third-millennium *Kranzhügel* economy, allowing for large settlement in this region. Why then this does not seem also to be the case in the second millennium remains a mystery.

[7] Which is to say that the possibility that other towns shared this function always exists, as with the case of Nabada (Tell Beydar) and Nagar (Tell Brak).

We know most about Der at Mari under Zimri-Lim, located on a wadi also known, strangely enough, as "Balikh" (Durand 2000: 124; idem 2004: 126). Durand (2004) supposes that this was the place where the Simalites first arrived under Yaggid-Lim prior to his capture of the *šakkanaku*'s Mari, and so named it after their point of origin to the north, and that it is for this reason that Der became the locus of the festivals which establish the power of the king, postulated to be duplicates of those performed at Der on the better-known Balikh (Durand and Guichard 1997: 39–40). But Der on that Balikh may not in fact be the starting point of this situation at all. It is not the earliest attested Der; nor is it mentioned in the Ebla archive (Bonechi 1993).[8]

Although it might not immediately be evident that it has any relationship with the Amorites of the Old Babylonian period, if the Transtigridian Der, the Der of the god Ištaran, is the Der restored (year 6) and then destroyed (year 21) by Šulgi in the Ur III period (Frayne 1997: 95, 103[9]), it is perhaps the most significant of the four. Transtigridian Der was a cult center and apparently a settlement of substantial size and *it* is perhaps the symbolic capital of Simalite identity, the one replicated in all the others despite the fact that academic tradition has long endeavored to associate the origin of the Amorites with a western location, a problematic endeavor in and of itself.[10] For the history of this Der is tied to Šulgi's conquest of the lands to the east of Mesopotamia, with its plains and highlands suitable for pastoralism, a conquest I argue (Porter n.d.) is intended primarily for the appropriation of the broad-range animal-husbandry of that region and its incorporation into the Third Dynasty of Ur's taxation system. This Der is a liminal place, physically, politically, and doubtless ideologically, lying on the frontier between Mesopotamia and the mountains. It is also this very region in which the Tidnum, the pastoralist group identified as Mardu and the subject of much Ur III calumny, were based (Michalowski 1976; Porter n.d.), for despite a general conflation of Mardu and Tidnum as synonymous renderings of the category Amorite, and the general confusion over whether the homeland of the Amorites should be the east or west, Ur III references to the Tidnum are specifically to the east (Porter n.d.; see Marchesi 2006 for a full discussion of this topic).[11] The Tidnum are no respecters of liminality, "returning from their mountain lands" (ETCSL n.d.)[12] to the lowlands under Ur III dominion, as part of, I argue, a regular seasonal migration that both Šulgi and Šu-Sin wish to impede. Hence the great wall was apparently built.[13]

---

[8] There seems to be consensus (contra Frayne 1997: 95) that BÀD[ki], mentioned in the Ebla texts and in association with Amorites (Owen 1995), although provocative, is not another writing of BÀD.AN.KI (that is, Der) or alternatively, BÀD.GAL.AN.KI.

[9] See there for additional bibliography.

[10] There has long been something of a contest between the three regions associated with Amorites in the texts — the area around Jebel Bishri, the Jebel Hamrin, and ancient Šimanum, located somewhere to the north of the Khabur triangle (see Sallaberger 2007 for a summary); in fact all are locations of Amorite groups and none may be seen as an original homeland.

[11] Of course the Tidnum are mobile and we only have the vaguest of indication as to their pastoral range, and the location of Der, while thought to be in the region of modern Badra (Heimpel 2003: 608; Frayne 1997: 95) is also speculative.

[12] Compare Michalowski (1976: 199), "coming."

[13] In fact this is not a simple matter either. Šulgi claims to have a built a "wall of the land" in year 37, and in literary letters argued to come from approximately the same time, mentions the Tidnum (Frayne 1997: 106; Michalowski 1976: 84), although they do not in fact state directly that the wall is for them. Subsequently Šu-Sin claims to have built a wall which he explicitly calls "that which keeps the Tidnum out." Following Michalowski (2005: 200), I am inclined to think that Šu-Sin simply appropriated the construction of his forebear, renaming it, and perhaps repairing it.

It is not beyond the realm of possibility that the disruption to the regular seasonal movements of the Tidnum wrought by not only the construction of the wall, but also by Ur's regular campaigns against the highlands (Frayne 1997), as well as the military control of pastoralism from that region (Van De Mieroop 2004: 75, map 4.1) led to the general migration of the Tidnum westward, so that although there is no explicit association between Tidnum and Der evident in the texts, that this was the origin of the significance of the place name should be considered.

In a way though it does not matter which Der came first — all that matters is what Der is, and what the rituals performed there, do. This is a complicated discussion and my recapitulation of the rituals is entirely reliant on the work of the Mari team, especially that of Durand (2005) and Durand and Guichard (1997), and although my interpretation of aspects of the meaning and significance of mirrored toponyms, locations of Der, and ritual practice differs somewhat from theirs, this is largely only because I approach these materials from the perspective of a different problem, and a different paradigm. For in the preserved ritual texts there is, I think, a complex system of religious practice that served multiple purposes, with one aspect or another perhaps uppermost at any given point in time, but all of which may be characterized as integrative. There is the justification of Zimri-Lim's usurpation of rule through religious continuity in the elements of conflation (Durand and Guichard 1997) between the festivals of the goddess Eshtar of Irradan, who originated at Ekallatum and was brought to Mari under Samsi-Addu's rule; and Deritum, the goddess of Der at the time of Zimri-Lim, and the performance of the rites are split between Mari, specifically the palace, and Der. This itself should be read as the incorporation of the mobile population with the urban, just as it is symbolic of the linkage of a new, and external, regime with its subjects, for Deritum goes into Mari, the goddess of Mari does not come into Der.

But the details of these rites to Eshtar/Deritum also include sacrifices to the dead and their commemoration by the erection of monuments. Vassals, allies, and kin had to attend, although they did not want to, and the sacrifices made, sacrifices to the dead, were rituals of blood — that is, blood in the sense of kinship. They defined both the identity of the group and established political allegiances and fealty by connecting people through shared ancestry (Durand 2005; Durand and Guichard 1997). And shared ancestry meant shared participation, if only through invocation of names, in the *kispu,* the monthly feast at which the living and their dead were both present (Charpin and Durand 1986; Tsukimoto 1985).

At the same time, the location of Der outside Mari, the performance in fact of the festival to Deritum, may be understood not as a city celebration, but as a Simalite one, where it is the descent group and its reciprocal rights and obligations that is foregrounded. The name Der itself is thus a symbol of religious beliefs and their synonymous sociopolitical relations, so that its invocation at multiple sites is a deliberate claim of shared identity, at the same time as its use establishes an old history in a new place. These rituals embodied the past in the future; and they embodied time in place — not only at the local level, serving to draw together the distant elements of Zimri-Lim's polity, but on a pan-regional level as well. For Der on the Balikh, Der at Mari, and even the Transtigridian Der become thereby one and the same, and thus the far-flung members of the Simalite entity are bound together in terms of social, even if not political, identity.[14]

---

[14] As an aside, there is a stone monument from Larsa on which year names are recorded that Durand and Guichard (1997: 41) suggest serves a similar function — the simple reading of the list serves to invoke the line of dead ancestors and is as well a recitation of the history of the country that brings a concept of time into the realm of religion.

There is a micro-level therefore on which time-space distanciation is accomplished, maintaining linkages between members of the same polity not always co-located; and a macro-level, where the respective locations of Der in the vicinity of Simalite pasturage takes on yet another dimension. Given the commemorative and mortuary aspect of the Der rituals on the two Balikhs, the dead are present at these sites at the very least symbolically. The presence of the dead may mark territorial and ancestral claims to lands only seasonally used, especially if in above-ground mortuary monuments (Porter 2002b); they also mark boundaries and inhibit their transgression through fear of the wrath of the dead. Der on the Balikh is close to the rival Yaminite consortium of Zalmaqum, always given that these locations are approximately right, Transtigridian Der in the vicinity of that perennial problem Ešnunna on the one side and Elam on the other. Der at Mari is bordered by Suhum, one-time possession of Ešnunna but populated by Simalites at the time of Zimri-Lim (Durand 2004: 155).

Of course it is this last caveat that should be emphasized — historical geography is a very speculative endeavor, but if the locations of most of these names is even vaguely appropriate, then the potential for the kind of relationships of place I have outlined is worth investigating. The fundamentals of interpretation — that kinship structures are manifest in place and perpetuated through the dead in order to build the ties that bind, perpetuating social and political identity thereby — is attested in the *hi'arum* ritual, the "exchange of blood" involving the sacrifice of donkeys, that creates family ties out of political accords, requiring participation in the ancestor traditions of one's new brother or father (Charpin 1993: 182–88; Durand 1992: 117; Durand and Guichard 1997: 40). The people of the second millennium at least understood that kinship was as much socially as biologically constructed, long before anthropologists came to the realization that Evans-Pritchard's (1969) segmentary opposition theory was by no means the end, or even the state, of the matter. Kinship itself was, and is, the means of time-space distanciation, functioning inclusively or exclusively according to contingent circumstances. The real question then is when, and why, kinship appears to operate as one or the other.

The understanding of how mobility works in the modern world — even since the Islamic conquests, in fact — largely, and I would argue inappropriately, shapes our understanding of mobility in the ancient world and its outcomes, leading to a reductionist view that there was only one such: a profound social and psychological separation between mobile populations and sedentary ones. But any situation, any constraint, always has multiple possible outcomes and/or resolutions, and which outcome eventuates is the product of a complex series of contingent factors, the proper subject of investigation. But it does not stop there. Outcomes have a dynamic of their own. Invoking a geographic kinship in order to counter potential fragmentation implicit in mobility fashioned spatial relationships and associated political interactions; invoking social kinship as politics produced overlapping networks of representation and identity that are the very reason we have such difficulty today in sorting out what it means to be Amorite.

TELL BANAT[15]

This idea of kinship and ancestry configured through relationships of place immediately evokes the implicit meaning of certain burial practices in the third millennium, at the same time as it adds another dimension to their understanding. I have spelled out the details of this elsewhere (Porter 2002b), but in brief, I have argued that the establishment of above-ground mortuary remains in the Euphrates River valley in the early third millennium B.C., and around which the settlement of Tell Banat was a little later to grow, was the materialization of a social system based on ancestors in order to establish a history of place in the face of competing claims to territory. Although we do not know the inhumation practices of the original burials at the heart of these mounds, the nature of the subsequent practices in their enlargement tells us that those ancestors were instrumental in maintaining certain conceptions — self-conceptions — of Banat society as a communitarian, kin-based group (Porter 2002a).

There is another site, however, that is not noted for its burial remains but that also shows the materialization of ideologies of kinship in its history and morphology in a number of ways. This is Tell Chuera, one of the largest of the third-millennium settlements in Syria (Meyer and Hempelmann 2006: 23),[16] located midway between the Balikh and Khabur rivers. There are three features that are very distinctive of, and perhaps peculiar to, Tell Chuera, other than its double wreath or *Kranzhügel* form. These are:

- the prevalence of domestic architecture across the site revealed through geomagnetic prospection and excavation, but especially at its center, where public buildings might be expected;

- the lack of any evidence as yet for a palace until just before the Akkadian period[17] (Pruss n.d. c);

- the ubiquity of the *in-antis* architectural form for non-residential structures.

Combined, these three things also suggest a particular self-conception — and realization — of a communitarian, kin-based society.

The first two factors are virtually self-explanatory: unlike many large-scale sites of this time period such as Ebla or Mari, the upper mound of the *Kranzhügel* is not given over to public, administrative function housed in massive buildings that dominate the symbolic heart of the site, its center, but rather to the domestic occupation in which the site seems to have its origins (Dohmann-Pfälzner and Pfälzner 1996; Hempelmann n.d. a–b; Pruss n.d. b).[18] For

---

[15] My thanks to the Directorate General of Antiquities and Museums, Syria, especially in the persons of past director-general Sultan Muhessen, and present director-general Bassam Gamous; directors of excavations Adnan Bounni and Michel al-Maqdissi, Damascus, and Wahid Hyatta and Nadim Fakesh, directors, Aleppo Museum, for their support of excavations and research at Tell Banat; also to my co-director of the Euphrates Archaeology Project, Thomas McClellan.

[16] Compare sites listed in McClellan and Porter 1995: 51; Stein 2004: 67.

[17] The details of the building beneath Palace F belonging to level 3 are insufficiently clear as yet to properly determine a function.

[18] See Meyer (n.d.) for a color plan of Tell Chuera showing the functions of different areas. However, Meyer and Hempelmann (2006) have a very differing interpretation of the organization of the inner part of the settlement; they propose that the linear depression evident in the contour plan at the center of the site is a defining characteristic of some *Kranzhügel* sites. They further propose (2006: 25) that this line links the public architecture at Chuera in a string (Palace F and the *Steinbau* complex are opposite each other) and is therefore evidence, in conjunction with the street layout, of an elite authority that can design and implement a city plan, conceiving the domestic housing as peripheral to that authority.

at the beginning of the third millennium, the new town was laid out over an even earlier tell, which had at its center a large open space constituting a public square surrounded on all sides by houses (Pruss n.d. b). This did not change even toward the end of the Early Dynastic period, when the first "official building," the precursor to the level 2 "palace," was constructed on the outer edge of the inner mound (Orthmann et al. 1995: 121–50; Pruss n.d. a, n.d. c) but remained the enduring core of the settlement.

The third factor, however, requires a little more discussion. The *in-antis* form, with its one long room and open forecourt, is commonly accepted as religious in function, and its deployment at Tell Chuera is quite informative. On the one hand, it is repeatedly used in a massive, monumental complex, *Steinbau* I through *Steinbau* IV, and each component might be thought to regulate access to the uppermost building in a kind of "via sacra" (Meyer n.d.; Pruss n.d. c). On the other hand, two small *in-antis* structures were embedded among domestic houses, the mudbrick *Kleiner Antentempel* (Dohmann-Pfälzner and Pfälzner 1996), in which a group of statues was found (Moortgat 1965), and opposite it, the stone-founded *Steinbau* VI (Pruss n.d.c). Both of them date originally to Tell Chuera (TCH) Period ID, although the antecedent structure of the *Kleiner Antentempel* precedes the construction of *Steinbau* VI which is the latest building in this form. The association of statues, residential housing, and temples suggest that the *Kleiner Antentempel* at least was the locus of ancestor practices, and serviced therefore a descent group, although we cannot know how that group was constituted. As has recently been argued, the statues, stylistically earlier than the context in which they were found, would have been handed down from generation to generation, at the same time as the structures in which they were housed were repeatedly rebuilt as occupation levels continued to amass (Hempelmann n.d.b). Both statue and structure underwent a commensurate transformation: as the statues became increasingly divorced from the human world, where they were originally representations of actual beings (perhaps even of the individuals buried beneath this house [Hempelmann n.d.b]), and more and more relegated to the other world, the earliest building in this sequence, founded in level 13/TCH IB, was transformed from domicile to religious structure in levels 3–1/TCH ID. Interestingly, while other houses underwent modification through these thirteen levels, the building beneath the *Kleiner Antentempel* did not (Hempelmann n.d. b). Hodder (n.d.) has called such long-lived buildings that contained socially and ideologically significant remains (burials in the case of Çatal Höyük) "history houses," that because they embodied and anchored the temporal and spatial identity of the group, served as magnets around which those who would associate themselves with that identity clustered, and this interpretation seems appropriate to the *Kleiner Antentempel* with its statues. If correct, the addition of a second *in-antis* structure, *Steinbau* VI, in the depression in the center of the site might suggest the emergence of competing views of social structuring as has been suggested for Tell Banat (Porter 2002a) at the same time. The discovery of a statue in *Steinbau* VI (Hempelmann, pers. comm.) is provocative, but further comment will have to await publication of the materials.

Outside the city is another *in-antis* structure, the *Aussenbau*, with its standing stones (Moortgat 1965: pls. 7–8). Statues and stones may equally constitute ancestor practices as

---

However, to my knowledge, Palace F is later than the *Steinbau* complex and *Steinbau* VI later still, and so these buildings were not instituted as a unit even if the street layout is indicative of a city plan, which can be accomplished by a community equally well as

by a centralized power, and thus far, domestic housing precedes any public construction at the site. But whatever one's interpretation of the layout of this site, it differs markedly from acropolis sites such as Ebla for example.

lineage definition and linkage albeit in different ways,[19] and it is tempting to suggest that the *Aussenbau* was so located to serve the seasonal needs of non-resident groups, just as the stele at Jebelet et-Beihda (McClellan 2004; Meyer 1997), and perhaps a similar connection is implicit in the standing stone found in the third-millennium temple complex at al-Rawda (Castel and Peltenburg 2007: 608, fig. 8). Lest a distinction is assumed here between the religious practices of nomads and those of the cities, however,[20] it must be remembered that a baetyl was found at Ebla in Temple N of the lower city (Matthiae 1980), and they were also placed in temples of the gods within the city of Mari as well (e.g., Margueron 2004: 263).[21]

There is no specific way at this point in time to prove the presence — or absence for that matter — of mobile pastoralists at Tell Chuera without texts, although the subject is under investigation at the Universities of Halle-Wittenberg and Leipzig (n.d.) and promising work is being done at other sites in distinguishing between the morphology of sheep/goat bones of locally grazed sheep and those taken long distances that may come to clarify the matter (Weber 2006). There is a certain environmental logic, though, that suggests pastoralism is a necessary component of risky agriculture. Chuera is located in a dry-farming zone where crop failure is a constant possibility, and today pastoralists move back and forth between that area and the Euphrates. The pre-Sargonic Beydar texts demonstrate an integrated, multi-component economy that is likely to serve as a model for this general region in two ways: the first in the decentralized organization of production that has multiple tiers of administration and responsibility distributed over quite extensive distances, from the first-order site of Nagar (Tell Brak) to the second-order site of Nabada (Tell Beydar) some forty kilometers away, to the multiple villages and hamlets administered by Nabada, as far as ten kilometers away (Sallaberger and Ur 2004); the second, in the integration of extensive and varied animal husbandries (sheep/goat and equids) with cereal production at Nabada and subordinates (Van Leberghe 1996; Porter 2007; Sallaberger 2004), textile manufacturing (Van Leberghe 1996: 121), and product distribution networks at Nagar itself (Archi 1998; Eidem, Finkel, and Bonechi 2001). The central role of the steppe in the economy of both Nagar and Nabada may also be adduced from the participation of Nagar's leader in rituals to Šamagan, the god of the steppe, at Nabada. Moreover, the only names of deities that appear in personal names at Nabada (apart, that is, from generic names for god such as *il* and *ilum*) are Šamagan and Dagan (Sallaberger 1996: 87).

There is another logic however, which is perhaps a backwards one, and it is this: if there is marked evidence of the kind of strategies that counter the *dis*-integrative effects of mobility, then there is probably a situation in place where mobility is an issue. According to most archaeological models, ideologies of kinship and descent are supposed to disappear as the state takes over. And although the models are just frankly wrong to my mind, at Chuera, which physically presents a very differing morphology to polities such as Ebla or Mari in its layout and organization, this is clearly not the case. Kinship systems are manifest in the nature and distribution of its religious architecture which center around the ancestors of descent groups, and the risk of fracture which this might present is countered by the temple *in-antis* located in a different performative and social context: the *Steinbau* complex. Unlike *Steinbau* VI in the domestic quarter, here the series of *in-antis* buildings are integrated into one large ritual

---

[19] See, for example, the extensive literature on Stonehenge and similar monuments such as Parker Pearson et al. 2006; Parker Pearson and Ramilisonina 1998.

[20] Such as Arnaud 1980.

[21] See Nicolle 2005 for a survey.

space through enclosure in a temenos wall at the edge of the site. While the *Steinbau* complex in its monumentality might be assumed simply to represent the public sector, a state authority, this deployment of the *in-antis* form brings the idea of the domestic into the public arena, and vice versa as the "history house" was transformed to a temple, and forms a communal space where all lineages could be represented.

If the *in-antis* structure is so strongly associated with this kind of socio-ideological formation, though, its distribution elsewhere is significant — and it is on the Euphrates that it is found (McClellan 1999: 424):[22] at Qara Qosak; Halawa Tell A, where, interestingly, Hempelmann (n.d. a) is proposing that a specific building that contained rudimentary statues is an ancestor place, although I would interpret it more as a mortuary room; and finally at Tell Banat, but outside the city at the satellite site of Tell Kabir (Porter 1995). This, in conjunction with the history of Banat and a strong degree of material overlap in ceramic assemblage and small finds, including a stone statue that fits somewhere between the Chuera statues and the Halawa ones in terms of style, warrants further consideration. For I think we might see here more than a shared cultural milieu. I think we might see the extension of the same ideologies of kinship and descent that are represented, in a different way, in the mirrored toponyms, ideologies invoked, moreover, for much the same reasons. But it all comes back to the nature of Banat.

With its mortuary complexity that goes beyond the simple functional aspects of a cemetery and its low-level administrative components, I propose that Tell Banat in essence functioned like the sites of Der. It was an ancestral site that anchored claims to place and political identity at the same time as it extended concepts of connectedness over considerable distances. The view that Banat is first and foremost an ancestral site rather than the center of an independent city-state arises from a revised understanding of the relationship between the large and complex building located in the middle of the town, called Building 7, and the mortuary material with which it is associated (McClellan and Porter 1999; Porter 2002a, 2008; Porter and McClellan 1998). There have always been three possible interpretations — that it is a secular structure, one that many would call a palace, but that I would simply call public; that it is a religious structure, that is, a temple to a god such as Dagan or Ishtar, or that it is in some way a mortuary structure — to commemorate the dead and service their needs after inhumation, as the mortuary house of the Hittite queen Ashmunikal, for example. Or perhaps it might have worked much like a modern-day funeral home, where the dead were prepared for burial. Current readings of the archaeological sequence of construction in this area incline McClellan and Porter to the idea that this is a commemorative mortuary structure.

The earliest remains found in the main settlement of Tell Banat in Area C consist of remnant parts of a mortuary mound (labeled II) rather like White Monument B at Tell Banat North, which was a man-made earthen hillock on which burial deposits had been placed in smaller tumuli, that was then encased in white terra pise built in successive bands from the bottom up (McClellan 1998). A gravel deposit some sixty meters in diameter and at the very least three meters deep was then placed over the top of the Area C mound, that is, Mortuary Mound II. Initially this deposit was interpreted as a construction fill to provide a somewhat more level surface for the subsequent building, but, on the basis of the relationship between the various features of Area C, we now understand that the gravel was mounded and was intended as an enlargement of the earlier mortuary mound in the same manner as the various

---

[22] Also at al-Rawda (Castel and Peltenburg 2007).

phases of the White Monument, although for whatever reason it never reached similar dimensions. The terracing of Building 7, one of the very distinctive features of this structure, was to accommodate the slope of the mound. Furthermore, rather than having been built over the mound with the uppermost terrace later eroded, Building 7 only ever encircled it and the two columns located on the upper terrace were in the open. This reconstruction resolves many of the small anomalies and puzzles presented by Building 7, including the fact that no traces of a wall delineating the eastern limits of the building, western limits of the gravel, was ever recovered. The question remains as to whether Building 7 was intended as an integral part of the enlargement, a service building acting as a monumental gateway to the mound; or whether in fact it was built at a later stage, incorporating, perhaps appropriating — even hiding — an earlier structure within its center. Peltenburg (2008) has put forward a persuasive argument that a regular process is visible in the Euphrates valley in the second half of the third millennium, whereby all monumental mortuary remains are appropriated and enclosed by the later structures of a secular authority. I am inclined to think that, if this were the case at Banat, the structure would bear closer affinities with other administrative buildings of the period.

The highly elaborate, stone-constructed tomb, Tomb 7, was part of this complex. Its massive roof of limestone slabs was visible in the open courtyard on the southern side of the mound. The tomb's entrance was a stone box that rose above ground level that could be opened and closed with the aid of levers. Around the tomb were a series of contemporaneous and later smaller graves, some of which had been opened, pots and jewelry left behind, bodies gone. On top of Tomb 7 were three bodies placed on open ground, in no container of any sort, and covered only with a few boulders to keep them in place. Clearly this area is marked by the taint of death, not after the time of the public buildings there, but during their use. It was also surrounded by the smelly, smoky refuse of pottery production, a factor that has always been difficult to reconcile with the housing of a ruling elite.

Recent excavations by the German team directed by Adelheid Otto and Berthold Einwag have raised another possible location for the administrative center of Tell Banat, and this is at the southern end of the site, on top of the mountain called Jebel (Tall) Bazi (Einwag and Otto in press; Otto 2006). Here a third-millennium building, also with unusual features, has been found. Otto and Einwag interpret this building as a citadel, although little enough of it has been recovered to make a definitive determination, and they date it to Banat Period III. As yet however there is no evidence of occupation at Bazi in the relevant period for this discussion, that is, the first period of occupation at Banat, in the time of Building 7.

It is certainly possible that the initial mortuary mounds, the first structures built at Banat, housed the dead of pastoral nomads unconnected to any other permanent settlement. Despite the fact that this fits the common perception of nomads roaming free of attachment, however, I contend that this would in fact be an unusual situation in antiquity. But whatever one's views here, the ritual texts from the Ebla archive (Fronzaroli 1992, 1993) provide evidence not just of ancestor *practices*, such as seen in lists of material (Archi 2002) given to the ladies — dead ladies — of Ebla, but of ancestral *places* critical in the constitution of rule there, just as in the Mari letters, albeit in a different manifestation. At the time of the royal funeral, or wedding and accession, for they are all part and parcel of the same process, King and Queen, God and Goddess travel across the countryside on a pilgrimage to a number of sites. Nenaš is one such site visited by the royal progression because of its association with previous rulers who are presumably buried there. At Ebla this ritual is enacted in the perpetuation and justification of rule as a question of descent whether or not rule is passed from father to son, which is in question, or perhaps precisely because it is not. And, as well as integrating rural members of the polity with the center, they also enable the ultimate form of social integration — between the gods and humans, between the living and the dead.

If in both major archives for the northern region, those of Ebla and Mari, archives that are supposed to attest to two very different types of political construction (although this I think is open to argument), external locations focused on death are seen to be critical to the integration and perpetuation of the polity, the possibility must be examined that Tell Banat was the ancestral site for another city, a site to which the leaders of that city also perhaps made pilgrimage. But how can it be determined which polity that might be?

There is no straightforward methodological answer to this question — even identical material assemblages and evidence of production in one center and transmission to the other may be explained by multiple reasonings. Statistical understanding of cultural relationships, while promising, are complicated to the point of current impossibility by discrepancies in publication practices, chronologies both real and applied, and contexts, which have been shown to be determinative of the nature of assemblages especially in terms of ceramic comparisons (Porter 1999). Nevertheless, Chuera and Banat have closely parallel, although not identical, histories that stand in some critical respects in contradistinction to other, neighboring sites.

Settlement at Tell Chuera was initially established at the beginning of the third millennium (Tell Chuera [TCH] stratum IA), on the upper mound only. Although precise correspondences will have to wait until more complete publication of the earlier pottery from Chuera, the mortuary mounds at Banat date at least as early as the beginning of TCH IB (Meyer and Hempelmann 2006: 34, table 1).[23] At approximately the same time as Chuera undergoes expansion with the construction of the outermost wall (Meyer and Hempelmann 2006: 23), that is, the end of TCH IB/beginning of TCH IC, Tell Banat comes into being as a major settlement with the construction of the gravel mound, Building 7, and the pottery production installations of Area D, that is, Banat Period IV (Porter and McClellan 1998). This is the time, as Meyer and Hempelmann note, when settlement numbers not only increase across northern Syria, but a number of sites are enlarged, at least in terms of the area enclosed by walls if not in terms of population (the outer ring at Beydar, for instance, appears to be empty at this point [Sallaberger and Ur 2004: 61]).

But the similarities are more pointed than that both sites are just part of a generalized development. In both cases there are depressions occupied with non-administrative structures at the center of each site although the depressions themselves differ in nature. At both sites the development and elaboration of non-administrative architecture is a major feature at this time in contrast to what seems to be the norm elsewhere. At Chuera, the *Steinbau* complex is begun, although the area had been occupied before it (Pruss n.d. c), and at Banat the enlargement of the White Monument in phase B, the piling of the gravel mound over Mortuary Mound II, and the emplacement of the associated complex of Building 7 and Tomb 7 occurs.

In Area F at Tell Chuera, the location of the Akkadian-period palace, material dating to TCH IC lies under a building constructed in TCH ID (Banat III) and characterized by the excavators as "official" or "public," but about which little is known at this point (Pruss n.d. c). Interestingly, the sequence here, although apparently later, parallels that in Area C at Tell Banat:

---

[23] Although in absolute terms Meyer and Hempelmann down-date their sequence compared to others.

Compare Schwartz and Miller 2007: 181; Porter 2007: 82.

TELL BANAT IV (= TCH IC)	TELL CHUERA ID (= BANAT III)
Area C	Area F
Construction of Mortuary Mound	—
Deposit of Massive Gravel Layer over Mortuary Mound	Construction of an Official Building (Level 3)
Construction of Terraced Building on Gravel Layer	Building of a Mudbrick Terrace
—	Erection of a Terraced Palace over Level 3 (Level 2b2) (Pruss n.d. c)

It seems that at Chuera, as at Banat, the period TCH ID/Banat III was a phase of major construction, revision, and expansion, with the building of the level 2 Palace F itself, *Steinbau* VI, and various changes to the *Steinbau* complex at Chuera; and at Banat, the addition of Building 6 over Building 7, the *in-antis* temple at Kabir, and the Bazi structure, among other innovations. The expansion of Banat in Period III may indicate that it did not remain only a mortuary site but perhaps became a kind of dual capital like Maškan Šapir for Larsa (Porter n.d.; Steinkeller 2004), representing what I term a "bifurcated polity." The situation did not last, however; Banat is abandoned a little before Chuera, at about 2300 B.C.

The fact that not all the features at Chuera and Banat, especially architectural ones, are as comparable as the *in-antis* form should not be taken as an argument against close connections between these sites for two reasons: (1) the function of Building 7/6, the *Steinbau* complex, Palace F, and the Bazi Building are all different; and (2) the expectation that people coming from one place will necessarily duplicate all facets of their material culture in another place is problematic. If different sites hold different roles in the polity, then their material remains are also likely to be different. For example, a primarily residential settlement versus a primarily special-function site will yield a different repertoire of ceramics and a different body of architecture; a mortuary facility will be different than the house of the god. What is more significant, similarity in public structures dissimilarity in residential ones? Or is it the other way around: is similarity in residential structures more significant than dissimilarity in public ones? If the same peoples live in two places do they necessarily build the same structures and make the same artifacts in each place? Some divergence might be predicted if what they did in each place was different. Other variables would include the nature of communication between the two places, whether it was a direct movement of peoples, movement of men versus women through marriage, or communications of officials and leaders only, not of the ordinary population. Frequency of material correlations may not adequately represent frequency or intensity of connections.

The more useful way forward, therefore, is theoretical, rather than methodological, and that is in trying to understand the meaning contained in material categories, in particular the material manifestations of a political ethos. By "political ethos" I mean the concatenation of political, social, and religious ideologies and practices that produce, and/or express, and/or perpetuate a group's self-conception, world views, place within that world, internal organization, and operation. In this framework the prime focus of neo-evolutionary archaeology, hierarchy, becomes just one element of consideration among many and must be understood not as a detached and self-perpetuating category of social reality, but in terms of its interaction with the other components that comprise political ethoi, ranging from (but by no means limited to) the multiple social networks to which individuals belong, to understandings of the way human existence is positioned in cosmological constructs.

Two things become evident from this perspective. First, in the case of third-millennium Syria, different conceptions of the nature of society are closely allied to different interactions with the other worlds, the world of the gods and the world of the dead, and these have different materialities. Second, those places that share a political ethos in its broadest, overarching sense, may be lumped together on a gross scale. At this level of analysis two basic groups are visible — one, where the dominant effect is the appearance of a communitarian ethos, the other, a hierarchical one. On a finer level there actually becomes considerable variation within these, variation that allows for more particular connections to be made, such as that I propose for Tell Banat and Tell Chuera, for their respective material remains reveal the same political ethos.

In arguing for a specific connection between these two settlements, it is not just that the *in-antis* temple is found in both, or that each has statues; it is rather in the rendering of the social world that the material culture of each site embodies and two very similar ideas about how society should be and how it is organized then emerge — ideas that stand in marked contrast to other polities such as third-millennium Ebla and Mari.[24] This does not mean that kinship and descent are not factors at Ebla, on the contrary they are very important, but the aspects of them that we see there do work differently. They work to construct a polity centralized around the institutions of the city that are largely contained by the city (as opposed to dispersed outside the city) in its administrative complex and religious architecture dedicated to the gods. The temples of major deities play a dominant role both spatially, in their place within the settlement, and sociopolitically, in the connection between public cult and secular authority. Admittedly, at Ebla the picture is clearer because of texts; the role of dead kings as ancestors would not otherwise be visible, nor would the complex relationship established between god, king, and throne. At the same time, the lack of a wide sample of mortuary remains makes it difficult to determine whether multiple ways of viewing and rendering social relationships are in evidence as they are at Banat, whether ancestors are operative in other social arenas. Nevertheless, the co-clustering of sacred and secular buildings on acropoleis is traditionally read as indicative of the collusive relationship between these two venues of power. Centralized administration and public cult are entirely implicated in each other in the conveyance of authority from above — quite literally — and this is a markedly different situation from one conveyed from below, as it were. For while Banat and Chuera are different in detail and different in nature, nevertheless at each site ancestors are the otherworldly beings that shape social and political life through the arena of what is traditionally called "domestic" religion, in distinction to, or at the very least in tension with, the public cults of the gods.

Moreover, ancestors at Banat do not seem to serve to privilege one lineage over another, perpetuating clear hierarchies as has been argued for the site of Jerablus Tahtani (Peltenburg 1999), where a group of individuated burials within the publically visible but spatially

---

[24] The relationships between the material remains of the city of Mari in the third and second millennia, the concept of political ethos, and sociopolitical organization under Zimri-Lim, require a very extensive discussion that cannot be undertaken here; suffice it to say that simply because Zimri-Lim is a pastoralist does not mean that his is a communitarian polity in any way — neither because he captured a city with an established system and merely perpetuated it, nor because this is how pastoralists are supposed to work.

segregated Tomb 302 asserts the dominance of one group over society. Rather, Banat bodies reproduce the idea of community through reducing individual identities over a multi-stage burial process (Porter 2002b; Wilhelm 2007) at the same time as they render an actual social complexity: different groups within society are presented as equally significant as each other in varying, but equivalent, burial displays. At Chuera, the public sector is, I argue, and contra Meyer and Hempelmann (2006), spatially subordinate to the residential one; and while the way the site developed over time might account for this, with "state formation" taking place within an established settlement, the emergence of a dominant group that appropriated power from the community unto itself would have physical, spatial, ramifications that are not in evidence. Instead, at least one lineage group focused on a "history house" co-existed with another centered around *Steinbau* VI, with no material indication that one asserted primacy over the others. And yet perhaps, as at Ebla, other Chuera ancestors are located far from the city itself: in this case at Banat.

Each site thus manifests a very similar communitarian ethos construed in both cases through ancestor practices, an ethos unlike that seen at other contemporaneous sites. This similarity is hardly fortuitous. If I were to propose a hypothetical reconstruction of how this situation came into being, I would suggest this: that Chuera was always a multi-component polity that included long-range pastoralism, as essential to it as any other form of productive activity. The Euphrates valley, sparsely occupied at this time, was an attractive source of summer pasture and supplemental cereals. But pastoralists from Chuera probably did not set up shop there permanently, at least at first. Rather, they would have sowed some seed, hoped for the best, and gone on about their normal seasonal pursuits. But if they were not there to stake claim to their land, what would prevent other people from taking it over? Here is where the above-ground mortuary mounds come into play — they are the first step in establishing a group's claim to place, who belongs to the group, and as well, to whom the group belongs. Banat, as previously argued, is the ancestral site that anchors someone else's territorial claim to the area in which it is situated, a claim that periodic use could not on its own establish, and through those very ancestors it transcends the distance between that territory and the someone else who claims it, by anchoring a political and social identity as well. Multi-component polities do not, of course, require bifurcation, but when bifurcation occurs, one way of dealing with the problems this presents is to constantly deploy kinship ideologies; the elaboration of the above-ground burial mounds into a ritual center is just such a response, but it is not the only one.

CONCLUSION

This paper will obviously be seen as a study in speculation in some regards, especially by archaeologists, and yet archaeologists are, by and large, far more vested in an anthropological approach to the Near East than Assyriologists. At the same time, the application of anthropological thought in Near Eastern archaeology has tended, still, to be restricted to neo-evolutionary perspectives on complex society. Whatever its limitations, this paper is intended as a demonstration of the potential of a broadened anthropological sensibility brought to both textual and material data, and it proposes ways of thinking about the relationship between material remains and political structures that go beyond material*ism*, historical or otherwise. It is also intended as a consideration of alternative analytical, and actual, spaces, ones where the lines *we* draw between urbanism and pastoralism are erased by reading *between* the lines, as it were. Because the foregoing discussion suggests that there is another spatial model of organization of the early polity to be added to the ones already established, that of the bi-furcated multi-component state, where the constraints of distance and dispersal wrought by groups moving far from home in pursuit of subsistence gave rise to the materialization of kinship ideologies in multiple ways of time-space distanciation. One way is in duplication of place names, another in the distribution of burial monuments, but in both ways, the essence of the practice was the creation of belonging through the extension and manipulation of kinship. Because such kinships are often obviously not actual, they are increasingly termed "fictive," something to be distinguished from the biological "realities" of family. Yet these idioms, which could be created in any number of ways ranging from adoption to sacrifice, were just as meaningful as those engendered in the time-honored way, and are therefore better rendered by the term "socially-constructed kinship." In both examples discussed here, socially-constructed kinship was deployed because these were kin-based systems, and so while there is a second model of polity, the one that I term communitarian, to be juxtaposed therefore with the tradi-tional one of hierarchically organized and driven early polities, perhaps what is at stake is not so much a redefinition of the state as it is a re-examination of archaeological ideas of kinship and its potentialities.

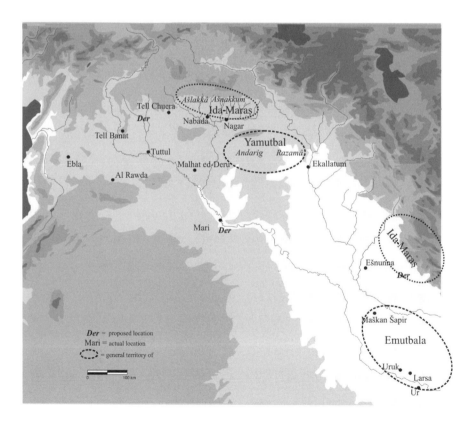

Figure 11.1. Map

BIBLIOGRAPHY

Abdi, Kamyar

2003   "The Early Development of Pastoralism in the Central Zagros Mountains." *Journal of World Prehistory* 17: 395–448.

Archi, Alfonso

1998   "The Regional State of Nagar According to the Texts of Ebla." In *About Subartu: Studies Devoted to Upper Mesopotamia*, edited by Mark Lebeau, pp. 1–16. Subartu 4/2. Turnhout: Brepols.

2002   "Jewels for the Ladies of Ebla." *Zeitschrift für Assyriologie* 92: 161–99.

2006   "Eblaite in Its Geographical and Historical Context." In *The Akkadian Language in Its Semitic Context: Studies in the Akkadian of the Third and Second Millennium BC,* edited by Guy Deutscher and N. J. C. Kouwenberg, pp. 96–112. Uitgaven van het Nederlands Instituut voor het Nabije Oosten te Leiden 106. Leiden: Nederlands Instituut voor het Nabije Oosten.

Arnaud, Daniel

1980   "Traditions urbains et influences semi-nomades à Emar, à l'âge du Bronze Récent." In *Le Moyen-Euphrate: Zone de contacts et d'échanges* (Actes du Colloque de Strasbourg, 10–12 March 1977), edited by Jean-Claude Margueron, pp. 245–64. Travaux du Centre de recherche sur le Proche-Orient de la Grèce antiques 5. Leiden: E. J. Brill.

Bonechi, Marco

1993   *I nomi geografici dei testi di Ebla*. Répertoire géographique des textes cunéiforme 12; Beihefte zum Tübinger Atlas des Vorderen Orients, Reihe B, Geisteswissenschaften 7. Wiesbaben: Dr. Ludwig Reichert.

Castel, Corinne, and Edgar Peltenburg

2007   "Urbanism on the Margins: Third Millennium BC Al-Rawda in the Arid Zone of Syria." *Antiquity* 81: 601–16.

Charpin, Dominique

1993   "Un souverain éphémère en Ida-Maraṣ: Išme-Addu d'Ašnakkum." *Mari: Annales de recherches interdisciplinaires* 7: 165–91.

2003   "La 'toponymie en miroir' dans le Proche-Orient Amorrite." *Revue d'Assyriologie* 97: 3–34.

Charpin, Dominique, and Jean-Marie Durand

1986   "'Fils de Sim'al': Les origines tribales des rois de Mari." *Revue d'Assyriologie* 80: 141–83.

Dohmann-Pfälzner, Heike, and Peter Pfälzner

1996   "Untersuchungen zur Urbanisierung Nordmesopotamiens im 3. Jt. v. Chr.: Wohnquartierplanung und städtische Zentrumsgestaltung in Tall Chuera." *Damaszener Mitteilungen* 9: 1–13.

Durand, Jean-Marie

1992   "Unité et diversités au Proche-Orient à l'époque Amorrite." In *La circulation des biens, des personnes et des idées dans le Proche-Orient ancien* (Actes de la 38ᵉ Rencontre Assyriologique Internationale, Paris, 8–10 July 1991), edited by Dominique Charpin and Francis Joannès, pp. 97–128. Paris: Éditions Recherche sur les Civilisations.

1997   *Les documents épistolaires du palais de Mari,* Volume 1. Littératures anciennes du Proche-Orient 16. Paris: Les Éditions du Cerf.

1998   *Les documents épistolaires du palais de Mari,* Volume 2. Littératures anciennes du Proche-Orient 17. Paris: Les Éditions du Cerf.

2000   *Documents épistolaires du palais de Mari,* Volume 3. Littératures anciennes du Proche-Orient 18. Paris: Les Éditions du Cerf.

2004   "Peuplement et sociétés à l'époque amorrite (I) Les clans densim'alites." In *Nomades et sédentaires dans le Proche-Orient ancien* (Compte rendu de la 46ᵉ Rencontre Assyriologique Internationale, Paris, 10–13 July 2000), edited by Christophe Nicolle, pp. 111–97. Amurru 3. Paris: Éditions Recherche sur les Civilisations.

2005   *Le culte des pierres et les monuments commémoratifs en Syrie amorrite.* Florilegium marianum 8; Mémoires de Nouvelles Assyriologiques Brèves et Utilitaires 9; Supplément à Mémoires de Nouvelles Assyriologiques Brèves et Utilitaires 2. Paris: Société pour l'étude du Proche-Orient Ancien.

Durand, Jean-Marie, and Michael Guichard

1997   "Les rituels de Mari (textes nᵒ 2 à nᵒ 5)." *Florelegium marianum* 3: 19–78.

Eidem, Jesper; Irving Finkel; and Marco Bonechi

2001   "The Third Millennium Inscriptions." In *Excavations at Tell Brak,* Volume 2: *Nagar in the Third Millennium BC,* by David Oates, Joan Oates, and Helen McDonald, pp. 99–120. McDonald Institute Monographs. Oxford: British School of Archaeology in Iraq.

Einwag, Berthold, and Adelheid Otto

In press   "Tall Bazi 2000 und 2001: Die letzten Untersuchungen auf der Zitadelle und in der Nordstadt." *Damaszener Mitteilungen* 15.

Electronic Text Corpus of Sumerian Literature (ETCSL)

n.d.   http://etcsl.orinst.ox.ac.uk/cgi-bin/etcsl.cgi?text=t.3.1.08&charenc=j#, 04/30/08.

Evans-Pritchard, E. E.

1969   *The Nuer: A Description of the Modes of Livelihood and Political Institutions of a Nilotic People.* Oxford: Oxford University Press.

Fleming, Daniel E.

2004   *Democracy's Ancient Ancestors: Mari and Early Collective Governance.* Cambridge: Cambridge University Press.

Frayne, Douglas

1990   *Old Babylonian Period (2003–1595 BC).* The Royal Inscriptions of Mesopotamia, Early Periods 4. Toronto: University of Toronto Press.

1997   *Ur III Period, 2112–2004 BC.* The Royal Inscriptions of Mesopotamia, Early Periods 3/2. Toronto: University of Toronto Press.

Fronzaroli, Pelio

1992   "The Ritual Texts of Ebla." In *Literature and Literary Language at Ebla,* edited by Pelio Fronzolari, pp. 163–85. Quaderni di Semitistica 18. Florence: Università di Firenze.

1993   *ARET* 11: *Testi rituali della regalità (Archivio L.2769).* Università degli studi di Roma la Sapienza 11. Rome: Missione archeologica italiana in Siria.

Giddens, Anthony

1981   *A Contemporary Critique of Historical Materialism,* Volume 1: *Power, Property and the State.* Berkeley: University of California Press.

Guichard, Michael

2002   "Le Šubartum occidental à l'avènement de Zimrî-Lîm." In *Florilegium marianum,* Volume 6: *Recueil d'études à la mémoire d'André Parrot,* edited by Dominique Charpin and Jean-Marie Durand, pp. 119–68. Mémoires de Nouvelles Assyriologiques Brèves et Utilitaires 7. Antony: Société pour l'étude du Proche-Orient Ancien.

Heimpel, Wolfgang

2003   *Letters to the King of Mari: A New Translation with Historical Introduction, Notes and Commentary.* Mesopotamian Civilizations 12. Winona Lake: Eisenbrauns.

Hempelmann, Ralph

n.d. a   "Die Ausgrabungen im Bereich K." In *Ausgrabungen in Tell Chuēra in Nordostsyrien*
II: *Vorbericht der Grabungskampagnen 1998–2004*, by Jan-Waalke Meyer. In
preparation.

n.d. b   "Domestic Cult of the Ancestors in Early Bronze Age Syria." In preparation.

Hodder, Ian

n.d.   "2007 Review." In *Çatalhöyük Archive Report 2007 (with Abstracts in Turkish)*,
pp. 1–4. Çatalhöyük Research Project. http://www.catalhoyuk.com/archive_reports/
05/28/08.

Ismail, Farouk; Walther Sallaberger; Philippe Talon; and Karel Van Lerberghe

1996   *Administrative Documents from Tell Beydar (Seasons 1993–1995)*. Subartu 2.
Turnhout: Brepols.

Kouchoukos, Nicholas

1998   Landscape and Social Change in Late Prehistoric Mesopotamia. Ph.D. dissertation,
Yale University.

Lees, Susan, and Bates, Daniel

1974   "The Origins of Specialized Nomadic Populations: A Systemic Model." *American
Antiquity* 39: 187–93.

Lyonnet, Bertille

1998   "Le peuplement de la Djéziré occidentale au début du 3ᵉ millénaire, villes circulaires
et pastoralisme: Questions et hypothèses." In *About Subartu: Studies Devoted to
Upper Mesopotamia*, Volume 1: *Landscape, Archaeology, Settlement*, edited by Marc
Lebeau, pp. 179–95. Subartu 4/1. Turnhout: Brepols.

2004   "Le nomadisme et l'archéologie: Problèmes d'identification. Le cas de la partie occidentale de la Djéziré aux 3ᵉᵐᵉ et début du 2ᵉᵐᵉ millénaire avant notre ère." In *Nomades
et sédentaires dans le Proche-Orient ancien* (Compte rendu de la 46ᵉ Rencontre
Assyriologique Internationale, Paris, 20–13 July 2000), edited by Christophe
Nicholle, pp. 25–49. Amurru 3. Paris: Éditions Recherche sur les Civilisations.

Marchesi, Gianni

2006   *LUMMA in the Onomasticon and Literature of Ancient Mesopotamia*. History of the
Ancient Near East, Studies 10. Padua: Sargon.

Margueron, Jean-Claude

2004   *Mari: Métropole de l'Euphrate au IIIᵉ et au début du IIᵉ millénaire av. J.-C.* Paris:
Picard/Éditions Recherche sur les Civilisations.

Matthiae, Paolo

1980   "Campagne de fouilles à Ebla in 1979: Les tombes princières et le palais de la ville
basse à l'époque amorrhéenne." *Comptes rendus de l'Académie des Inscriptions et
Belles-Lettres* 1980: 94–118.

McClellan, Thomas

1998   "Tell Banat North: The White Monument." In *About Subartu: Studies Devoted to
Upper Mesopotamia*, Volume 1: *Landscape, Archaeology, Settlement*, edited by Marc
Lebeau, pp. 243–71. Subartu 4/1. Turnhout: Brepols.

1999   "Urbanism on the Upper Syrian Euphrates." In *Archaeology of the Upper Syrian
Euphrates, the Tishrin Dam Area* (Proceedings of the International Symposium at
Barcelona, 28–30 January 1998), edited by Gregorio del Olmo Lete and Juan-Luis
Montero-Fenollós, pp. 413–25. Aula Orientalis Supplementa 15. Barcelona: Editorial
AUSA.

2004   "Funerary Monuments and Pastoralism." In *Nomades et sédentaires dans le Proche-
Orient ancien* (Compte rendu de la 46ᵉ Rencontre Assyriologique Internationale,
Paris, 20–13 July 2000), edited by Christophe Nicholle, pp. 63–67. Amurru 3. Paris:
Éditions Recherche sur les Civilisations.

McClellan, Thomas, and Anne Porter
  1995   "Jawa and North Syria." *Studies in the History and Archaeology of Jordan* 5:
                  49–65.
  1999   "Survey of Excavations at Tell Banat: Funerary Practices." In *Archaeology of the
                  Upper Syrian Euphrates, the Tishrin Dam Area* (Proceedings of the International
                  Symposium at Barcelona, 28–30 January 1998), edited by Gregorio del Olmo Lete
                  and Juan-Luis Montero-Fenollós, pp. 311–20. Aula Orientalis Supplementa 15.
                  Barcelona: Editorial AUSA.

McCorriston, Joy
  1997   "The Fiber Revolution: Textile Intensification, Alienation and Social Stratification
                  in Ancient Mesopotamia." *Current Anthropology* 38: 517–49.

Meyer, Jan-Waalke
  1997   "Djebelet el-Beda: Eine Stätte der Ahnenverehrung?" *Altorientalische Forschungen*
                  24: 294–309.
  n.d.   http://web.uni-frankfurt.de/fb09/vorderasarch/tch3jt.htm, 05/28/08.

Meyer, Jan-Waalke, and Ralph Hempelmann
  2006   "Bemerkungen zu Mari aus der Sicht von Tell Chuera — Ein Beitrag zur Geschichte
                  der ersten Hälfte des 3. Jts v. Chr." *Altorientalische Forschungen* 33: 22–41.

Michalowski, Piotr
  1976   The Royal Correspondence of Ur. Ph.D. dissertation, Yale University.
  2005   "Literary Works from the Court of King Ishbi-Erra of Isin." In *"An Experienced
                  Scribe Who Neglects Nothing": Ancient Near Eastern Studies in Honor of Jacob
                  Klein*, edited by Yitzhak Sefati, Pinhas Artzi, Chaim Cohen, Barry Eichler, and Victor
                  Hurowitz, pp. 199–211. Bethesda: CDL Press.

Milano, Lucio; Walther Sallaberger; Philippe Talon; and Karel Van Lerberghe
  2004   *Third Millennium Cuneiform Texts from Tell Beydar* (*Seasons 1996–2002*). Subartu
                  12. Turnhout: Brepols.

Moortgat, Anton
  1965   *Tell Chuera in Nordost-Syrien: Bericht über die vierte Grabungskampagne 1963.*
                  Wissenschaftliche Abhandlungen der Arbeitsgemeinschaft für Forschung des Landes
                  Nordrhein-Westfalen 31. Cologne: Westdeutscher Verlag.

Nicolle, Christophe
  2005   "L'identification des vestiges archéologiques de l'aniconisme à l'époque amorri-
                  te." In *Le Culte des pierres et les monuments commémoratifs en Syrie amorrite*, by
                  Jean-Marie Durand, pp. 177–89. Florilegium marianum 8; Mémoires de Nouvelles
                  Assyriologiques Brèves et Utilitaires. Paris: Société pour l'étude du Proche-Orient
                  Ancien.

Orthmann, Winfried; R. Hempelmann; H. Klein; C. Kühne; M. Novak; A. Pruss; E. Vila; H.-M. Weicken;
and A. Wener
  1995   *Ausgrabungen in Tell Chuēra in Nordost-Syrien*, Volume 1: *Vorbericht über die
                  Grabungskampagnen 1986 bis 1992.* Vorderasiatische Forschungen der Max Freiherr
                  von Oppenheim-Stiftung 2. Saarbrücken: Saarbrücker Verlag.

Otto, Adelheid
  2006   "Archaeological Perspectives on the Localization of Naram-Sin's Armanum." *Journal
                  of Cuneiform Studies* 58: 1–26.

Owen, David
  1995   "Amorites and the Location of BÀD^ki." In *Immigration and Emigration within the
                  Ancient Near East: Festschrift E. Lipiński,* edited by Karel Van Lerberghe and Antoon
                  Schoors, pp. 213–19. Orientalia Lovaniensia Analecta 65. Leuven: Uitgeverij Peeters
                  en Department Oriëntalistiek.

Parker Pearson, Mike; Josh Pollard; Colin Richards; Julian Thomas; Christopher Tilley; Kate Welham; and Umberto Albarella

2006   "Materializing Stonehenge: The Stonehenge Riverside Project and New Discoveries." *Journal of Material Culture* 11: 227–61.

Parker Pearson, Mike, and Ramilisonina

1998   "Stonehenge for the Ancestors: The Stones Pass on the Message." *Antiquity* 72: 308–26.

Peltenburg, Edgar

1999   "The Living and the Ancestors: Early Bronze Age Mortuary Practices at Jerablus Tahtani." In *Archaeology of the Upper Syrian Euphrates, the Tishrin Dam Area* (Proceedings of the International Symposium at Barcelona, 28–30 January 1998), edited by Gregorio del Olmo Lete and Juan-Luis Montero-Fenollós, pp. 427–42. Aula Orientalis-Supplementa 15. Barcelona: Editorial AUSA.

2008   "Enclosing the Ancestors and the Growth of Socio-Political Complexity in Early Bronze Age Syria." In *Sepolti tra i vivi: Evidenza ed interpretazione di contesti funerali in abitato; Atti del Convegno Internazionale*, edited by Gilda Bartoloni and Maria Gilda Benedettini, pp. 91–123. Scienze dell'Antichità 15. Rome: Edizioni Quasar.

Porter, Anne

1995   "The Third Millennium Settlement Complex at Tell Banat: Tell Kabir." *Damaszener Mitteilungen* 8: 125–63.

1999   "The Ceramic Horizon of the Early Bronze in the Upper Euphrates." In *Archaeology of the Upper Syrian Euphrates, the Tishrin Dam Area* (Proceedings of the International Symposium at Barcelona, 28–30 January 1998), edited by Gregorio del Olmo Lete and Juan-Luis Montero-Fenollós, pp. 311–20. Aula Orientalis-Supplementa 15. Barcelona: Editorial AUSA.

2002a   "Communities in Conflict: Death and the Contest for Social Order in the Euphrates River Valley." *Near Eastern Archaeology* 65: 156–73.

2002b   "The Dynamics of Death: Ancestors, Pastoralism and the Origins of a Third Millennium City in Syria." *Bulletin of American Schools of Oriental Research* 325: 1–36.

2007   "You say Potato, I Say … Typology, Chronology and the Origin of the Amorites." In *Sociétés humaines et changement climatique à la fin du troisième millénaire: Une crise a-t-elle eu lieu en haute-Mésopotamie?* (Actes du colloque de Lyon, 5–8 December 2005), edited by Catherine Kuzucuoglu and Catherine Marro, pp. 69–115. Varia Anatolica 18. Istanbul: Institut Français d'Études Anatoliennes-Georges Dumezil.

2008   "Evocative Topography: Experience, Time and Politics in a Landscape of Death." In *Sepolti tra i vivi: Evidenza ed interpretazione di contesti funerali in abitato; Atti del Convegno Internazionale*, edited by Gilda Bartoloni and Maria Gilda Benedettini, pp. 71–90. Scienze dell'Antichità 15. Rome: Edizioni Quasar.

n.d.   *Mobilizing the Past*. In preparation.

Porter, Anne, and Thomas McClellan

1998   "The Third Millennium Settlement Complex at Tell Banat: Results of the 1994 Excavations." *Damaszener Mitteilungen* 10: 11–63.

Pruss, Alexander

n.d. a   http://www.orientarch.uni-halle.de/digs/chuera/chu96_e.htm, 05/28/08.

n.d. b   http://www.orientarch.uni-halle.de/digs/chuera/chu97_e.htm, 05/28/08.

n.d. c   http://www.orientarch.uni-halle.de/digs/chuera/chu98_99/98_99eng.htm, 05/28/2008.

Ristvet, Lauren, and Harvey Weiss

2005   "The Häbür Region in the Late Third and Early Second Millennium B.C." In *The History and Archaeology of Syria*, Volume 1, edited by Winfried Orthmann, pp. 1–26. Saarbrücken: Saarbrucker Verlag.

Sallaberger, Walther

1996   "Calendar and Pantheon." In *Administrative Documents from Tell Beydar* (*Seasons 1993–1995*), edited by Farouk Ismail, Walther Sallaberger, Philippe Talon, and Karel Van Lerberghe pp. 85–87. Subartu 2. Turnhout: Brepols.

2004   "A Note on the Sheep and Goat Flocks. Introduction to Texts 151–167." In *Third Millennium Cuneiform Texts from Tell Beydar* (*Seasons 1996–2002*), edited by Lucio Milano, Walther Sallaberger, Philippe Talon, and Karel Van Lerberghe, pp. 13–21. Subartu 12. Turnhout: Brepols.

2007   "From Urban Culture to Nomadism: A History." In *Sociétés humaines et changement climatique à la fin du troisième millénaire: Une crise a-t-elle eu lieu en haute mésopotamie?* (Actes du colloque de Lyon, 5–8 December 2005), edited by Catherine Kuzucuoglu and Catherine Marro, pp. 417–56. Varia Anatolica 18. Istanbul: Institut Français d'Études Anatoliennes-Georges Dumezil.

Sallaberger, Walther, and Jason Ur

2004   "Tell Beydar/Nabada in Its Regional Setting." In *Third Millennium Cuneiform Texts from Tell Beydar* (*Seasons 1996–2002*), edited by Lucio Milano, Walther Sallaberger, Philippe Talon, and Karel Van Lerberghe, pp. 51–71. Subartu 12. Turnhout: Brepols.

Schwartz, Glenn, and Naomi F. Miller

2007   "The 'Crisis' of the Late Third Millennium B.C.: Ecofactual and Artifactual Evidence from Umm el-Marra and the Jabbul Plain." In *Sociétés humaines et changement climatique à la fin du troisième millénaire: Une crise a-t-elle eu lieu en haute mésopotamie?* (Actes du colloque de Lyon, 5–8 December 2005), edited by Catherine Kuzucuoglu and Catherine Marro, pp. 179–204. Varia Anatolica 18. Istanbul: Institut Français d'Études Anatoliennes-Georges Dumezil.

Stein, Gil

2004   "Structural Parameters and Sociocultural Factors in the Economic Organization of Northern Mesopotamian Urbanism in the Third Millennium B.C." In *Archaeological Perspectives on Political Economies*, edited by Gary M. Feinman and Linda M. Nicholas, pp. 61–79. Foundations of Archaeological Inquiry. Salt Lake City: University of Utah Press.

Steinkeller, Piotr

2004   "A History of Mashkan-shapir and Its Role in the Kingdom of Larsa." In *The Anatomy of a Mesopotamian City: Survey and Soundings at Mashkan-shapir,* by Elizabeth C. Stone and Paul E. Zimansky, pp. 26–42. Winona Lake: Eisenbrauns.

Tsukimoto, Akio

1985   *Untersuchungen zur Totenpflege* (kispum) *im alten Mesopotamien*. Alter Orient und Altes Testament 216. Kevelaer: Butzon & Bercker.

Universities of Halle-Wittenberg and Leipzig

n.d.   "Difference and Integration: Interaction Between Nomadic and Settled Forms of Life in the Civilisations of the Old World." Collaborative Project, Universities of Halle-Wittenberg and Leipzig. http://www.nomadsed.de/en_index.html 06/01/08.

Van De Mieroop, Marc

2004   *A History of the Ancient Near East, ca. 3000–323 B.C.* Blackwell History of the Ancient World. Malden: Blackwell.

Van Lerberghe, Karel

    1996   "The Beydar Tablets and the History of the Northern Jazirah." In *Administrative Documents from Tell Beydar* (*Seasons 1993–1995*), edited by Farouk Ismail, Walther Sallaberger, Philippe Tallon, and Karel Van Lerberghe, pp. 119–22. Subartu 2. Turnhout: Brepols.

Weber, Jill

    2006   Economic Developments of Urban Proportions: Evolving Systems of Animal-Product Consumption and Distribution in the Early and Middle Bronze Ages in Syro-Mesopotamia. Ph.D dissertation, University of Pennsylvania.

Weiss, Harvey; M.-A. Courty; W. Wetterstrom; F. Guichard; L. Senior; R. Meadow; and A. Curnow

    1993   "The Genesis and Collapse of Third Millennium North Mesopotamian Civilization." *Science* 261: 995–1004.

Wilhelm, Susanne

    2007   "Ancestral Bones: Early Bronze Age Human Skeletal Remains from Tell Banat, Syria." *Baghdader Mitteilungen* 37: 359–80.

12

KINGSHIP OF CITY AND TRIBE CONJOINED: ZIMRI-LIM AT MARI

DANIEL E. FLEMING, NEW YORK UNIVERSITY

In discussion of ancient society, as examined in the broadest possible framework, all terms are up for negotiation. It is not even clear how and to what extent our categories are meaningful in these distant settings. The "state" may be archaic, but the tiered relationships of ancient kingdoms may not best be understood as truly fixed hierarchies with dominant power flowing down from above. The "city" may not involve a concentrated population, and its residential aspect may even be incidental to its administrative and ritual functions. There are political entities that may overlap multiple kingdoms, bound by ties that do not depend on geographical proximity, whether or not they are best considered "tribal." Large populations move through the back country with their flocks and herds, but they are so closely integrated socially and politically with settled peoples as to test the utility of the word "nomad."

In a re-evaluation of kinship studies based on his own research in the Pacific Caroline Islands, David Schneider reflected on the inadequacy of his own analytical framework until he paid attention to the indigenous vocabulary for social organization. When he first evaluated the evidence that he gathered from ethnographic work, he treated a category called the *tabinau* as a patrilineage, in purely kinship terms. Later, returning for a closer look at actual usage, he concluded that his preconceived notions of society had impeded his ability to build a picture of social organization from the ground up. The *tabinau* had different meanings in different settings: a dwelling, persons related through ties of land, a group living together with different ties to the same land, or a place where something is founded, but never land without people.[1]

For ancient societies, careful attention to language should likewise challenge preconceived reconstructions. The problem is that indigenous information about mobile herding peoples can be hard to come by, with texts generally produced in settled centers, and "nomads" treated as outsiders. In the midst of such perspectives, the archives of early second-millennium Mari have long offered something different, in which the pastoralists are more visible if not more accessible. Along with thousands of palace administrative records, 3,000–4,000 letters were collected by Mari's kings, mostly in the thirteen-year reign of Zimri-Lim, its final ruler.[2] The letters offer unparalleled access to a range of social situations in a landscape that includes every sort of political affiliation encountered by the Mari leadership.[3]

---

[1] Schneider 1984: 21–23.

[2] For a basic historical review of Mari as known from its early second-millennium archives, see Charpin and Ziegler 2003. Charpin has also published an overview of Mesopotamian political history for the larger period (see Charpin 2004: 25–480).

[3] The bibliography for society as viewed from the Mari archives is enormous. A convenient bibliography of the most important materials is found in Charpin 2004: 453–75. The following publications relate especially to mobile herding populations and social organization in what are usually understood as "tribal" terms: Kupper 1957; Luke 1965; Rowton 1967: 109–21; idem 1973: 201–15; idem 1974: 1–30; and several related pieces; Charpin and Durand 1986: 141–83; Anbar 1991; Nicolle 2004 (and especially articles by Durand, Fleming, and Albà in Nicolle 2004); Fleming 2004.

The Mari archives allow us to approach a conversation about nomads, tribes, and the state with access to the political and social vocabulary of the peoples themselves. Such written evidence presents a host of obstacles to our comprehension, both by the distance from modern settings and by the need to disentangle who speaks from what perspective. The indigenous voices nevertheless offer a constant challenge to each generation of our social reconstructions. With the most recent Mari research, it is becoming evident that under king Zimri-Lim, the categories commonly isolated as "tribe" and "state," along with "nomad," "pastoralist," and the like, came together in a single social web.[4] In Zimri-Lim's kingdom, these were not merely mutually dependent, as envisioned by Michael Rowton.[5] The categories, so far as they apply, were dimensions of a social unity that incorporated elements of them all.

The city of Mari was located upstream of Babylonia on the Euphrates, just below where the Ḫabur flows into it from the hills to the north. Through several decades and two separate political administrations, the Mari kingdom bridged the eastern Mesopotamian powers and the great Syrian centers of Aleppo and Qatna.[6] Mari's rulers had dealings with peoples from the Persian Gulf to the Mediterranean, with particular interest in the swath of land north of the Euphrates and filling the Ḫabur drainage and surrounding steppe. Mobile herding groups constituted a major component of the region's population in this period, and they form a constant presence in the archives.

POLITICAL AND SOCIAL CATEGORIES IN THE MARI ARCHIVES

Although the Mari archives were discovered in the 1930s and their remarkable royal correspondence has been published in tantalizing morsels through the decades that followed, the basic social framework for their production is only beginning to become evident.[7] The progress proceeds from the past generation of publication and analysis under the leadership of Jean-Marie Durand, the results of which leave an unavoidable influence on my own work.

---

[4] This became evident first of all with the discovery by Charpin and Durand that Zimri-Lim identified himself with the Binu Sim'al people, one of the "tribal" groups that had always been considered separate from and often at odds with state centers like Mari. Zimri-Lim was thus a king both of Mari and of the Binu Sim'al together, with tangled political results (Charpin and Durand 1986, above).

[5] Rowton distinguished the nomadism seen in the Mari archives as "enclosed" and "dimorphic": established in the spaces between heavily settled areas and participating directly in that sedentary society. For Rowton, Mari was an intermediate dimorphic state, a territorial state within which tribal and dimorphic chiefdoms played a prominent role, but whose own authority stood apart as centralized bureaucracy (Rowron 1973: 203–04; Rowton 1976: 27–28).

[6] The city of Mari that produced the archives came to prominence under Yaḫdun-Lim, who ruled about seventeen years and was followed by a son who ruled at most two (ca. 1810–1794 and 1793–1792, by the Middle Chronology). Mari fell to Samsi-Addu, who

came to dominate much of upstream Mesopotamia, and he only turned his attention to the city several years later, when he established his younger son, Yasmaḫ-Addu, there as king. Yasmaḫ-Addu ruled slightly more than ten years (ca. 1785–1775) but could not maintain power after the death of his father. Zimri-Lim, the heir of Yaḫdun-Lim, then reigned at Mari for slightly more than thirteen years (ca. 1775–1763).

[7] Mari was first excavated and identified in 1933–34, and early publication of texts emerged only in articles, interrupted by the war (see Dossin 1938: 105–26; idem 1939: 97–113). After the war, texts were published under the leadership of Dossin in the series Archives Royales de Mari (ARM), from 1946 to 1977 (I–XIX); publication continued under the leadership of Maurice Birot and then Jean-Marie Durand. Durand's tenure began in the early 1980s, and publication has diversified into new series, along with ARM. The principal venue has become *Florilegium marianum*, along with *Mari: Annales de Recherches Interdisciplinaires* (*M.A.R.I.*) and Amurru.

In the Mesopotamian world viewed through the remarkable royal correspondence of Mari, all the key categories of common discussion find some counterpart. The indigenous vocabulary offers one avenue for re-evaluating assumptions about how ancient society aligns with the frameworks of city and state, nomad and tribe. Nothing quite matches, or should be taken to match, if we allow the ancient terms to take priority in shaping our analysis.[8]

- The main building block of regional politics was the *mātum*, usually translated "land," which most often defined the population of a kingdom, although three Mesopotamian *mātum*s were ruled by alliances of kings.[9] No *mātum* was subordinate to a higher political category, although the king of one *mātum* could be vassal to another. Some of these "lands" could be small, without the formal administrative tiers of a larger kingdom like the one centered at Mari.[10] Was this a "state"? Any entity capable of bearing the "state" label would have been a *mātum*, but the word itself had broader application and reflected no consciousness of the particular organizational demands embodied in the modern category.

- Every settlement in this world was capable of being identified as an *ālum*, the word usually translated as "city." The *ālum* referred to the body of residents that acted as a unit with reference to some settled center, whatever the size.[11] It did not have to be fortified, nor was size a criterion. Nothing in this word or any other recognized the essential difference of any concentration of people that would achieve separate designation as a larger "city," as opposed to a town, village, or hamlet.

- Certain populations were identified by names that were not coterminous with any one *mātum*. In some cases, a kingdom could be named for the town at its center and a *mātum* with such an extended application: Kurdâ and the *māt Numḫâ*, Andarig and the *māt Yamutbalim*. The Numḫâ and the Yamutbal people, however, were not confined to these kingdoms, and the kings of Kurdâ and Andarig did not rule all of the peoples identified as Numḫâ and Yamutbal.[12] The best attested such groups were paired as

---

[8] The perspectives presented here reflect the work published in Fleming 2004, and extensive reflections on each category may be found there. At the same time, some ideas explored for this article move beyond positions taken in that earlier work.

[9] The three *mātum* alliances, each governed as one "land" by a coalition of separate city centers and their kings, were Zalmaqum, Ida-Maraṣ, and Šubartum. Zalmaqum consisted of four towns in the upper Baliḫ River system (see Kupper 1998: 35–36); Ida-Maraṣ was a larger coalition of ten or more centers in the region of the Ḫabur River's tributaries (Fleming 2004: 126–27); and Šubartum was one step farther east, on the eastern side of the Tigris River, north of the Diyala (see Steinkeller 1998: 76–78).

[10] It is difficult to evaluate the administrative structures of lands for which we have no archives, and judgment of what constitutes a "small" *mātum* is largely a matter of extrapolation. For instance, the land of Kurdâ, which itself could be subordinate to Mari, is said to suffer the revolt of another *mātum*: "The land of Adna has rebelled against Ḫammurabi

king of Kurdâ" (ARM II 50:5–6; republished in translation in Durand 1998, no. 601, p. 262).

[11] The political nature of the town can be seen in the fact that one may write a letter simply to a town by name. Šadum-labua king of Ašnakkum writes to Zimri-Lim, "I did not (previously) write to Eluḫut, but now I will write to Eluḫut" (ARM XXVIII 104:33–36). The ruler or group of leaders may be the intended recipient, but it is the town as such that is understood as the political actor. Elsewhere, we hear that "Urgiš" has taken over half the possessions of an assassinated king (ARM XXVIII 98:13–20).

[12] The strongest evidence for this may be a letter in which Zimri-Lim's earliest second-in-command, a man named Bannum, defends his prior status as regional Chief-of-Pasture (*mer'ûm*) by recounting his oversight of three different groups, the Binu Sim'al, the Numḫâ, and the Yamutbal (Villard 1994: 297, n. 3, A.1098:10'). The Binu Sim'al are Zimri-Lim's own core population, not defined by association with Mari, and Bannum asserts authority over both this group and the two associated with other settled kingdoms.

Binu Yamina and Binu Sim'al, "Sons of the Right (Hand)" and "Sons of the Left." Detail from the Mari documentation allows distinction of component groups to each of these, so that the higher order categories may be understood as confederations.[13] I have described these groups while entirely avoiding the term "tribe," although this is their common identification, including my own work. Unlike the *mātum* and the *ālum*, the language had no generic word for such peoples. The component groups of the Binu Yamina and the Binu Sim'al appear to have been the *li'mum* and the *gayum* respectively. Even within these two confederations, no evidence demonstrates a family framework for explaining bonds between groups. It may finally be appropriate to use "tribal" terminology for these important constituents of the Mesopotamian population, in part for lack of a better modern category, but it is worth maintaining particular caution regarding the political and social reality.

- Finally, several words apply to the herding communities that moved about the back country, the people who could be associated with "nomadism." Outsiders who move in and out of the southern desert were called Sutû and were not considered part of the local Mesopotamian societies.[14] Occasionally, the mobile herding communities would be identified by the domain they inhabited, the *nawûm* grazing land itself.[15] Most often, however, mobile herding groups were Ḫana, a category so entirely accepted by the Mari writers that they most often used it in place of the Binu Sim'al group affiliation, while maintaining the assumption of mobility inherent in the Ḫana term.[16] Although not all Binu Sim'al in fact lived in mobile communities, they were all sometimes treated as such under the Ḫana name. Durand proposes that the word *ḫanûm* was derived from a West Semitic root associated with encampment, or life in tents.[17] Whether or not this is correct, and it is plausible, the messy application to all Binu Sim'al peoples suggests caution in simple equation with "nomads."

ZIMRI-LIM, NOMAD KING

In his favorite titulary, Zimri-Lim identified himself as "the king of Mari and the *māt Ḫana*."[18] If we allow the word Ḫana its common meaning, Zimri-Lim was a nomad king who

---

[13] For detailed discussion of this pair, within the framework of "tribal" terminology, see Fleming 2004: 43–63.

[14] See, for instance, a letter to king Yasmaḫ-Addu that reports attacks by Sutû on the land of Qatna (near Hama in western Syria) and on Palmyra and its neighborhood (Durand 1998: p. 507, no. 745, A.1098:10'; cf. Ziegler 2004).

[15] The term is common, and its particular nuance cannot always easily be isolated by reference to the flocks, the steppe, or the herding community. Nevertheless, the people themselves are often in view. For instance, one letter from an associate of Zimri-Lim to his lord recounts a conversation with king Ḫammurabi of Kurdâ in which the king fears a mixing of military and herding groups in his territory. "Send

away your troops with Atamrum, and send away your herding community (*nawûm*) that is encamped in my district" (ARM XXVI 392:38–40).

[16] One confirmation of this identification is found in the brief victory report sent by a military leader to Zimri-Lim, which begins, "The Ḫana are well; the troops of my lord are well," and concludes, "The troops are well and the Sim'alites are well" (Guillot 1997, *FM* III 135:4, 5').

[17] Durand 1992: 13–14.

[18] See Charpin and Durand 1986: 152–55. The title comes first of all from Zimri-Lim's predecessor, Yaḫdun-Lim, who applied it to himself in the Šamaš temple dedication inscription (Dossin 1955: 1–28, i:17–19).

ruled "the land of the mobile herdsmen" from the old administrative center of Mari. As just observed, Zimri-Lim used the Ḫana category to name his entire Binu Sim'al power base, yet this did not dilute the word's association with mobile herdsmen. Rather, the Binu Sim'al were thus proudly identified as a nomad people.[19]

The Ḫana in Zimri-Lim's royal titulary present an awkward and unexpected social construction. In the context of any single kingdom, the *mātum* was separate both from the king who ruled it and from his royal capital. As target of attack, or as seedbed of rebellion, it was the population of the land outside the king's administrative base.[20] Most often, the constituent parts of the *mātum* were its "towns" (*ālum*).[21] In the case of Zimri-Lim's domain, the standard patterns of usage for the words *mātum* and Ḫana ought to have disallowed their combination. We never find "towns of the Ḫana," who were mobile herdsmen, yet Zimri-Lim could lead a *māt Ḫana*.

One answer to this conundrum is the fact that in this context, the Ḫana were in fact the Binu Sim'al people, one part of whose population did live in towns. In my study of Mari political society, I understood Zimri-Lim's titulary to reflect his two main constituencies, the people whom he came to rule by conquest of Mari and his Binu Sim'al kinsmen, so "Mari" and "the land of the Ḫana."[22] On reconsideration of the Ḫana terminology, it strikes me that I underestimated the force of this word. I refused to accept the direct meaning of Zimri-Lim's titulary because it seemed not to fit the political reality displayed in the archives as a whole. Elsewhere, the people acquired by Zimri-Lim with his conquest are especially inhabitants of the river valley, which was called the Aḫ Purattim or "Banks of the Euphrates."[23] The Aḫ Purattim was governed by a system of districts and governors in an administrative structure

---

[19] Durand (1991) has gathered a set of Mari texts that record procedures for swearing loyalty-oaths, with various constituencies in view. The oath for Zimri-Lim's Ḫana people divides the voice of the kingdom's population between the "Ḫana of the steppe (*nawûm*)" and "the townsmen" (literally, "men of the towns"): "I shall hereby [never] commit offense against Zimri-Lim my lord, and when I hear an unfriendly word, either from the mouth of the Ḫana of the steppe or in the mouth of the townsmen, saying, 'Zimri-Lim [and] his offspring shall not rule us,' I shall hereby not join in bringing trouble on Zimri-Lim [and] his offspring ..." (M.6060:20'–27'; idem 1991: 50–52).

[20] The mood of the *mātum* was a constant concern. The *mātum* could be considered rebellious (ARM XXVI 382:3', 412:23, 31; ARM XXVII 132:11), anxious (verb *dalāhum*, ARM IV 25; ARM XIII 146; ARM XXVI 323, 542, 548; verb *hašûm*, ARM XXVI 210), or calm (verb *nâhum*, ARM I 43; ARM II 16; ARM IV 57; ARM VI 76; ARM XXVI 411, 430, 519).

[21] A governor of the most distant Mari district writes back to the king, "On the side of the land (*mātum*) of Yassan and on the side of the land (*mātum*) of Apum, there are reliable towns. That is why Qarni-Lim is

staying behind to guard the land (*mātum*)" (ARM XXVII 72–bis:24'–27'). Charpin (1990: 71, A.315+) mentions "the towns that are in the land of Kaḫat" (line 16) and proceeds to list them, concluding that these towns are run down.

[22] See Fleming 2004: 164–65, especially the section entitled, "The Two Rivers of Zimri-Lim."

[23] The letter of Bannum, mentioned above in note 12, contrasts his role as Chief-of-Pasture over the Binu Sim'al, the Numḫâ, and the Yamutbal, with his entry into an alternate world, conquered on behalf of Zimri-Lim: "And if the Ḫana press you to appoint another Chief-of-Pasture, saying, 'Now that Bannum, our Chief-of-Pasture, lives in the Aḫ Purattim, we should appoint another Chief-of-Pasture'; you — answer them this way: 'Previously, he lived in the steppe, and he maintained the status of the Sim'alites, the Numḫâ, and the Yamutbal. Then, he left for the Aḫ Purattim, where he forced open the fortified towns and so has secured your status in the Aḫ Purattim. Now, because I myself have come here, I have left this man in the Aḫ Purattim in order to hold the fortified towns. Now, as soon as I reach (Mari), I will send you back your Chief-of-Pasture.' Answer them this way!" (Villard 1994, A.1098:6'–15').

that mirrored the palace and its ruler for the kingdom as a whole.[24] All the people of the districts were accounted for by their settlements, and ideally, they would not move without the permission of governor and king.[25] The population of these districts fit the normal content of a *mātum* "land," and yet this was not the *mātum* of Zimri-Lim in his royal title as "king of Mari and the *māt Ḫana*."

In general, the city named with its *mātum* stood for no more than the single administrative center of a kingdom. The people ruled by the king could then be named variously; most often, the *mātum* was simply identified with the central city.[26] In some cases, the primary power base could be named as a kinship group known outside the context of this one kingdom, as with Andarig and the *māt Yamutbalim* or Kurdâ and the *māt Numḫâ*.[27] In neither of these other kingdoms do we have any evidence to suggest that the towns of Andarig and Kurdâ designated parallel populations, governed by districts like Mari's Aḫ Purattim. In light of these analogies, the Aḫ Purattim cannot be represented by "Mari" alone, and it seems to be ignored entirely in Zimri-Lim's titulary. Rather, Zimri-Lim regarded his essential "land" as identified with his tribal base, which he identified in turn by their mobile herding component. In conception, Zimri-Lim was a nomad king. He has not been regarded as such because the evidence from his palace archives so obviously assumes an institutionalized urban setting like those known across early Mesopotamia. Nevertheless, we gain by taking seriously the language of this ancient figure on his own terms.

GOVERNANCE OF AḪ PURATTIM AND ḪANA

If the kingdom of Zimri-Lim were allotted a territory, as for a modern state, the region would extend up and down the Euphrates and Ḫabur rivers, mostly upstream from Mari itself. The area of Suḫû was situated downstream from Mari, where there were few major towns and a strong herding presence in the steppe north and south of the narrow Euphrates valley.[28] Zimri-Lim's core dominion was administered through four district centers that followed a line up the Euphrates and then the Ḫabur from Mari to Terqa, Saggaratum, and Qaṭṭunan. Further up the Euphrates were Dur Yaḫdun-Lim and the old town of Tuttul, and Zimri-Lim

---

[24] On the administration of Zimri-Lim's kingdom by its districts, see Lion 2001: 141–209. ARM VII 277 lists a sequence of local "palaces" at Mari, Terqa, Saggaratum, Dur Yaḫdun-Lim, and Qaṭṭunan (v':2–6). Four of these represent the primary district centers of Zimri-Lim's kingdom, with Dur Yaḫdun-Lim usually treated as part of the Saggaratum district. It nevertheless enjoyed some special prestige and importance, as demonstrated by one reference to a joint district of Saggaratum and Dur-Yaḫdun-Lim (ARM XXIII 69:1–2), and another to a "district of Dur-Yaḫdun-Lim" on its own (ARM XXVI 76:23–24).

[25] One letter from the governor of the Qaṭṭunan district to Zimri-Lim recalls instructions from the king to arrest local villagers who try to leave without permission (ARM XXVII 26:14–19). This is not easy to do, especially when local crops have been ruined by a locust plague.

[26] Examples include the *māt Ekallatim* (ARM II 18:4; ARM XXVI 425:8; etc.); the *māt Babilim* (ARM II 25:15'); the *māt Ešnunna* (ARM X 155:9; ARM XXVI 376:10; etc.); and the *māt Larsa* (ARM XIII 27:15; ARM XXVI 385:41'; etc.).

[27] For the *māt Yamutbalim*, see ARM X 84:24; ARM XXVI 383:7, 432:8'; ARM XXVIII 172:8'–9'; the *māt Numḫâ*, ARM XXVI 358:9', 521:11; Joannès 1985: 109, A.3209. These names should not be regarded as fixed titles, however. It was also possible to name the same political entities by their governing centers, as with Babylon and Ešnunna, as *māt Andarig* (ARM I 132:6; ARM IV 31:9; ARM XXVI 430:33) and the *māt Kurdâ* (ARM II 23:11').

[28] Joannès (1996: 334) considers the Suḫûm a "zone under control" rather than fully part of the Mari kingdom. During the reign of Zimri-Lim, before Babylon's conquest of the larger region, Mari, Ešnunna, and Babylon contested the territory.

retained influence as far as Imar on the great elbow of the Euphrates, where it drops out of the northern hills and turns east toward the Persian Gulf.[29] Up the Ḫabur, the last district center of Qaṭṭunan was still below the confluence of the various tributaries. Beyond Qaṭṭunan, the busy region represented especially by the eastern and central parts of the Ḫabur drainage displays a strong affinity between Zimri-Lim and various independent centers, with one large association defined as a *mātum* of plural kings under the name of Ida-Maraṣ.[30]

As a whole, the territory ruled by Zimri-Lim from Mari appears to have been called the Aḫ Purattim, Banks of the Euphrates. It is then striking and strange that Zimri-Lim would bypass this entire agglomeration of settled peoples in the definition of his kingdom by the *māt Ḫana*.[31] The reality of this political bifurcation is confirmed in the many references to the separate governance of the Aḫ Purattim and the Ḫana under Zimri-Lim.[32] While the Aḫ Purattim districts had palaces and governors, with town leaders called *sugāgum*s, the Ḫana were led by one or possibly two powerful "chiefs of pasture" (*mer'ûm*), with the smaller-scale *sugāgum* leaders defined without reference to settlements.[33] Under their *mer'ûm*, the Ḫana reported directly to Zimri-Lim, bypassing entirely the governors of the Aḫ Purattim.[34]

In this system, the Ḫana enjoyed a political existence completely unlike that of the Aḫ Purattim. Whereas the residents of the Aḫ Purattim were not supposed to move without

---

[29] For the complicated political situation of Imar on the elbow of the middle Euphrates, see Durand 1990: 42–53. Imar and Tuttul had natural associations, yet Imar remained outside the direct influence of Zimri-Lim's kingdom, falling instead within the circle of Yamhad, to the west.

[30] Ties with the region north of Qaṭṭunan, among the tributaries of the Ḫabur, appear to have been based on common connection to the Binu Sim'al population. One text creates an opposition between the Binu Yamina range in the western lands of Yamhad, Qatna, and Amurrum, while the Ḫana, or Binu Sim'al, are defined by a range in Ida-Maraṣ (Fleming 1998: 61, n. 91).

[31] Zimri-Lim's predecessor, Yaḫdun-Lim, considered the Aḫ Purattim to be conquered territory. He claims in the Šamaš temple inscription that "he established control over the Banks of the Euphrates" (iv 4), an achievement that he celebrates in his epithet in the Dur Yaḫdun-Lim building inscription, as "the one who established control over the Banks of the Euphrates" (*kišād purattim*, lines 7–8). In the long version of his royal seal, Zimri-Lim likewise presents the Aḫ Purattim as a separate entity from the *māt Ḫana*, with the following titulary: "Zimri-Lim, appointed by Dagan, beloved of Enlil, who established control over the Banks of the Euphrates (Aḫ Purattim), king of Mari and the *māt Ḫana*, son of Yaḫdun-Lim" (Frayne 1990, 626, E4.6.12.4).

[32] There are many expressions of this overall division. One explicit reference, cast in exactly these terms, is found in a reply from Zimri-Lim to another king who has requested military aid. The Mari king has at the core of his force 100 Ḫana and 100 "of my servants of the Aḫ Purattim," who together represent "the heads of my land" (ARM XXVI/2, p. 33, A.2730:80–10). Another example, with slightly different terminology, occurs in a letter from one of Zimri-Lim's district governors, who exhorts him to remember that he is first of all "the king of the Ḫana" and secondly "the king of the Akkadian(s)" (ARM VI 76:20–21). It appears that the second category refers to the territory conquered by Zimri-Lim and his people from Yasmaḫ-Addu, which included Mari and the settled areas of the river valley that were dependent on it, so the Aḫ Purattim.

[33] The parallel and contrasting political domains within Zimri-Lim's kingdom are cast in particularly sharp relief with the office of *sugāgum*, which held a place in both systems. This figure has been understood entirely in terms of town leadership (see Nakata 1989: 113–18). Plural *sugāgū* are listed together with "elders" as the core leadership of tribally defined populations: e.g., the Binu Yamina (ARM XXVI 24:11), the Numḫa (Lafont 1994, *FM* II 117:30–31), the Mutebal (Lafont 1994, *FM* II 116:10–11). "Ḫana" leadership may be identified specifically as *sugāgū* (Guichard 1994, *FM* II 123:27'–28'; Charpin 1992: 98, A.2119:29–31).

[34] Governors of the Aḫ Purattim districts complained to their king about the activities of the Ḫana's *mer'ûm* leaders, who were responsible directly to Zimri-Lim. In ARM XXVII 151, the governor of Qaṭṭunan rails against the *mer'ûm* Ibal-pi-el, because he has supposedly tried to claim authority over non-Ḫana troops in the campaign against Elam.

reporting to the governor, the normal life of the Ḫana involved movement. Loyalty and service were expected based on personal ties, managed through the leadership of *sugāgum* and *merʾûm*. In time of war, the districts and their settlements would all be counted by census, so that contributions to the king's forces could be tracked by formal records.[35] We have no evidence for any Ḫana census under Zimri-Lim.[36] Ḫana fighters formed the backbone of Zimri-Lim's military, but it appears that he received their backing without the pressure of this writing-based accountability.[37] I have said that under Zimri-Lim, "Ḫana" can be shorthand for "Binu Simʾal," the people of the king. Although it is certain that the settled population of the kingdom included Binu Simʾal towns,[38] we never hear of any town or group under district governance identified as Binu Simʾal. This stands in contrast to the oft-mentioned "towns of the Binu Yamina," the outsider complement to the people of Zimri-Lim.[39] While the Binu Yamina had to accept administration through their settled towns, where they could be counted and managed through the Aḫ Purattim districts, the king's Binu Simʾal kinsmen seem to have been left free with their mobile Ḫana affiliates.

The *merʾûm* was a figure of impressive power. He reported directly to the king, sometimes to the frustration of district governors who had to deal with Ḫana traversing their domains. The separate lines of relationship are visible in one letter from the governor of Qaṭṭunan to King Zimri-Lim: "I was not forceful with Ibal-el (the *merʾûm*). It is to be feared that I would be forceful, and then he would complain about me (to the king)."[40] The governor requests Zimri-Lim to issue the forceful request that can only come from him. Frequently, the governors report warily what they know of the *merʾûm*'s movements and activities. The district rulers know that they have no authority over the Ḫana leader, and the governors' letters imply such an independence that even the king may not have full knowledge of the *merʾûm*'s affairs.[41]

Both the centrality of the Ḫana as Zimri-Lim's core constituency and the power of their *merʾûm* are underscored by a series of letters that recount stages in the confirmation of an alliance between the joint *mātum* of Ida-Maraṣ, in the central Ḫabur drainage, and the Ḫana.[42]

---

[35] On the census in Mari texts, see Durand 1998: 332–53. During the reign of Zimri-Lim, there appear to have been two major episodes of census-taking, one just after the war with Ešnunna (year 5) and the other in preparation for war against Elam, together with the Babylonians (year 10; idem 1998: 347).

[36] Before Zimri-Lim, king Yasmaḫ-Addu reports to his brother that the land has been counted by census, defined by the two categories of "land" (*mātum*) and "Ḫana" (ARM IV 57:9–10); for Ḫana census, see also ARM I 82:14–15, 87:4–5; ARM II 1:10, 24–25.

[37] In the treaty offered to Zimri-Lim by king Ibal-pi-el II of Ešnunna, Zimri-Lim's military forces are listed by category, beginning with "the army (or, batallion) of Mari" and "the army of the Ḫana" (Charpin 1991: 141–44, A.361 iii:13′–15′). See the discussion of the Ḫana army in Fleming 2004: 85–87.

[38] One of the clearest examples is Sapiratum in the region downstream from Mari, which is mentioned in a text that makes explicit connection with one of the Binu Simʾal constituent groups (see Charpin 1997: 341–66; ARM VIII 85+).

[39] There was a particular concentration of Binu Yamina population in the district of Terqa, the governor of which made frequent reference to these people as "the towns of the Binu Yamina" (e.g., ARM II 92:12–13, 102:19–23; ARM III 6:5–13, 70+:8–14), and other governors use the same phrase.

[40] Guichard 1997, *FM* III 20:rev.2′–4′.

[41] Another governor of Qaṭṭunan sends a report to Zimri-Lim about a meeting between Ibal-el the *merʾûm* and the king of Ašnakkum, one of the principal centers of Ida-Maraṣ, north of Mari. The governor writes as if his lord would not necessarily know what transpired at such a "meeting of the Ḫana," and he will want to get reliable information from an independent source (Durand 1994, *FM* II 63; cf. another reference to the same event in ARM II 33).

[42] The documents are gathered in Charpin 1993: 165–91. See especially text nos. 2, 3, 6, 7, and 9. Throughout, the treaty is defined as binding the Ida-Maraṣ coalition and the Ḫana — not Mari, or even Zimri-Lim; see idem 1993, text no. 2 (A.2326):8–10, and text no. 8 (= ARM II 37), throughout.

Ida-Maraṣ related to Zimri-Lim as a fluid vassal collective, and this event reaffirmed the relationship as if it only encompassed the king and his Ḫana people, just as presented in the royal titulary. It is as if the Aḫ Purattim did not exist, except perhaps as a separate set of vassals to Zimri-Lim and the Ḫana. The very lands that we are inclined to regard as defining a Mari-based kingdom had nothing to do with the core political identity of Zimri-Lim's domain. In the arrangement of this alliance, the Ḫana and Zimri-Lim were represented by Ibal-el the *mer ʿûm*. Various kings and key leaders from Ida-Maraṣ gathered before the *mer ʿûm*, who oversaw the transaction and who felt free to change the ritual procedure undertaken by the visitors, without writing first for royal instruction.[43]

THE CONSTRUCTION OF ZIMRI-LIM'S KINGDOM

In a world divided into kingdoms, where the governing center may often be distinguished from the *mātum* governed, it is easy to envision a simple political structure based on a hierarchy of authority descending from the monarch. The Mari evidence shows that this impression of a hierarchical pyramid of power can be deceiving. Zimri-Lim ruled an amalgam of peoples through separate relationships, with each group directly accountable to himself. At the center stood Zimri-Lim's own people and power base, the Binu Sim'al, whom he permitted to identify themselves by their mobile Ḫana component. In the end, Zimri-Lim considered himself the king of the Binu Sim'al Ḫana, with Mari as his royal seat. All other constituencies stood outside this central relationship.

With the Ḫana at center, the people of the Aḫ Purattim, for all their fixed commitment to Mari-based leadership, were relegated to something more like vassal status, forced to swear fealty through local leaders. In real terms, the local leaders of the Aḫ Purattim were probably the *sugāgum*s of individual towns, who only occasionally acquired their positions by outside appointment.[44] These were overseen by the district governors who represented the king's management, in a system that did not originate with Zimri-Lim and that may have been passed on with conquest of the Euphrates valley territory. For Zimri-Lim, despite the seeming intimacy of their reliance on the Mari center, this population was more foreign to him than were the Ḫana.

So far as we understand the basic relationship of the Aḫ Purattim people with their king as similar to that of vassals, then the main criterion for distinguishing them from independent vassal realms appears to be distance. The Aḫ Purattim was bound to the Mari capital in a geographical unity that permitted a more direct involvement in its regular affairs, expressed through the district governors and their local palaces. The difference between a governor and a vassal king was that the governor was appointed by Zimri-Lim without evident input from

---

[43] The negotiations over final treaty arrangements are described in a letter from Ibal-el to Zimri-Lim (Charpin 1993, text no. 7, A.2226).

[44] All *sugāgum* leaders had to pay the king a fee called the *sugāgūtum* in maintenance of their position, and royal approval was certainly standard (Fleming 2004: 70–75). Nevertheless, the appointment of Asqudum, a powerful associate of Zimri-Lim, to be *sugāgum* of Ḫišamta in the district of Terqa appears to be

exceptional (ARM XXVI 5:12–21, etc., 6:53–57). Bannum, the lead *mer ʿûm* of the Binu Sim'al, protests vehemently, and it is clear that the appointment is a benefit granted to an influential person with no prior link to the town. Despite the *sugāgūtum* fee, then, the position must be considered a financial benefit. It seems that the *sugāgum* could raise the fee from his constituents and pay the king a fraction of the quantities received.

the local leadership, whereas the rule of vassal kings was only ratified by their overlord.[45] It does not appear that Zimri-Lim could simply appoint one of his circle to rule an allied center, such as one of the small constituents of the Ida-Maraṣ coalition.[46] According to the norms of political terminology, only peoples with leaders who could claim status as "kings" (*šarrum*) would be regarded as *mātum*s, and a separate word was coined for "districts" under the king at Mari.[47]

Zimri-Lim thus enjoyed the longer-distance support of various peoples who maintained their own local leadership. The largest of these was the alliance of ten or more kings in the Ḫabur under the name of Ida-Maraṣ. Other northern kings accepted Zimri-Lim's leadership on individual terms. The second direction of Zimri-Lim's influence was up the Euphrates toward the Baliḫ River. One basis for this more distant connection seems to have been the location of an old Binu Sim'al center at the town of Der, just north of the Euphrates on the Baliḫ.[48] With Zimri-Lim's interest in that area, the town of Tuttul, at the confluence of the two rivers, naturally fell under his sway as well, though with its tradition of governance by plural elders, the royal interest was represented by a long-term envoy called the *ḫazzannum*, distinct from governors and vassal kings.[49] Outside of Zimri-Lim's political power base of the Binu Sim'al Ḫana, both the Aḫ Purattim districts and all these subordinated peoples stood at one remove from the core definition of the realm as "Mari and the *māt Ḫana*."

As a whole, the Mari archives of King Zimri-Lim show one configuration by which mobile pastoralists, the population that we come to regard as "nomads," could be integrated into a political network that included settlement-based kingdoms. In common modern parlance, with all its flaws, the nomads were bound up with both city and state, even as the nomad category was idealized as distinct. They could even dominate a political landscape of cities and states. In the standard language of early second-millennium Akkadian, the mobile Ḫana could not be identified with towns (*ālum*), but Zimri-Lim could rule a Ḫana land (*māt Ḫana*). The political category that allowed the combination of mobile Ḫana and settled populations in a close-knit core of Zimri-Lim's people was represented by the Binu Sim'al and its subgroups, which may be considered "tribal," without limitation as primitive and egalitarian. Through this tribal organization, the herding communities of early second-millennium Mesopotamia could participate in regional politics at every level without binding themselves irrevocably to the definition of power by city-based kingdoms.

---

[45] Durand's suggestion that kingship had to be approved by the suzerain seems to apply specifically to Ida-Maraṣ leaders under Sim'alite Mari rule, and it is not clear from the published evidence whether the practice extended further afield (see Durand 1997: 207, 467).

[46] A letter from an erstwhile vassal with more independent status suggests a more likely scenario. A former king of Kurdâ is reported to ask for help from Zimri-Lim in regaining his throne. He is evidently a product of the local political scene, asking for outside help, including the powerful influence of

the Binu Sim'al *mer'ûm* (A.1215, cited in Guillot 1997: 276).

[47] The "district" was called a *ḫalṣum*, and its "governor" was a *šāpiṭum*; see Fleming 2004: 133–39.

[48] On the status of the western Der, with its apparent relationship to Zimri-Lim's Mari, see Durand and Guichard 1997: 39–41.

[49] Zimri-Lim's influence at Tuttul was less direct than that of his predecessor Yaḫdun-Lim, who considered the town to be the western base for his Binu Sim'al kingdom; see Charpin and Ziegler 2003: 182.

ABBREVIATIONS

ARM I   *Correspondance de Šamši-Addu et de ses fils.* Georges Dossin. Archives Royales de Mari 1. Paris: Imprimerie National, 1950.

ARM II   *Lettres diverses.* Charles-F. Jean. Archives Royales de Mari 2. Paris: Imprimerie National, 1950.

ARM III   *Correspondance de Kibri-Dagan, Gouverneur de Terqa.* Jean-Robert Kupper. Archives Royales de Mari 3. Paris: Imprimerie National, 1950.

ARM IV   *Correspondance de Šamši-Addu.* Georges Dossin. Archives Royales de Mari 4. Paris: Imprimerie National, 1951.

ARM V   *Corresopondance de Iasmah-Addu.* Georges Dossin. Archives Royales de Mari 5. Paris: Imprimerie National, 1952.

ARM VI   *Correspondance de Bahdi-Lim, Préfet du palais de Mari.* Jean-Robert Kupper. Archives Royales de Mari 6. Paris: Imprimerie National, 1954.

ARM VII   *Textes économiques et administratifs.* Jean Bottéro. Archives Royales de Mari 7. Paris: Imprimerie National, 1957.

ARM VIII   *Textes juridiques.* Georges Boyer. Archives Royales de Mari 8. Paris: Paul Geuthner, 2003.

ARM X   *Correspondance féminine.* Georges Dossin and André Finet. Archives Royales de Mari 10. Paris: Paul Geuthner, 1978.

ARM XIII   *Textes divers.* Georges Dossin, Jean Bottéro, M. Birot, M. Lurton Burke, Jean-Robert Kupper, and André Finet. Archives Royales de Mari 13. Paris: Paul Geuthner, 1964.

ARM XXIII   *Archives administratives de Mari* I. Guilliaume Bardet, Francis Joannès, Bertrand Lafont, Denis Soubeyran, Pierre Villard. Archives Royales de Mari 23. Paris: Éditions Recherche sur les Civilisations, 1984.

ARM XXVI   *Archives épistolaires de Mari* I. Jean-Marie Durand. Archives Royales de Mari 26. Paris: Éditions Recherche sur les Civilisations, 1988.

ARM XXVII   *Correspondance des gouverneurs de Qaṭṭunân.* Maurice Birot. Archives Royales de Mari 27. Paris: Éditions Recherche sur les Civilisations, 1993.

ARM XXVIII   *Lettres royales du temps de Zimri-Lim.* Jean-Robert Kupper. Archives Royales de Mari 28. Paris: Éditions Recherche sur les Civilisations, 1998.

FM   *Florilegium marianum.* For *FM* II, see Durand 1994, Guichard 1994, and Lafont 1994; for *FM* III, see Guichard 1997 and Guillot 1997.

BIBLIOGRAPHY

Anbar, Moshe
　1991　　　*Les tribus amurrites de Mari.* Freiburg: Universitätsverlag; Göttingen: Vandenhoeck
　　　　　　& Ruprecht.

Charpin, Dominique
　1990　　　"A Contribution to the Geography and History of the Kingdom of Kahat." In *Tall al-*
　　　　　　Ḥamīdīya 2 (Recent Excavations in the Upper Khabur Region, Symposion, December
　　　　　　9–11, 1986), by Seyyare Eichler, Markus Wäfler, and David Warburton, pp. 67–85.
　　　　　　Orbis Biblicus et Orientalis, Series Archaeologica 6. Freiburg: Universitätsverlag;
　　　　　　Göttingen: Vandenhoeck & Ruprecht.
　1991　　　"Un traité entre Zimri-Lim de Mari et Ibâl-pî-El II d'Ešnunna." In *Marchands, di-*
　　　　　　plomates et empéreurs: Études sur la civilisation mésopotamienne offertes à Paul
　　　　　　Garelli, edited by Dominique Charpin and Francis Joannès, pp. 141–44. Paris:
　　　　　　Éditions Recherche sur les Civilisations.
　1992　　　"De la vallée du Tigre au 'triangle du Habur': Un engrenage géopolitique?" In
　　　　　　Recherches en Haute Mésopotamie: Tell Mohammed Diyab; Campagnes 1990 et
　　　　　　1991, edited by Jean-Marie Durand, pp. 97–102. Mémoires de N.A.B.U. 2. Paris:
　　　　　　Société pour l'étude du Proche-Orient ancien.
　1993　　　"Un souverain éphémère en Ida-Maras: Išme-Addu d'Ašnakkum." *Mari: Annales de*
　　　　　　Recherches Interdisciplinaires 7: 165–91.
　1997　　　"Sapīratum, ville de Suhûm." *Mari: Annales de Recherches Interdisciplinaires* 8:
　　　　　　341–66.
　2004　　　"Histoire politique du Proche-Orient amorrite (2002–1595)." In *Mesopotamien: Die*
　　　　　　altbabylonische Zeit, edited by Dominique Charpin, Dietz Otto Edzard, and Martin
　　　　　　Stol, pp. 25–480. Orbis Biblicus et Orientalis 160/4. Freiburg: Universitätsverlag;
　　　　　　Göttingen: Vandenhoeck & Ruprecht.

Charpin, Dominique, and Jean-Marie Durand
　1986　　　"'Fils de Sim'al': Les origines tribales des rois de Mari." *Revue d'Assyriologie* 80:
　　　　　　141–83.

Charpin, Dominique, and Jean-Marie Durand, editors
　1994　　　*Florilegium marianum* II: *Recueil d'études à la mémoire de Maurice Birot.* Mémoires
　　　　　　de N.A.B.U. 3. Paris: Société pour l'étude du Proche-Orient ancien.

Charpin, Dominique, and Nele Ziegler
　2003　　　*Florilegium marianum* V: *Mari et le Proche-Orient à l'époque amorrite: Essai d'his-*
　　　　　　toire politique. Mémoires de N.A.B.U. 6. Paris: Société pour l'étude du Proche-Orient
　　　　　　ancien.

Dossin, Georges
　1938　　　"Les archives épistolaires du palais de Mari." *Syria* 19: 105–26.
　1939　　　"Les archives économiques du palais de Mari." *Syria* 20: 97–113.
　1955　　　"L'inscription de fondation de Iahdun-Lim, roi de Mari." *Syria* 32: 1–28.

Durand, Jean-Marie
　1990　　　"La cité-État d'Imâr à l'époque des rois de Mari." *Mari: Annales de Recherches*
　　　　　　Interdisciplinaires 6: 42–53.
　1991　　　"Précurseurs syriens aux protocoles néo-assyriens: Considérations sur la vie politique
　　　　　　aux Bords-de-l'Euphrate." In *Marchands, diplomates et empereurs: Études sur la*
　　　　　　civilisation mésopotamienne offertes à Paul Garelli, edited by Dominique Charpin
　　　　　　and Francis Joannès, pp. 13–71. Paris: Éditions Recherche sur les Civilisations.
　1992　　　"Unité et diversités au Proche-Orient à l'époque amorrite." In *La circulation des biens,*
　　　　　　des personnes et des idées dans le Proche-Orient ancien (Actes de la 38ᵉ Rencontre

Assyriologique Internationale, Paris, 8–10 juillet 1991), edited by Dominique Charpin and Francis Joannès, pp. 13–14. Paris: Éditions Recherche sur les Civilisations.

1994   "Administrateurs de Qaṭṭunân." In *Florilegium marianum* II: *Recueil d'études à la mémoire de Maurice Birot*, edited by Dominique Charpin and Jean-Marie Durand, pp. 83–114. Mémoires de N.A.B.U. 3. Paris: Société pour l'étude du Proche-Orient ancien.

1997   *Documents épistolaires du palais de Mari*, Volume 1. Littératures anciennes du Proche-Orient 16. Paris: Éditions du Cerf.

1998   *Documents épistolaires du palais de Mari*, Volume 2. Littératures anciennes du Proche-Orient 17. Paris: Éditions du Cerf.

Durand, Jean-Marie, and Michaël Guichard

1997   "Les rituels de Mari." In *Florilegium marianum* III: *Recuil d'études à la mémoire de Marie-Thérèse Barrelet*, edited by Dominique Charpin and Jean-Marie Durand, pp. 19–82. Mémoires de N.A.B.U. 4. Paris: Société pour l'étude du Proche-Orient ancien.

Fleming, Daniel E.

1998   "Mari and the Possibilities of Biblical Memory." *Revue d'Assyriologie* 92: 41–78.

2004   *Democracy's Ancient Ancestors: Mari and Early Collective Governance*. Cambridge: Cambridge University Press.

Frayne, Douglas

1990   *Old Babylonian Period (2003–1595 BC)*. Royal Inscriptions of Mesopotamia, Early Periods 4. Toronto: University of Toronto.

Guichard, Michaël

1994   "Au pays de la dame de Nagar." In *Florilegium marianum* II: *Recueil d'études à la mémoire de Maurice Birot*, edited by Dominique Charpin and Jean-Marie Durand, pp. 235–72. Mémoires de N.A.B.U. 3. Paris: Société pour l'étude du Proche-Orient ancien.

1997   "Le sel à Mari (III): Les lieux du sel." In *Florilegium marianum* III: *Recueil d'études à la mémoire de Marie-Thérèse Barrelet*, edited by Dominique Charpin and Jean-Marie Durand, pp. 167–200. Mémoires de N.A.B.U. 4. Paris: Société pour l'étude du Proche-Orient ancien.

Guillot, Isabelle

1997   "Les gouverneurs de Qattunân: Nouveaux textes." In *Florilegium marianum* III: *Recuil d'études à la mémoire de Marie-Thérèse Barrelet*, edited by Dominique Charpin and Jean-Marie Durand, pp. 271–90. Mémoires de N.A.B.U. 4. Paris: Société pour l'étude du Proche-Orient ancien.

Joannès, Francis

1985   "Nouveaux mémorandums." In *Miscellanea Babylonica: Mélanges offerts à Maurice Birot*, edited by Jean-Marie Durand and Jean-Robert Kupper, p. 109. Paris: Éditions Recherche sur les Civilisations.

1996   "Routes et voies de communication dans les archives de Mari." In *Mari, Ébla et les Hourrites: Dix ans de travaux*, Part 1 (Actes du colloque international, Paris, mai 1993), edited by Jean-Marie Durand, pp. 323–61. Amurru 1. Paris: Éditions Recherche sur les Civilisations.

Kupper, Jean-Robert

1957   *Les nomades en Mésopotamie au temps des rois de Mari*. Paris: Les Belles Lettres

1998   *Lettres royales du temps de Zimri-Lim*. Archives Royales de Mari 28. Paris: Éditions Recherche sur les Civilisations.

Lafont, Bertrand

1994   "L'admonestation des anciens de Kurdâ à leur roi." In *Florilegium marianum* II: *Recueil d'études à la mémoire de Maurice Birot*, edited by Dominique Charpin and

Jean-Marie Durand, pp. 209–20. Mémoires de N.A.B.U. 3. Paris: Société pour l'étude du Proche-Orient ancien.

Lion, Brigitte
  2001   "Les gouverneurs provinciaux du royaume de Mari à l'époque de Zimrî-Lîm." In *Mari, Ebla et les Hourrites: Dix ans de travaux*, Part 2 (Paris, mai 1993), edited by Jean-Marie Charpin and Dominique Charpin, pp. 141–209. Amurru 2. Paris: Éditions Recherche sur les Civilisations.

Luke, J. T.
  1965   Pastoralism and Politics in the Mari Period. Ph.D. dissertation, University of Michigan.

Nakata, Ichiro
  1989   "A Further Look at the Institution of *sugāgūtum* in Mari." *Journal of the Ancient Near Eastern Society* 19: 113–18.

Nicolle, Christophe, editor
  2004   *Nomades et sédentaires dans le Proche-Orient ancien* (Compte rendu de la 46ᵉ Rencontre Assyriologique Internationale, Paris, 10–13 juillet 2000). Amurru 3. Paris: Éditions Recherche sur les Civilisations.

Rowton, Michael B.
  1967   "The Physical Environment and the Problem of Nomads." In *La civilisation de Mari* (15ᵉ Rencontre Assyriologique Internationale), edited by Jean-Robert Kupper, pp. 109–21. Les congrès et colloques de l'Université Liège 42. Liège: Les Belles Lettres.
  1973   "Urban Autonomy in a Nomadic Environment." *Journal of Near Eastern Studies* 32: 201–15.
  1974   "Enclosed Nomadism." *Journal of the Economic and Social History of the Orient* 17: 1–30.
  1976   "Dimorphic Structure and Topology." *Oriens Antiquus* 15: 17–31.

Schneider, David M.
  1984   *Critique of the Study of Kinship*. Ann Arbor: University of Michigan Press.

Steinkeller, Piotr
  1998   "The Historical Background of Urkesh and the Hurrian Beginnings in Northern Mesopotamia." In *Urkesh and the Hurrians*, edited by Giorgio Buccellati and Marilyn Kelly-Buccellati, pp. 76–78. Malibu: Undena.

Villard, Pierre
  1994   "Nomination d'un scheich." In *Florilegium marianum* II: *Recueil d'études à la mémoire de Maurice Birot*, edited by Dominique Charpin and Jean-Marie Durand, pp. 291–97. Mémoires de N.A.B.U. 3. Paris: Société pour l'étude du Proche-Orient ancien.

Ziegler, Nele
  2004   "Samsî-Addu et les Bédouins." In *Nomades et sédentaires dans le Proche-Orient ancien* (Compte rendu de la 46ᵉ Rencontre Assyriologique Internationale, Paris, 10–13 juillet 2000), edited by Christophe Nicolle, pp. 95–109. Amurru 3. Paris: Éditions Recherche sur les Civilisations.

13

FROM PASTORAL PEASANTRY TO TRIBAL URBANITES: ARAB TRIBES AND THE FOUNDATION OF THE ISLAMIC STATE IN SYRIA

DONALD WHITCOMB, UNIVERSITY OF CHICAGO

INTRODUCTION

"Establish for the Bedouin (al-ʿarab) *who are with you a place of settlement* (dār al-hijra)." (Letter of the Caliph ʿUmar to Saʿd; al-Ṭabari 1879: i/2360)

The *dār al-muhājirīn* or *dār al-hijra*, abode of the emigrants (Crone 1994: 356–57), is defined succinctly by Athamina (1986: 190) as "a center of immigration to which Muslims should move, according to principles of the new faith."[1] One must wonder whether the use of *dār al-hijra* in this letter, in evoking the powerful religious concept of the *hijra*, in the sense of moving into a new life and community,[2] refers to the establishment of Islamic settlements called *amṣār* (singular *miṣr*), usually described as garrisons or cantonments.[3] With the possible exception of al-Jabiya, the initial Muslim settlement in Syria (Bilad al-Sham) appears to have been in explicit contrast to such foundations but pursued a more complex interaction within or adjacent to established cities.

Some light may be shed by considering pre-Islamic settlements around the classical cities, a phenomenon known as the *parembole nomadon* or extra-mural camp of Arabs (in Arabic, the *ḥāḍir*). Recent archaeological investigation of village sites suggests patterns of organization which may be directly linked to the pastoral camp, as delineated in the archaeological studies of Cribb and a number of ethnographers working in Syria. There had been several episodes of sedentism of Arab tribes in Syria before Islam, particularly under the Banu Ghassan who controlled much of the region as eparchs under the Byzantines. In contrast, it seems that the majority of Arab tribes that settled in Syria after the Muslim conquest originated from the relatively urbanized South Arabia, as well as the Hijaz. The former were peasantry associated with those cities, while the latter were more pastoral in their dominant economy.

The interaction of these newly Islamicized tribes with older Ghassanid tribes may be seen in the early *qaṣr* of Sinnabra (now identified with the site of Khirbet al-Karak). This was a seasonal palace of Muʿāwiya and later Umayyad caliphs (ca. 640–705) and may be related to other *quṣūr* or "desert castles," a term which encompasses a variety of palaces, baths, and

---

[1] In the words of Paul Wheatley (2001: 41): "by the time the *amṣār* were being established, *hijra*, the sundering of bonds of family and lineage for the sake of lodging in a permanent settlement, was being exalted as the consummate symbol of submission to the will of the One God."

[2] The reference is to the *hijra* of the Prophet from Mecca to Yathrib (later called Madina). This has usually been

translated as a "flight," or "emigration," in fact an exodus, in the sense of abandoning an old life for a renewed faith in a new "land of milk and honey." Extension of this concept for the *amṣār* and later emigration is the subject of discussions in Crone 1994 and Madelung 1986.

[3] The most famous and oft-cited are Kufa, Basra, and Fustat (Cairo), but this definition must be used with caution.

other architectural elements of country estates. These *quṣūr* may have functioned as settlements for Umayyad leaders and their followers and, like the Roman villa, had the potential to
take many urban characteristics.

Settlement of large numbers of Arab tribesmen meant development of the *amṣār* and social
adjustments which Athamina has explored. The distinctive patterns in Syria suggest changes
within the matrix of older, classical cities. An interesting example involves the ancient city of
Emesa, the Islamic Hims (now Homs). In the absence of archaeological information, one may
turn to specific reports and other documentation on the town and evaluation of the caliphate of
Muʿāwiya. With his famed successor ʿAbd al-Malik, the Umayyad state would build on these
foundations, and tribal characteristics would be subsumed under political factions.

EVOLUTION OF SETTLEMENT STRUCTURE: THE HADIR

"Few are the towns of any importance in Islam that do not have a campsite
(maḍrib) *there for their inhabitants"* (al-Muqaddasi 1906: 76).

The great Arab geographer, Muhammad ibn Ahmad al-Muqaddasi, notes that a feature
of Islamic urban structures was an adjacent camp. This was a feature of pre-Islamic cities in
Bilad al-Sham and has been examined as the *ḥāḍir*.[4] Composite settlements show the use of
tents in a sedentary context as well as trends toward adoption of permanent structures. There
is a tendency to see the "desert castles" as country estates (Northedge 1994) and indeed
settlement in private estates seems to have been a widespread pattern (such as the *qura* in
Khurasan; Athamina 1986: 188–89).

The early Islamic city of Qinnasrin became the administrative center of the northernmost
military district (*jund*) of al-Sham, probably under Yazīd ibn Muʿāwiya. In this function
Qinnasrin replaced the Byzantine city of Chalcis. The two cities have been assumed to be the
same, unexcavated ruins; unfortunately this massive citadel and lower town revealed almost no
evidence of Islamic occupation. However, about four kilometers to the east is a large village
called al-Hadir, a mound covered with late Byzantine and early Islamic materials (Whitcomb
2000b: fig. 1).

Chalcis was a classical city of some culture and sophistication, as suggested in the
Syriac story of Rabbula who came from an aristocratic family in Qinneshrin (Kennedy and
Liebeschuetz 1988). Beyond this relation of a conversion to Christianity is an implication of
the existence of a separate Qinnesrin and its association with Arab tribes. This corroborates
reports that by the latter half of the sixth century, the Banū Tanūkh and Banū Ṭayyiʾ had
settled at Chalcis.[5] The modern Byzantine historian John Haldon (1995: 416) has noted,
"substantial Arab settlements already existed near a number of cities [in Syria], and prior
to conquest, very considerable numbers of Arabs ... were based at these sites, serving the
Romans as federate or allied troops."

This suggests that Qinnasrin may be viewed as a military camp, a *ḥāḍir*. Such camps no
doubt also served as extramural commercial centers for the Arab-dominated caravan trade.
Thus, for Shahid, the *ḥāḍir* was an ethnic suburb with permanent architecture, the locus of
tribal sedentarization. This seems to be the idea expressed in the classical term, *parembole*

---

[4] This subject was first delineated in Whitcomb 1994 and
considered in light of nomad settlement in Whitcomb
2006.

[5] Banū Tanūkh and Ṭayyiʾ tribes were later conceived as
elements in the Qays (Muḍar) and Yaman (Kalb) confederacies; these had become political factions by the period of the Qinnasrin evidence at hand; see Cobb 2001.

nomadon, as a periurban settlement[6] rather than Helms' broader interpretation. In the case of the *ḥāḍir* of Chalcis, this camp retains its name in the modern town of Hadir (fig. 13.1).

The first excavations at Hadir Qinnasrin exhibited a classic example of luck: one of the trenches revealed a peculiar residence (fig. 13.2). The architectural plan of area K shows a structure of two rectangular rooms, made first in mudbrick and then duplicated in stone cobbles. Artifacts associated with these architectural remains, both ceramics and coins, fall into two phases: an earlier of the late seventh and early eighth century, and a second phase of the later eighth and early ninth century (pre-Samarran). The smaller of the rooms has a couple of ovens and storage vessels. The southwest wall of both rooms was very fragmentary with a series of column bases and seems to have been mostly open. These features add up to a very specific house form, a type derived from the "black" tent used by Arab tribes in the recent and immediate past. The translation of a nomad tent into more permanent material is not so uncommon. Ethnographic study of nomad tribes in Syria has documented a temporary house called a *sibāṭ* (Daker 1984: 54–56, fig. 3) used for seasonal occupation and very similar to the remains uncovered at Hadir Qinnasrin (fig. 13.3).

The interpretation of excavated remains from Hadir Qinnasrin as an example of sedentism is important for the history of Qinnasrin.[7] There are a number of archaeological projects in Syria which have produced evidence of contemporary, early Islamic sedentism (see below). Before turning to these archaeological remains, one might consider two ethnoarchaeological aspects of such settlements.

1. *Architectural Change*. The process of gradual loss of mobility, what Daker (1984: 51–53) calls the "fixed tent," may begin with the tendency to re-occupy earlier camping sites and to utilize elements of previous residences. Cribb (1991b) notes a tendency to use such "fixtures," leveled floors, storage platforms, hearths, ditches, etc.; not the least important are pre-existing wall footings. "The use of substantial stone walls to enclose tent sites is so common that it must be considered a standard feature in the repertoire of tent architecture" (Cribb 1991b: 88). This characteristic of built walls has led Cribb to a typology of residence in which the tent evolves into a more permanent walled structure, first with a tenting roof and then with more permanent materials. Organization of space within tents and village houses is very similar (Watson 1979: 280), due in part to the persistence of nomad traits among sedentary populations (Cribb 1991b: 97). There seem to be sequential stages for *composite settlements*, explored by Sweet, Daker, and especially Jarno.[8] The intermediate stage is most revealing, with social activities (men's domain) retained within the tent, and food preparation and storage activities (women's domain) in fixed structures.

2. *Change in Settlement Structure* (fig. 13.4). Transitional settlements begin to have a history when continuities in social relationships are reflected spatially in clustering, changes in the acceptable *density* of occupation. As Barth (1961) notes, physical distance correlates with social distance in the layout of settlements (Cribb 1991b: 371). Increasing this *density threshold* may be a matter of increased *security*, among other social factors. The implication for an evolving settlement structure is one of

---

[6] The term "periurban" is taken from Glick's (2002) discussion of *huertas* around early Islamic cities in Spain.

[7] The second season of excavations in the year 2000 produced a set of similar buildings. These structures, in area A2b, were less well preserved and their interpretation not as persuasive.

[8] See Whitcomb 2006 for further bibliography.

territoriality and, more immediately, mechanisms and attitudes toward property and land ownership. These changes are facilitated by supra-kinship spatial relationships of *tribal* organization in terms of land and urban-based state formations (Marx 1996: 104). Acceptance of an increasing density threshold suggests, in spatial terms, the movement to pastoral peasantry and ultimately toward tribal urbanites.

A recent study by Jodi Magness (2004) on the Palestinian site of Khirbet Abu Suwwana, east of Jerusalem, offers another example of a peripheral settlement of the early Islamic period. The site was excavated by Sion (1997) and may be dated to the eighth century for phase 1 and the ninth–early tenth for phase 2. The plan of Abu Suwwana is the cumulative result of a long occupation (fig. 13.5).[9] Analysis of the peculiar clustering of structures suggests several developmental layers. Without the in-filling of vacant areas and definition of courtyards, one may perceive modular architectural units, a standard pattern of plus/minus five rooms in-line and opening in the same direction (here east). These units average 4×20 m. These buildings expand by doubling some rooms and by extension of one or more wings to form a courtyard. The original units appear to be spaced between 10 and 20 m apart from one another (a spacing ethnographically confirmed [Cribb 1991a]).

Magness notes several other sites with such modular architectural units, more often as isolate structures due to preservation and other factors. These include 'Ein 'Aneva and Elot village (R. Avner 1996: figs. 128–29). This latter settlement lies in the immediate vicinity of early Islamic Ayla (Aqaba) and has been suggested as a composite settlement with tents (R. Avner 1998) and an example of Bedouin sedentism (Avner and Magness 1998: 40). About 20 km north of Ayla was another early Islamic settlement with modular architecture (Yisrael 2002); in this case, there seems an association with copper smelting from the famous Timna mines of contemporary (as well as earlier) date.

The intensive surveys of the western Negev revealed extensive camps and settlements between 20 and 30 km south of the Byzantine/early Islamic cities in the region. Avni (1992) and Haiman (1990, 1995) clearly outline the association of these settlements with agricultural terracing in the same Byzantine and early Islamic period. Haiman (1995: 35) describes these farmsteads as "nucleus units," forming a square of one to three rooms and a courtyard; the size compares closely with the modular units of Abu Suwwana and elsewhere.[10]

Berthier identifies a number of sites on the middle Euphrates as seasonal (Berthier 2001: 156–60). These were modular units (3×4, 8, 12, 16 m) and apparently repeatedly occupied, first in the Abbasid (period Ib = 750–900) and then in the Middle Islamic period (III–VI; 1000–1300). Rousset (2005: fig. 2, though dated somewhat earlier) notes a similar site at Wadi al-Amur 2. Many other examples may come to be identified with these patterns in mind;[11] one is tempted to re-examine Poidebard's aerial photographs of remains in the desert for post-Roman sedentism (cf. Dentzer 1994).

---

[9] Adjacent structures to the house at Hadir Qinnasrin, not discussed here, may indicate a similar in-filling during its occupation.

[10] Both Magness (2004) and Haiman (1995: 41) see this type of modular house as reflecting the egalitarian social structure and as expression of the Bedouin "paternal house."

[11] The author presented a preliminary study of similar settlements near the Euphrates at the Middle East Studies Association meeting in 1998, "Two Abbasid Farmsteads near Tell Sweyhat." This material was based on field-work in 1973 and study of older aerial photographs; these were sites 7 and 11 in Wilkinson's study of the Sweyhat region (Whitcomb 2004). I wish to thank Asa Eger for reminding me of these parallels.

Helms' (1990) monograph entitled *Early Islamic Architecture of the Desert* is an account of his survey and excavations at al-Risha, located about 200 km southeast of Damascus. He describes the site of al-Risha as a collection of modular architectural structures (fig. 13.6); the site is remarkably similar to Abu Suwwana in the linear arrangement of buildings of comparable (though slightly larger) size. The ceramics indicate a similar dating to the eighth and early ninth century; the relative lack of in-filling and contiguous courtyards may suggest a shorter duration of occupation. There is a variety of plans including an enclosed "khan" (structure C), which recalls the architecture of nearby Jebel Says (Helms 1990: 94). On the other hand, he suggests that the mosque may have had a tent roofing. The mosque, as manifestation of cult, is curiously peripheral to the camp or derived settlement, as exemplified in Abu Suwwana and typically in the Negev (e.g., Be'er Ora). This may indicate only a lack of planned nucleus for the settlement.[12]

This archaeological site takes a particular interest in light of Helms' (1990: 3) interpretation as "a unique opportunity to examine the effects of the coming of Islam on the Bedouin tribes." Having worked on a Bronze Age site with urban characteristics also in the desert, Helms has developed a detailed seriation of relationships between steppe and cultivated, settled lands. Thus there is a widespread pre-Islamic phenomenon of the *parembole nomadon*, which may be reduced to the simple syllogism, "it exists in the desert, therefore it is Bedouin" (Helms 1990: 20).

PALACES FOR THE TRIBAL STATE

It is reported that Muʿāwiya occupied the palace of Sinnabra on the south coast of lake Tiberias during the winter, and that the practice continued under ʿAbd al-Malik.[13] As Robinson (2005) notes, during the early period of his reign, ʿAbd al-Malik followed many of Muʿāwiya's practices. Among his innovations was the *maqṣūra*, tentatively defined as "a columned bay ... enclosed by a railing or screen against which Muʿāwiya leaned while hearing petitions" (Whelan 1986: 210–11) and the *miḥrāb* which has associations with the apsidal form in royal palaces, just as Khoury (1993: 60) has suggested.

Khirbet al-Karak is a small site located on the southern shore of the Lake of Galilee, 5 miles south of Tabariyya (Tiberias), capital of the *jund* of al-Urdunn (fig. 13.7).[14] The excavations by the Oriental Institute of the University of Chicago discovered a Byzantine church with substantial re-occupation in the early Islamic period (Delougaz and Haines 1960).[15] This Islamic structure seems to be a *dār* or residence of a type described by Hirschfeld (1995: 82–84, fig. 59) as a villa rustica or manor house. South of this was a second structure described as a Roman fort (*qaṣr*) with a synagogue inside and bath (*hammam*) attached; this

---

[12] This pattern of peripheral location for the mosque occurs in most of the "desert castles" and Abbasid caravanserais, where the mosque is on the exterior and near the principal entrance (Whitcomb 1996).

[13] Mayer (1925) discusses the Arabic reports of al-Sinnabra, "a place in al-Urdunn province, opposite ʿAqabat Afīq, a distance of three miles from Tabariyya." Sinnabra appears to have been a seasonal capital during the Umayyad period. See Whitcomb 2002 for further references. The caliph Marwan ibn al-Hakam is reported to have stayed there and may have died in this palace.

[14] The site is better known as Beth Yerah, famed for its ceramics characteristic of the Early Bronze period. An initial description of the Islamic remains may be found in Whitcomb 2002.

[15] In the words of Delougaz and Haines (1960: 59, n. 6), "the designation 'church' applies strictly to architectural remains, not to objects; the latter are not associated with the church as such but are later."

identification was challenged by Reich (1993) and analysis of the architecture and artifacts clearly indicate an Umayyad date for the complex (Whitcomb 2002).[16]

The association of the bath, the internal decorations, and the apsidal building within fortified walls forms a structural complex with characteristics that recall the palaces of the so-called desert castles (*quṣūr*) of the Levant (fig. 13.8).[17] Unlike many of the *quṣūr*, Khirbet al-Karak does not seem to feature a series of *buyūt* arranged around a central courtyard; this suggests a different function, perhaps more "urban" in the sense of a design comparable to ʿAnjar (Hillenbrand 1999: 72) or more palatial as at Qasr ibn Wardān. On the interior, the large apsidal element may be compared with the "palace" within the southwestern quadrant of ʿAnjar. Perhaps more interesting is the apse of al-Mundhir's building at Rusafa (Ulbert et al. 1986: 122, fig. 69), which Sauvaget (1939) saw as an audience hall and Shahid (1995: 501–05) as a praetorium of the late sixth century.[18] The parallels adduced, palace structures, would recall Sauvaget's discussion of the apsidal form as the inspiration of the *miḥrāb*. Khoury (1993: 60) has also noted the connection of the meanings of the term *miḥrāb* with royalty and palaces such as the Ghumdan. Recently Cytryn-Silverman has identified a structure at Tabariya with very similar form to Khirbet al-Karak as the *dār al-imāra* of that city.[19]

As Kennedy (1992: 294) has noted, "the Umayyad *quṣūr* were the product of peculiar and particular social and economic conditions." It may follow that this type of *qaṣr* may represent a seasonal court as part of the process of tribal settlement and creation of a tribal state under Muʿāwiya. The palace of Mshatta and that on Amman citadel may be variants of Umayyad courts in both the *quṣūr* and urban settings (Whitcomb 2000b: fig. 9).

TRIBAL GOVERNANCE

"... during the first civil war, many tribal sub-groups left the amsar *of Iraq and joined the camp of Muʿāwiya in Syria. There they were settled by Muʿāwiya in Qinnasrin which from then on was a* misr*"* (Athamina 1987: 24).

As Crone interprets the same report, upon Muʿāwiya's accession he established a military district at Qinnasrin for populations from Kufa and Basra, who had abandoned their *hijra*. The terms used by Tabari are *maṣṣarahā wa-jannadahā*, from *miṣr* and *jund* (Crone 1994: 360). The combination of these terms suggests that the creation of a separate military district north of Hims was an administrative operation and distinct from the creation of a new urban entity (*miṣr*), necessarily residential in nature.[20] The meaning of *miṣr* has prompted much discussion and the common understanding as a military camp or garrison may be too limiting and probably inaccurate. The cognate word *tamṣīr* seems to have referred to the establishment of such camps, but also the transformation of sections of those camps into quarters of a city (Bosworth 1991). Use of the term *miṣr* did not cease with the decline of the militaristic role of such urban structures; rather *miṣr* came to mean any large and important city[21] and eventually

---

[16] More recently, the ceramics from the early excavations have been found to confirm this dating (Greenberg, pers. comm.).

[17] The fortified perimeter closely duplicates the *qaṣr* recently discovered by Leisten (1999–2000) at Balis.

[18] This neglects the debate on the possible function as a church and the interactions of religious and secular functions in light of tribal practice (Fowden 2000).

[19] Personal communication. The latest phase of this building was described by Hirshfeld as a praetorium.

[20] Likewise, other reports cited by Crone (1994: 357) use *dār hiğra wa-manzil ğihād* and *dār hiğra wa-qayrawān*, implying a separation of the *dār al-hijra* from the military camp.

[21] Bosworth (1991) sees a generic usage in hadith and notes a lexicographic usage as "an exactly delineated and demarcated territory." This definition comes remarkably close to the meaning of *khiṭṭa* according to Akbar (1989: 82–84).

to refer to a "capital city," as in al-Hamdani's (1885: 57–58) list of the seven *amṣār* of ʿUmar. Thus when al-Muqaddasi (1906: 47) presents four definitions of the term *"miṣr,"* one finds an evolution of the meaning for an almost invariably successful program of settlement of large tribal populations, the foundation of great Islamic cities.[22]

Athamina has carefully examined Islamic policy toward nomads and policies designed to secure loyalty toward the state. The massive movement to the *amṣār* (*hijra*) was implemented as a process of settlement and new identity as *muhājirūn* (Athamina 1987: 9). Questions of loyalty persisted in denigration of individuals with nomad background (*aʿrāb*) and avoidance of conferring positions of authority to such leaders (Donner 1981: 263ff.). Significantly Muʿāwiya seems one of the first to systematically deviate from this policy (Athamina 1987: 16). One mechanism was the disruption of tribal hospitality (*dīyāfa*) and establishment of the *dār al-aḍyāf* by governors in the *amṣār*; ultimately this began to weaken the attachment to traditional tribal leaders (Athamina 1987: 20–21). Athamina notes other essential attributes of tribal authority, such as generosity with properties (*inhāb al-rizq*) and granting protection to weak individuals, were undermined through state policies and laws (Athamina 1987: 22). Likewise, development of the *shurṭa* (police force) bypassed traditional tribal authorities (Humphreys 2006: 95). Control over the annual stipends by an official called the *ʿarīf* further eroded the power of the tribal leaders (*raʾīs*) and all these factors culminated in the power to appoint those leaders by the state (Athamina 1987: 19, 22–23).

These mechanisms have been suggested for the "classic amṣār" (Basra, Kufa, and other locations) and the application to the tribal composition within Syrian cities has not been as clearly delineated. Thus one might return to urban settlement as *dūr al-hijra*, encouraged "as a requisite for full membership in the Ummah" (Duri 1980: 52–53). This underlying concept suggests that settlement was an important and structured matter for the community of believers, and careful description of the settlements is a fundamental step toward understanding the earliest phase of the "Islamic city."[23]

MUʿĀWIYA, HIMS, AND THE TRIBAL STATE

The preceding archaeological aspects of sedentarization have turned on the role of the first Umayyad ruler, Muʿāwiya ibn Abī Sufyān, who ruled as governor of Syria for twenty years and as caliph for another twenty years (ca. A.D. 640–680). Muʿāwiya was reputed to have built up a system of tribal alliances based on acceptance from the Kalb in the south and the Tanukh in the north. In his recent study, Humphreys (2006) casts Muʿāwiya as a kind of tribal sheikh who understood the nature of tribal society but desired only "stability and peace."[24] Key to understanding his rule was the move of the political capital from Madina to Damascus, the focus of residence and political authority in a new Syrian *dīyār al-hijra* (realm

---

[22] "The earliest [*amṣār*] were those established in Syria during the campaigns undertaken at the conclusion of the Riddah wars, namely al-Jābiya, Ḥimṣ, ʿAmwās (capital before al-Ramla), Tabariya, al-Ludd, and al-Ramla" (Wheatley 2001: chapters 2, 24). This program may have anticipated the foundation of Kufa and al-Basra by a year or two.

[23] There exists an archaeological myth, often adopted by historians, that, by the mid-eighth century, the displacement of the Caliphate from Umayyad Damascus to

Abbasid Baghdad meant a shift in political patronage resulting in severe decline or stagnation in Syrian cities. This is often mistakenly interpreted to mean an abandonment in urban culture and life, and literally, a corresponding rise in nomadism (Whitcomb 1995; 2000a).

[24] "Should we regard Muʿāwiya as a state-builder [or merely] a gifted politician?" (Humphreys 2006: 93 and 110). The alternative depiction of Muʿāwiya is one of a great centralizer, or implicit state-builder (Keshk 2002: 102, n. 3 for further references).

of emigration). When Muʿāwiya made Qinnasrin a *miṣr* and a *jund* (as reported above), he divided this northern territory from the *jund* of Hims. This narrative information on Hims, and archaeological inferences, may indicate some patterns of tribal settlement in Syrian cities.

From the time of Sasanian control in the early seventh century through the Byzantine reoccupation (of about five years), increased garrisons in Syria seem to have been within the city walls (Kaegi 1992: 100–09). One of the implications is the problem of billeting, either in competition with numerous civilian refugees, or within improvised barracks. In either case, the Byzantine evacuation by Heraclius in A.D. 636[25] must have left large vacancies in Emesa and other cities. Thus the report of occupation states the Muslims "divided [Emesa] up among the Muslims in lots (*khiṭaṭ*), so that they might occupy them; and he settled them also in every place whose occupants had evacuated it and in every abandoned yard" (Donner 1981: 245–47). Thus unlike many other regions, occupation brought the Arab tribes into the classical cities.

This quotation from al-Baladhuri is one of the rare references to the use of *khiṭaṭ* other than in association with the classic *amṣār*. It suggests that, in the first place, open, ruinous areas within the city were marked out in a systematic fashion and that the holding of grants of land (*qaṭīʿa*) or dwellings (*dār*) was not confined to abandoned properties. A careful examination of modern maps of Hims reveals copious traces of the Hellenistic/Roman plan.[26] Unlike the great cities of Aleppo and Damascus (where Sauvaget used this methodology so successfully), the plan of classical Hims looses definition toward the middle of the city, where an alternative grid (fig. 13.9), oriented north–south and approximating the direction of *qibla*, may be discerned.[27] This extreme case, where the inner city seems to have been changed or replanned, may not have been so unusual; one prime example may have been Jerusalem, where the Haram al-Sharif (Rosen-Ayalon 1989) and much of the eastern part of the Byzantine city was ruinous enough to allow Muslim reconstruction (fig. 13.10; Whitcomb n.d. a).[28]

The case of Hims is particularly important for the processes of settlement and political evolution. The tribes that settled in Hims after the conquest were from South Arabia, Yemen, and the Hadhramaut, considered Qahtanid.[29] Arab tribes that had already moved into Syria were Quḍāʿa and with other Syrian Arab tribes "were in the Umayyad age, for political reasons, genealogically linked with the South Arabian emigrants and counted as originally South Arabian" (Madelung 1986a: 142).[30] The town was a strong supporter of Muʿāwiya, especially given the prosperity during his reign (Madelung 1986a: 147). Madelung has noted

---

[25] The reduction of walled cities seems to have involved a siege, sometimes of several months, and a treaty; the violent conquest of Caesarea Maritima in A.D. 640 seems to have been an exception.

[26] This reconstruction is based on an unpublished study by Paul Cobb, "The Missing *amsar* of Syria: Alternative Urbanization at Hims," presented to Middle East Studies Association meetings, Washington, 1991. Probably wisely, Cobb refrained from proposing a central replanning by the Muslims.

[27] Among the central open areas was that in which Hisham constructed suqs; see Madelung 1986a: 171.

[28] What is needed is an archaeology of his years of rule. As an example, Muʿāwiya replaced ʿAmr ibn al-ʿĀṣ at the siege of Caesarea and thus might claim its conquest. He is reported to have found a large number of Arabs

living there, presumably in a *ḥāḍir* (al-Baladhurī 1968: 141; Whitcomb n.d. b). This city was the last Byzantine capital and may have impressed Muʾāwiya, especially the shrine on the Temple Mount and praetorium to the south; this configuration may anticipate the Dome of the Rock and Umayyad buildings south of the Haram al-Sharif (Whitcomb 2007).

[29] The governor of Hims under Muʿāwiya was al-Simṭ b. al-Aswad of the Kinda.

[30] A major influence in the social history of Hims was the presence of Kaʿb al-Aḥbār, the Jewish convert and advisor to Umar, who belonged to the Himyarite clan of Dhū Ruʿayn and provided escatological and apocalyptic prophesies in Hims. He died in 654 and his tomb remains a shrine in the town (Madelung 1986a: 143).

that "*muhājirūn*, emigrants, was the honorific title which the Arab settlers like to apply to themselves." He continues with the revealing report that "the prime hadith of the Prophet which ... affirmed its continuation ... was transmitted from the caliph Muʿāwiya in Hims" (Madelung 1986a: 163).

The report of this hadith is remarkable in a town famous for its apocalyptic prophesies during the Umayyad period. Kaʿb al-Aḥbār gave the dire prediction that, in the final battle with the Byzantines, "no owner of a feddan or of a tent pole will remain, but they will join the Rum." This indicates "the bias of the Yemenite town dwellers against the Bedouin Arab tent dwellers and against peasant farmers" (Madelung 1986a: 164). What Kaʿb al-Aḥbār saw as tribal perfidy, one might suggest as a more generic reassertion of tribal options toward a semi-nomad lifestyle. In a statement strangely anticipating Ibn Khaldun, he says:

> when they have become numerous, they will leave the towns, communities, and mosques and lead a Bedouin life .... But God has never established a caliphate or kingship except among the people of towns and civilization (Madelung 1986a: 165).

An achievement is implicit in this assessment, that the faithful Yemeni tribes successfully transitioned into the urban settlement initiated by Muʾāwiya. It follows that research into the archaeology of his reign should yield further evidence of the tribal beginnings of the Islamic city.

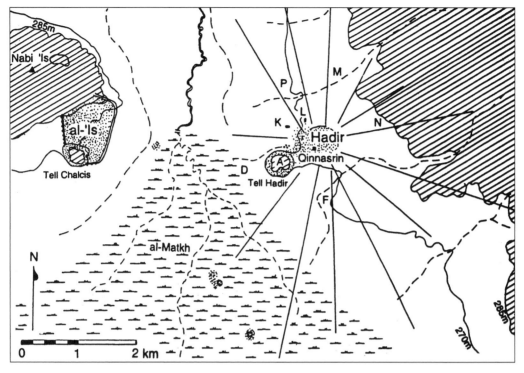

Figure 13.1. Map of Qinnasrin area, with Tell Chalcis and Hadir sites

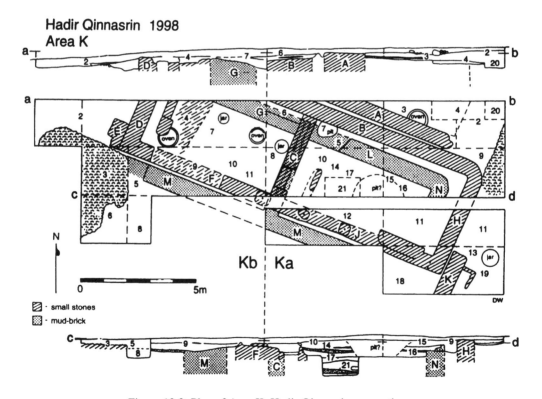

Figure 13.2. Plan of Area K, Hadir Qinnasrin excavations

Figure 13.3. Winter residence near Hadir Qinnasrin (after Charles 1939: pl. X)

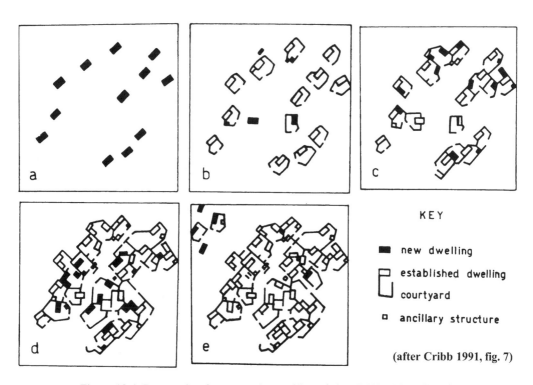

Figure 13.4. Progression from tent site to village (after Cribb 1991a: fig. 7)

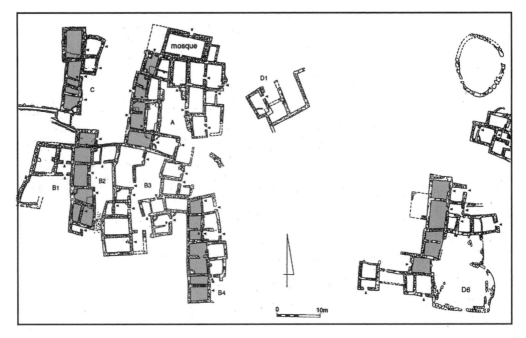

Figure 13.5. Khirbet Abu Suwwana (after Sion 1997: fig. 3)

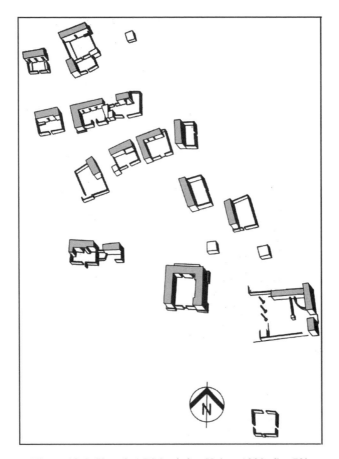

Figure 13.6. Site of al-Risha (after Helms 1990: fig. 72)

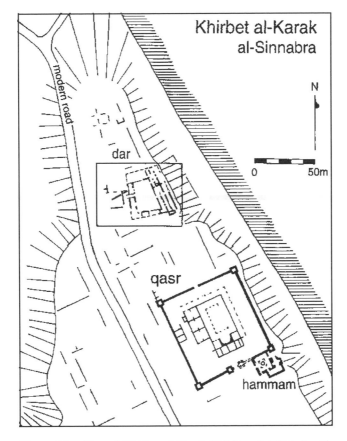

Figure 13.7. Plan of Khirbet al-Karak (Whitcomb 2002: fig. 2)

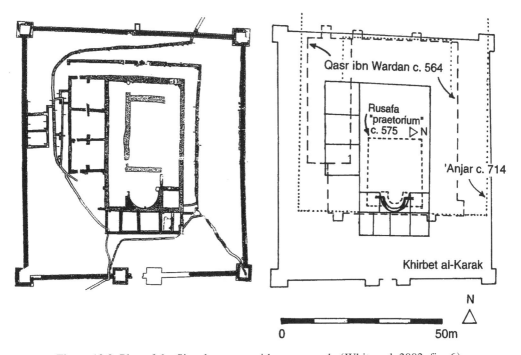

Figure 13.8. Plan of the Sinnabra *qasr*, with comparanda (Whitcomb 2002: fig. 6)

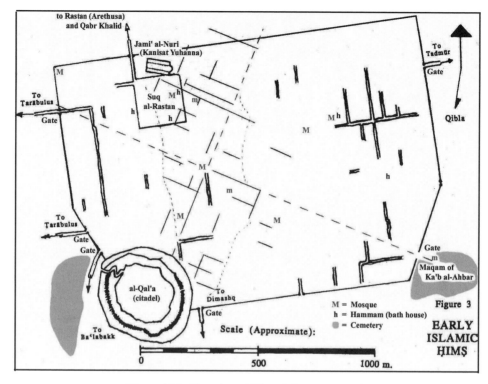

Figure 13.9. City plan of Hims (after Cobb n.d.)

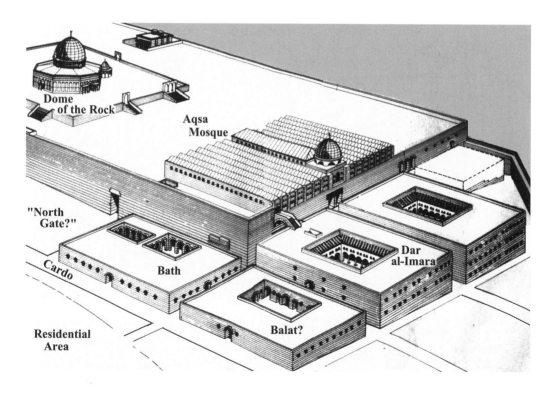

Figure 13.10. Reconstruction of Early Islamic Jerusalem (after Bahat 1996: 82–83)

BIBLIOGRAPHY

Akbar, Jamel
  1989   "Khatta and the Territorial Structure of Early Muslim Towns." *Muqarnas* 6: 22–32.

Athamina, Khalil
  1986   "Arab Settlement during the Umayyad Caliphate." *Jerusalem Studies in Arabic and Islam* 8: 185–207.
  1987   "*A'rab* and *Muhajirun* in the Environment of the *Amsar.*" *Studia Islamica* 66: 5–25.

Avner, Rina
  1996   "Elat." *Excavations and Surveys in Israel* 15: 119–21.
  1998   "Elat-Elot: An Early Islamic Village." *Atiqot* 36: 21*–39* [124–25]. [in Hebrew]

Avner, Uzi, and Jodi Magness
  1998   "Early Islamic Settlement in the Southern Negev." *Bulletin of the Schools of Oriental Research* 310: 39–57.

Avni, Gideon
  1992   "Survey of Deserted Bedouin Campsites in the Negev Highlands and Its Implications for Archaeological Research." In *Pastoralism in the Levant: Archaeological Materials in Anthropological Perspectives*, edited by Ofer Bar-Yosef and Anatoly M. Khazanov, pp. 241–54. Monographs in World Archaeology 10. Madison: Prehistory Press.

Bahat, Dan
  1996   *The Illustrated Atlas of Jerusalem*. Jerusalem: Carta.

al-Balādhurī, Aḥmad b. Yaḥyā
  1968   *Kitāb Fatūḥ al-Buldān*. Edited by M. J. Goeje. Leiden: E. J. Brill. Reprint.

Barth, Fredrik
  1961   *Nomads of South Persia: The Basseri Tribe of the Khamseh Confederacy*. Brown Series in Anthropology. Boston: Little Brown.

Berthier, Sophie
  2001   *Peuplement rural et aménagements hydroagricoles dans la moyenne vallée de l'Euphrat, fin VIIe–XIXe siècle*. Publications de l' Institut français d'études arabes de Damas. Damascus: Institut français d'études arabes de Damas.

Bosworth, Clifford Edmund
  1991   "Misr." *Encyclopedia of Islam* (2nd edition): 146.

Charles, Henri
  1939   *Tribus moutonnières du Moyen-Euphrate*. Documents d'études orientales 8. Beirut: Institut français d'études arabes de Damas.

Cobb, Paul M.
  1991   "The Missing *amsar* of Syria: Alternative Urbanization at Hims." Unpublished paper given at the Middle East Studies Association meetings.
  2001   *White Banners: Contention in Abbasid Syria, 750–880*. State University of New York Series in Medieval Middle East History. Albany: State University of New York.

Cribb, Roger
  1991a   "Mobile Villagers: The Structure and Organization of Nomadic Pastoral Campsites in the Near East." In *Ethnoarchaeological Approaches to Mobile Campsites: Hunter-Gatherer and Pastoralist Case Studies*, edited by Clive S. Gamble and William A. Boismier, pp. 371–93. Ethnoarchaeological Series 1. Ann Arbor: International Monographs in Prehistory.
  1991b   *Nomads in Archaeology*. New Studies in Archaeology. Cambridge: Cambridge University.

Crone, Patricia
    1994   "The First-Century Concept of *Higra*." *Arabica* 41: 352–87.

Daker, Naoras
    1984   "Contribution à l'étude de l'évolution de l'habitat bédouin en Syrie." In *Nomades et sédentaires: Perspectives ethnoarchéologiques*, edited by Olivier Aurenche, pp. 51–79. Éditions Recherche sur les Civilisations, Mémoire 40; Centre Jean Palerne 4. Paris: Éditions Recherche sur les Civilisations.

Delougaz, Pinhas, and Richard C. Haines
    1960   *A Byzantine Church at Khirbet al-Karak*. Oriental Institute Publications 85. Chicago: University of Chicago Press.

Dentzer, Jean-Marie
    1994   "Khåns ou casernes à Palmyre? À propos de structures visibles sur des photographies aériennes anciennes." *Syria* 71: 45–112.

Donner, Fred M.
    1981   *The Early Islamic Conquests*. Princeton: Princeton University.
    1989   "The Role of Nomads in the Middle East in Late Antiquity (400–800 C.E.)." In *Tradition and Innovation in Late Antiquity*, edited by Frank M. Clover and R. Stephen Humphreys, pp. 73–85. Wisconsin Studies in Classics. Madison: University of Wisconsin.

Duri, Abdel-Aziz
    1980   "Governmental Institutions." In *The Islamic City: Selected Papers from the Colloquium Held at the Middle East Centre, Faculty of Oriental Studies at Cambridge, United Kingdom* (19–23 July 1976), edited by R. B. Serjeant, pp. 52–65. Paris: UNESCO.

Fowden, Elizabeth Key
    2000   "An Arab Building at al-Rusafa — Sergiopolis." *Damaszener Mitteilungen* 1: 303–24.

Glick, Thomas F.
    2002   "Tribal Landscapes of Islamic Spain, History and Archaeology." In *Inventing Medieval Landscapes: Senses of Place in Western Europe*, edited by John Howe and Michael Wolfe, pp. 113–35. Gainesville: University of Florida.

Haiman, Mordechai
    1990   "Agricultural Settlement in Ramat Barne'a in the Seventh–Eighth Centuries C.E." *Atiqot* 10: 111–25. [in Hebrew]
    1995   "Agriculture and Nomad-State Relations in the Negev Desert in the Byzantine and Early Islamic Periods." *Bulletin of the American Schools of Oriental Research* 297: 29–53.

Haldon, John
    1995   "Seventh-Century Continuities: The Ajnåd and the 'Thematic Myth.'" In *The Byzantine and Early Islamic Near East*, Volume 3: *States, Resources and Armies*, edited by Averil Cameron, pp. 379–423. Princeton: Darwin.

Ibn al-Faqih al-Hamdani
    1885   *Kitab al-Buldan*. Edited by M. de Goeje. Bibliotheca Geographorum Arabicorum 5. Leiden: Brill.

Helms, Svend
    1990   *Early Islamic Architecture of the Desert: A Bedouin Station in Eastern Jordan*. Edinburgh: Edinburgh University.

Hillenbrand, Robert
　1999　　　　　"'Anjar and Early Islamic Urbanism." In *The Idea and Ideal of the Town Between Late Antiquity and the Early Middle Ages*, edited by Gian Pietro Brogiolo and Bryan Ward-Perkins, pp. 59–98. The Transformation of the Roman World 4. Leiden: Brill.

Hirschfeld, Yizhar
　1995　　　　　*The Palestinian Dwelling in the Roman-Byzantine Period*. Collectio minor 34. Jerusalem: Israel Exploration Society.

Humphreys, R. Stephen
　2006　　　　　*Mu ʾawiya ibn abi Sufyan: From Arabia to Empire*. Makers of the Muslim World. Oxford: Oneworld.

Kaegi, Walter Emil
　1992　　　　　*Byzantium and the Early Islamic Conquests*. Cambridge: Cambridge University.

Kennedy, Hugh
　1992　　　　　"The Impact of Muslim Rule on the Pattern of Rural Settlement in Syria." In *La Syrie de Byzance à l'Islam, VIIe–VIIIe siècle* (Actes du colloque international Lyon-Maison de l'Orient méditerranéen, Institut du monde arabe, Paris, 11–15 September 1990), edited by Pierre Canivet and Jean-Paul Rey-Coquais, pp. 291–97. Damascus: Institut français de Damas.

Kennedy, Hugh, and J. H. W. G. Liebeschuetz
　1988　　　　　"Antioch and the Villages of Northern Syria in the Fifth and Sixth Centuries A.D.: Trends and Problems." *Nottingham Medieval Studies* 32: 65–90.

Keshk, Khaled
　2002　　　　　The Depiction of Mu ʾawiya in the Early Islamic Sources. Ph.D. dissertation, University of Chicago.

Khoury, Nuha N. N.
　1993　　　　　"The Dome of the Rock, the Ka'ba, and Ghumdan: Arab Myths and Umayyad Monuments." *Muqarnas* 10: 57–65.

Lecker, Michael
　1989　　　　　"The Estates of 'Amr b. al-'As in Palestine: Notes on a New Arabic Inscription." *Bulletin of the School of Oriental and African Studies* 52: 24–37.

Leisten, Thomas
　1999–2000　"Balis: Preliminary Report on the Campaigns 1996 & 1998." *Berytus* 44: 35–55.

Madelung, Wilfred
　1986　　　　　"Has the *Hijra* Come to an End?" *Revue des Études Islamiques* 54: 225–37.

Magness, Jodi
　2004　　　　　"Khirbet Abu Suwwana and Ein 'Aneva: Two Early Islamic Settlements on Palestine's Desert Periphery." In *Changing Social Identity with the Spread of Islam: Archaeological Perspectives*, edited by Donald S. Whitcomb, pp. 11–23. Oriental Institute Seminars 1. Chicago: The Oriental Institute.

Marx, Emanuel
　1996　　　　　"Are There Pastoral Nomads in the Arab Middle East?" In *The Anthropology of Tribal and Peasant Pastoral Societies: The Dialectics of Social Cohesion and Fragmentation*, edited by Ugo Fabietti and Philip Carl Salzman, pp. 101–15. Studia Ghisleriana. Pavia: Collegio Ghisliari.

al-Muqaddasi
　1906　　　　　*Kitab ahsan al-taqasim fi ma'rifat al-aqalim*. Edited by M. J. de Goeje. 2nd edition. Bibliotheca Geographorum Arabicorum 3. Leiden: Brill.

Northedge, Alastair
    1994   "Archaeology and the New Urban Settlement in Early Islamic Syria and Iraq." In *The
                    Byzantine and Early Islamic Near East,* Volume 2: *Land Use and Settlement Patterns*
                    (Papers of the Second Workshop on Late Antiquity and Early Islam), edited by G. R.
                    D. King and Averil Cameron, pp. 231–65. Studies in Late Antiquity and Early Islam
                    1. Princeton: Darwin.

Reich, Ronny
    1993   "The Bet Yerah 'Synagogue' Reconsidered." *Atiqot* 22: 139–44.

Robinson, Chase F.
    2005   *'Abd al-Malik.* Makers of the Muslim World. Oxford: Oneworld.

Rosen-Ayalon, Myriam
    1989   *The Early Islamic Monuments of al-Haram al-Sharif: An Iconographic Study.* Qedem
                    28. Jerusalem: Hebrew University.

Rousset, Marie-Odile, and Catherine Duvette
    2005   "L'élevage dans la steppe à l'époque byzantine: Indices archéologiques." In *Les
                    Villages dans l'Empire byzantine, IV*e*–XV*e *siècle,* edited by Jacques Lefort, Cécile
                    Morrisson, and Jean-Pierre Sodini, pp. 485–94. Réalités byzantines 11. Paris:
                    Lethielleux.

Sauvaget, Jean
    1939   "Les Ghassanides et Sergiopolis." *Byzantion* 14: 115–30.

Shahid, Irfan
    1992   "Ghassanid and Umayyad Structures: A Case of *Byzance après Byzance.*" In *La Syrie
                    de Byzance à l-Islam, VII*e*–VIII*e *siècle* (Actes du colloque international Lyon-Maison
                    de l'Orient méditerranéen, Institut du monde arabe, Paris, 11–15 September 1990),
                    edited by Pierre Canivet and Jean-Paul Rey-Coquais, pp. 299–307. Damascus: Institut
                    français de Damas.

    1995   *Byzantium and the Arabs in the Sixth Century.* Washington: Dumbarton Oaks.

Sion, Ofer
    1997   "Khirbet abu Suwwana." *Atiqot* 32: 183–94. [in Hebrew, English summary, p. 50*]

al-Ṭabarī, Abū Jaʿfar Muḥammad b. Jarīr (d. 310/923)
    1879–1901   *Ta'rīkh al-rusul wa al-mulūk.* 13 volumes. Edited by M. J. de Goeje et al. Leiden: E.
                    J. Brill.

Ulbert, Thilo; I. Bayer; P. L. Gatier; D. Grosser; R. G. Khoury; M. Mackensen; and C. Romer
    1986   *Resafa,* Volume 2: *Die Basilika des Heiligen Kreuzes in Resafa-Sergiupolis.* Mainz
                    am Rhein: Philipp von Zabern.

Watson, Patty Jo
    1979   *Archaeological Ethnography in Western Iran.* Viking Fund Publications in
                    Anthropology 57. Tucson: University of Arizona.

Wheatley, Paul
    2001   *The Places Where Men Pray Together: Cities in Islamic Lands, Seventh Through the
                    Tenth Centuries.* Chicago: University of Chicago.

Whelan, Estelle
    1986   "The Origins of the Mihrab Mujawwaf: A Reinterpretation." *International Journal
                    of Middle East Studies* 18: 205–23.

Whitcomb, Donald
    1994   "*Amsar* in Syria? Syrian Cities After the Conquest." *ARAM* 6: 13–33.
    1995   "Islam and the Socio-Cultural Transition of Palestine, Early Islamic Period (638–1099
                    C.E.)." In *The Archaeology of Society in the Holy Land,* edited by Thomas E. Levy,
                    pp. 488–501. New York: Facts on File.

1996   "The Darb Zubayda as a Settlement System in Arabia." *ARAM* 8: 25–32.

2000a   "Archaeological Research at Hadir Qinnasrin, 1998." *Archéologie Islamique* 10: 7–28.

2000b   "Hesban, Amman, and Abbasid Archaeology in Jordan." In *The Archaeology of Jordan and Beyond: Essays in Honor of James A. Sauer*, edited by Lawrence E. Stager, Joseph A. Green, and Michael D. Coogan, pp. 505–15. Harvard Semitic Museum Publications; Studies in the Archaeology and History of the Levant 1. Winona Lake: Eisenbrauns.

2002   "Khirbet al-Karak Identified with Sinnabra." *al-Usur al-Wusta* 14/1: 1–6.

2004   "Khirbet Dhiman (SS 11) and Khirbet al-Hamrah (SS 7) (Sweyhat Survey Period XIV)." In *On the Margin of the Euphrates: Settlement and Land Use at Tell es-Sweyhat and in the Upper Lake Assad Area, Syria*, edited by Tony J. Wilkinson, pp. 98–100, 124–31. Excavations at Tell es-Sweyhat, Syria 1; Oriental Institute Publications 124. Chicago: The Oriental Institute.

2006   "Archaeological Evidence of Sedentarization: Bilad al-Sham in the Early Islamic Period." In *Die Sichtbarkeit von Nomaden und saisonaler Besiedlung in der Archäologie: Multidisziplinäre Annäherungen an ein methodisches Problem*, edited by Stefan R. Hauser, pp. 27–45. Orientwissenschaftliche Hefte 21; Mitteilungen des SFB "Differenz und Integration" 9. Halle: Orientwissenschaftliches Zentrum der Martin-Luther-Universität Halle-Wittenberg.

2007   "An Urban Structure for the Early Islamic City: An Archaeological Hypothesis." In *Cities in the Pre-modern Islamic World: The Urban Impact of Religion, State and Society*, edited by Amira K. Bennison and Alison L. Gascoigne, pp. 15–26. Society for Oriental and African Studies and Routledge Studies on the Middle East 6. London: Routledge.

n.d. a   "Jerusalem and the Beginnings of the Islamic City." In *Jerusalem in Perspective: 150 Years of Archaeological Research*, edited by K. Galor.

n.d. b   "Qaysariya as an Early Islamic Settlement." In *Shaping of the Middle East: Christians, Jews, and Muslims in an Age of Transition, ca. 550–750 C.E.*, edited by K. Holum.

Yisrael, Yigal

2002   "Be'er Ora (Southeast)." *Excavations and Surveys in Israel* 114: 102*–104* [125–129].

14

PASTORAL MOBILITY AS AN ADAPTATION

FRANK HOLE, YALE UNIVERSITY

INTRODUCTION

In this short follow-up to my role as discussant in the seminar, I shall range broadly over topics related to pastoral nomadism. My remarks are based on papers in the seminar as well as personal experience with transhumant pastoralists in Iran, and long-term, but more casual observation of nomads and their camps elsewhere in the Near East. Rather than comment specifically on particular papers, I have chosen to organize this paper topically, referring to seminar papers as needed.

During the seminar I was particularly struck by the lack of emphasis, or absence of discussion in most of the papers, on the impact of terrain and climate in the formation and nature of nomadic societies. This is not to disparage sociopolitical factors that also loom large, but to recognize that landscape and climate are important parts of the adaptation of pastoral people. Nomads range over terrain as varied as the great Nefud Desert of Arabia to the grasslands of northern Mesopotamia, to the steep, folded mountains of the Zagros and the endless grasslands of Central Asia. Climate along with topography constrain nomadism to longer or shorter migrations, and the use of one or another species of livestock. Because of the need to sustain herds in a generally arid, strongly seasonal environment, mobility is essential, but the pace and distances over which it occurs, as well as the resources that are available, differ greatly among the principal habitats. Landscape and climate provide a structure and partial rationale for my topical discussions that follow.

CLIMATE

The climate in the Near East is one of extremes between wet, cool winter months and hot, dry summers. For farmers and herders the growing season is winter/spring. This is when the annual grasses, forbs, and crops grow. By late spring this vegetation has begun to turn brown as it ripens and withers with the rapidly rising temperatures. Precipitation is highly variable and, along with cooler winter temperatures, the principal determinant of a successful growing season. Without going into detail (see Sanlaville 2000a–b; Wirth 1971), it suffices to say that the boundary between rain-fed agriculture and steppe pastoralism fluctuates today, so that in regions of 300 mm average annual precipitation, in three years out of ten crops may be lost. In zones where average annual precipitation is less than 150 mm, success can be anticipated in only one out of ten years. Late winter frost or a prolonged cold spell may delay the critical period of seed growth and expose plants to premature desiccation. The variables are too many to detail here; the point is that in an agriculturally marginal zone, pastoral mobility provides more security than fixed-place agriculture.

This is true today and we know that climate has fluctuated in the past, sometimes with devastating impact (Hole 1997). Whether or not one agrees that desiccation caused the collapse of the Akkadian empire, it is incontestable that the Khabur basin suffered a drought that led to the virtual abandonment of settlements (Lyonnet 1998; Sallaberger 2007; Weiss 1997; Wilkinson 2000a–b). That the drought was preceded by a lengthy period when precipitation exceeded that of today is also widely recognized (Riehl 2007; Riehl, Bryson, and Pustovoytov 2008). Clearly, mobile pastoralists had the potential to adapt more quickly to such changes than did people who lived in large nucleated settlements dependent on agriculture. In a fundamental sense, nomadic pastoralism is an adaptation to aridity and uncertainty and, as we shall discuss, to many other potential factors.

MOBILITY

Mobility stands in contrast to immobility or settlement. It implies a movement *through* space rather than a place *in* space. Mobility is an adaptation to the terrain, climate, species of livestock, quality of natural resources, other mobile people, local settlements, and external forces, including economy, politics, and hostilities. Mobility is an adaptation to different configurations of these variables, which helps to ensure the livelihood of people and flocks.

There are two aspects of mobility that deserve emphasis: environment and distance. Mobile people occupy terrain that is generally not suited to fixed-place agriculture, usually due to lack of precipitation or seasonal extremes of temperature. Mobile people thus occupy an environmental niche that cannot support subsistence-level agrarian settled life. Of course there is some mingling of niches, and boundaries between the desert and the sown have shifted, but the generalization holds: mobile people occupy land that is not suited to agriculture. On the other hand, they occupy land that can support herds of animals and supply various wild products that may be needed or desired by both settled and mobile people. In many cases, as I shall discuss later, it is possible for settled and mobile people to sustain lives without necessary economic interaction.

The second aspect of mobility is distance, or the size of the sustaining area. Bedouin Arab camel-riding tribes might cover hundreds of miles in their annual movements, whereas vertical transhumant pastoralists might move a few days' walk to reach seasonally suitable pastures. The environment determines which of these patterns *can* obtain, given appropriate species of livestock and means of human transport.

A brief description of Luri pastoralists in the central Zagros Mountains of Iran illustrates the role of terrain and distance (Hole 1978, 1979). The Zagros Mountains of Luristan, Kurdistan, and Bakhtiyari are rugged, often without surface water, blanketed with snow in the winter, and difficult to access because of the terrain (fig. 14.1). At the base is the Susiana plain and eastern Mesopotamia, low-lying land, blazing hot in the summer, but relatively mild in winter. The contrast with the mountain zone could not be more stark, yet it is but a short walk from plain to peak, for those nimble enough to negotiate the landscape. A similar movement from the Jezirah of north Mesopotamia into the Taurus and northern Zagros Mountains was long practiced by Kurdi tribes. Interestingly, even when I first worked in Iran, there were still herds of gazelle, wild sheep and goats, pigs, bears, and wild cats available to hunters. Moreover, the elevated slopes of the Zagros also supported wild barley and wheat, along with almonds, pistachios, figs, jujubes, and abundant oaks that produced large and succulent acorns. In short, even in the mid-twentieth century, the central Zagros had rich, edible wild resources that could supplement both herding and agriculture.

When I traveled with the Baharvand tribe I watched the people glean food along the way. Streams and pools supplied greens, while unripe almonds, as well as acorns, could be eaten without processing. According to older men, in the past they had hunted, harvested wild cereals, and collected acorns as a staple food. The women confirmed this and they showed me acorn roasting ovens and grinding mills (fig. 14.2) and gave me recipes for cooking acorn meal. They said they now planted small fields in both their winter and summer pastures because it is now safe; moreover, a planted field produces well in a confined area, whereas wild stands may be thin and scattered, and acorn meal is considered less palatable than bread. Nevertheless, we know from ethnography that acorns could be a staple food, as for non-agricultural California Indians (Driver 1953; Gifford 1936; Mason 1995). The need for security was echoed by others. In Luristan in the 1930s, Erich Schmidt's team observed that crops were harvested green and piled on roofs to secure them (Schmidt, van Loon, and Curvers 1989). I was told a similar story — that men would go out and hand strip the heads of grain and hurry home with them for fear that a hostile tribe might burn the crop. The point is that while nomads might survive without cultivated grain, they prefer its ease of preparation, taste, and convenience, so long as there is security. In other words, farming is not inherently antithetical to mobile pastoralism.

ARCHAEOLOGICAL EVIDENCE

Some have maintained that nomadic people leave little residue for archaeologists to find and, relative to settled villagers, this is true. However, there *are* remains if one knows what to look for and where to find sites. Both Tom Levy and Steve Rosen (this volume) have shown that it is possible to find sites of nomads, especially in the very arid parts of the southern Levant, and sites have also been found in Jordan (Betts and Russell 2000), and Iran (Abdi 2002; Hole 1974; Mashkour 2002; Mashkour and Abdi 2002; Mortensen and Mortensen 1989). The mobility of pastoral people requires them to occupy many sites during the seasonal round, and it remains for archaeologists with an understanding of terrain and herd behavior to piece together a convincing annual cycle of sites for any particular group.

Any campsite is only one stopping point on a migration, whether it be long or short. Even though the Baharvand Lurs could reach their destination in a few days of walking, they stop along the way for longer or shorter times, depending on the weather, the proximity of other camps, and condition of the pastures. At each stop they configure the camp differently. When they are hunkered down for the winter, their tents are enclosed by stone walls and are sited for protection from the wind (fig. 14.3). As the weather eases, they may move a short distance to a clean spot, away from the build-up of dung and fleas. During migration, they may simply set up screens around each family's site and build a small fireplace (fig. 14.4). When they reach their destination, there are many opportunities for the composition of the camp to change, as families from many small camps have the opportunity to intermingle. Depending on the season, tents may be oriented differently — protection from wind, or to take warmth or shade from the sun. In all cases, however, tent sites are within easy vocal communication.

Camps also vary with the seasonal needs of the livestock (Digard 1975; Hole 2004). For protection, the tents may surround an open corral (fig. 14.5), and in the spring, when there are lambs and kids, each tent may have an annex to shelter them. In Luristan the floor is covered with branches and there are small canals to allow for the drainage of liquid waste (fig. 14.6). Saidel (this volume) shows campsites with small corrals that look very much like what one sees in the Zagros during springtime and it will be interesting to discover whether his sites are specific to the season. In addition to tent sites, nomads may also leave other traces, such as feed troughs (fig. 14.7), grain storage bins (fig. 14.8), bird traps (fig. 14.9), and corrals

(Fujii 2007). During migration, some of the tribe placed a stone on piles when they crossed particularly difficult summits (fig. 14.10).

My personal experience is primarily in the Zagros, but I have also observed and obtained some ethnographic information from former nomads on the north Syrian steppe. This did not entail vertical transhumance; rather it was a movement from riverine sites to the steppe during the wetter seasons. While I found a number of modern camps during my surveys, I found few convincing ones from prehistory. There are a couple of factors that may be pertinent. First, stone is not commonly found over most of the steppe, so that the evidence of campsites may be restricted to fireplaces, ovens, and perhaps ditches. A more serious factor is that the land surface has changed markedly over the millennia and has likely either buried or eroded traces of sites. Alizadeh and colleagues (Alizadeh et al. 2004) have shown this to be true in Susiana. Modern land use also contributes to geomorphic changes and has caused irreparable damage to archaeological traces (Kouchoukos 1998; Kouchoukos and Wilkinson 2007).

TENTS AND SHELTERS

The two prevailing types of nomad dwelling are the black tent (fig. 14.11) and the yurt (Cribb 1991a–b). In the Near East the black tent is near universal while the yurt is confined to Turkic-speaking peoples of Anatolia and Central Asia. Whenever people were mobile they had to have some kind of shelter. From Paleolithic times onward in regions where plant material was available it was probably used; in some cases animal skins might have sufficed. What is different and significant about woven tents is that they can be moved from place to place. However, some have maintained that the black tent could not have been used before the use of pack animals. There is no question that a black tent, woven of goat hair, is heavy and cannot be carried easily by humans (fig. 14.12). However, it is composed of long strips of cloth, each of which can be handled separately and reassembled with pins, still heavy, but manageable. I maintain that the tent could be of any age — certainly weaving was known and sophisticated long before the Neolithic (Soffer, Adovasio, and Hyland 2000). I have also maintained that the tents need not be moved, at least in the Zagros, where ethnographic nomads constructed shelters of reeds or of oak branches for summer use, leaving their tents cached in their winter pastures or in nearby settlements. Black tents are good for shade but they get very hot in summer. The *kula*, or bowers as early travelers described them, are tent-size shelters used in the summer, composed only of a roof of branches (fig. 14.13). As I have observed, the floor plans of these are identical to tent sites.

LIVESTOCK

In the seminar there was little discussion of the habits and needs of the different species of livestock. Khazanov noted the incompatibility of camels with sheep, for example, although some camel-riding nomads on the Syrian steppe were also sheep herders. Nevertheless, there is a line of demarcation where one species prevails over the other. Goats, because of their physiological differences from sheep, are more at home in the mountains than on the steppe. Moreover, sheep prefer green annual vegetation while goats are content with the drier shrubs, although there is cross-over between the two species as fodder is available (Betts and Russell 2000). Camels, on the other hand, prefer salty desert shrubs. Cattle are quite another matter. Ritner (this volume) describes the Libyan herders of cattle in much the same way as we read of sheep herders, yet cattle require different modes of herding and access to water and forage than do sheep or goats, let alone camels. While it is true that cattle herding may have been done long before agriculture in the Sahara, this could only have been carried out with the extensive use of native plants for human consumption (Wendorf, Close, and Schild 1987; Wendorf, Schild, and Close 1984). This prehistoric pattern is certainly *not* what the Libyans practiced, but the question is, what *was* their mode of subsistence? It seems likely that they depended on settlements along the coast which are known to have been capable of producing grain, albeit at some distance from Egyptian eyes.

RITUAL

Ritual is an important topic, but largely ignored except by Anne Porter, who attempts to show that rituals carried out at the various Der sites were one of the ties that bound the Hana. As she put it, these Ders were a "symbol of religious beliefs and their synonymous sociopolitical relations, so that its invocation at multiple sites is a deliberate claim of shared identity, at the same time as its use establishes an old history in a new place" (Porter, this volume). The far-flung members of the Simalite entity are bound together through these rituals, as well as through a shared way of life, whatever sub-unit they belonged to. I am reminded of the Early Bronze Age shrine at Jebelet ed Beidha on the south flank of the Jebel abd al-Aziz. A less hospitable locale could scarcely be imagined today, yet it overlooked a steppe that stretched to the horizon and may have held hundreds of tents of pastoralists in the spring. Among the third-millennium *Kranzhügel* sites, Tell Chuera and Tell Beydar are known to have had temples at which ceremonies were held periodically. We may imagine similar gatherings at later shrines, as Porter claims. That her reconstruction bears some semblance to reality is made clear by Fleming (this volume) who fleshes out the social and geographic structure of the Hana through careful examination of the native terms. As such, his paper complements Porter's by showing the underlying social structure that she claims was held together in part through shared ideology. While there is textual evidence for ritual locations in the third and second millennia B.C., elements of ritual among nomadic pastoral people may have a very long history. Stone structures found in the southern Levant, certainly constructed by nomadic people over the millennia, may go back to the Neolithic (Avner 1990, 2001; Rosen et al. 2007).

CENTER-BASED PASTORALISM

Only in the western drainage of the Khabur River of northeastern Syria is there a pattern like that described by Lyonnet (this volume), where herders clustered in walled towns (*Kranzhügel*) and, so far as I know, this is a historically unique and geographically limited phenomenon (Akkermans and Schwartz 2003: 256–59). The excavated sites so far have featured palaces, administrative buildings, warehouses, and tightly clustered residential houses (Pfälzner 1997). Lyonnet makes a persuasive case that these are centers that controlled livestock production, largely carried out by mobile herders (Lyonnet 1996, 1998, 2001, 2004). This is not entirely surprising, for mobile herders on the steppe may have used settlements as bases at which to store goods as early as the Neolithic, as at Sabi Abyad (Akkermans and Duistermaat 1996) and Umm Dabaghiyah (Kirkbride 1974).

As this settlement system is unique it is worth an extended discussion. Third-millennium texts from Tell Beydar (ancient Nabada) tell of herding on the steppe, apparently commissioned by the kingdom of Nagar (Tell Brak) (Van Leberghe and Wambacq 1996). This emphasizes the fact that by the mid-third millennium B.C., wool production had become a commodity and that sheep herding was no longer just a subsistence pursuit. It is probable that these *Kranzhügel* sites were installations *designed* and specifically built for exploiting steppe grazing where there were few earlier or contemporary settlements. This is not to assert that wool had not previously been a valued item in trade; rather that its commodification had now become institutionalized (Kouchoukos 1998; McCorriston 1997). The site of Beydar, on the steppe northwest of Hasseke in the Khabur River drainage of northeast Syria, is informative because of the large number of pre-Sargonic texts that have been recovered and translated. These texts describe food rations to both people and livestock, especially donkeys, but they also refer to wool plucking and agriculture. From the texts, two important roles stand out: the production of wool and hides, and the raising of the hybrid onager/ass, an equid that was highly prized by Eblaites and used for pulling chariots. Tell Beydar consists of a ring wall, apparently dating to the earliest occupation around 2800–2700 B.C., and a central mound on which a "palace" and several "temples," along with workshops, have been excavated. Additionally there is a granary, a possible sheepfold, and an area of residential houses. The excavated remains of these constructions post-date 2500 B.C. and it is not clear what structures preceded them on the central mound that stands some 27.5 m above the surrounding plain. Tell Beydar has sherds from the Ubaid period through the later third millennium on the surface, but the nature of these earlier occupations is not known (Lyonnet 2000: figs. 4–6, 8).

Nabada had within its immediate area a number of other "cities" of smaller scale, some of which are probably recorded on Wilkinson's survey (Wilkinson 2000a). According to the texts so far recovered, it seems that five individuals controlled draft animals and workers and were responsible for dispersing grain rations to persons of varied occupations as well as to livestock (Van Leberghe 1996a–b). The town appears to have been home primarily to workers, managed by a small, but not royal, group of men and persons responsible for the cult activities at the temples. In short, the site has the appearance of a community organized for a specific role, as a central place on the steppe for a dispersed population.

The organization of Beydar cannot be reconstructed from existing documents or archaeology; however, one may make some inferences. The most compelling information is that certain men controlled the economy (Van Leberghe 1996b: 117) and there is a "palace-scale" structure sharing space on top of the mound with a temple. Domestic structures that might be suited to high officials are absent. It is noteworthy that Nabada did not have a "ruler"; rather the *en* came periodically to Nabada for the annual festival of Samagan and perhaps for an assembly of "rulers" (Sallaberger 1996: 106; Van Leberghe 1996b: 121). Although a number of "cities" in the sphere of Nabada are listed, and some may be tell sites, it is possible (see Fleming, this volume) that they refer to herding camps headed by "rulers" who assembled at Nabada (Van Leberghe 1996b: 117; Sallaberger and Ur 2004). It is curious, in view of the assignment of several buildings to the role of temple, that cultic objects have not been found. In the absence of domestic facilities, it is not unlikely that these structures were temples, but it is odd that they contained no ritual objects. The contrast with Chuera is striking, but perhaps not unexpected in view of the great disparity in scale between the two sites.

This review essentially confirms what Lyonnet claims, that Beydar and other *Kranzhügel* sites are centers in the steppe around which agriculture and herding took place. It may be, however, that the grain produced was primarily for local consumption by the residents, visiting dignitaries, and laborers who came seasonally to harvest crops and pluck sheep (Betts and Russell 2000; Sallaberger 1996, 2004; Sallaberger and Ur 2004; Van Lerberghe 1996a–b; Van Leberghe and Wambacq 1996). In view of terrain surrounding the *Kranzhügel* sites, it is likely that detached pastoralists planted fields along the many streams (now dry) that coursed the steppe. The herding camps were built in the few favorable drainages where enough water could be secured to ensure an agricultural crop and domestic use (Kouchoukos 1998). Most of the livestock were pastured away from these sites.

The rationale for these sites seems clear. The demand for wool, hides, and hybrid asses led to the establishment of what we might think of as central-placed herding camps, composed of managers and essential craftsmen, farmers, and herders. Such sites may have been established by local tribal leaders who maintained economic relations with Nagar and other third-millennium cities. I suspect that there is no modern counterpart to these sites, although some analogies might be drawn. The fact that these sites were all founded before the middle of the third millennium, and they follow a common pattern, suggests that their construction was part of an overall plan for the exploitation of the steppe during a particularly favorable climatic period. The excavation of earth to construct the perimeter walls required a huge investment in labor. At Beydar, the kilometer-long wall was the first construction; then similarly massive labor was required to build the central mound, also walled, which stands today some 27.5 m above the plain. The labor to build Mabtuah Sharki was even greater, but Chuera may have been the most labor-intensive of all, considering that much of its citadel consists of basalt structures. The labor force required to build such sites without the aid of machinery cannot be accounted for by settlement at the sites themselves or the small, satellite sites. It must have come from populations that are presently invisible archaeologically. Unfortunately, the texts so far recovered give no clue, although the fact that harvest crews were given rations suggests that there were large numbers of pastoralists in the vicinity who could be pressed into seasonal labor.

What does this say about pastoral nomadism? It says that the leaders of the western Khabur in the third millennium invented a new form of livestock management in which steppe and settlements were integrated economically, socially, and ritually. From the point of view of the herders, for want of a better term, we might call the system center-based pastoralism. Why was such an investment put into these sites when it might have been possible to raise livestock in less visible and expensive ways? A clue is in the political relations of the third millennium, during which frequent warfare seems to have been the norm (Sallaberger 2007: 423). The sites were visible symbols of strength, ritual centers, rallying points for the troops, and strongholds against attack. So far none of these sites has been discovered to have been destroyed. The downfall of the system may well have resided in a combination of climate change and fluctuating political and economic fortunes, a synergistic convergence that proved fatal when Sargon arrived.

HISTORY

When we consider the history of nomadism we must be careful to strip away conceptions that are based on modern peoples whose lives are constrained in ways that may not always have obtained in the past. For instance, much has been made of the symbiotic relationships between pastoral and farming peoples. It is generally agreed that nomads need grain, while farmers require products available to nomads that they cannot find or raise in their settlements. Neither of these assumptions, in my view, has relevance to the earliest stages of nomadism.

Concerning the early history of nomadic pastoralism, I put forward the site of Tepe Tula'i in northwest Susiana as evidence that precedes Hakalan and Parchineh, as well as Dar Khazineh on the Gargar channel of eastern Susiana (Alizadeh et al. 2004; Hole 1974, 1975).

The site, on the upper Khuzistan steppe, outside the zone of rain-fed agriculture, consists of a number of stone constructions that are the same size and layout of nomad tents in Iran (fig. 14.14). Tula'i is a convincing tent camp, whether one believes that it represents migratory people or not (Bernbeck 1992; Wheeler Pires-Ferreira 1975–1977). Because of the summer weather of Khuzistan, which people endure but herds do not, I believe it is a winter/spring herders' camp of people who migrated into the mountains around 8,000 years ago. This is some 1,500 years later than the first evidence for domesticated sheep and goats in Iran (Zeder in press; Zeder and Hesse 2000).

ADAPTIVE CO-EVOLUTION

Adaptation is a general term for the way people react to their physical and social situations. It is useful, however, to think of it over the length of history, as a process of co-evolution. Co-evolution is a powerful concept in evolutionary biology and I think it has some pertinence to our discussions of the relations among farmers, herders, and their livestock. If we allow that each of these groups may interact with others of its own kind and the environment, then over time we may see the rationale for the kinds of economic and social mixes that are described in this seminar. Rather than trying to identify types and to see cases of nomadism as a unity, we should bear in mind what evolutionary biologists know well: that both the physical and social environments of each case are different and consequently affect the adaptive stance that each "species" takes.

In the long history of pastoral adaptations, there have been several significant innovations that have altered mobility, social structure, and relations with other mobile herders and people of the settlements. Among these, but scarcely discussed in the seminar because of its focus on narrow slices of time, are the following, not necessarily in historical order:

The keeping of dogs

The use of pack animals, especially donkeys

The introduction of the woven tent

The introduction of horses and camels for riding

The introduction of pick-up trucks and roads

The commodification of wool

Markets in which to sell and buy goods

The introduction of tea and coffee

The introduction of firearms

The forced settlement of nomads — state control

Circumscription of pastures through changes in land tenure

Availability of wage labor

Provisioning of livestock and people with feed and water

Loss of land to agriculture and degradation of pastures

Changes in demand for pastoral products

Access to education for pastoralist children (fig. 14.15)

Police states with close control over nomads

In the twenty-first century, all these factors obtain for nearly all pastoralists. Eight thousand years ago, when the herders of Tepe Tula'i ventured from the steppe and into the Zagros Mountains, none of these obtained. The history of pastoral nomadism is one of adaptation to these factors, which affected both mobility and social life.

Despite such changes, there is a core adaptation that cannot have changed because the most fundamental of the factors — climate, terrain, species of livestock, and vegetation — have not changed significantly. That is not to say that they have been constant; rather that any changes have occurred within narrow limits. In the Near East, these factors necessitate mobility and flexibility in the conformation of social groups.

THE FUTURE OF NOMADIC STUDIES

I see pastoralism in its various forms as examples of adaptation to environmental and social conditions within a mixed agro-pastoral economy. Each observed situation is an accommodation to opportunities and limitations. The spectrum from specialized farming to specialized herding and combinations thereof represents an organic whole, each part of which is vital to, and determined by, the other components of the system. The pastoralists observed historically and ethnographically should be seen in this rubric. This implies that typological categorization of the separate components is not very productive. Unfortunately, because pastoralists have usually not been literate and their physical traces are hard to find and interpret, we tend to see only the agricultural side of the system and to give it priority in interrelationships. Although there are numerous texts that establish the contributions of livestock to cities, and the strict accounting that went into controlled production, there is nothing written from the pastoralists' point of view.

Apart from their raising of livestock, pastoral people, as they do today, might have contributed to seasonal agricultural labor and to armies. Moreover, as these dispersed people tend to be healthy, they serve as a ready supply of immigrants into disease-depleted cities. Pastoralists were also in a position to supply aromatic resins, medicinal herbs, minerals, and similar resources that were desired in the cities and towns. As Levy has indicated, they might be pressed into labor for smelting, an occupation that might also confer on them some economic and political advantage. In modern times, many work seasonally in wage labor.

The pastoralists that we see today have worked out highly effective divisions of labor with towns, agriculturalists, and craftspersons. Two examples from my fieldwork illustrate this. The Luri people of western Iran manufactured little of consequence other than woven tents, carpets, bags, and rope (fig. 14.16). For wooden and metal utensils they depended, as did most ethnographically known pastoralists in the Near East, on "gypsies." These folk were sometimes integrated into tribes as clients, but they also made rounds among tribes. A second, related occupation is that of musician. These same outcast people, regarded as unclean, nevertheless played the music at celebrations, and they performed other services such as circumcision and prostitution.

While the gypsies are generally thought to have emigrated from India, perhaps as late as the sixteenth century A.D., it is interesting to ask whether they created a new niche in the adaptive system or occupied one previously held by the pastoralists themselves. A change to an outside supplier could have been very rapid, as it offered distinct advantages. If we had archaeological sites, we might be able to see this transition. I recall that when I first went to Iran, the bazaar in Dizful was lined with shops of craftsmen. A couple of years later, the craftsmen had largely disappeared and the market was flooded with goods manufactured in

China. These are examples of adaptation to the forces that impinge on the structure and inter-relations among the various groups in the Near East.

Far from a unity, nomadic pastoralists are, as Khazanov says, joined by the focus on herding for subsistence and the needs of the livestock to find suitable forage. These factors also require a flexible social structure that can accommodate fission and fusion. At each moment in time there is a process of adaptation, because the determining factors are always changing, if only in subtle ways. In short, in most cases we have an agro-pastoral economy, whether it exists on the scale of a small hamlet or village or a Mari-scale kingdom. In a fundamental way, it seems likely that so long as the economy was based on subsistence farming and herding there was no necessary separation of the two. Settled folk were farmers and held livestock which they pastured nearby. However, if seasonal changes in pastures required movement, then some or all of a community might move seasonally, without necessarily cutting social ties. It is probably true, as some have claimed, that "specialized" pastoralism — the permanent detachment of some of the population from settlements — occurred only when products of the livestock — meat, fat, wool, milk — became commodified, thus ensuring a source of "income" that could secure needed grain and crafts. The wealth of a community, whether from intensive irrigation agriculture, manufacturing, or trade, would enable such a separation. In the modern world, global economy, interstate rivalries, national boundaries, mixed ethnic and religious communities, availability of wage labor, use of pick-up trucks, and so on both circumscribe the economy of pastoralists and afford alternative opportunities and limitations to migration.

Figure 14.1. Winter camp of the Baharvand Lurs in the Zagros Mountains, Iran (This and all photographs taken by the author in Iran in 1959–1960 and 1973)

Figure 14.2. Acorn crusher in Luristan

Figure 14.3. Remnant of winter camp. When occupied, stone walls are covered with a black tent

Figure 14.4. Typical campsite during migration. The woman on the left is cracking a sugar cone with an adze, while the other woman is pouring milk into a pot to prepare yoghurt

Figure 14.5. Kurdi tents surrounding a corral during spring migration

Figure 14.6. Stone and brush-covered tent annex for penning of lambs and kids

Figure 14.7. Feed troughs for sheep and goats at a temporary camp

Figure 14.8. Grain bins for storing the winter crop during migration

Figure 14.9. Dead fall bird trap. Hunter waits until a bird goes under the rock to get a piece of corn; he then pulls a cord to drop the rock on the bird

Figure 14.10. Typical pile of stones atop a difficult pass. People add a stone when they reach the summit and many offer a prayer

Figure 14.11. Typical Luri black tent made of strips woven from goat hair. Sections of tent are pegged together at the ridge. Live chickens are carried in the basket lying in front of the tent

Figure 14.12. Donkey loaded with strips of tent cloth, reed screens, tent poles, and a kid. All such equipment must fit onto a donkey or horse

Figure 14.13. *Kula*, a summer shelter which would have surrounding reed screens when in use. A mud manger is in the background

Figure 14.14. Tepe Tula'i, an 8,000-year-old pastoral campsite. The stone chul is a typical emplacement inside a tent for keeping bedding off the ground

Figure 14.15. Tent school for Luri pastoralists in the winter camp ground

Figure 14.16. Goat-skin bag used to churn milk. Tripod, ropes, and bag are
made locally and are easily transported on donkey back

BIBLIOGRAPHY

Abdi, Kamyar
    2002   *Strategies of Herding: Pastoralism in the Middle Chalcolithic Period of the West Central Zagros Mountains.* Ann Arbor: University of Michigan.

Akkermans, Peter M. M. G., and Kim Duistermaat
    1996   "Of Storage and Nomads: The Sealings from Late Neolithic Sabi Abyad, Syria." *Paléorient* 22: 17–44.

Akkermans, Peter M. M. G., and Glenn M. Schwartz
    2003   *The Archaeology of Syria: From Complex Hunter-Gatherers to Early Urban Societies (ca. 16,000–300 BC).* Cambridge World Archaeology. Cambridge: Cambridge University Press.

Alizadeh, Abbas; Nicholas Kouchoukos; Tony Wilkinson; Andrew Bauer; and Marjan Mashkour
    2004   "Human-Environment Interactions on the Upper Khuzistan Plains, Southwest Iran, Recent Investigations." *Paléorient* 30: 69–88.

Avner, Uzi
    1990   "Ancient Settlement and Religion in the Uvda Valley in Southern Israel." *Biblical Archaeologist* 53: 125–41.
    2001   "Sacred Stones in the Desert." *Biblical Archaeology Review* 27: 31–41.

Bernbeck, Reinhard
    1992   "Migratory Patterns in Early Nomadism: A Reconsideration of Tepe Tula'i." *Paléorient* 18: 77–88.

Betts, Allison V. G., and Kenneth W. Russell
    2000   "Prehistoric and Historic Pastoral Strategies in the Syrian Steppe." In *The Transformation of Nomadic Society in the Arab East*, edited by Martha Mundy and Basim Musalam, pp. 24–32. Cambridge: Cambridge University Press.

Cribb, Roger
    1991a   "Mobile Villagers: The Structure and Organization of Nomadic Pastoral Campsites in the Near East." In *Ethnoarchaeological Approaches to Mobile Campsites*, edited by Clive S. Gamble and William A. Boismier, pp. 371–93. Ethnoarchaeological Series 1. Ann Arbor: International Monographs in Prehistory.
    1991b   *Nomads in Archaeology.* New Studies in Archaeology. Cambridge: Cambridge University Press.

Digard, Jean-Pierre
    1975   "Campements Baxtyar: Observations d'un ethnologue sur des matériaux intéressant l'archéologue." *Studia Iranica* 4: 117–29.

Driver, Harold E.
    1953   "The Acorn in North American Indian Diet." *Proceedings of the Indian Academy of Sciences* 62: 56–62.

Fujii, Sumio
    2007   "Wadi Abu Tulayha and Wadi Ruweishid ash-Sharqi: An Investigation of PPNB Barrages Systems in the Jafr Basin." *Neo-Lithics* 2: 6–17.

Gifford, Edward W.
    1936   "Californian Balanophagy." In *Essays in Anthropology Presented to A. L. Kroeber in Celebration of His Sixtieth Birthday, June 11, 1936*, edited by Robert H. Lowie, pp. 87–98. Berkeley: University of California.

Hole, Frank
    1974   "Tepe Tula'i, an Early Campsite in Khuzistan, Iran." *Paléorient* 2: 219–42.

1975   "The Sondage at Tappeh Tula'i." In *Proceedings of the Third Annual Symposium on Archaeological Research in Iran*, pp. 63–76. Tehran: Iranian Center for Archaeological Research.

1978   "Pastoral Nomadism in Western Iran." In *Explorations in Ethnoarchaeology*, edited by Richard A. Gould, pp. 127–67. School of American Research Advanced Seminar Series. Albuquerque: University of New Mexico Press.

1979   "Rediscovering the Past in the Present: Ethnoarchaeology in Luristan, Iran." In *Ethnoarchaeology: Implications of Ethnography for Archaeology*, edited by Carol Kramer, pp. 192–218. New York: Columbia University Press.

1997   "Evidence for Mid-Holocene Environmental Change in the Western Habur Drainage, Northeastern Syria." In *Third Millennium BC Climate Change and Old World Collapse*, edited by H. Nüzhet Dalfes, George Kukla, and Harvey Weiss, pp. 39–66. NATO ASI Series 1; Global Environmental Change 49. Berlin: Springer.

2004   "Campsites of the Seasonally Mobile in Western Iran." In *From Handaxe to Khan: Essays Presented to Peder Mortensen on the Occasion of His 70th Birthday*, edited by Kjeld von Folsach, Henrik Thrane, and Ingolf Thuesen, pp. 67–85. Aarhus: Aarhus University Press.

Kirkbride, Diana V. W.
1974   "Umm Dabaghiyah: A Trading Outpost?" *Iraq* 36: 85–92.

Kouchoukos, Nicholas
1998   Landscape and Social Change in Late Prehistoric Mesopotamia. Ph.D. dissertation, Yale University.

Kouchoukos, Nicholas, and Tony Wilkinson
2007   "Landscape Archaeology in Mesopotamia: Past, Present, and Future." In *Settlement and Society: Essays Dedicated to Robert McCormick Adams*, edited by Elizabeth C. Stone, pp. 1–18. Ideas, Debates, and Perspectives 3. Los Angeles: The Cotsen Institute of Archaeology, University of California; Chicago: The Oriental Institute.

Lyonnet, Bertille
1996   "Settlement Pattern in the Upper Khabur (N.E. Syria), from the Achaemenids to the Abbasid Period: Methods and Preliminary Results from a Survey." In *Continuity and Change in Northern Mesopotamia from the Hellenistic to the Early Islamic Period* (Proceedings of a Colloquium at the Seminar für Vorderasiatische Altertumskunde, Freie Universität Berlin, 6–9 April 1994), edited by Karin Bartl and Stefan R. Hauser, pp. 349–61. Berliner Beiträge zum Vorderen Orient 17. Berlin: Dietrich Reimer Verlag.

1998   "Le peuplement de la Djéziré occidentale au début du 3ᵉ millénaire, villes circulaires et pastoralisme: Questions et hypothèses." In *About Subartu: Studies Devoted to Upper Mesopotamia*, Volume 1: *Landscape, Archaeology, Settlement*, edited by Marc Lebeau, pp. 179–93. Subartu 4. Turnhout: Brepols.

2000   "Méthodes et résultats préliminaires d'une prospections archéologique dans la partie occidentale du Haur-Khabur, depuis le Néolithique jusqu'à la fin du IIᵉ millénaire av. n. è." In *La Djéziré et l'Euphrate syriens: De la protohistoire à la fin du IIᵉ millénaire av. J.-C.: Tendances dans l'interprétation historique des données nouvelles*, edited by Olivier Rouault and Markus Wäfler, pp. 241–53. Subartu 7. Turnhout: Brepols.

2001   "L'occupation des marges arides de la Djéziré: Pastoralisme et nomadisme aux débuts du 3ᵉ et du 2ᵉ millénaire." In *Conquête de la steppe et appropriation des terres sur les marges arides du Croissant fertile*, edited by Bernard Geyer, pp. 15–26. Travaux de la Maison de l'Orient 36. Lyon: Maison de l'Orient.

2004   "Le nomadisme et l'archéologie: problèmes d'identification; Le cas de la partie occidentale de la Djéziré aux 3ᵉ et début du 2ᵉ millénaire avant notre ère." In *Nomades et sédentaires dans le Proche-Orient ancien* (Compte rendu de la 61ᵉ Rencontre

Assyriologique Internationale, Paris, 10–13 July 2000), edited by Cristophe Nicolle, pp. 25–49. Amurru 3. Paris: Éditions Recherche sur les civilisations.

Mashkour, Marjan
> 2002   "Chasse et élevage au nord du plateau central Iranien entre le Néolithique et l'Âge du Fer." *Paléorient* 28: 27–42.

Mashkour, Marjan, and Kamyar Abdi
> 2002   "Archaeozoology and the Question of Nomadic Camp-Sites: The Case of Tuwah Koshkeh (Kermanshah, Iran)." In *Archaeozoology of the Near East,* Volume 5: *Proceedings of the Fifth International Symposium on the Archaeozoology of Southwestern Asia and Adjacent Areas*, edited by Hijlke Buitenhuis, Alice M. Choyke, Marjan Mashkour, and Abdel Halim al-Shiyab, pp. 211–27. ARC Publications 62. Groeningen: ARC.

Mason, Sarah L. R.
> 1995   "Acornutopia? Determining the Role of Acorns in Past Human Subsistence." In *Food in Antiquity*, edited by John Wilkins, F. David Harvey, and Michael Dobson, pp. 12–24. Exeter: Exeter University Press.

McCorriston, Joy
> 1997   "The Fiber Revolution: Textile Extensification, Alienation, and Social Stratification in Ancient Mesopotamia." *Current Anthropology* 38: 517–49.

Mortensen, Inge D., and Peder Mortensen
> 1989   "On the Origin of Nomadism in Northern Luristan." *Archaeologia Iranica et Orientalis* 2: 929–51.

Pfälzner, Peter
> 1997   "Wandel und Kontinuität im Urbanisierungsprozess des 3. jtsds. v. Chr. in Nordmesopotamien." In *Die orientalische Stadt: Kontinuität, Wandel, Bruch* (First Internationales Colloquium der Deutschen Orient-Gesellschaft in Halle/Saale, 9–10 May 1996), edited by Gernot Wilhelm, pp. 239–65. Colloquien der Deutschen Orient-Gesellschaft 1. Saarbrücken: Saarbrücker Druckerei und Verlag.

Riehl, Simone
> 2007   "Archaeobotanical Evidence for the Interrelationship of Agricultural Decision-Making and Climate Change in the Ancient Near East." *Quaternary International* doi:10.1016/j.quant.2007.08.005: 1–22.

Riehl, Simone; Reid A. Bryson; and Konstantin Pustovoytov
> 2008   "Changing Conditions for Crops During the Near Eastern Bronze Age (3000–1200 BC): The Stable Carbon Isotope Evidence." *Journal of Archaeological Science* 35: 1011–22.

Rosen, Steven A.; Yoav Avni; Fanny Bocquentin; and Naomi Porat
> 2007   "Investigations at Ramat Saharonim: A Desert Neolithic Sacred Precinct in the Central Negev." *Bulletin of the American Schools of Oriental Research* 346: 1–27.

Sallaberger, Walther
> 1996   "Grain Accounts: Personnel Lists and Expenditure Documents." In *Administrative Documents from Tell Beydar* (*Seasons 1993–1995*), edited by Farouk Ismail, Walther Sallaberger, Philippe Tallon, and Karel Van Lerberghe, pp. 89–106. Subartu 2. Turnhout: Brepols.
> 2004   "A Note on the Sheep and Goat Flocks: Introduction to Texts 151–167." In *Third Millennium Cuneiform Texts from Tell Beydar* (*Seasons 1996–2002*), edited by Lucio Milano, Walther Sallaberger, Philippe Talon, and Karel Van Lerberghe, pp. 13–21. Subartu 12. Brussels: Brepols.
> 2007   "From Urban Culture to Nomadism: A History of Upper Mesopotamia in the Late Third Millennium." In *Sociétés humaines et changement climatique à la fin*

du troisième millénaire: Une crise a-t-elle eu lieu en haute Mésopotamie? (Actes du colloque de Lyon, 5–8 December 2005), edited by Catherine Kuzucuoglu and Catherine Marro, pp. 417–56. Istanbul: Institut Français d'Études Anatoliennes-Georges Dumezil.

Sallaberger, Walther, and Jason A. Ur

2004 "Tell Beydar/Nabada in Its Regional Setting." In *Third Millennium Cuneiform Texts from Tell Beydar (Seasons 1996–2002),* edited by Lucio Milano, Walther Sallaberger, Philippe Talon, and Karel Van Lerberghe, pp. 51–71. Subartu 12. Brussels: Brepols.

Sanlaville, Paul

2000a "Environment and Development." In *The Transformation of Nomadic Society in the Arab East,* edited by Martha Mundy and Basim Musallam, pp. 6–16. Cambridge: Cambridge University Press.

2000b *Le Moyen-Orient arabe: Le milieu et l'homme.* Série Géographie. Paris: Armand Colin.

Schmidt, Erich F.; Maurits N. van Loon; and Hans S. Curvers

1989 *The Holmes Expeditions to Luristan.* 2 volumes. Oriental Institute Publications 108. Chicago: The Oriental Institute.

Soffer, Olga; James M. Adovasio; and David C. Hyland

2000 "The 'Venus' Figurines: Textiles, Basketry, Gender, and Status in the Upper Paleolithic." *Current Anthropology* 41: 511–37.

Van Leberghe, Karel

1996a "The Beydar Tablets and the History of the Northern Jazireh." In *Administrative Documents from Tell Beydar (Seasons 1993–1995),* edited by Farouk Ismail, Walther Sallaberger, Philippe Tallon, and Karel Van Lerberghe, pp. 119–26. Subartu 2. Turnhout: Brepols.

1996b "The Livestock." In *Administrative Documents from Tell Beydar (Seasons 1993–1995),* edited by Farouk Ismail, Walther Sallaberger, Philippe Talon, and Karel Van Leberghe, pp. 107–17. Subartu 2. Turnhout: Brepols.

Van Leberghe, Karel, and Patrick Wambacq

1996 "Administrative Documents from Tell Beydar, Digitized Images." In *Administrative Documents from Tell Beydar,* edited by Farouk Ismail, Walther Sallaberger, Philippe Tallon, and Karel Van Lerberghe, plates 56–85. Subartu 2. Turnhout: Brepols.

Weiss, Harvey

1997 "Late Third Millennium Abrupt Climate Change and Social Collapse in West Asia and Egypt." In *Third Millennium BC Climate Change and Old World Collapse,* edited by H. Nüzhet Dalfes, George Kukla, and Harvey Weiss, pp. 711–23. NATO ASI Series 1; Global Environmental Change 49. Berlin: Springer-Verlag.

Wendorf, Fred; Angela E. Close; and Romuald Schild

1987 "Early Domestic Cattle in the Eastern Sahara." In *Palaeoecology of Africa and the Surrounding Islands* 18, edited by Johanna A. Coetzee, pp. 441–48. Rotterdam: Balkema.

Wendorf, Fred; Romuald Schild; and Angela E. Close

1984 *Cattle-Keepers of the Eastern Sahara: The Neolithic of Bir Kiseiba.* Dallas: Southern Methodist University Press.

Wheeler Pires-Ferreira, Jane

1975–1977 "Tepe Tula'i: Faunal Remains from an Early Camp Site in Khuzistan, Iran." *Paléorient* 3: 275–80.

Wilkinson, Tony J.

2000a   "Archaeological Survey of the Tell Beydar Region Syria, 1997: A Preliminary
             Report." In *Tell Beydar: Environmental and Technical Studies*, edited by Karel van
             Leberghe and Gabriella Voet, pp. 1–37. Subartu 6. Turnhout: Brepols.

2000b   "Settlement and Land Use in the Zone of Uncertainty in Upper Mesopotamia." In
             Rainfall and Agriculture in Northern Mesopotamia (Proceedings of the Third MOS
             Symposium, Leiden 1999), edited by Remko M. Jas, pp. 3–35. MOS Studies 3;
             Uitgaven van het Nederlands Historisch-Archaeologisch Instituut te Istanbul 88.
             Istanbul: Nederlands Historisch-Archaeologisch Instituut te Istanbul.

Wirth, Eugen

1971   *Syrien. Eine Geographische Landeskunde*. Wissenschaftliche Länderkunden 4/5.
             Darmstadt: Wissenschaftliche Buchgesselschaft.

Zeder, Melinda

In press   "A View From the Zagros: New Perspectives on Livestock Domestication in the
             Fertile Crescent." In *New Methods and the First Steps of Animal Domestications*,
             edited by Jean-Denis Vigne, Daniel Helmer, and Joris Peters. London: Oxbow.

Zeder Melinda A., and Brian Hesse

2000   "The Initial Domestication of Goats (*Capra hircus*) in the Zagros Mountains 10,000
             Years Ago." *Science* 287: 2254–57.

INDEX